DUNKIRK
TO
BELSEN

The Soldiers' Own Dramatic Stories

DUNKIRK TO BELSEN

The Soldiers' Own Dramatic Stories

JOHN SADLER

*Dedicated to all who served in the
Durham Light Infantry –
'Faithful'*

Foreword by General Sir Mike Jackson

BOOKS

First published in Great Britain in 2010 by

JR Books, 10 Greenland Street, London NW1 0ND

www.jrbooks.com

A catalogue record for this book is available from the British Library.

ISBN 978-1-906779-87-0

1 3 5 7 9 10 8 6 4 2

Printed in the UK by the MPG Books Group

Waiting

*I wanted to beg you to say, instead I smoothed my apron and
watched you walk away*

*I wanted to fall down on my knees and cry and scream and plead
and plead and plead*

*Instead I boiled water, made tea while you fastened braces,
polished boots, shone buttons.*

*'I'm more likely to die down that bloody pit,' you said, we both
knew it wasn't true. 'This is our way out, our chance to get
away, from the grime and the dirt and the same places, faces
day after day.'*

*You always thought you were better than our little town, where
we grew up side by side.*

*Always the tallest, strongest, fastest and bravest lad at school.
Born for better things.*

*I knew you all my life, loved you since you were fifteen, and now
I had to say goodbye. 'It's not for long, love,' you said, 'we'll
be home by Christmas love.' You kissed me, held my gaze with
those blue, blue eyes and turned and walked away.*

*I held that image in my mind till this day, you striding down the
street, proud to be in khaki, prouder still of the red cap
covering your sandy, blonde hair.*

*Played it over and over in my mind over the years, wondered if I
could have changed things in any way.*

*Sixty-five years to the day I watched you stroll down our street
round the corner, gone.*

I'm old now, Johnny, and now at last, I hope soon to see you again.

Samantha Kelly

Contents

Foreword

The traditional role of the infantry is to take and hold ground, a function which requires the infantry soldier to engage his enemy in close-quarter battle – often in difficult and demanding terrain and in all weathers. It is dangerous and dirty work.

Dr John Sadler's *Dunkirk to Belsen: The Soldiers' own Dramatic Stories* tells the story of the British Infantry in World War 2 as seen through the eyes of the Durham Light Infantry. It is a story of great courage and determined perseverance, and a moving demonstration of the extraordinary bonds forged between soldiers in battle.

There were few regular soldiers in the DLI – they fought the war and then returned to civilian life. The harrowing description of the horrors of Belsen when liberated by the Durham Light Infantry shows why they fought and died to achieve the Allied Victory.

General Sir Mike Jackson
20th September 2010

Acknowledgements

This book is the product of a lifetime's obsession with World War Two and the role of the British infantrymen who, as Montgomery pointed out, were not, in the main, the members of a professional *corps d'élite* as the Wehrmacht might seek to assert but essentially citizens under arms. In the main they were a conscript army, young men dragged from occupations and professions distant from bearing arms. War for most would be a challenging, infinitely tedious, often disagreeable and occasionally terrifying experience. Their enemies – German, Italian and Japanese – were formidable, the ground over which they fought often hostile and yet, despite dreadful defeats and infinite hardship, they prevailed and emerged victorious. Yet these victors had become different men, forged in the fires of the greatest and most destructive conflict mankind had yet enacted.

Thanks are due to a great many people without whose willing and generous contribution the work could not have been completed. These include: Steve Shannon, Alistair Bowden, Liz Bregazzi and Gill Parkes of Durham County Council, Peter Hart and Emma O'Brien of the Imperial War Museum, Richard Groocock of the National Archives, Amy Cameron of National Army Museum, Anna Flowers of Newcastle Central Library, David Fletcher of the Tank Museum Bovington, Roberta Twinn of Tyne and Wear Museums, Rod Mackenzie of the Argyll and Sutherland Highlanders' Museum, Thomas B. Smyth of the Black Watch Museum, Paul Evans of the Royal Artillery Museum, Christopher Dorman O' Gowan, Sir David Kelly, Sir Lawrence Pumphrey, Christopher and Margaret Vane, Timothy Norton, John Stelling, Mark Pinkney, Sir Paul Nicholson, Major Chris Lawton MBE, Colonel Arthur Charlton, General Mike Jackson, Trevor Sheehan of BAE Systems, Terry Deary, Graham Trueman, Adam Barr, Colonel Anthony George, Colm O'Brien, John Fisher, John Shepherd, Brian Ward, Jennifer Harrison, Rosie Serdiville, Chloe Rodham, and to Samantha Kelly for original verse. Particular thanks are due to my agent Kate Hordern for her enthusiasm and unflagging zeal; to Jeremy Robson of JR Books; lastly, and as ever, to my wife Ruth for her habitual patience during the birth of yet another history. The author remains responsible for all errors and omissions.

The Author is grateful to the following for permission to quote extracts from previously published works; To Arrow Books for the passage from *Other Times* by L. Thomas; To Pen & Sword for passages from *Churchill's Underground Army* by J. Warwicker and *El Alamein: Recollections of the Heroes* by P. Warner; To Richards Literary Agency for passages from *Rommel's Army* by D. McGuirk; to Random House for passages from *Forgotten Voices of the Second World War* by M. Arthur, *The Pendulum of War; the Three Battles of El Alamein* by N. Barr and *After Daybreak; the Liberation of Belsen 1945* by B. Shepherd; to Harper Collins for passages from *Quartered Safe out Here* by G.M.Fraser and *Nemesis* by Sir Max Hastings; to Thomas Nelson for passages from *Faithful; the Story of the Durham Light Infantry* by S.G.P. Ward; to the London Stamp Exchange for passages from *Into Battle with the Durhams* by Majors Lewis & English; to MacMillian & Co for passages from *The Imperial War Museum Book of the Desert war* (ed.) A. Gilbert; to the History Press for passages from *The Handbook of the British Army 1939 – 1945* by G. Forty and to Headline for passages from *The Autobiography of the British Soldier* by J. Louis-Stempel. The author and publishers take copyright matters seriously and the author has made every endeavour to avoid missing attributions or adding those which are incorrect, apologies are thus tendered for any errors or omissions which, if drawn to the author's attention will be rectified.

John Sadler
Northumberland, summer 2010

Maps

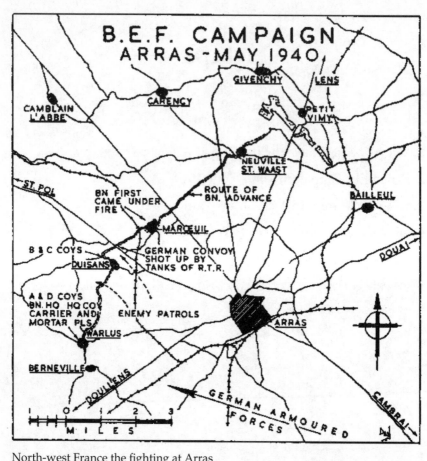

North-west France the fighting at Arras

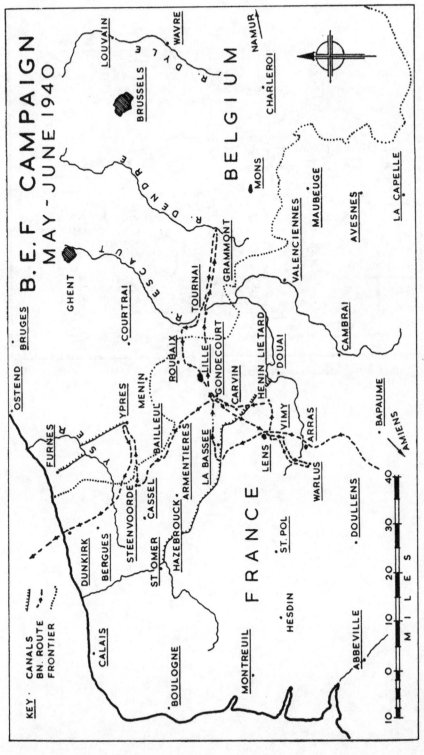

The BEF Campaign, May – June 1940

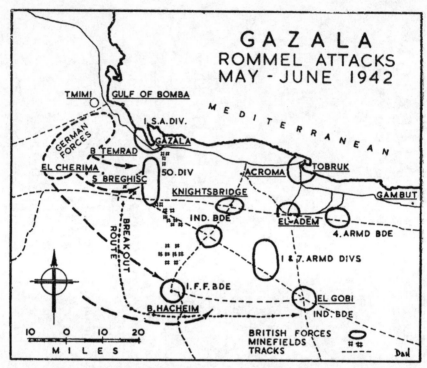

Gazala, Rommel attacks, May – June 1942

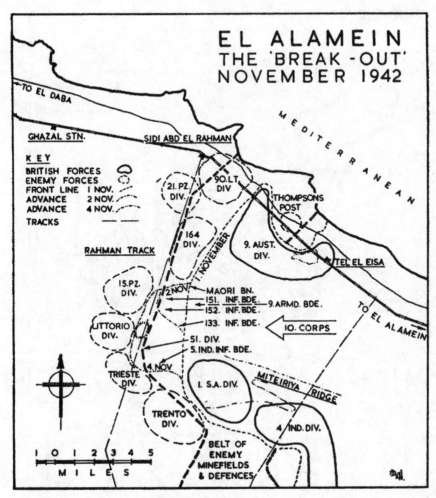

El Alamein – the Breakout, November 1942

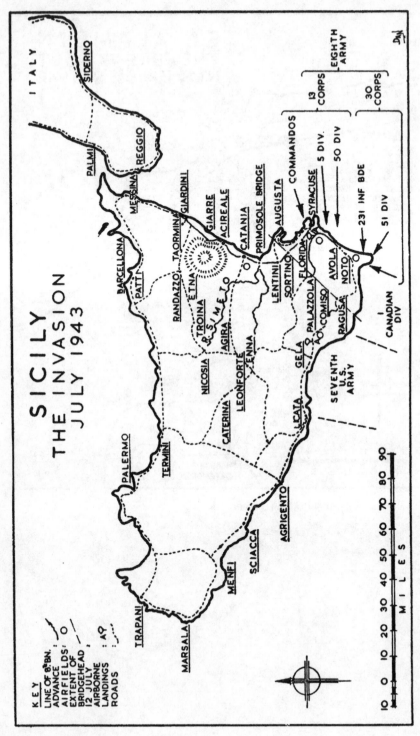

Sicily, Primosole Bridge, July 1943

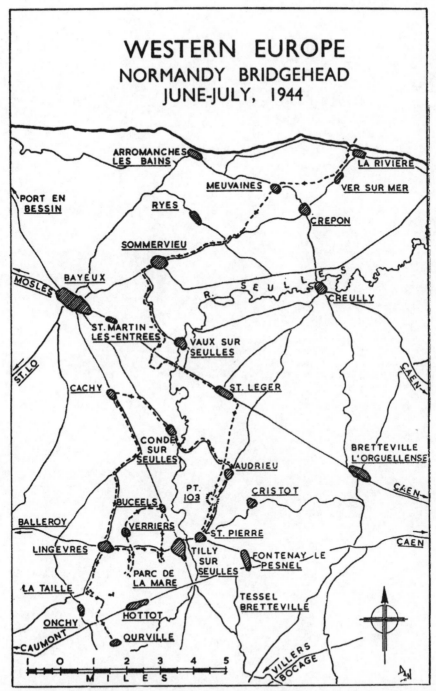

WESTERN EUROPE
NORMANDY BRIDGEHEAD
JUNE-JULY, 1944

Western Europe, Normandy Bridgehead, June – July 1944

Chapter 1

'Phoney War', 1939–40

It was at 11.00am on 3 September 1939 that Britain entered a new era. The transition from peace to war was swift and dramatic. The country had put on uniform. The sky over the cities was dotted with balloons. Everywhere people were digging trenches, filling sandbags. Gas masks were given out. There was a rush for black paper and cloth to screen windows and skylights. Grim, grey vehicles thundered along the roads on mysterious errands. There was in the air a feeling of change – complete, inevitable, tremendous.

Putting on uniform

A generation before, war had come in cloudless August, greeted by vast, thronging crowds intoxicated with an almost transcendent spirit of patriotic fervour. Young men queued to volunteer in their tens of thousands. Their children, who listened to Neville Chamberlain's radio broadcast, greeted the business of war in an altogether different mood. The Prime Minister's voice, scratchy and somehow rather feeble over the airwaves, conveyed a sombre note of resignation. This time there would be no great rush of enthusiasts off to biff the 'Beastly Hun'.

That the Hun was still beastly was beyond question. Their conduct in Poland, which was swiftly overrun and then murderously oppressed, hammered into a Dark Age vision of servility, left no room for doubt. Appeasement was definitely out of fashion: 'I remember the bother with Czechoslovakia, and we thought there was going to be a war. My father certainly did – and we were quite prepared for it. Then of course it all blew over temporarily, and I remember Dad bought us a dolly each to celebrate, because it seemed as if it was going to be alright – and of course, it wasn't.'[1]

I remember vividly 'Peace in our Time' – Neville Chamberlain coming back from Munich. We thought, 'Thank God, it's going to be peace, it's not going to be war.' But of course events proved [*sic*] wrong. I began thinking, 'Is it going to be like the First World War, when thousands of men were killed? In a way they were human fodder.' I thought, 'Is it going to be a repeat? What's going to happen to my brothers?'[2]

Britain was two very different countries in the 1930s. Both north and south had been badly affected by the great depression with unemployment in the latter reaching 13.5 per cent. But the decade had seen a revival of economic prosperity throughout the Home Counties, with new manufacturing such as electrical goods and a burgeoning motor industry. Leafy and pleasant suburbs spread outwards and standards of living soared; electric cookers, washing machines and radios filled kitchens in garden townships. In the north a very different picture emerged. Here, traditional industries such as coal mining, shipbuilding, textiles and engineering were in marked decline; unemployment spread like contagion. Millions existed in cramped, unsanitary housing on means-tested handouts, eating in communal soup kitchens; with poverty and squalor spread disease: scurvy, rickets and tuberculosis.

The Great War of 1914–18 had been billed as 'the war to end all wars' and David Lloyd George had promised a 'land fit for heroes'; both had proved illusory. The 'heroes' of the Western Front were seen begging on street corners and pawning their medals to survive, and now another war was brewing. Guernica had shown what indiscriminate horrors modern strategic bombing could unleash. The only thing certain about this war was that it would be very much worse than the last: 'Looking round, I could see that we were quite unprepared to enter a war of any magnitude – we just weren't ready. We never had the kit and we never had the men. We never had anything – we had so far lagged behind.'[3]

Ready or not

Britain had 'won' the First World War but what was the face of victory? A whole generation of young men blighted in what seemed, in retrospect, a bickering between members of a dysfunctional pan-European royal family. There was a feeling that the huge, titanic effort expended during the war was somehow a one-off. The scale, suffering and sheer pointlessness of the whole ghastly mess had led to a view, not surprisingly, that such a thing could simply never again occur, must never be allowed to recur:

> It is not therefore surprising that, as the horrific experience of war receded, to be replaced by the onerous problems of peacetime soldiering, the feeling should grow that the unprecedented war effort of 1914–18 had been unique, even an aberration. No less an authority than the Chief of the Imperial General Staff, Sir George Milne, endorsed this view in 1926 when he described the recent war as 'abnormal'. At present he added, the army could not even mobilise a single corps; it was most unlikely ever again to be required to fight a European War. The phrase 'Never Again' was frequently used about such a nightmarish prospect; politicians implied scornfully that they would not send troops to 'the trenches' and even the use of the term 'Expeditionary Force' was deplored in government discussions and official reports.[4]

Life was hard in the north-east during the depression and after. The Jarrow March passed into legend as the potent symbol of a north/ south divide. In such difficult times, Sir Oswald Mosley's British Union of Fascists was able to make significant gains in terms of a popular following. Modelled on and extolling the perceived virtues of Mussolini's Italy, membership rose as high as 50,000 and produced an equally aggressive response from Jewish leftist groups. The north-east was by no means immune and there were violent clashes between both factions in Newcastle upon Tyne.

One further consequence, particularly for northern regiments such as the Durham Light Infantry, was an abundance of recruits. Economic necessity was, as ever, a powerful driver to enlistment:

> Durham being one of the counties hardest hit by the economic depression as well as being one in which unemployment gave a welcome, however regrettable, stimulus to enlisting; the Regiment could have recruited itself six times over. Recruiting had even to be suspended for several months in the year. As it was, recruits were so numerous that the old militia barracks at Barnard Castle were opened up as additional accommodation.[5]

Raised in 1758 as the 68th Foot, the Durham Light Infantry served across the breadth of the rapidly expanding British Empire, from raiding the French coast in the Seven Years' War to the malarial heat of the Carribean, through Walcheren and the Peninsula, the Crimea, New Zealand, India and South Africa. In 1914–18 the Regiment raised no fewer than 43 battalions, of which just over half fought in one or more theatres.[6]

From 1939–45 the experience of the men serving in the DLI battalions mirrors that of the British Army as a whole. They fought in France in 1940, throughout the Desert War, battled across Sicily, slogged through Italian mud, battled in the bocage and in the jungles of Burma. When it all seemed to be over, one of their battalions uncovered the horrors of Belsen. Not all of Britain's youth were unblooded – those who had already fought in the Spanish Civil War knew far better what to expect:

> We had no illusions on that score. However, I answered the call the same as many thousands of others and reported myself at Winchester, and were there a total of two days. Everything was in chaos…You can imagine the chaos as literally hundreds and hundreds were pouring through the gates those first three days – all reserves answering the call.[7]

That distinguished popular historian Arthur Bryant expressed the tradition most perfectly, writing in 1948:

> John Moore's[8] tradition, though often neglected and obscured, survived in two great branches of the army – the Rifles and the Light Infantry. Widely applied in 1914 and still more in the years after 1940, it enabled men untrained in war to become superb soldiers and to defeat the finest veterans of the continent. Their victories are now as much a part of history as Waterloo and Agincourt. Though wars pass, the British soldier remains. His weapon and uniform may be changed, his tactics superseded, his body threatened with death and mutilation by new, though not more fearful weapons, but the factor of his spirit is constant.[9]

It was Haldane's reforms of the early 20th century that created the basis for territorial forces but these have an ancient, militia lineage, in the case of the Durhams, certainly as far back as 1685. Alarums during the Napoleonic Wars when it seemed, as later in 1940, that Britain might be invaded by a strong continental foe, spurred recruitment of Volunteer Companies, though this faded away rather after the demise of the threat in 1815. A general revival occurred in the late 1850s and after 1908 four territorial battalions (the 6th, 7th, 8th and 9th) were formed into 151 Brigade, which was to serve with considerable distinction in both World Wars.[10] World War Two would arguably be the most testing time of all for the Durhams and the whole of Britain's citizen army, pitted against one of the most monstrous and brutish tyrannies in history. The years 1939–45 would witness both the nadir and zenith of military achievement, from the scarred and bitter sands of Dunkirk, the crucible of the Western Desert, the long slog up the spine of Italy, the Normandy beaches, the slopes of Kohima and the doleful gates of Bergen-Belsen.

Call to arms

Unlike those resounding fanfares of 1914, the nation came to arms in 1939 with an air of weary resignation. Many had accepted for some time that war was inevitable and that Munich was but a stopgap. Despite 'Peace in our Time', the number of territorial battalions had been doubled from 13 to 26 in March 1938. Partial mobilisation had been anticipated by the passing of the Military Training Act 1939. No sooner had Chamberlain issued his mournful declaration of war than the National Service (Armed Forces) Act – conscription – came into immediate effect. If there was to be no spectacular rush to the colours this time around, there was at least a steady trickle. Men came forward to enlist voluntarily, more in a spirit of stoical acceptance than in any marked swell of patriotic fervour: 'It was a silent audience which heard the Prime Minister announce quietly that a state of war existed between Great Britain and Germany, and just that evening the various companies heard HM the King speak to his people throughout the British Empire. The challenge from Nazi Germany had been accepted.'[11]

In September 1939 there was a total of eight DLI Battalions; the 1st was in distant Tientsin, with the 2nd rather nearer to hand in less exotic Woking. Of the five territorial formations, two (the 5th and 7th) had been diverted to Air-Defence-Great-Britain.[12] The remaining three (the 6th, 8th and 9th) would form 151 Brigade with a further three reserve Battalions, the 10th, 11th and 12th (Tyneside Scottish).[13] All who served in these units were by definition volunteers: professionals and territorials. There would be no Second World War equivalent of the Kitchener formations. The 'Dunkirk' Battalions, raised by conscription, might be the nearest in concept, and of these DLI formed the 14th, 16th and 17th Battalions which were to serve as 206th Independent Infantry Brigade:[14]

As one of the three DLI battalions of 151 Infantry Brigade of 50 Division, the 8th, like so many other territorial units, had its teething troubles during those first hectic weeks after the declaration of war. To Captain A.B.S. Clarke the adjutant and others on the administrative side must go much of the credit for the smooth running of the unit. They brought order out of chaos during that critical period of the Battalion's history. September was indeed a month when there was so much to do and so little time in which to do it. Trenches were dug and sandbags filled as part of the air defence scheme, dozens of indents were sent in by the harassed Q.M. [Quartermaster] for the many and varied stores needed to bring the unit up to its war establishment and the medical officer was busy all day, inspecting, inoculating and vaccinating hundreds of tough-skinned miners.[15]

Despite the exigencies of a life and death struggle, the army's capacity for bureaucratic officiousness never dimmed:

When, for instance, in a practice, all the fire hoses were found to be defective, the barrack-master at Shorncliffe, an old soldier of some 40 years' service, issued a new one but 'on condition,' as he said, 'you never use it for water but let it stand on the wall.' Views, too, on the advantages and disadvantages of the various defences were apt to change with each new commander. One liked such and such pillboxes; another did not; and one day spent painting them with the letters A (approved), B (requiring strengthening), C (not wanted) or X (loop-holes not wanted) might be followed by another spent in painting C on those already marked A or B or in painting out the Xs. But one of the most rewarding moments in a commanding officer's service came on 10 May 1941 when the Battalion was visited by the General Officer

Commanding the XII Corps, General Bernard Law Montgomery, whose decided opinions on all matters had already made a refreshing impact on his command. After watching the Battalion for some time he rose to go, saying as he did so, 'Well, that's very good. You could do anything with that lot.'[16]

Preparation

This is the safety catch, which is always released
With an easy flick of the thumb. And please do not let me
See anyone using his finger. You can do it quite easy
If you have any strength in your thumb. The blossoms
Are fragile and motionless, never letting anyone see
Any of them using their finger.

Henry Reed, 'Naming of Parts'

It had not been anticipated that a shrunken and emasculated army of those grim inter-war years would need to answer a fresh and all-consuming summons. The UK was divided into a total of eight military districts, each of which could field its quota of regular and territorial divisions. The whole of the north-east region was within Northern Command. At the outset virtually all available regular and TA formations would be required to fill the ranks of the BEF being sent to France.[17] At the same time Britain still maintained vast overseas commitments within the Empire. The Second World War was viewed at the time, and more so in the rosy glow of hindsight, as a crusade, the Western democracies tilting against a totalitarian regime, the most brutal and repugnant in history. This was not necessarily immediately apparent at the time:

When war was declared, I was in bed having a lie in, which one did after a late Saturday night. My mother called upstairs to tell me, and said there was someone using a rattle, which was the signal for gas being used. This was the state of tension which existed at the beginning. But no gas was ever used so here was I, in a reserved occupation, wanting to go into the armed forces, but unable to do so…The recruiting officer asked us our occupations, and told us we were in reserved jobs, and he couldn't take us. So that was the first rejection. One might ask why did I want to go into the forces, when I could continue in a fairly safe job? Well, the forge work was very hard and dirty, and the thought of getting away from it, without considering the dangers, was all I could think of. It must be remembered having a job before the war was something to hold on to...[18]

Peter Williams was a youthful volunteer with an ambition to serve in the Royal Armoured Corps. He found his introduction to the soldier's life something less than Homeric:

Thus began our eight weeks of basic training, which was to make a young offender's institution seem like a holiday camp by comparison. Each hut had 20 two-tier bunks to hold 40 troopers but no other furniture except for the scrubbed trestle table which was in the central pathway. At reveille we had to fold our blankets and lay out our kit on the bunk ready for inspection. Then we had to sweep the hut, ;bumper; the floor, scrub the table and we even had to scrub the back of the scrubbing brush (this latter took some ingenuity and we resolved it by cooperating with the next door hut).

We were drilled from 6.00am to 8.00pm and, apart from marching drill on the parade ground, we had to go everywhere at the double. We were marched to all meals in the cookhouse; to the camp barber's shop that first week; to the camp tailor (a German prisoner of war) to have our best battledress altered to fit; to the medical officer for fitness tests, inoculations, tetanus toxoid, TAB, typhus; and we were even marched to the ablutions block for a daily cold shower. The haircutting parades were probably a racket as we were deducted 6d from our pay for each haircut and I'm sure that the infantry sergeants in charge of us had some sort of rake-off. Because of lack of earlier dental hygiene (we had only visited the dental clinic if we had toothache), I spent many sessions in the dental chair during those first weeks and I have every reason to be grateful to the Army for correcting the many years of neglect.[19]

Part of the limitations in British and French tactical thinking throughout 1939 and 1940 was that this war would be a re-run of the last and that it would become a static affair of trenches. That the break-in battles of 1918 had shown potential for the use of mass-armoured forces seemed to have been overlooked. Tanks were to be used in penny packets for infantry support, rather than in large independent formations, capable of exercising strategic impact:

> I think we rather thought that it would be very like the First War – there'd be the rush forward by the Germans – we'd hold them. Then trench warfare would come about as it was. We did realise that there'd be much more bombing from the air – in fact, we thought it would be much greater than it was to start off with. Gas – so everybody had gas masks.[20]

No amount of training, as the draft manual readily concedes, could offer a substitute for action: 'Everything else is make-believe. It follows therefore that the more practically and realistically troops are taught when they are not fighting the better they will perform when they are, and the impact of battle will be less strange to them.' The British Army of 1939 would go to France as the most mechanised in history though, tragically, virtually all of these vehicles and equipment would be lost there. So much British kit was abandoned in Norway, France and later Greece that, when attacking Crete in 1941 from the air, the Luftwaffe parachuted crates of spare parts for Allied vehicles! Despite this and despite the fact the vast majority of Axis forces still relied upon transport of the equine variety, British arms were defective in certain key respects. Infantry tanks, the Matilda particularly, were slow-moving and under-gunned, though their thick armour would give the Germans a fright at Arras.

Anti-tank weapons relying upon the same two-pounder gun were ineffective and the anti-tank rifle obsolete. The Bren light machine-gun was a fine weapon but the Wehrmacht possessed the fast-firing MG34 and lots of them. British Lee-Enfield rifles were, as ever, rugged and reliable, but our infantry lacked handy and versatile submachine-guns.[21]

> One of the things we were told – the sort of rumour that was going round – was that the Germans couldn't possibly have built up an army since 1933, in six years. People even said that, when the Germans paraded their tanks through the cities of northern Germany, some of them were made of cardboard. That is the sort of rumour one heard.[22]

There was also the problem of space: where were all these hordes of khaki heroes going to sleep? Britain, unlike the continent, had no tradition of mass armies; unlike the USA, there was no abundance of ground where vast, tented cities could spring up unimpeded. Barracks were relatively few and more could not be constructed overnight; most of those standing dated from the 18th or 19th centuries. The swelling battalions thus had to be accommodated on a rather ad hoc basis, billeted in private and large country houses, hotels, village halls and schools, an administrative nightmare and grossly inefficient. As a nation we tend to pride ourselves, not without justification, for our capacity simply to 'muddle through'. At this time Britain was on the cusp of experiencing her most severe test of nationhood since Bonaparte.

In 1939, the introduction of Infantry Schools lay three years distant. For that first desperate half of the war Britain remained on the defensive. One disaster followed another: Norway, France and Belgium, Greece, Crete, the fall of Malaya, Burma and Singapore. Cities were pounded during the Blitz, U-boat wolf packs stalked Atlantic convoys; defeat, starvation and ruin filled our horizons. It was not until October 1942 that the 'End of the Beginning' heralded the 'Beginning of the End'. Montgomery's great victory at El Alamein, though costly, ended Rommel's long run of successes, and disaster in the East at Stalingrad gave Germany a taste of what lay in store. Fortress Europe no longer seemed impregnable.

Training

> Will young soldiers pause, while I tell them two laws
> Of the rear, which should cause no surprise.
> The first of the two is called 'cover from view',
> And the second is 'cover from flies'.
>
> When you've done all you can in a bucket or pan,
> Don't think it a terrible bore
> To sprinkle some sand on the top with your hand,
> From a box you'll find on the floor.
>
> Now flies my with ease spread a lot of disease,
> So from this it's perfectly clear,

Conceal your excreta, it looks so much neater,
And keep flies away from the rear.

Laws of the Rear[23]

For those answering the call at the outset, training took place at Infantry Training Centres, essentially just a reclassification of regimental depots. Training was thus 1914–18 vintage. 'Battle Drill' did not appear until after 1942 when the School of Infantry was established:

> On receiving my call-up papers, I started to prepare for the life ahead. I had not much idea of army life, but I did my best to visualise it. The fateful day came…I left home about 7am, which had meant getting up at what, at that time, seemed an unearthly hour but I was soon to learn that reveille at 06.00 hours was quite the usual thing in the army. We changed trains at Durham and boarded a train to Brancepeth Castle. Spirits were high and there were some real characters. On arrival at Brancepeth we left the train and began our tramp down the straight road to the castle. At the Castle we were hanging about for quite a time before being issued with a meat pie. I remember that more than half the lads left theirs, while some finished off a second. We also received a mug of cocoa which I think was made of red limestone![24]

These training centres (64 in number in 1939)[25] by their very nature tended to be situated in large urban areas and thus unsuited to coping with a very substantial influx of untrained recruits. Peter Anderson continues:

> At this point we were issued with kitbags, which were soon to be filled up with kit. We followed each other through the corridors having equipment and clothing thrown at us from all directions. When we had got all the kit we were marched away to the camp, which was about half a mile away. It was a Durham Light Infantry camp and the Duke of Wellington's Infantry (No. 4 Infantry Training Camp, 54 Primary Training Wing). After we had managed to carry all our kit to the camp, we were sorted into companies. Each of the four companies had two squads each. I was in 'C' Company 19 Squad. We were then given palliasses, which we had to fill with straw, quite a job that was! We then

received a mug, plate, knife, fork and spoon and other equipment, including a bed!

During the next few days we were marched all over camp for various things. We went to the tailor who marked one of our battledress suits for altering where necessary. We also went to the shoe repairer who put 13 studs in each of our boots. We went to the barber's and all had haircuts. It was really funny to watch some of the chap's expressions when they felt their hair being separated from their heads: some of them looked as if they hadn't had their hair cut for months! We were then taken to the M.I. room for inoculations: TAB and TT, and were confined to barracks for 48 hours. We found out why the next day: our arms were very stiff and everyone felt ill, with one or two chaps passing out during the day.[26]

Such rapid expansion inevitably resulted in an acute shortage of officers. An initial response was to establish cadet formations nationwide 'where the emphasis was placed more on technical efficiency and physical endurance rather than on character and leadership'.[27] As the war progressed a more considered approach was adopted, with those selected being sent to Officer Cadet Training Units; for infantry the course duration was normally 17 weeks.[28] Many infantry recruits would find the training and fitness regime extremely tough and for many this was their first taste of regular exercise and equally regular rations:

I was drafted to an infantry training regiment in Scotland. Every recruit had to have basic infantry training. I weighed only nine stone when I went into the army, that being due to the working conditions and food shortages. I did really thrive on the fresh air, exercise, food and training. I can honestly say that I have never felt fitter than at that time, or since in my life. It was hard work but interesting, and it suited me down to the ground.[29]

Peter Anderson recalls how little leeway was afforded to new recruits:

We had fairly decent meals at the camp all cooked by ATS cooks. We had kit inspections every week. The army authorities watched our every move during this part of army training. One night some of us went into nearby Crook for the evening and walked home eating fish and chips. We were stopped by army redcaps (military police) and told in no uncertain terms that this was not acceptable behaviour.[30]

That period of 'Phoney War' that followed the fall of Poland, the 'First Ally' as the exiled government would come to be known, did not long endure. Germany's triumph there had been the product of superior infantry tactics on the Hutier model from the last war. The world had yet to witness blitzkrieg. The Allies, now Britain and France, would not be kept waiting unduly.

Colonel W.I. Watson
Durham County Record Office D/Cl 27/278/402

Notes

1   Arthur, M., *Forgotten Voices of the Second World War* (London, 2005), p.5.
2   Ibid.
3   Ibid.
4   Bond, B., 'The Army Between the Two World Wars 1918–1939' in *The Oxford History of the British Army* (Oxford, 1994), p.257.
5   Ward, S.G.P., *Faithful – A History of the Durham Light Infantry* (Durham, 1962), p.449.
6   Ibid. p.333.
7   Arthur, p.10.
8   General Sir John Moore, killed at Corunna in 1809.
9   'A History of the Light Infantry', *Illustrated London News* 20 November 1948.
10 Ward, p.333.
11 Lewis, P.J. & English, I.R., *Into Battle with the Durhams: 8 DLI in World War Two* (London, 1990), p.2.
12 Air-Defence-Great-Britain – An RAF command function which combined Army and RAF elements for the defence of the UK (1925).
13 Ward, p.461.
14 Ibid. pp.460–6.
15 Lewis & English, p.2.
16 Ward, p.462.
17 Forty, G., *British Army Handbook 1939–1945* (Stroud, 1998), chapter 3.
18 BBC, WW2 People's War A8557103.
19 Ibid.
20 Arthur, p.19.
21 The Maschinenpistole MP38 and MP40 were superior to anything the UK possessed at the start of the war. The development of the ubiquitous Sten gun was a response.
22 Arthur, p.19.
23 *Laws of the Rear* – popular army doggerel
24 BBC, WW2 People's War A3696087.
25 Forty, pp.28–29.
26 BBC, WW2 People's War A3696087.
27 Forty, p.13.
28 Ibid.
29 BBC, WW2 People's War A8557103.
30 Ibid. A3696087.

Chapter 2

The Battle of Arras: 151 Brigade in France, 1940

It [the Durham Light Infantry] is a magnificent regiment, steady as a rock in battle and absolutely reliable on all occasions. The fighting men of Durham are splendid soldiers; they excel in the hard fought battle and they always "stick it out to the end".

Montgomery of Alamein

A sense of moral duty
Drove Britain into War
When Hitler grabbed for booty
The Polish Corridor.
No man of honour doubted
That we were in the right.
When guarantees are flouted,
The guarantor must fight.

For ours is not the quarrel
By fleeting passion stirred
For us the issue moral
Is – that we keep our word
Casus Belli (Polish Ambassador of the exiled government, 1940)

In 2006 the DLI celebrated 250 years of service.[1] It and its successor regiments have remained amongst the proudest formations in the British order of battle. Nicholas Harman, whose revisionist history *Dunkirk, the Patriotic Myth*[2] appeared in 1980, accused 151 Brigade – particularly the 6th and 8th Battalions (the 9th being in reserve) – of an atrocity against German POWs perpetrated in the course of the Battle of Arras in May 1940. Veterans, outraged at these assertions, based on the most circumstantial of evidence, collected eyewitness testimony from survivors to refute the allegations. For a variety of reasons their findings were not publicised and the slur remains. Harman would have been likely to raise hackles in Durham even without such heinous charges – he describes the two battalions as being comprised of largely uneducated mineworkers led by supercilious 'toffs', the classic southerner's stereotype.

Harman claims to have gleaned his information from unnamed survivors who were not themselves witnesses but heard of the alleged war crime from a third party who was. Nonetheless, he asserts quite emphatically that they [the DLI] could not take the prisoners with them so they killed them rather than set them free to fight again. Later allegations, building on the initial claim, aver that the murdered Germans were Waffen SS and the killings formed justification for two subsequent and notorious massacres of British prisoners.[3]

Blitzkrieg

> *Hitler has only got one ball,*
> *Goering's got two but very small,*
> *Himmler is very similar,*
> *And poor old Goebbels' got no balls at all.*
>
> > Marching song, to the tune of 'Colonel Bogey'

The men of the three Durham Battalions were not regular soldiers, they were all territorials. An order to mobilise all TA formations had gone out as early as 1 September 1939. 'The Battalion was concentrated in Gateshead, "D" Company was sent to Sunderland, "A" Company to South Shields, "C" Company was at Felling, "B" Company, "HQ" Company and Battalion HQ were at the Drill Hall Gateshead.'[4] The three Durham units – 6th Battalion (Lieutenant-Colonel H. Miller), 8th Battalion (Lieutenant-Colonel A. Leybourne) and the 9th (Lieutenant-Colonel W.F. Simpson) – were in fact overstocked with recruits, sufficient to form a reserve unit for each of the front-line formations, the 10th, 11th and 12th.[5] The three Durham battalions formed 151 Brigade of 50th Northumbrian Division. Over the next six years of war these Geordie soldiers would be tested in the fires of every sphere of combat; never would they be found wanting. By October the Division was training in the gentle folds of the Cotswolds and Brigadier J. Churchill had been appointed to lead 151 Brigade.

One of the BEF's most fully motorised formations, 50th Division, began to disembark in France from January 1940.

Having deployed after the 2nd Battalion, the men of 151 Brigade noticed a far greater ambivalence in the attitudes of their French hosts, whose enthusiasm for the BEF had moderated somewhat over the winter. The French had also developed a marked passion for grandiose compensation claims, as 8th Battalion discovered in St. Remy:

> The buxom Frenchwoman who ran the village *estaminet* was disgusted with the behaviour of the Battalion, for nothing she could say or do would persuade the troops to raid her wine cellar. The previous battalion billeted in St. Remy – a hard-drinking Scottish unit – carried out a lightning raid one night and lifted some hundreds of bottles which the messing officer paid for at retail prices. Madame quickly stocked her wine cellars again when the arrival of Captain Dixon and Lieutenant Pitt made it evident that another battalion was going to be billeted in St. Remy, but the opportunity of selling her stock wholesale at retail prices did not occur again, in spite of her frantic unofficial appeals to the troops to help themselves.[6]

On 10 May 1940 when the German Blitz erupted, 151 Brigade was in reserve. A series of manoeuvres and counter-manoeuvres followed, with the brigade deploying west of Brussels on the River Dendre, before a general withdrawal commenced on 18 May. It was a very warm spring, the cobbled roads unyielding in fierce sun, crammed with desperate refugees. By the 19th the Durhams were in the region of La Bassee Canal. It would not have required an abundance of strategic insight to realise the overall situation was unfavourable. The BEF was strung out in a defensive arc along the line Douai–Peronne, shielding Arras. This mining country of Artois would have been familiar to the previous generation who'd fought so hard there in the Great War and the region resonated with names such as Vimy and Neuville St. Vaast.

The Durhams had been digging in with their habitual industry, as Captain John James March, 9th Battalion adjutant, recalled:

> We were in the Lille area and some visiting politicians and generals came to visit us, my platoon. The Brigadier was there

and, I think General Martel [GOC 50th Division]. Well, my
Durham miners could dig very quickly, their movements with
the pick were those they used to hew coal, short strokes. 'This
won't do,' said the General, 'they're not digging the army way.'
'No sir,' I replied, 'they're miners and they can dig faster than
anybody else.' 'Carry on' was all he said! All of our miners were
transferred out just afterwards tho' theirs was a reserved
occupation – they became the Bevan Boys.[7]

By now the Germans had passed Cambrai, scene of the first great
tank battle in 1917, thus piercing the Peronne–Cambrai gap, and the
French armies appeared to be faltering. Weygand had succeeded
Gamelin as C-in-C of French forces but the collapse of their 9th
Army had opened up a yawning chasm in the overextended Allied
line, threatening the Channel ports, driving a wedge between the
BEF and French formations. The generally agreed strategy was for
both British and French forces to march towards the old Somme
battlegrounds and link with units there, but in Whitehall rumblings
of alarm were already sounding and the notion that the BEF might
have to be withdrawn by sea already forming. The situation was
grave and yet there was a clear opportunity to strike a blow against
the right flank of the German penetration which, if successful, could
sever their communication and supply, depriving the offensive of
the necessary 'oxygen'. It would also then be possible to effect a
junction with Allied forces further south. Major-General Harold
Franklyn was to lead two divisions (the 5th and 50th) supported by
74 British tanks from 1st Army Tank Brigade and 60 French Chars.

Arras itself, at this point, was held by a rather ad hoc formation,
designated 'Petreforce' after its commanding officer, General Petre.
As the blow was to be delivered by a full two-divisional battlegroup,
151 Brigade was allotted a secondary role, resting on the defensive
along La Bassee Canal. This ambitious plan was soon radically
scaled down, with only the three Durham battalions to provide the
infantry component. In the balmy pre-dawn light of 21 May, 151
Brigade was formed up to the north of Vimy Ridge – emotive
ground. HQ was set up in Petit Vimy with two battalions attacking
using the axis of the Arras–Doullens Road as a start line. The blow
would fall south and south-east of Arras, intending to penetrate
toward the banks of the River Sensee. John March, with most of his
brother officers, remained lamentably in the dark: 'Counter-attack,

nobody knew what the hell was happening. It didn't help that we were constantly disrupted by retreating Belgians, absolutely useless and always in the way. I drew my pistol on some once. I didn't actually fire of course; I remembered they were supposed to be our allies!'[8]

The Battle of Arras

> *Frankfurt has only one beer hall*
> *Stuttgart, die Munchen all on call,*
> *Munich, vee lift up our tunich,*
> *To show vee 'Cherman' have no balls at all*
> Sung to the tune of 'Colonel Bogey'

Of the two battalions 'up', 8 DLI would take the right, moving through Maroeuill, Warlus and Vailly to reach Boisleux-au-Mont. On the left, 6th Battalion would advance past Ecurie, Achicourt and Beaurains toward Henin. Each flank attack would have the support of a battalion of tanks. These would comprise Infantry or 'I' tanks: 58 Matilda Mark I armed only with machine-guns and 16 Mark II variants equipped with the two-pounder cannon, a well-designed and efficient gun but of limited effectiveness against German tanks. The Matildas were both heavy and slow, though their substantial armour would cause grave initial consternation. Throughout the assault 9th Battalion would remain in reserve, posted to the right rear.

From the outset the attack was driven by the dire expediency of confusion. A single brigade could not really expect to achieve the great things expected of two full divisions. The Durhams had marched long and hard to gain their present positions and could look forward to a further eight miles in the warming day, just to reach the start line. Orders did not come through till 09.45 hours, requiring the attack to begin at 14.00 hours. Cooperation with the accompanying tanks was presumed rather than rehearsed. Little was known of enemy strength and dispositions.[9] It was an inauspicious beginning.

It was nearer 11.30 hours that the columns finally moved forward, their timetable already disrupted; unbeknown to them the Germans were already dug in north of the presumed start line. These forward elements were bumped by 4th RTR preceding 6th DLI. Lumbering

'I' tanks, moving like armoured leviathans, cut a swathe through the unsuspecting Axis, lulled by the swiftness and ease of their advance. The Matildas shot up soft-skinned vehicles, killed numbers of the enemy and precipitated something of a panic amongst the survivors. As the Durhams pushed on behind the tanks, they mopped up around Dainville and took several hundred dejected prisoners.[10] Though the start line was not reached until an hour and a half past deadline, these early successes proved heartening and, by 17.00 hours, the battalion was in possession of Beaurains. Major Allison was amongst those officers taking part, at that time a 2nd Lieutenant in 'C' Company 6th DLI:

> My platoon went after about 50 Germans hiding in a summer house. They all came out with their hands up. A sergeant and some men captured another 50 or so nearby, so in all we had about a hundred prisoners. At this stage the Stukas started to make things unpleasant…It was decided that we had better get the prisoners well to the rear. I was ordered to take charge of a 10-soldier escort. The prisoners were quite cheerful, certainly in better shape than we were, and some of them said they were Austrians. We gave the prisoners cigarettes and quite a bit of talk took place between the escort and the prisoners…At Battalion HQ we were told to get them back to Brigade HQ. This was a place north of Arras, about two hours' march away. I shared a motorcycle with another man and we rode up and down the column keeping it on the move. The only hint of trouble came when passing through the French villages where civilians shouted insults at the 'Boche'. At 151 Brigade HQ we duly handed over the prisoners. They were now out of the hands of the DLI and were the responsibility of Brigade and 50th Division HQ.[11]

Private Iceton was driver/batman to Major Jeffreys, Second-in-Command 6th Battalion, and followed the advance of 'D' Company 'as close as possible bearing in mind the difficulties with the roads. I made numerous trips back to Advance Battalion HQ with wounded.' As the Durhams cleared Achicourt and advanced on Beaurains, Iceton found himself targeted by German gunners, 'so I sped along the road until I found a junction with a dirt road going south'. Presently he came upon another gun emplacement with a handful of infantry. He signalled to them to surrender as they appeared to have no fight left in them, even though he forgot to take his rifle as he dismounted! 'Turning my back on them I walked the 10 to 20 yards back to the truck, got my rifle, made a point of loading a bullet and returned, indicating what I wanted with the rifle muzzle..."C" Company then took my prisoners and proceeded towards Beaurains...Throughout there was no thought in the battalion of treating the prisoners other than correctly.'[12]

On the right, 8th Battalion were finding matters altogether more trying. From the outset contact with the supporting armour of 7th RTR was lost as the tanks charged ahead without attempts at contact or cohesion. As the Durhams moved forward across the line of the Arras–St. Pol road, they followed in the wake of their armoured comrades whose path, marked by a slew of twisted metal and corpses, was not difficult to discern. 'B' Company, clearing woods around Duisans, netted some captives and the battalion took charge of more corralled by French tanks. Major Pitt, intelligence officer 8 DLI, recalled these events:

We came to the cemetery at Duisans just after some French tanks had attacked German motorised infantry along the adjacent road (Arras–St. Pol). There were many German vehicles on fire. One German sergeant in a pitiful condition with both legs severed looked up at me and said 'Shoot me', but I could not do it. Some Germans who had escaped the hail of French fire had run into the cemetery and were hiding among the gravestones. Our French liaison officer came up to me and said, 'Look, our tanks have got some Germans bottled up in the cemetery but our men don't want to have to get out of their tanks to flush them out. Will your men come and get them out?' I went into the cemetery with a Frenchman. The First World War gravestones were freshly chipped with machine-gun bullets from the French tanks. There must have been 18 to 20 very frightened young Germans lying there. Brandishing my .38 revolver, I shouted 'Heraus! Heraus!' The Germans scrambled up with their hands above their heads. 'You English?' one man asked me. After the hammering they had taken from the French, they seemed relieved to see an English soldier; we marched them out. A French sergeant appeared and we handed the prisoners over to him. He started to push them around a bit and made them strip to their underpants and lie down on the road. I thought all this was a bit unnecessary though, of course, we were in the middle of a fluid battle situation and this was an effective way of making POWs immobile.'[13]

At this point both 'B' and 'C' companies, under the Second-in-Command Major McLaren, remained in the village whilst Colonel Beart led the rest on toward Warlus. Still acting in concert with the French Chars, 'C' Company stormed the village cemetery where the remnant of the German garrison appeared dug in as described above. Already depleted by the whirlwind advance of the British armour, the survivors quickly surrendered; only some 20 per cent of the company-sized unit had survived. By the time mopping up was complete, the remainder of the battalion under the CO had occupied Warlus. It was now 17.15 hours. Corporal Self of 8 DLI also took part in this brisk action:

The prisoners taken on 21 May 1940 were handed over to the French army, who were in reserve to the 8th Battalion DLI. From my position, which was about 300 yards down the road from the French, I saw them embussed into transport, and taken to the rear. What happened to the prisoners after that I have no idea, but certainly the Durhams had no contact with them...One of my company platoons attacked the vicinity of a cemetery from which there was firing on our position behind three French tanks. It was estimated that about a hundred Germans were killed and about 20 prisoners taken. These prisoners were also handed over to the French...I was quite surprised to find the German prisoners were much the same as ourselves; I saw no ill-treatment of them.[14]

Cheering as such gains were, it was becoming clear that so limited a force could not hope to reach the final objective. German formations, if initially caught off-guard, could be expected to steady and counter-attack, whilst the Luftwaffe reigned in the clear blue skies above. Rommel's 7th Panzer (nicknamed the 'Ghost' division, so swift had been its advance) found their 37mm Pak 36/37 anti-tank guns ineffective against the slow but seemingly invulnerable Matildas. With the dash and resourcefulness that were soon to be his trademarks, Rommel ordered his 8.8cm Flak cannon and field guns to be switched to the anti-tank role, the first use of the redoubtable and deadly '88s'. These swiftly began to turn the tide, hammering the grinding and exposed Matildas, whose rush had carried them largely beyond infantry support.

Warlus, at around 17.45 hours, was subjected to the unwelcome attentions of Stukas and strafing fighters, prelude to a determined counter-attack by Axis infantry with tank support. The Durhams met this thrust with a skilled defence, repelling all attempts and accounting for a number of panzers. With darkness came fresh attempts, driving in outposts and virtually encircling the village. As Axis units filtered forward they were able to interdict the line of the Warlus–Duisans road and further isolate British forces in the latter hamlet. Over on the left a similar picture was emerging – aerial bombardment followed by ground assault. Feeling the strain, 6th Battalion was obliged to quit Beaurains and fall back upon Achicourt, a difficult manoeuvre, not accomplished without loss.

The village of Neuville St. Vast held potent memories and ample testimony to the fierce fighting there in the previous war. ninth DLI found the place looted and largely empty, unmilked cows, disconsolate in abandoned fields, provided refreshment, as did stocks of food and wine the Germans had neglected to pilfer. Apart from the unwelcome attentions of prowling Stukas, the battalion was largely left unmolested and it was not until 16.00 that the Durhams were moved up to form a perimeter around Maroeuil. Here a sharp-eyed driver, tracking the fall, saved Major Battiscombe from an Axis bomb. As they moved into position, a stream of shot-up and damaged Matildas were struggling back through the narrow streets, testimony to the savagery of the contest being waged further forward.

The massacre that never was

Lieutenant-Colonel H.S. Snell was then transport officer for 151 Brigade:

As the Brigade Transport Officer and as part of the Brigade Battle Drill I was, in this period, checking the roads in the forward areas to confirm the suitability for supply points – air cover, turning circuits etc. and to note alternative routes for use in the event of air or enemy interference. After reporting the position to Brigade Battle HQ, I returned to main HQ at Vimy via 9 DLI Givenchy road at 22/23.00 hours. Some little time later I was asked by the staff captain if transport was available for evacuation of prisoners. I advised no...

At this time a section of military police were in the area and the D.A.P.M. [Provost Marshal] was either present or had recently visited. He could have a call on the TCL's at Hullock via Division. The prisoners being reported on the main road, I went at once and found them halted in close formation guarded by a few soldiers. The CMP's were all present and in charge. I understand that the prisoners were an amalgamation of those taken by both the 6th and 8th DLI. It was my job to see them off to 50 Division HQ, and I was advised that Captain Buckmaster, the divisional intelligence officer, would be interrogating a selection of them. As I walked down the column I did not hear any protest or see any signs of distress. I explained the transport position to an NCO in charge and he reported the prisoners all fit to march. A detachment of military police then took charge of the prisoners and I watched them march off well clear of the brigade area. That was the end of the matter of the prisoners as far as brigade was concerned.

I would stress the following:

- I did see and have some contact with the prisoners.
- The few soldiers who were present had slung rifles and no automatic weapons.
- The prisoners were under control of the military police.
- The proceedings were orderly and silent. No comments, gestures or demonstrations were made by the prisoners or to them during their halt at Vimy.
- I had travelled the roads from Vimy to the forward areas at the relevant times and had seen nothing untoward and had seen the prisoners out of the area under the proper authority. I had traversed the ridge after the battalions had left and picked up the stragglers.
- The timetable...shows the time and distance element; the troops were at all times engaged in the enemy operation and in disengaging from them. Any allegations concerning misconduct by the Durham Light Infantry at this time are a myth.[15]

As the Axis pressure steadily built up, any question of continuing the advance vanished. It was a question now of extracting the survivors and forming a defensible line in the area of Vimy Ridge. Eighth Battalion was ordered to fall back though the 9th dug in around Maroeuil, whilst the survivors in Warlus, their ammunition stocks virtually expended, began to plan a break-out. Still supported by French tanks and with the blessed arrival of a brace of armoured troop carriers, the Durhams crammed into every serviceable or near-serviceable carrier and truck to run the gauntlet of enemy fire. Though Colonel Beart was incapacitated by wounds and the baton of command passed to Ross McLaren, the withdrawal was successfully accomplished.

In this storm of fire and steel the Battle of Arras was fought out. The attackers had lost perhaps 100 or more casualties, the Germans several times that number with some 400 captured; 35 of the British 'I' tanks had been destroyed whilst the Germans lost rather fewer. Field Marshall von Runstedt later admitted 'a critical moment in the drive came just as my forces had reached the Channel. It was caused by a British counter-stroke southward from Arras towards Cambrai on May the 21st. For a short time it was feared that our armoured divisions would be cut off before the infantry divisions could come up to support them. None of the French counter-attacks carried any serious threat such as this one did.'[16] Rommel made a diary entry wherein he confirmed the losses for his division as including 89 killed, 116 wounded and 173 missing.[17] There is the suggestion, which Harman puts forward erroneously, that the majority of German prisoners came from SS Totenkopf.[18]

The most thorough English-language study of the 'Death's Head' division and which draws heavily on German archival sources deals with the view 'from the other side of the hill'. The account incorrectly identifies the British attackers but, no doubt correctly, portrays the near-panic which ensued: 'The confusing battle of tanks, armoured cars and infantry that followed was a sobering experience for the men in the Totenkopf Division.'[19] The main blow seems to have landed squarely on the anti-tank battalion whose guns proved ineffective against the Matildas, 'which inflicted heavy losses especially upon the Third Company of the Tank-Destroyer Battalion. After watching helplessly while their shells bounced off the enemy tanks, a number of the gun crews were blasted to pieces at close range or crushed beneath the treads of the relentless Matildas.'[20]

Having been thus surprised, the SS fell back to regroup, abandoning their guns – this sounds very much like a rout. Having rallied, and bringing up mortars and heavy machine-guns, the Death's Head renewed the fight but the Matildas ground on, inflicting yet heavier losses. Only the deployment of the heavier Flak and field guns tipped the balance. Recorded losses were 39 dead, 66 wounded and 2 missing,[21] which would clearly support the contention that the bulk of prisoners taken by the Durhams came from 7th Panzer and not Totenkopf. The SS, whilst prepared to admit to an element of panic, appeared to consider their resilience superior to that of Rommel's men: '…And if there was momentary panic in SSTK, it was nowhere near as serious as the chaos that prevailed in Rommel's 7th Panzer Division, which absorbed the centre and left of the British attack. According to Rommel's own version of events, the condition of his troops for a while was critical, verging on hysteria.'[22]

Two other factors are relevant in that the later atrocity at Le Paradis perpetrated by SS Totenkopf appears to have been motivated by mounting frustration at the heavy losses inflicted by successive British rearguards. This notorious massacre occurred after the BEF withdrew from Bethune and formed a new defensive line along the banks of the Canal de Lawe. There does not appear to be any specific assertion that this act was a reprisal for similar outrages committed by the Durhams earlier at Arras. It seems more to have been a local reaction, instigated by the company commander, SS Obersturmführer Fritz Knochlein. At his subsequent trial fellow officers sought, not perhaps unexpectedly, to distance themselves from Knochlein; there does seem to have been a widespread revulsion at the murder of British POWs, even to a degree within the SS, not famed for their sensibilities.[23]

A very clear contrast emerges, from the German side, of how their own men were treated when captured. The SS were treated well, given food and cigarettes:

> According to their own version of the captivity, they were not mistreated by the British. At one point, British soldiers even saved the prisoners from a French mob that tried to lynch them after the Luftwaffe had destroyed a small village and killed several civilians. Thereafter, they were dressed in British greatcoats and helmets so as not to attract the attention of the French population. The SS men finally escaped when the British soldiers guarding them simply walked away in the confusion to join the last units being evacuated from Dunkirk.[24]

One of those who interrogated the captured Germans was Colonel M.J. Buckmaster,[25] then a captain and acting as an intelligence officer with 50th Division:

> I examined three men of the 8 Schutzen Regiment [lorry-carried infantry] captured near Maroeil and one man of the 6 Schutzen Regiment captured near Arras. These examinations took place at about 04.00 hours on the 22nd May...They were all communicative and answered questions without reluctance. Morale seemed fairly good. There was no vindictiveness shown against England or France or resentment at being captured. The men were mostly very young; they came from all parts of Germany but principally the Cologne area...Our prisoners were given normal civilised treatment. Talk of a massacre by the Durhams is nonsense.[26]

As the Durhams fell back on Vimy after the battle, their withdrawal was covered by elements of the French 3rd Light Mechanised Division, whose surviving tanks provided an invaluable screen which blunted the cutting edge of Axis pursuit. On 23 May, the French put in a further attack but could make no headway; the die was now irrevocably cast. The Durhams might have thought they'd make a stand on the hallowed ground and commanding reaches of Vimy but this was not to be. The strategic situation was crumbling and a further withdrawal inevitable. The road to Dunkirk was fast becoming the only one available.

What then had been achieved? The enemy had received a rude shock and a bloody nose. Losses in terms of men and materiel had been inflicted. More importantly, 'this limited counter-attack probably delayed the German advance to Calais by some two days, with a corresponding effect on the successful evacuation at Dunkirk.[27] Despite the paucity of forces committed, the attackers had caused deep consternation – Axis reports were suggesting some five full divisions had been committed! The three Durham battalions engaged had displayed stamina, endurance, resilience and considerable courage. They had fought doggedly and determinedly, carrying out skilful withdrawals under the noses of German guns. This was not the conduct of ill-trained or poorly led soldiers. Their task was essentially an impossible one, attempting, with but a single brigade, to accomplish a design intended for two divisions. Liaison with the armour had admittedly been poor – a lack of coordination that was to bedevil infantry/tank cooperation till the second Battle of El Alamein in October 1942.

Is there any evidence to suggest 6th and 8th Battalions DLI murdered Axis prisoners at Arras? The answer has to be that there is none. The Durhams, thrown into the fight in an ad hoc and ill-planned attack, conducted themselves in an exemplary fashion, both officers and men. Resolute in attack and tenacious in defence, they exhibited skill and professionalism. None of the German sources appears to suggest that any atrocity occurred; SS Totenkopf appears to have lost only a couple of men captured, and their own well-attested subsequent outrages do not appear to have occurred as any form of reprisal. On balance there is nothing to suggest the Durhams behaved in anything other than an exemplary fashion. The accusations levelled cannot be substantiated unless dramatic new evidence emerges and any slur should be completely effaced.

The retreat to Dunkirk

As the Durhams pulled back to Vimy Ridge they would be in the shadow of the vast Canadian memorial which dominates the high ground and Plain of Douai below. This dazzling stele commemorates the heroism of those Canadians who took the ridge in 1917 and records the many sons of Canada who failed to return home. What fearful irony that the BEF should now be retreating over such hallowed ground won at dreadful cost. Arras would be a last gambit; from now on there would be only retreat. It must have seemed as though the enormous sacrifice of the previous generation was undone, rendered meaningless.

Orders were followed by counter-orders as the strategic situation began to unravel; it did not require the insight of a master tactician to appreciate that matters were becoming increasingly fraught. Having dug in at Vimy, the Durhams were to act as a prop to the BEF's southern flank;[28] 'received message that Vimy Ridge would be held to the end, last man last round'.[29] On 24 May the 'last man, last round' order was rescinded yet they were already in danger of being encircled and the division was obliged to withdraw smartly. For once, the Germans were laggardly as everyone slipped out of the net. Nonetheless, the great mass of Allied vehicles was clogging the roads, intermingled with the sorry wrack of refugees. John March was one of those who found the ground at Vimy rather surreal: 'Vimy Ridge was an amazing sight; the French had preserved and rebuilt these pristine trenches and the place was full of souvenir shops. Trouble was the old trenches faced the wrong way; this time the Germans were coming from the other direction!'[30]

Harry Sell, undertaking a final sweep over the abandoned perimeter, discovered two happy souls still blissfully sleeping. As he drove on into the flaming ruins of Givenchy he met a German reconnaissance unit coming the other way. This was clearly the limit and 'he beat a hasty retreat'.[31] As he sped free of danger and joined the retreat he came upon 8th Battalion's mess vehicles with the exhausted cooks snoring peacefully within. Bleary-eyed, the tired men were instantly galvanised by the magic incantation 'Boche tanks!' The situation was growing steadily more critical. 'Battalion ordered to withdraw to rest behind La Bassee Canal at La Courriere, all bridges to the west having been blown. Owing to the fact that no transport was available, most of the stores except weapons and ammunition had to be abandoned, weapons etc, being carried.'[32]

John March was one who recalled the terrifying wail of the German dive-bombers, now as thick as locusts:

> When you hear the bloody awful howling Stukas diving, then you were literally shit-scared. And what you did was this. You got yourself flat in a trench or some puddle in the road, or a fence or ditch; and I can assure you I was damn lucky because each time they had a Stuka attack they missed me, but they got friends of mine. It's quite, quite frightening; the worst thing is the noise.[33]

A current fantasy in the disintegrating realm of Franco-British cooperation was the Weygand Plan, which sought to combine a strong, southerly thrust with a French advance from the Somme region. On paper, this was eminently sound as the German advance had indeed left their forward units exposed to just such a deployment. In the real world, the Belgians were already flaky and their abandonment of the Lys Canal threatened to uncover the whole of BEF's left:

We had dug in near the River Lasne when my company commander sent me to get in touch with the Belgian Army on our left. I found them lined up on the road, not far from our position. I was somewhat surprised to see this, as it rather looked like the end of an exercise in England. So, I said to an officer, 'Where are your positions going to be?' as he obviously had none. And he just said they were *'finis'*.[34]

By late evening on 25 May Lord Gort had taken the momentous and correct decision to plug this yawning gap whilst withdrawing towards the coast; both the 5th and 50th Divisions were to redeploy and cover this exposed left flank. For the Durhams this might be rather more easily ordered than accomplished. German pressure south of La Bassee Canal was developing, and the 8th and 9th Battalions had both sent their carriers[35] to assist their hard-pressed French allies in the line. The Brigade extracted itself with some difficulty and marched towards Ypres, heavy with memory. Few cities have witnessed such a vast effusion of British and imperial blood than that which is inextricably linked with the campaigns of the BEF from 1914–18. In five great battles the Germans had failed to eliminate the salient there – might the DLI be about to fight a sixth? Men walked on exhausted, asleep on their feet. John March recalls: 'One didn't eat or sleep, seemingly for days, a lot of heavy equipment was dumped. But you had a job to do; you simply had to keep awake. One has a responsibility to the men. The refugees were particularly distressing, clogging the roads, but what can one do, unless you're completely ruthless?'[36]

The retreat was never a rout but it was frequently chaotic. The Luftwaffe was in constant and jubilant attendance; shooting at refugees to cause stampedes and further clog the roads was a given tactic. German ground forces seldom allowed a respite:

Nearby there was a Vickers pom-pom[37] on blocks of wood manned by three gunners. A mortar bomb hit it and the three blokes were just shattered. I ran over to them, and I looked at one poor fellow – his face – his eyes staring up at me. And I thought, 'Well I can't do anything for him.' I ran back again, and there was this chap, dragging himself on his elbows. He was sobbing and there were two lines in the sand from his legs – but there were no feet on the end of his legs…Then I saw this rifleman running in front of me.

One minute he was there – there was a terrific explosion – next minute he was in bits. How can a man fully clothed in webbing, uniform, a belt round his waist, gas mask, boots and everything else, within seconds be lying there without a stitch of clothing on him? He was totally in pieces with his head lying on his neck, eyes open. The skin of his belly was taken right off – and there were his intestines; just like you see in a medical book.[38]

Of more immediate concern was the incessant bombing by the Luftwaffe – JU87s, the terrifying Stuka[39] and roaring ME109s[40] raked the congested roads and sprayed every field and ditch. Much was said, unfairly, of the RAF at this time – 'Rare as fairies' was just one of the more repeatable versions. There are few worse experiences for an infantryman than to be attacked relentlessly from the air, when he is virtually defenceless. As the Durhams sought to disengage, Germans surged forward and captured the town of Carvin from the French. The 8th Battalion was ordered to put in a counter-attack to shore up the overall position. Of the three battalions, only the 6th was able to continue the march towards Flanders and, though 8th Battalion's attack was successful, their comrades in the 9th suffered heavily, both from enemy strikes across the canal and a continual plague of Stukas. After dark on the 26th the survivors were able to break off. Trucks were found and both battalions, with the 6th, were to be found digging in afresh around Ypres on the morning of 27 May.

And there were still these hapless refugees, human flotsam thrown up by the scale and suddenness of the German attack:

The roads were absolutely jammed with civilians of all ages – mostly very young and very old. The old people I shall never forget because it's something I've never seen before – never thought I'd see. Some of them must have been in their eighties, with huge bundles on their backs, bowed right over walking along those hot roads...There were mothers pulling prams piled up with belongings, little children hanging on their skirts crying. They weren't walking – they were just trudging along in the heat, virtually worn out.[41]

Tales circulated of German snipers and saboteurs dressed as women or priests – in the fevered atmosphere of retreat anything seemed credible: 'Then a rifleman next to me shot an old woman that ran out of a house – and I cursed him for what he'd done. I thought it was unnecessary to shoot an old lady – but he said, "I'm sorry, that was my orders. Anyone dressed as old women, nuns or priest or civilians running about, gets shot. Five of my company had been shot by Germans dressed as nuns."'[42]

Evidence of this fifth-column activity appeared to be everywhere:

There were some Belgians – but they may have been Germans – who were ploughing a field down two sides so that the corner pointed towards our HQ. This was for the benefit of enemy aircraft, which duly arrived and plastered our HQ out of existence. We lost our first colonel through that. It was somewhere between the Oudenaarde and Ypres areas. The ground had been ploughed in the form of an arrow, aiming straight at our HQ. No farmer ploughs his land that way. After that, when I noticed anyone ploughing wrongly, he got shot. I shot two of them who were doing that. They knew what they were doing – I knew what they were doing – so there was no need to say anything.[43]

By the following morning the Belgians had finally thrown in the towel and the divisional commander, General Martel, made the fateful announcement that evacuation was now inevitable. Though being taken off by sea might be hoped for, it was not necessarily guaranteed. The line was thin and by no means watertight; German pressure was increasing as the bridgehead collapsed. Ypres was left behind; there would be no fresh battle there. That night the Durhams slipped away, and then into the Dunkirk perimeter itself on the night of the 29th/30th. The Germans perceived the threshold of a historic triumph; pressure from the air and the relentless onrush of ground forces never diminished. As the 8th Battalion fell back, 'C' Company forming the hinge with another battalion was surrounded and obliged to fight a hopeless night-long battle against mounting odds that could have only one outcome.

For the survivors, the coastal plain was anything but inviting: the hordes of desperate refugees had thinned but the featureless expanse offered little or no cover from the fury of Axis planes, which swarmed, largely unchallenged, like angry hornets. Abandoned vehicles and smashed equipment offered dire testimony to the unfolding tragedy. French units, too, were crowding in, exhausted men and horses adding to the congestion. Sappers were busy in great dumps of vehicles, systematically wrecking what could not be saved. At night, mild, opalescent spring skies were lit as fierce as day by the funeral pyres of BEF stores. As dawn rose on 30 May, 6th and 8th Battalions were dug in along the Bergues Canal, 9th Battalion behind by the Ringsloot waterway. German troops were pressing hard, survivors of the 9th under fire even as they were digging in. This was the testing time; men were exhausted, losses were heavy and the enemy's barrage from land and skies unending.

A frequent comment from survivors of the retreat is on the apparent superiority of German equipment:

The Germans had brought the tanks in and they were blasting. They knew when they brought those damned great big tanks in, that was it. I actually fired the Boys anti-tank rifle[44] for the first time in my life – a terrifying weapon. To even fire, you had to hang on to it, like grim death, because it would dislocate your shoulder if you didn't. I fired at a tank coming over the bridge that wasn't blown – and I couldn't miss it from about 50 yards away. An officer was right beside me, and I saw this hit the tank and all it had done was to just about knock the paintwork off. It made a noise like a ping-pong ball. The officer who was beside me said, 'Leave the blessed thing there, get the hell out of it!' And we did – and only just in time. We scarpered – quick! We just disappeared off the other side of the bridge only just in time, because this fellow opened up and he blew half the coping of the bridge off with this terrible big gun on the front of the tank.[45]

On the last day of May, earmarked for the 50th Division's escape from the trap, the Durham battalions were again hard pressed, though reinforcements did come up from the second line. They would be needed, for elements of the 9th Battalion were pushed back and were subsequently ordered to counter-attack and hold the canal line. Two companies – 'A' and 'D' – were detailed for the job, attacking by Bulscamp Bridge. John March had been commanding a platoon here at Bulscamp:

We had a very wide frontage, some 150–200 yards, and the Germans came at us in force. Most of the men were killed or captured and it was here I was wounded. I felt a blow on my tin helmet and there was a large hole clear through it. I remember my batman asking if he could have my lanyard and whistle. 'Whatever for?' I managed to ask. 'Something to remember you by sir,' he replied![46]

Despite all their intense fatigue and shrunken numbers, the Durhams charged manfully, led by Captain Wood and Sergeant-Major Kemp. Such was their elan they swept the enemy from their objectives and re-established the shrinking line.[47] Nonetheless, Brigadier Churchill ordered a further withdrawal and sent two companies of the Royal Northumberland Fusiliers, together with a Guards Battalion up in support of the 6th Durham Battalion. It was, through all this, impossible not to have some grudging admiration for the German fighting man:

> I remember being very impressed with these German soldiers at the time – how bloody tough they looked. How efficient they seemed, relative to us. They were so businesslike, and how very smart the officers seemed by comparison. Everything seemed so much better than what we had. They were professional by comparison to us. I'd never seen anything like them.[48]

By evening, the Durhams, with their reinforcements, were still clinging tenaciously to the canal line. Brigadier Churchill created three marching formations from his mixed bag and, at 20.00 hours, gave the order for a final retreat on to the beaches – there was nowhere left to go. It now all depended on the Navy – Operation Dynamo.

The beaches

It seemed, to these begrimed, unutterably wearied men that their ordeal might be almost over: it was either escape or capture, they themselves had done all that could have been done. And yet perhaps not quite; one final lunatic plan was hatched to deploy 151 Brigade in mounting a last-ditch diversionary attack. They would form two formations, one in trucks the other on foot, and strike at the enemy closing the ring, throwing them off guard and buying precious time to aid the evacuation. Happily, by 14.30 hours on 1 June, this suicidal mission was aborted:

...the final move to the Dunkirk beach began. No weapons that could be carried were abandoned. Indeed Sergeant Joseph Malone of the 8th carried a heavy old Lewis gun which he had picked up in the early stages of the fighting and which he said he preferred as 'something solid rather than them new-fangled Brens!'; while Lance-Corporal Edward Wilson, the canteen steward, had an alarm clock round his neck and a sandbag full of £40 of French currency.'[49]

By midnight, all of 50th Division had embarked and were taken off, the last to leave. They would be back. Surveying the dreadful wreckage of the BEF at Dunkirk – miles of abandoned and shattered vehicles; guns, their bust barrels pointing skywards in mute testimony; corpses; filth; and mountains of abandoned stores – few would have thought that, four years later almost to the day, 50th Division would return to the beaches of France.

Notes

1   The Durham Light Infantry was raised as the 68th Foot in 1758, though the county link was not cemented till 1881. Following amalgamation in 1968, it became 4th Battalion the Light Infantry (now the Rifles).

2   Harman, N., *Dunkirk, the Patriotic Myth* (London, 1980).

3   SS Totenkopf was responsible for the murder of 97 British POWs from the 2nd Battalion Royal Norfolks at Le Paradis on 27 May 1940. It was alleged the British had been using dumdum bullets. The following day, Liebstandarte SS Adolf Hitler likewise murdered some 80 POWs from the Royal Warwicks, Cheshires and Royal Artillery at Wormhoudt.

4   Major R.C. Kelly, unpublished diary.

5   12th Battalion, 1st Tyneside Scottish were attached to the Black Watch.

6   Lewis, P.J. & English, L.R., *Into Battle with the Durhams: 8 DLI in World War Two* (London, 1990), p.9.

7   DLI Sound Recording Project.

8   Ibid.

9   Rissik, D., *The DLI at War – History of the DLI 1939–1945* (Durham, 1952), p.25.

10   Ibid. p.26

11   Major T. Allison, DLI Unpublished Archive.

12   Private G.E. Iceton MM, DLI Archive.

13   Major R.I. Pitt, DLI Archive.

14   Corporal G. Self DCM, DLI Archive.

15   Lieutenant-Colonel H.S. Sell OBE MC, DLI Archive.

16   Rissik, p.28.

17   Harman, p.101.

18   SS Totenkopf, formed October 1939.

19   Sydnor, C.W., *Soldiers of Destruction – the SS Death's Head Division 1933–1945* (Princeton, 1977), p.95.

20   Ibid. p.95.
21   Ibid. p.96.
22   Ibid. p.96.
23   Ibid. pp.106–7.
24   Ibid. p.102.
25   Maurice James Buckmaster went on to head the French Section of SOE.
26   Colonel M.J. Buckmaster, DLI Archive.
27   Rissik, p.28.
28   Ibid. p.29.
29   Major Kelly.
30   DLI Sound Recording Project.
31   Rissik, p.29.
32   Major Kelly.
33   DLI Sound Recording Project.
34   Arthur, M., *Forgotten Voices of the Second World War* (London, 2005), p.50.
35   A lightly armoured family of tracked vehicles, manufactured by Vickers Armstrong, used mainly for transport of men and equipment.
36   DLI Sound Recording Project.
37   'Pom-pom' probably means here a 40mm Vickers anti-aircraft auto-cannon.
38   Arthur, p.51.
39   JU87 dive-bomber.
40   German fighter aircraft, one of the best of the war.
41   Arthur, p.50.
42   Ibid. p.51.
43   Ibid. p.53.
44   Correctly, the Boys .55 cal. anti-tank rifle; obsolescent.
45   Arthur, p.63.
46   DLI Sound Recording Project.
47   Rissik, p.33.
48   Arthur, p.55.
49   Rissik, p.35.

Chapter 3

'Jerry Beat to a Frazzle': 2nd Battalion on the River Dyle, France, 1940

Land of soap and water,
Hitler's having a bath,
Churchill's looking through the keyhole,
Having a jolly good laugh
                    Sung to the tune of 'Land of Hope and Glory'

On 25 September 1939, the 2nd Battalion DLI sailed for France. Poland, Britain's 'First Ally', was prostrate, her lands carved up between two grand and greedy dictators, arguably the two most criminal regimes in history. The Battalion, together with the 1st Royal Welsh and 1st Royal Berkshires, formed 6th Brigade of 2nd Division – it would remain with this formation till the end of the war. Most of the teaching given prior to embarkation referred to the intricacies of trench warfare and was delivered by officers who had learnt their trade in that earlier conflict.[1] That this war might prove altogether different did not appear necessarily to be on anyone's radar at that time; evil consequences would follow. At the outset, arrival at Cherbourg and the journey to Chauteney, in the vicinity of Sable, proved agreeable. There was not a hint of what was to come.

At this point, French civilians were enthusiastic, choosing to believe the politicians' bombast that their great Maginot Line[2] was impregnable. This was the 'Phoney War' – there was no invasion, no conflict, the rumble of the guns was far to the east and unheard in that mellow autumn. War was known to be terrible but its full horrors were as yet unseen, although the savage bombing of Guernica, the Basque citadel, during the Spanish Civil War had given some warning of the impact of saturation bombing. Only the most perceptive or pessimistic could foresee a Europe laid so completely in ruins.

Next the Durhams marched on to Arras in Artois, scene of such bloody fighting in the previous war with the monuments of that colossal carnage all around them, the neat CWGC cemeteries, in the sere autumnal bloom of an English garden. A vast effusion of French, German, British and Commonwealth blood had taken place here and the ancient town, with its extensive and beautiful gabled squares, had assumed an almost mythic significance. From here, these men's fathers had burrowed through chalk, linking age-old workings to form a vast underground labyrinth from which they could issue forth into the very faces of the Germans, like the dragon's seed.

Vimy Ridge, the highest point, had been won through a magnificent and superbly executed effort by the Canadian Corps, not without significant cost. From the downlands the Battalion next advanced to the Belgian frontier and winter quarters. Winter proved less congenial; that of 1939–40 was bitterly cold, one of the worst remembered, perhaps a fitting harbinger for the tragedy about to unfold in the spring. Here they dug, standard fare when the High Command has nothing to suggest. The line was more in name than concrete; some early French bunkers were standing but little else by way of concentrated defences. Any who recalled Flanders from the First War would not easily forget that unforgiving, sodden clay, the ice-bound easterlies and the winter drabness of a flat, largely destroyed land. Lille was the nearest big city that offered a full range of diversions to young soldiers with pay in their pockets.

Major Robert ('Bobby') Simpson took over as CO, when his predecessor succumbed to illness and was repatriated. The Battalion was ready if ever something should happen; however, nothing did. The long, cold and weary months of bitter winter finally gave way to the wet spring of that region. The war might have seemed 'phoney' but it was very real and this unnatural calm would not prevail. Any who were anticipating a return to the static warfare of 1914–18 – and these were many, amongst both British and French officers – would find themselves violently deluded.

In the inter-war years, British theorists such as J.F.C. Fuller and Basil Liddel-Hart, echoed by a then-unheard-of French officer, one Colonel Charles de Gaulle, became champions of a fluid school of warfare based upon the use of massed armoured forces. This doctrine had been set aside by others who preferred to exalt the traditional supremacy of the horse and ignore the lessons of barbed wire. In Germany, however, matters stood very differently. Here, Heinz Guderian had initiated a school of armoured warfare that would employ ground attack aircraft as 'flying artillery' to overcome the tanks' dependence on supporting guns. This doctrine was defined as 'Lightning War' – blitzkrieg. On 10 May 1940, the Allies would discover precisely what this doctrine implied.

The onslaught

During the warming spring evening of 9 May, sounds of distant bombing could plainly be heard like some far-off fearful overture. There was an alarum over possible parachutists but none materialised. By first light, noise of aero-engines swelled like the devil's dawn chorus. Belgium was most clearly being attacked; her hoped-for neutrality disappeared, fled like a phantom in the night: the country was, once again, the front line. It was therefore time for the BEF to move up towards positions along the River Dyle – where Plan D of the joint Anglo-French strategy proposed the Allied armies would stand. In what seemed like an unreal calm, Battalion transport moved off at dusk on the 11th, no wailing dirge of Axis bombs interrupted and civilians cheered the Allies on. By the following evening the Durhams were digging in on the banks of the river, with Battalion HQ located in the village of La Tombe – the name was perhaps unfortunate.

Sergeant-Major Martin McLaine, a career soldier, was serving with 2nd Battalion and commanding a mortar platoon:

It was a narrow valley, bounded by hills; you got down into the position over a narrow track, not suitable for lorries. My platoon had been used on fatigues; dig here and dig there – I went to see the Company Commander and said I want to get my men forward so they can use the gun [mortar] and do the job they're trained to do. We were really something new, the mortar platoon and we had two dedicated trucks with all our ammo and warlike stores aboard. We had to hump the gun and ammo down to Mr. Annand's [2nd Lieutenant, later Captain Richard Annand] position. When we got down to the bridge we saw the vanguard coming in and the RE blew the bridge. Bang! We began digging in, no use this as a forward OP – the Germans commanded the position, they could see everything we were doing. There was constant sniping. Nobody was keen to help us – fact was they didn't want us; once we fired, we acted as a magnet for shells and mortars![3]

The ground was undistinguished and the Battalion was responsible for a 2,000-yard frontage. This otherwise level and largely featureless terrain was defined by twin obstacles of river and railway line. Behind the plain the land began to rise toward low, wooded hills and 'C' Company, as reserve, entrenched here. They were not expected to stand but to provide timely warning of any attack. In fact, the water and railway line formed a shallow 'X' shape with the crossing point towards the Durhams' left flank, itself bisected by a lateral road which crossed both obstacles by bridges. 'A' Company held the right, 'B' the centre across from the loop in the river, and 'D' far left on the south bank, covering these crossings. The position overall lay in a dip between timbered slopes and was largely bare of cover. Belgian sappers had constructed a number of pillboxes and slit trenches but these were rather ad hoc and without depth. Again the Durhams dug, in the fond expectation this would be the front line: 'it was suggested that there would probably be 10 to 14 days to prepare the area before any attack was likely'.[4] In this, the Germans were to prove most disobliging.

Martin McLaine recalls:

'D' Company was at the foot of the valley. There was a long winding track and the bridge across the river. It had a balustrade, very ornamental, about 50 yards long and maybe eight wide, probably went with the big house behind us; the road was dead straight down to it, the bridge was dead straight and so was the road beyond! The crossroads beyond was very busy with refugees, rumbling along in carts, continuously. The French had built a fortress [bunker] near us with a stupid little pillbox. A platoon was on the left behind this fortress. We got no orders from the CO and we had to carry down a large amount of ammo, each bomb weighed 10 pounds or so and we had to organise carrying parties. We were shelled all the way down and one of my men was wounded. 'Look,' I said to him, 'we're going to have to leave you here for a while till we get all this ammo down to the position.' He was the only casualty we had then. We just had one gun, and no night lamp and aiming post so we could shoot at night.[5]

First, there were the refugees pouring down the roads, an almost biblical exodus of traumatised and desperate people, carrying everything they could on their backs or on carts: 'The Battalion had received a somewhat strange and unexplained warning that any carrying red blankets were likely to be fifth columnists.'[6] Quite why this was so was never fully explained; nor was the illogical assumption that enemy agents would be so keen to advertise themselves; in the event, large numbers of people did appear to have brightly coloured cloths. The injunction was ignored. On 14 May both bridges were blown.

Defending the Dyle

The standard Hollywood image of a German panzer formation is of a rush of armoured leviathans. This is not, in practice, anything like reality. First would come pathfinders on fast motorcycle combinations, then armoured cars (four- and eight-wheeled SdKfz-222s and 234s), a barbed screen behind which rode motorised infantry, either in trucks or half-tracks. Their function was to engage unarmoured gun teams and transport whilst covering their own anti-tank weapons, at this point mainly Pak38s. Around 16.00 hours on the 14th these Axis elements bumped 'C' Company. Captain Blackett and his men, who had hurriedly thrown an improvised barricade across the road, met them with a well-directed hail of small arms and anti-tank rifle fire. Their role was to harass rather than resist so the Company withdrew in an orderly manner, disengaging without loss. La Tombe had to be hurriedly evacuated, shocked families stumbling dazed from their homes, orderly lives suddenly turned topsy-turvy, their settled existences seeming extinguished in an instant: 'In the small house where was Battalion HQ the occupants left at only a few minutes' notice; they took almost no belongings and the evening meal was still cooking on the fire after they and their small children had tearfully left their little home.'[7]

Realising they faced a major challenge, the Germans spent a cautious night. They probed around the Durhams' left but were soon discouraged. The short spring night was enlivened by staccato bursts of random fire and bright comets of tracers. At dawn, the situation changed as a determined attack overran one platoon of 'B' Company, dug in near the remnants of the destroyed bridge. Martin McLaine and his mortar platoon did good service: 'Next day the shooting match proper started. We had only the one gun and zeroed in on the crossroads, and provided supporting fire wherever we thought it was needed. We used HE rounds and still sent the odd stray round towards that crossroads; we stopped a whole lot of German traffic.'[8]

Well-trained Axis infantry had maximised the use of cover afforded by some derelict buildings to rush the river crossing, using a handy weir that had proved difficult to slight. The fight lasted several hours, by which time most of the platoon had been knocked out. Second Lieutenant John Hyde-Thompson remained on his feet and took the Axis on single-handed, dropping their officer with his Webley pistol and seeing off the survivors with grenades. He then organised the right-flank platoon to put in a counter-attack, which, though vigorous, failed to restore the situation. Nonetheless, he did manage to occupy a fall-back position which effectively denied the enemy a consolidated foothold.[9]

At around 11.00 hours 'C' Company was sent in to bolster the line and see the Germans back across the water. One platoon was decimated but Sergeant-Major Pinkney managed to establish a hold on the railway embankment with a handful, whose well-directed fire forced the enemy to cede the riverbank. The predictable German response was to intensify a furious barrage of MG fire and mortars, which thoroughly stonked the Durhams. Captain Tubbs, leading 'B' Company, was wounded and evacuated; losses were so high that 'C' and 'B' Company survivors were formed into a single composite. Sergeant Pinkney's survivors, who had fought long, hard and well, were able to withdraw, save for a single section north of the railway, which had to wait until cover of darkness.

Pressure had also been mounting against 'D' Company on the Durhams' left. Captain Hutton was disabled by wounds, and the fury of the assault intensified. One section was completely cut off, holding a bunker by the river's edge. Their ammunition exhausted, the men, under Corporal Thompson, made a run for it; none survived. Sergeant-Major Norman Metcalfe at Company HQ used his initiative to send in the reserve platoon, which effectively shored up the threatened position. The line held but only just; losses were high, the remnant spread awfully thin and now with no reserves. Brigade responded to requests for assistance and sent forward a detached company from 1st Royal Welsh Fusiliers. It was no later than noon and the Durhams had, at some cost, given the enemy a severely bloodied nose. German casualties were high enough to deter further attacks. Through the long spring afternoon, troops were machine-gunned, mortared and sniped at – less costly than all-out assault but still nerve-grinding and relentless.

Darkness brought no relief. Once again a fairy-like web of tracers criss-crossed the night sky, mortar shells crashed down and frequent, fresh probes were launched. The stump of the slighted bridge to 'D' Company's front proved especially attractive, but the Germans had to contend with Captain Richard ('Dickie') Annand. Sergeant-Major Metcalfe was a witness:

> In they came with a vengeance, and weren't they socked with a vengeance. They were bumped off like ninepins in bundles of ten. They seemed determined to get that bridge and therefore reinforcements were simply piled up with casualties. There must have been thousands of them; the position we had couldn't have been better. Jerry couldn't move old 'D'. We had casualties, especially 16 Platoon, but they were wonderful. Mr. Annand, Batty, Wood, Surtees – they just went mad. Jerry got up to the other side of the bridge, to their sorrow; they must have thought they had demons in front of them. Mr Annand and Co. just belted them and they even got on to the parapet to be able to pitch grenades. For two hours it was all hell let loose, then Jerry gave up and withdrew. I could hardly believe it when we checked up: we'd only about 16 casualties. We fired over 20,000 rounds and over 100 grenades had been used.[10]

Martin McLaine was another witness to this astonishing feat:

> The Germans had got into the river bed; they were too near to use the mortar, too close to our men. Captain Annand kept

going forward; remember, it was a straight road – a miracle he wasn't hit. He went across and threw grenades at the bridging party beneath. He must have caused devastation; we could hear the German wounded screaming for their mothers. We think he killed about 40 of them aside from the wounded. That stopped all work and, though this wasn't in the citation, Captain Annand took a party to recapture that silly pillbox. My mate Corporal Bell, an ex-TA man, went with him. Bell was killed though.[11]

This was only a respite. The Germans came on again, regardless of loss. Again Richard Annand saw them off. Terry O'Neill (who lost an arm in this fight) recalled: 'Mr. Annand came to me and asked for a box of grenades as they could hear the Germans trying to repair the bridge. Off he went and he must have given them a lovely time because it wasn't long before he was back for more.'[12] A section of German pioneers managed to cling to the bridge footings but the British officer again dashed forward, a sackful of grenades bouncing, and pelted them regardless of the storm of fire bursting around. At least another score of Germans were blasted to oblivion before Annand, now wounded, withdrew.

Once his injuries had been tended, he returned to the fight. In the fury and fog of battle he learnt, as the battalion was finally withdrawing, that his batman, badly hurt, had been left behind. Despite severe wounds Annand attempted to bring the injured man off in a commandeered wheelbarrow before collapsing from blood loss:

> He went back alone to look for Private Hunter, found him, put him into a wheelbarrow, and set off up the forest path after the rest. Then they came to a fallen tree that blocked the path. Richard Annand was so weak from the loss of blood that he finally left Private Hunter and went for help. Before he could be rescued, Private Hunter was taken prisoner and later died of his wounds.[13]

Despite the enormous gallantry of the Durhams and the significant losses they had inflicted, the overall position was fast unravelling. Pressure was continuing to build and snipers were active – whether these were from front or rear was unclear; suspicion was growing that fifth columnists were indeed active. The Battalion was deployed thinly, with no reserves and no second line. In the small hours of 16 May an order to disengage was transmitted from Brigade – 'then came the rotten order to withdraw. We were dumbfounded. We had Jerry beat to a frazzle.'[14] The Durhams were not to know of the disaster at Sedan which had determined the outcome of the campaign even as they fought so hard to hold the Dyle.

Martin McLaine was one of those astonished:

I was back outside Battalion HQ; the Germans overran some of our positions. I saw some of the Royal Welsh pass in front of us. The mortar had been sent back but we couldn't dig out the base-plate – it was driven too far into the earth. Still, we had a spare. I was convinced I could hit the Germans. We had no wireless so commands could only be relayed back from as far as your voice would carry. At that moment the Royal Welsh attacked and the mortar rounds knocked some of them down. It was terrible; I felt like shooting myself. I'd actually drawn my revolver when one of my men, Private Jones it was, restrained me – 'It's not your fault,' he said.[15]

After all this McLaine could not believe they were about to retreat:

We had the Germans beat, our counter-attacks recovered the ground lost, and we'd lost our transport. I saw the Company Commander but he just gave me a rollicking; but we did find a big grey horse attached to a milk cart in one of the barns in La Tombe, so we loaded the three-inch mortar and ammo and that was our transport till the horse near collapsed. Then we were ordered to dump our heavy weapons and we became riflemen. Nobody gave clear orders; we had no idea where we were headed most of the time. It wasn't the fault of the battalion officers; it was just the way the army was then. Shame to lose all that valuable kit: we smashed the sights and destroyed the elevating screws then threw the barrels into a ditch.[16]

Retreat

With the stench of burning materiel and abandoned vehicles, heralds of defeat, the 2nd Battalion commenced its withdrawal at 01.30 hours. Darkness was lit by the fires of an army in retreat;

flames from the ancient chateau at Ottenburg seared the night. Everywhere roads were clogged with a mass of men and vehicles. The Battalion could muster around 450 effectives, there was a shortage of both small-arms ammunition and grenades, and all non-riflemen were integrated into four somewhat ad hoc fighting companies; mortars were left behind. A new line was determined and as quickly abandoned. Captain Pearson, the quartermaster, performed prodigies to provide hot food for the desperately tired marching men. Two companies became detached in the enveloping fog of retreat and were not seen for several days. Fifth columnists appeared to be active in the Forest of Soignies as the Durhams passed through, the leafy canopy of spring leaves offering shade from a warming sun. In 48 hours the companies marched nearly as many miles; transport scheduled to arrive never did and drivers were falling asleep at the wheel, adding to lengthening tailbacks. As they tramped across the Brussels–Charleroi Canal, engineers were already packing demolition charges.

Martin McLaine and his platoon, now riflemen rather than artillerists, marched with the rest:

I was attached to Battalion HQ. The enemy were dropping three-inch mortars around us, terrific bang but little else. Oddly, I wasn't afraid; I had a belief I'd be alright as long as I stayed standing, didn't dive for cover – daft you might think but it worked. Getting out was tricky; whilst we were fighting adrenalin kept us going but now we were all dead tired. We hadn't sustained that many casualties, none in my platoon, apart from that fellow who'd been injured. Nobody was giving us any orders and, frankly, we were afraid of German tanks. The only weapon we had was the useless A/T rifle – couldn't penetrate the armour, it was there for morale not effect; anybody who said it would work should have been made to use one against a Jerry tank.[17]

Early morning on 19 May and Tournai was engulfed in flames. To add to the prevailing madness, inmates from the local asylum were wandering the shattered streets; these had to be rounded up and secured in the museum. Now the Durhams were expected to hold the line of the Escaut Canal – an uneventful four days, largely undisturbed by enemy activity, save for random long-distance shelling and a barrage of rumours. So potent were these that bridges were blown on the strength of them and precious vehicles abandoned. McLaine and his men were attached to 'D' Company:

> We were commanded by Lieutenant Gregson now. Captain Hutton had been injured; his kneecap blown off. We had a full company with everyone added in, now in three platoons with us mortar-men as reserve. We still didn't know where we were going but everyone, officers and men, were behaving well, no signs of any panic anywhere. We crossed some ground where 'C' Company had put in a bayonet charge, blood everywhere, lots of it, blood and bodies; one of my best friends was killed there. A lad called Rutherford, a fireman I think before, was collecting in abandoned rifles, most with bayonets attached, thick with blood.[18]

A further withdrawal followed and the Battalion was soon marching through a landscape they'd advanced over barely 10 days before; no cheering crowds this time. On the 24th, Bethune fell and the fog of war shrouded more closely. Nerves were stretched taut as enemy fire might erupt at any time – German or fifth columnists. Martin McLaine again:

> We came under MG fire and dived into ditches. I could see a fellow apparently directing fire from an open hayloft. I was getting ready to pot him when the CSM stopped me, said the fellow was probably just a Belgian farmer. I wasn't so sure but I didn't shoot. Later we came across the French – what a shambles, you never saw anything like it: some were barefoot, their clogs around their necks, some pushing prams or carts, no sign of order. It was disheartening I tell you, none of them was going to fight! None of what we did bore any resemblance to our training. We were told to prepare to ambush tanks. How do you ambush tanks? I improvised a barricade across the road, just took the French farmer's cart and bales; he was very unhappy about it! I put a couple of men in a hayloft ready to drop grenades into the tank hatches. We couldn't dig in, we had no tools, our ammo was down to what we had in our pouches and we'd few grenades.[19]

Nemesis

When the Durhams entered Calonnes-sur-Lys, locals advised them Axis forces had preceded them. Confusion prevailed and the Battalion moved to occupy St. Venant on the following evening. Enemy were very close; any daytime manoeuvre was accompanied by an unhealthy overture of mortars and MG fire. It soon became apparent the Durhams' left flank was rather in the air – the ominous and unmistakeable resonance of German armour could be clearly discerned. That night it seemed to the men of 2nd Battalion, like Homer's Greeks before Troy, that enemy campfires ringed them all around; more and hard fighting clearly loomed.

Martin McLaine was again in the press of the action:

The place was just a scattering of farm buildings along a single road with one big house. We dug in around this – I say around as we didn't go into the houses. The British Army didn't like to disturb residents and people were still in their homes. Not like Jerry, he'd have turned each house into a fortress; we should have done the same. We weren't receiving many orders so I went out for myself to do a recce. I came to a small humpbacked bridge, the whole area was waterlogged, deep streams and generally uncultivated, more animal pasture. I went around to make contact with the other platoons; we had no Brens only rifles. Jerry started shelling and again I was lucky. I met our officer, Lieutenant Gregson; he had his briar walking stick I remember. He asked me what I was doing there and I told him – suddenly there was a terrific bang as a shell landed nearby and he went down. I ran over to him, he was screaming and a bowl-shaped lump of shrapnel was wedged into the base of his spine. He was in terrible pain and I saw he was trying to pull out his revolver, I think to shoot himself. I took the pistol away and tried to pull out the shrapnel but it was red-hot! We had no field dressings left by then and I ran to get stretcher-bearers. Sergeant-Major Metcalfe sent out a party and gave me a cup of tea. The CSM said, 'Look Martin, there are no officers left; I'm in command and you're now Second-in-Command.' I protested there were PSMs [Platoon Sergeant-Majors] senior to me. 'Doesn't matter', he said, 'that's it.' They brought Lieutenant Gregson in, carried on a five-barred gate; poor fellow, he died. Later, I remember his mother sent out five embossed silver cigarette cases for the stretcher party.[20]

Sergeant McLaine now had to tell the other PSMs he was in charge;

> and they didn't all take too kindly to that. I sent Corporal Donaldson and a patrol forward, sent out the 'bad boys' – those who were habitually in trouble. Private Whitely, the battalion boxer, went with them. They were back in two hours, said they thought the whole German army was out there, and on this side of the canal as well. I let CSM Metcalfe know and he said we'd defensive fire behind us, guns and mortars, ha.[21]

In the filtering light of dawn 'A' Company was attacked when the Durhams brushed a fighting patrol. A savage firefight erupted and the Axis was driven off with loss, though not without the Durhams sustaining some casualties. Next came armour; the British two-pounder A/T gun was largely ineffective – those that existed were swiftly knocked out, leaving only anti-tank rifles. The Royal Welsh Fusiliers were also under pressure; matters were becoming serious.

> The CSM ordered stand-to at dawn, there was a terrific enemy barrage and we could then hear tanks in the distance. Well, rifles were no good against these steel monsters; men weren't willing to fight – it wasn't cowardice, there was just nothing you could do. The German infantry came on in the usual way, small groups using cover. I had a German rifle then, as I'd given mine to a fellow who had lost his. I got up into a corner of the barn; I was a marksman, and I put down seven Germans. A Lieutenant – never mind his name – came in and asked if he could fire a shot. Well, he did and next thing he was squatting in the corner, trousers down doing his business. Now I never saw that before – the books and films talk about that but it never happens in reality. Never seen a fellow fill his trousers; I just got on with the shooting. Men were starting to run from the tanks, there really was nothing you could do; men were running everywhere.[22]

2nd Battalion HQ was concentrated in a stout barn just off the road passing through St. Venant and south of the canal of that same name. Barricades were hastily flung across roads and trackways, the available gunners were firing over open sights as German tanks, like hungry sharks, closed in on the position. A brace of panzers began pounding the defenders from the left bank of the canal whilst more stormed 'A' Company's position. At least one Axis crew was dispatched by fire from an anti-tank rifle but the end was never in doubt: they hosed down the Durhams with MG fire and ground remorselessly over slit trenches, some of whose occupants died horribly yet others miraculously survived.

'D' Company was also being pulverised and soon down to single platoon strength with Sergeant-Major Metcalfe still the senior man left standing. Despite these mounting odds, the Durhams were still fighting, Metcalfe ordering Sergeant-Major Pearson to counter-attack with his shrunken platoon and seal a looming gap on one flank. This gallant but doomed attempt cost all their lives. When orders, via the Berkshires, came to fall back, Metcalfe could barely muster 25 men and retreating meant somehow getting over the canal. Martin McLaine:

> Saw my platoon running back now as well; one of our men had been shot through the head by a sniper and killed, this had unnerved the rest. I was disgusted. Some, a couple, were wounded, the blood running in channels down their trousers. CSM Metcalfe called for a counter-attack. 'But with what?' I said. The Germans were coming on, they had automatic weapons, Tommy guns. I was out of ammo for my German rifle and had only my pistol. I gave the order it was every man for himself.[23]

For the rest, the Axis net had already tightened too far. Some 'B' echelon transport had managed to cross the St. Venant Bridge and escape the trap; for the remainder it was now a question of selling their lives as dearly as possible. They now possessed no single anti-tank weapon and a handful of Axis tanks was rumbling through the shattered village. One simply stormed the bridge, hosing down any defenders, pumping high explosive into buildings. An 18-pounder, WWI vintage, somehow knocked this first panzer out but there were plenty more behind.

Those who were still able prepared to mount a final stand around the barn and Battalion HQ. Colonel Simpson fought with his revolver, despite injuries. Smoke and fumes clogged the air; hay and straw were everywhere on fire. It was soon ended: German tanks and infantry surged over the dwindling remnant; for 2nd Battalion the battle was over. Sergeant McLaine and his few survivors made a run for it:

> Across corn fields. I think it was corn, standing crops anyway. The men ran anyways and I ordered them to zig-zag, run and lie flat. Whitely was one of those hit. I went back to him; 'Leave me,' he said, 'I'm finished.' He was: I could see his injuries. He was a very brave man. As we crossed the field we came across a lorried Vickers MG section, just sitting around calm as you please. They pretty soon mounted up and scarpered. 'Don't go that way,' I yelled, 'you'll drive into an ambush.' They went anyway. Of 120 men in 'D' Company, nine of us got out.[24]

Their trials were not ended: 'We came to a canal, the Lys I think; half the men, including CSM Metcalfe, couldn't swim so I removed my webbing, got into the water and swum across. It was difficult; the far bank was concreted but I found a small boat and managed to paddle back over, so we got everyone across. Never got my webbing back tho.'[25] After exhausting marching, catching up with their own 'B' echelon and being under near-arrest in a barn, accosted by an officer who clearly had not seen action, the handful were saved. Those who survived were pitifully few: Metcalfe and McLaine's survivors from 'D' company, transport and 'B' echelon, wounded already evacuated, some on leave or LOB in England. The enemy might think they had heard the last of 2nd Battalion DLI – they most assuredly had not.

Notes

1   Rissik, D., *The DLI at War – History of the DLI 1939–1945* (Durham, 1952), p.5.
2   Named after French minister André Maginot; a vast line of forts, ideal for 1914 but completely outmoded by 1940.
3   DLI Sound Recording Project.
4   Rissik, p.11.
5   DLI Sound Recording Project.
6   Rissik, p.11.
7   Ibid.
8   DLI Sound Recording Project.
9   He was later captured.
10 Rissik, p.14.

11 Durham Sound Recording Project.
12 Deary, T., *Dirty Little Imps – Stories from the DLI* (Durham, 2004), p.46.
13 Ibid.
14 Rissik, p.15.
15 DLI Sound Recording Project.
16 Ibid.
17 Ibid.
18 Ibid.
19 Ibid.
20 Ibid.
21 Ibid.
22 Ibid.
23 Ibid.
24 Ibid.
25 Ibid.

Chapter 4

Western Desert: the 'Gazala Gallop', 1942

What did I see in the desert today,
In the cold pale light of the dawn?
I saw the Honeys creaking out,
Their brave bright pennants torn;
And heads were high against the sky,
And faces were grim and drawn.

L. Challoner, 'Desert Victory' 1943

The Western Desert has been described as a land only fit for war:

A few yards from where I was standing there was a depression in which there were several bodies hastily covered with sand, here and there a leg or arm protruding and part of a machine-gun barrel also sticking up. I was idly watching these as the last of the vehicles passed, and was waiting to be picked up. My opposite number was on the British side of the minefields some distance away, also waiting. It had been very hot, around 100 degrees I should think, but now the sun was beginning to set and it was getting colder. I put on my greatcoat, although I had been wearing shorts and khaki shirt all day, when I noticed the arm that was sticking out of the sand with its fingers outstretched. As I looked I saw the fingers slowly close to a clenched position. I felt my hair bristle as I was certain the poor fellow must be dead underneath the sand, for the hand was already turning black. I felt very relieved when I suddenly remembered the sharp difference in temperature that was causing this contraction. However, I was glad when our relief truck arrived and picked me up.[1]

Into the 'Blue'

The great swathe of the Sahara Desert covers a vast expanse. It has an enduring aura of romance and exoticism, experienced by very few of those who fought in the Desert War. Desert ('the Blue') threw up a whole catalogue of factors to hinder military activity and increase the misery of individual combatants. For these, British and Dominion, the Germans, Italians, French, Greeks and others, it seemed they had arrived in the very cauldron of a particular version of hell:

> ...my three strongest recollections are: the heat, sweat pouring and oozing from me, until I ached and itched with it...the strange lack of fear...the seemingly endless hours of utter boredom, observing a low ridge about 2,000 yards away with nothing moving, nothing happening, except the sun beating mercilessly down and one's eyes straining (as I remember our gunner putting it) 'at miles and miles of f*** all'.[2]

A captain recorded his first impressions of this alien terrain:

> The first time one goes up into the desert one is completely amazed by the flat terrain. We used to motor around the desert finding our way by sun compass. It was a gadget which had been produced by British officers in the 1930s. It was a very accurate compass. Roughly, the sun marked the gnomon – the same piece of equipment you have on a sundial clock – which threw a shadow, and if your compass was correctly set, that was the mark you kept your direction on.[3]

Along the Mediterranean coast runs the fertile coastal strip, along which most of the main settlements are located. This agreeable plain is bounded inland by a line of limestone cliffs, steep and bare, dragged through with narrow defiles or wadis. Atop the cliffs and running southwards in a gentle decline is a bare plateau, scorched by the hot sun and scoured by millennia of harsh winds. The surface is comprised of rock and layered grit, like the topping on a primeval cake, varying in depth from metres to centimetres. Where the base rock is denser, low hills have been left, insignificant humps or irregular ridges, possession of which was to be vital to the armies and demand a vast sacrifice in blood and materiel.

Though unremittingly harsh the desert was not devoid of either flora or fauna, or, for that matter, inhabitants: '... there was virtually no animal or insect life. Just the occasional jerboa – the desert rat (a nice friendly little fellow) – the scorpion and an occasional gazelle. The Arabs and their camels kept well out of the way.' Gazelles were game and a variant to the harsh ration diet. Hunting itself was a useful diversion:

We spied six of them in a line. The distance was only about 500 yards. All of us fired at once, hitting three. One went down on the spot, another kept limping on and the third kept falling and rising alternately. When we arrived we found the fallen gazelle still alive but unable to get up as his leg had been blown off. Nevertheless he made frantic, pathetic efforts to do so. As I watched him I was struck with pity for the little animal. But the fact that we were in need of meat put salve on my conscience...I shall never forget the death of that animal. At first we decided to blow its brains out at close range but somebody said it would make too much of a mess that way, so Skinner elected to stand 10 yards away and put a bullet through the brains. Skinner fired, the head was hit, thick blood spouted from the hole but the gazelle didn't die. It began to jerk and quiver spasmodically...[4]

Flies were another indigenous if less attractive feature: 'Flies were a terrible nuisance. More often than not you'd be drinking a cup of tea and you would have to put your hand over the top and sip it between the thumb and forefinger to stop the flies, otherwise they would be lining up around the rim to dive in.'[5] George Chambers, a Major serving in 8th Battalion, recalls: 'The water ration was about half a gallon a day. We had a system of filtering water through stones...we ended up using the same water again and again. You suffered from thirst but it was bearable. Flies were always a problem.' Beer was in fairly short supply: 'we had the occasional issue of cans of beer. They got so hot that when you pulled the ring, the contents shot up into the air, there was so much fizz; best thing was to leave the cans beneath a truck overnight so they'd cool down a bit.'

During the summer months, from May to October, the climate is scorching hot under a blistering and relentless sun, furnace bright and searing dry. Only in the evenings before the dark cold of night, before the sun sinks, is the broiling fire of day mellowed into evening cool. Winters are drear and damp with frequent heavy downpours. Torrents flow down the scree-riven wadis but water is soon soaked up by the parched and greedy desert. There is great and ascetic beauty and the desert can exert a powerful, almost obsessive pull. Dawn and sunset can be infinitely memorable and the stars glow with a clear, cold light that conjures biblical images. Soldiers were thrown back on their recall of heroic conflicts as depicted in the *Iliad*:

> Wilfrid Owen said that the poetry is in the pity; but that was in another war. This later war was one of great distances and rapid movement and for me the poetry came when least expected, in the interstices of a generally agitated existence, in the rush of sudden contrasts, and the recognition that, whatever else changes, one's own mortality does not.[6]

Moving over this great and shifting waste, where tracks were few and landmarks fewer, became an art in itself. One of those officers from 8 DLI who experienced the desert for the first time when 151 Brigade deployed was Major Harold Sell:

> If you're moving in a large formation across the desert it's not easy, so you'd have navigating officers using the sun compass. But the average driver had to improvise. They would put a string from the bonnet of the vehicle up to a row of nails on top of the cab and every hour they switched the string one notch along. The driver simply drove along the shadow on top of the bonnet and that kept him in the right direction. You had to stop every hour to check your tyres and let some air out or else they burst with the heat. Then you had to check to see the sand hadn't got into the carburettors. All this maintenance went on every hour you drove. At the same time you adjusted your compasses and checked your weapons. It was a drill which was carried out without any bother. You checked your petrol, you checked your oil, you checked your water.[7]

Subsistence

Q: 'Were they good days for you?'
A: 'Oh yes. Happy days with my men...I have always longed to meet them again. Where are all the Geordie men I loved and commanded now?'[8]

The desert offered little to sustain man. Rations, which inevitably come to prominence in the minds of fit young men, deprived of alluring sustenance, became a focal point for 'grousing', the litany of complaint which is the birthright of all soldiers:

> *You can stew it, you can fry it*
> *But no matter how you try it*
> *Fundamentally it remains the same,*
> *You can hash it, you can slash it,*
> *With potatoes you can mash it,*
> *But when all is done you've only changed the name.*
>
> 'A Cook's Thoughts on Bully'

Battles were large and terrifying though relatively rare. Smaller actions at platoon or company level were far more common and there was a constant need for patrolling, either light reconnaissance or the beefier and bristling fighting patrol.

> Recce patrols were messy affairs if we had to go through the pockets of some poor devil who had been killed and had been left lying out in the sand for a couple of days. People talk about rigor mortis, but after a day or two the limbs were flexible again and indeed, after a week or so, a quick pull on an arm or leg would detach it from the torso. Two-day-old corpses were already fly-blown and stinking. There was no dignity in death, only masses of flies and maggots, black swollen flesh and the body seeming to move, either because of the gases within it or else the thousands of maggots at work. We had to take documents, identity discs, shoulder straps, anything of intelligence value. Pushing or pulling these frightening dead men to reach their pockets was sickening. Of course, we couldn't wash our hands – one rubbed them in sand – sometimes we rubbed them practically raw if it had been a particularly disgusting day.[9]

'Desert Rose' sounds like an attractive form of flora. To the Allied army, however, it denoted an altogether more basic convenience – the field latrine. For temporary arrangements the hollow shell of a petrol container was buried with another laid on top at a suitable angle to form a urinal. Where more creature comforts were needed a deep trench was sunk with a hessian sheet on a timber frame arranged above. Chlorine was applied liberally. Cleanliness and hygiene were essential in the desert climate where dysentery and other horrors stalked, and the tending of these facilities was not itself without hazard.[10]

In such surroundings the comradeship of war was inevitably heightened. Men might express fine sentiments and extol the nobility of sacrifice but such poetic expressions soon wilted in the face of reality. Endless hours of tedium, dirty, sweaty, beset by a constant and ravenous horde of flies, troubled by looseness of the bowels and all the other complaints that add endless misery to a soldier's life, enlivened only by odd moments of sheer terror. The code of behaviour which evolved was dictated by pure pragmatism:

> Your chief concern is not to endanger your comrade.
> Because of the risk that you may bring him, you do not
>   light fires after sunset.
> You do not use his slit trench at any time.
> Neither do you park your vehicle near the hole in the
>   ground in which he lives.
> You do not borrow from him, and particularly you do not
>   borrow those precious fluids, water and petrol.
> You do not give him compass bearings which you have not
>   tested and of which you are not sure.
> You do not leave any mess behind that will breed flies.
> You do not ask him to convey your messages, your gear or
>   yourself unless it is his job to do so.
> You do not drink deeply of any man's bottles, for they may
>   not be replenished. You make sure that he has many
>   before you take his cigarettes.
> You do not ask information beyond your job, for idle talk
>   kills men.
> You do not grouse unduly, except concerning the folly of
>   your own commanders. This is allowable. You criticise
>   no other man's commanders.
> Of those things which you do, the first is to be hospitable
>   and the second is to be courteous…there is time to be
>   helpful to those who share your adventure. A cup of tea,
>   therefore, is proffered to all comers…

This code is the sum of fellowship in the desert. It knows
no rank or any exception.[11]

Krieg ohne Hass ('War without Hate') was a description attributed to
Rommel himself and insofar as war can ever truly be said to
represent chivalry, then it was here. The British had a high regard
for the Desert Fox, both as a fighting soldier of the highest calibre
and a man of impeccable honour. Some years after the war
Lieutenant-General Johann von Ravenstein observed:

> If the warriors of the Africa Campaign meet today anywhere in
> the world, be they Englishmen or Scots, Germans or Italians,
> Indians, New Zealanders or South Africans, they greet each other
> as staunch old comrades. It is an invisible but strong link which
> binds them all. The fight in Africa was fierce, but fair. They
> respected each other and still do so today. They were brave and
> chivalrous soldiers.[12]

Humour, as ever, was the soldier's balm. 'A typical example of the
sort of thing that amused us was the story that Hitler had secretly
contacted Churchill with the offer to remove Rommel from his
command in return for Churchill retaining all his generals in theirs.'[13]

Though the soldiers in the line observed a strict blackout procedure,
the sky to the east was lit up with the rich glow of the Delta cities.
The brightness and gaiety of easy living these represented could not
have contrasted more tellingly with the drab but dangerous austerity
of the front. The contrast between the rigours of the line and the
luxury of Cairo – the 'Unreal City' – could not have been greater: as
water in the desert was the most scarce and precious of commodities
at the same time as being the prime essential, troops at the front
were given extra cause to despise the 'desk wallahs' in Cairo,
enjoying their very different war. Harold Sell recalls:

> We imagined that every staff officer in Cairo lived in the lap of
> luxury, that was to say he had water. I remember on one of
> the circulars that came round, a wag had written a long poem
> about these staff officers in Cairo, who he called the 'Gaberdine
> Swine' – as their uniforms were made from gaberdine material.
> At the end of every stanza he had put in a chorus: 'And every

time they pulled the chain/Went three days rations down the drain.'[14]

As the desert campaign ground on, undistinguished places in that barren landscape, hitherto barely heard of, would become household names:

We got out of our trucks and turned off to the left at a crossroads. Presently, we drew up at the empty sidings. There was a sort of goods yard and a compound surrounded by barbed wire on a line of crazy poles. Behind the station buildings stood a row of shattered shacks with their doors hanging open. The whole place was littered with empty barrels and broken crates, and everywhere the brickwork was chipped and pockmarked by machine-gun bullets. Where the road crosses the metals stood a signal, its arm inappropriately set at 'safety'. The entire neighbourhood seemed to be completely deserted and, as I mounted the platform, I read on the front of the building the name of the place, 'ALAMEIN.'[15]

Prior to the Desert War, few people had heard of this insignificant halt some 50 miles west of Alexandria. Indeed, there was little to see. This rather shabby halt had the advantage of being close to the sea and it was possible to access the beach. This provided a welcome and refreshing experience for weary and dusty soldiery.

The Durhams deploy

Despite all the horrors of Dunkirk, morale in 151 Brigade was constant. Three territorial battalions had shown they could do as well as the regulars, pass through the fires and emerge. After rest and retraining they were earmarked for North Africa. To many this seemed like a far-off exotic land, seen only in movies. Reality was somewhat more sobering:

The convoy arrived off Suez early in July and the Brigade was decanted into Quassasin Camp. It began arriving at Quassasin station early one morning just as the village was waking up; and this introduction to the ways of the East showed the troops what they and others were to learn very rapidly: that Egypt is – apart from Cairo, Alexandria and a few other large towns – a land of dirty native villages inhabited by a disease-ridden population, plagued by flies and smelling to high heaven.[16]

Providentially, the Durhams were permitted a far gentler acclimatisation than their comrades in what would become the 8th Army, currently the Western Desert Force, as they were immediately shipped to Cyprus, that warm and verdant island, feared, after the debacle of Crete, to be the Axis's next target. The rather rough and ready methods employed by matelots to unload gear provided employment opportunities for enterprising locals: 'Inevitably something ended up in the water; but this was put right by a certain fat Cypriot who appeared every morning at daybreak and for a suitable fee dived into the harbour to retrieve anything from ammunition boxes to anti-tank rifles!'[17]

Thus the summer of 1941, whilst great battles raged in the Western Desert, was spent on the gilded shores of this enchanted island, reeking of antiquity. In November the Durhams moved again, this time towards Palestine and Iraq when it was feared German successes against Soviet Russia imperilled oil supplies. Should the Axis assault through the Caucasus burst through the bastion of Rostov and into Persia then 151 Brigade, who spent a winter very far from home by the banks of the Great Zab River, would have been there to resist this offensive. George Chambers remembers: 'We thought we might join up with the Russians; whether this was true or not we never found out – after all we were only two Brigades, us and 69 Brigade.' As it was, no threat transpired and by February 1942, the Brigade, as part of 50th Division, was deployed to relieve the 4th Indian Division in the Western Desert – the honeymoon was over. Few would have heard of the Gazala Line on the Egyptian–Cyrenaican frontier. It was a place they would come to know intimately.

As ever the Durhams adapted to their new environment. Harold Sell quickly metamorphosed into an 'old' desert hand:

Everybody had a tin like a petrol can in which he kept his water for washing in. We used captured Italian gas masks, took the filters off them – which were very good – and put them in the top of the tins. When you had your water bottle ration – and you had to be very meagre with it – you cleaned your teeth, swilled your mouth out and spat it into the filter to run back into the can. When you had built up half a can of water you washed your face in it then back into filter again. So you had a perpetual motion of water recycling; the water in your can might be weeks old.[18]

Deployment in the close confines of brigade or battalion 'boxes'[19] created sanitation difficulties and disease was an ever-present hazard. Harold Sell again:

> Latrine provision had to vary according to what sort of soil you were on. If some part of the area was relatively soft you could dig down latrines. Otherwise you had to use thunder boxes and carry them to these places. But the drill was always the same: every morning the sanitary squad would go round with tins of petrol, pour it into the latrine and light it to burn everything up. And then you had what they called the 'desert rose' – the urinals. They used to put one tin on top of another, and clip them together with another big tin on the top, stuck into the sand.[20]

Sell, like many in the 8th Army, was not enamoured of the locals:

> We had to throw a perimeter around the camps and drive round them in vehicles fitted with miniature searchlights and Bren guns to deal with the marauding Egyptians, who were always running around thieving. They were mainly looking for things like rifles, which they were very adept in stealing. A man could put his rifle down with a chain around it and he would wake up next morning and find it gone. So it was quite necessary to have these aggressive patrols who could fire at them without any hesitation.[21]

For a while there was quiet before the storm and the Brigade engaged in some aggressive patrolling against the Axis. Captain Maurice Kirby of 6th Battalion took a mortar section with the weapon mounted on a truck bed, portee fashion;[22] they rained down a hail of bombs on to the plump target of an Axis supply convoy: 'after 12 rounds, the whole horizon was ablaze'. Company-sized detachments were used to form the infantry element of all arms or 'Jock' columns;[23] Harold Sell relates:

> The job of a Jock column would be either to patrol an area and be sufficiently strong to take on any enemy reconnaissance unit, or

go out on a specific mission such as beat up an enemy airstrip or get some prisoners. Generally, the idea was to dominate the whole of no-man's-land between you and the Boche. They consisted of a company of infantry, a portee anti-tank detachment, some 25-pounders and carriers with three-inch mortars. We might have South African Marmon Herrington armoured cars or light tanks called 'Honeys' for back up.[24]

Though the columns frequently enjoyed success, this was offset by failures, as Sell continues:

We had a disaster with what we call Rosscol, commanded by Major Ross McLaren. The first thing we knew about it was a message from two or three men who had infiltrated the wire stating that the column had been overwhelmed four or five miles out in the desert. Immediately a relief column was sent out and discovered that Rosscol had been ambushed by German Mark IV tanks. They'd shot the whole lot up; apart from a few survivors who'd made it back, they'd either killed or taken everyone prisoner, including Ross McLaren. That, of course, was a flap in the land of flaps.[25]

Rommel attacks

The pendulum that was the kernel of the Desert War was in full swing. General O'Connor's winter offensive against the Italians in 1940, 'Operation Compass', had achieved great things and given Britain a victory when desperately needed. Any gains had been offset by Hitler's reluctant decision to support his tottering ally and send Rommel to North Africa with limited forces. The dynamism injected by the 'Desert Fox' quickly restored Axis fortunes. General Archibald Wavell was replaced as C in C by Sir Claude Auchinleck ('the Auk'), who planned a further, major offensive for autumn 1941. On the surface, it appeared that the 'Crusader' battles had resulted in a significant victory for the 8th Army but this was largely illusory and the thinning of British dispositions left the gains in Cyrenaica, so dearly won, again at hazard: 'To supply the 13th Corps and its attached troops...required some 1,400 tons [of supplies] a day. The average daily amounts received at Tobruk by sea and by lorry convoys...together came to 1,150 tons...there was thus a shortfall of some 250 tons on daily needs alone...The fact is the administrative resources of 8th Army were now stretched to the limit.'[26]

Rommel had also noted these deficiencies and a subtle shift in the balance of resources provided him with an opportunity – one which he, as an arch-opportunist, was not about to ignore: 'At a staff conference held on 12th January his senior intelligence officer, Major F.W. Von Mellenthin, predicted that for the next fortnight the Axis forces would be slightly stronger than the British immediately opposed to them.'[27] On 21 January, the Desert Fox threw two strong columns into an attack, one advancing along the coast road, the other swinging in a flanking arc, north of Wadi el Faregh. Caught off guard and dispersed, British units began to fall back. General Ritchie, commanding the 8th Army, was, at this time, far to the rear in Cairo and disposed to regard these moves as nothing more than a raid or reconnaissance in force. He and General Sir Claude Auchinleck, the C-in-C, did not detect the tremors of disquiet that commanders on the ground were experiencing. Early cables suggested the situation might be ripe for a strong riposte.

It has been said of military matters that 'too often the capacity to advance is identified with the desirability of advancing'.[28] Never was this truer than in the Desert War and the reality was that Rommel had seized and was maintaining the initiative. DAK had also perfected its offensive tactics, as panzer officer Heinz Schmidt recorded: 'With our 12 anti-tank guns we leapfrogged from one vantage point to another, while our panzers, stationary and hull-down, if possible, provided protective fire. Then we would establish ourselves to give them protective fire while they swept on again.'[29]

Lieutenant D.F. Parry, commanding the maintenance section of an anti-aircraft battery based in Benghazi, was one who realised matters were turning grave, despite more cautious official communiques:

It took over 24 hours for the news of the disaster in the south to filter through to Benghazi and as always the news was played down: 'There has been a slight penetration of our lines at Sirte but necessary measures are being taken to restore the situation.' This was followed by: 'It has been found necessary to form defensive positions to the east of Sirte; however, the situation is stabilising and Benghazi is not in any danger.' Some days later: 'As a precautionary measure steps will be taken to evacuate Benghazi', followed by 'Your workshop will leave Benghazi and proceed to Tobruk.'[30]

By the 24th the 'Auk' was sending signals in an altogether more sober tone. Rommel was still advancing, his own supply difficulties notwithstanding. When one officer had the nerve to point out fuel stocks were critical he received the curt advice, 'Well go and get it [fuel] from the British.' Within a day there were plans to evacuate Benghazi, producing a rather plaintive cry from Whitehall '… why should they all be off so quickly?' Both Ritchie and Auchinleck flew to the front but the local commanders, their instincts more finely tuned, were preparing for withdrawal. The 4th Indian Division was pulling out from Benghazi as 1st Armoured prepared to regroup near Mechili.

Swift as a terrier, Rommel, alerted by wireless intercepts, planned a double-headed thrust. One pincer swept along the coast road whilst the second, the 'Fox' in the lead, pushed over higher ground to sweep around and come upon the port from the south-east. A dummy lunge toward Mechili was intended to fool Ritchie, and succeeded. He dispatched his armour, leaving Benghazi exposed. General Tuker, commanding 4th Indian Division, whose appreciation of the unfolding tactical situation jibed with that of his superiors, lamented: 'We rang Army – and learnt to our consternation that the whole of the eastern flank had gone off on a wild goose chase after a phantom force of enemy armour falsely reported to be moving on Mechili…Dispersion, dispersion, dispersion.'[31]

Von Mellenthin, commenting on the effectiveness of the panzer tactics and the speed of the British withdrawals, observed scathingly: 'the pursuit attained a speed of 15 miles an hour and the British fled madly over the desert in one of the most extraordinary routs of the war'.[32] If Ritchie was groping in the fog of war thrown up by his brilliant opponent, Rommel himself faced other enemies much nearer home. General Bastico had become alarmed because the limited spoiling attack, to which he had agreed, was turning into a full-blown offensive of which he strongly disapproved. He signalled his fears to Comando Supremo and asked that General Rommel should be made to take a more realistic view. This brought Marshal

Cavallero to Rommel's headquarters on 23 January, accompanied by Field Marshal Kesselring (nicknamed 'Smiling Albert' by Allied troops) and bearing a directive from Mussolini. In this it was stated that there was 'no immediate prospect of sending supplies and reinforcements to Africa in the face of present British naval and air opposition'.[33]

Rommel was instructed to halt further attacks and establish a defensive position. Despite the weight of the delegation ranged against him, he demurred and reminded his superiors that only the Führer himself could apply restraint. Kesselring, who was inclined to back Cavallero and no particular admirer of Rommel, could not move the General and the party were sent packing, 'Smiling Albert' now growling in frustration. Meanwhile, and without armour, Tuker could not maintain a viable defence and quite rightly withdrew. The 7th Indian Brigade was garrisoning the port whilst the remainder of the division was holding a line east of Barce. These troops encountered the sweeping arm of Rommel's flanking move in a series of sharp encounters and escaped the net only with difficulty.

The 'Msus Stakes'

On 29 January Rommel rode triumphantly into Benghazi whilst the 8th Army scattered back to a defensive position astride the line from Gazala in the north to Bir Hacheim, '… back in fact to the very place where, only seven weeks before, General Rommel had broken away because he judged the tactical balance to be against him'.[34] This need not imply that all was entirely well on the other side of the wire:

> The [Axis] chain of command creaked from time to time, but the firm hand of General Rommel made up for its many weaknesses. He was not the C-in-C, it is true, but he was emphatically the man whose views mattered, for he did what he felt to be militarily right in spite of the frequent protests of his superior, General Bastico. And then, having made up his own mind on the policy, he had a habit of becoming a tactical leader, and by taking command personally at the most important spot, ensuring that his ideas were carried out.[35]

Rommel's own postmortem on the fighting up till early February, forming a portion of his official report, whilst allowing for some artful editing, contains a very fair assessment of British short-comings:

> The assembly of all the forces for the autumn offensive was cleverly concealed (wireless deception was also used) and was favoured by the weather. The attack therefore came as a complete surprise, but although the British command showed skill and prudence in preparing the offensive they were less successful when it came to carrying it out. Disregarding the fundamental principle of employing all available forces at the most critical point...Never anywhere at any time during the fighting in Libya did the British High Command concentrate all its available forces at the decisive point...British troops fought well on the whole though they never attained the same impetus as the Germans when attacking...The military result was that the British 8th Army was so severely beaten that it was incapable of further large-scale operations for months afterwards.[36]

Despite being penned by the enemy, this was by no means an overly harsh assessment. Throughout the 'Msus Stakes' (a name given to the rather precipitate rout) the 8th Army had been hamstrung by inaccurate intelligence, uncertainties of supply, inadequate training and a total lack of flexibility. The retreat resulted in the loss of 1,400 men, 70 tanks and 40 guns,[37] General Sir Alan Brooke, now Chief of the Imperial General Staff, confided to his journal: '... It was his [Churchill's] darkest hour...The weight of his burden would have crushed any other man.'[38] By late February, Brooke was warning that Malta's position was extremely precarious and the outcome doubtful, 'unless we could recapture Benghazi before May at the very latest'.[39] On 29 January, Auchinleck had sent a cautious if not disingenuous cable: 'It must be admitted that the enemy has exceeded beyond his expectations and mine and that his tactics have been skilful and bold.'[40] His next communication, a bare 24 hours later, sounded a rather more dolorous note: 'I am reluctantly compelled to [the] conclusion that to meet German armoured forces with any reasonable hope of decisive success our armoured forces, as at present equipped, and led must have at least two to one superiority.'[41]

Rommel consistently displayed the remarkable ability to convert limited tactical successes into major gains. His policy of leading from the front, though fraught with risks, had so far paid handsome dividends. Even though 8th Army Command might be depressing the War Cabinet with what appeared to be excessive caution, Auchinleck and General Ritchie[42] were if anything understating British weaknesses. The policy of senior officers to lead from a distance placed a greater burden on corps and divisional commanders. When the latter painted a sombre picture of the true state of their units, these assessments, though valid, were hardly ever greeted with rapture. Lieutenant General Sir Frank Messervy temporarily in command of 1st Armoured Division, when reporting his tanks to be in far worse state than Ritchie was wont to assume, felt his observations were considered 'subversive'.[43] General Tuker was no less outspoken: 'You will notice also that the principle of security was neglected, for nowhere west of Tobruk was there a firm base on which 13 Corps could fall back, or behind which it could be ready for a counter-offensive.'[44]

On 26 February, the Prime Minister sent a peevish telegram to the C-in-C Middle East: 'According to our figures, you have substantial superiority in the air, in armour and in other forces…The supply of Malta is causing us increasing anxiety…Pray let me hear from you.'[45] To afford the island fortress much needed relief, Whitehall needed an offensive in mid-March or early April at the latest. Auchinleck would not agree a date before the middle part of May. Lyttelton had meanwhile returned to England to become Minister of Production; his successor as Minister of State in Cairo was the Australian Richard Casey. A part of Auchinleck's difficulties was the mechanical inferiority of his tanks. Simply to have more machines than your opponent was of no consequence if those you had were unreliable. British tanks, particularly the Crusader, were markedly outclassed by German models and mechanically unsound to boot. Lyttelton was acutely aware of these shortcomings:

> On top of this mechanical failure must be reckoned the superior gun position of the German tanks…the Germans had developed a better form of tactic in the employment of their armoured formations; their tanks moved slowly from position to position, waiting till they had discovered the location of our artillery and anti-tank weapons…They kept out of range of the latter and suffered little damage from the former.[46]

Churchill, though he railed at the bad designs, continued to press Auchinleck for an early offensive and the Auk, to his credit, remained obdurate. A snappish exchange of cables ensued: 'We consider [3rd March] that an attempt to drive the Germans out of Cyrenaica in the next few weeks is not only imperative for the safety of Malta on which so much depends, but holds out the only hope of fighting a battle while the enemy is still comparatively weak...'[47] 'We are agreed [8th March] that in spite of the risks you mention you would be right to attack the enemy and fight a major battle.'[48]

When the Auk refused to bend and declined to hazard Egypt to succour Malta, he was summarily ordered home. He demurred, leaving Churchill with the choice of either 'backing him or sacking him'. Brooke and other wise counsels prevailed against the latter course and Auchinleck won his breathing space. Clement Attlee had been nominated to chair an enquiry into the mechanical defects of the British tanks which found the C-in-C's concerns fully justified. The Prime Minister's personal emissaries, Sir Stafford Cripps and General Sir Archibald Nye, vice-CIGS, were minded to side with Auchinleck. Their representations earned a sarcastic reply:

> I have heard from the Lord Privy Seal [Cripps]. I do not wonder everything was so pleasant, considering you seem to have accepted everything they said, and all we have got to accept is the probable loss of Malta and the army standing idle, while the Russians are resisting the German counter-stroke desperately, and while the enemy is reinforcing himself in Libya faster than are we.[49]

151 Brigade and the 'Gazala Gallop'

Auchinleck quickly found that he could not hope to meet his own deadline of mid-May; mid-June looked possible but a delay till August could not be fully discounted. Rommel, disobligingly, intended his own imminent assault to be directed in the south swinging on the pivot of Bir Hacheim, which he expected to overcome without undue difficulty. The attacks in the centre and north would, in the case of the former, be secondary and, in the latter instance, a mere feint. The 'Fox' himself would lead the main armoured thrust in the south which would, having dealt with the Free French at Bir Hacheim, sweep around behind the 8th Army and begin rolling up the line. Italian armour would attempt to batter through British minefields in the centre whilst General Cruewell would command joint infantry forces in the north. Ritchie's deployments were piecemeal and ill-considered. In the north, 13 Corps was spread in a series of defensive 'boxes' with 30 Corps to the south disposed by brigades together with the bulk of available armour.

Auchinleck, in all fairness, was not unaware of the current failures in British tactical doctrine:

> The experience of the winter fighting had taught General Auchinleck to decide upon two important changes in the organisation of the army. It was not only the enemy who had noticed that the British armour, artillery and infantry had often been unsuccessful in concerting their action on the battlefield. General Auchinleck accordingly made up his mind "to associate the three arms more closely at all times and in all places". He thought that the British type of armoured division would be better balanced if it had less armour and more infantry – like a German Panzer Division. In future, therefore, an armoured division would consist basically of one armoured brigade group and one motor brigade group. The former would contain three tank regiments, one motor battalion, and a regiment of field and anti-tank guns, and the latter three motor battalions and a similar artillery regiment. In addition, both types of brigade group would include light anti-aircraft artillery, engineers, and administrative units. The Army tank brigades, each of three regiments of 'I' tanks, would not form part of a division, but would continue to be allotted as the situation demanded.[50]

Major Bill Watson of 6th Battalion had also been unimpressed with the effectiveness of Jock columns: 'I suppose they kept the chaps occupied when we were in a defensive position but I won't say they did a lot of good, other than to keep the Germans on their toes.'[51] Allied defensive measures were no more popular:

> We lived in those days in what were called defensive boxes which were supposed to be more or less self-contained, protected by the most enormous minefield of up to three or four miles across in front of us. It was thought to be virtually impregnable. In the event it didn't prove to be so…The major problem was that the

boxes were too far apart, so that when the great attack came at the end of May there just wasn't the coordination between adjacent boxes...This lack of support meant one was really fighting an individual battle, which was a disaster if Rommel decided to turn his full might on you – which is exactly what happened to our brigade.[52]

Michael Ferens (later Colonel), serving with 6th Battalion, was one who had experience of beating up enemy transport:

We loaded mortars on the back of 15cwt trucks and set off after the recce party, once we got into range we turned about so the back of the trucks were facing the enemy. At the signal we loaded and fired three-inch bombs as fast as we could, kept on doing so till we saw the first one burst, then we started the trucks and left...a Jock column under Ross McLaren was less fortunate... retreated in some disorder shall we say; not many casualties but definitely in some disorder – there was an enquiry.'

Rommel's offensive and the Battle of Gazala, dubbed 'the Gazala Gallop or Stakes' by the 8th Army, can be divided into three phases: (1) Rommel launches his flank attack, 26–29 May, attempting to overrun British defences from behind; (2) fighting in the 'Cauldron' – Rommel tries to resupply and consolidate his forces; and (3) the reduction of Bir Hacheim, and the pounding of British armour, 11–13 June, followed by withdrawal from the Gazala line. A fourth and final phase of this battle was the subsequent storming of Tobruk. The Durhams would be fully and dramatically engaged; their role and subsequent breakout forming one of the legendary episodes in the Desert War.

At this time John Hackett, of Arnhem renown, was serving as a Major in the 8th King's Royal Irish Hussars; he was in a 'Honey'. Again, whilst armoured operations are not our prime concern, the infantry and tank battle were closely connected. On 27 May his mission was to check out the intended Axis thrust south of the Free French redoubt:

I got 'C' squadron on the move very quickly – they were a very handy lot. We went up a slope in this typically undulating desert country, and as I reached the top of this rise the commanding officer said to me over the radio: "Report when you first see them." I came over the top and there in front of me was the whole bloody German army, as far as I could see, coming my way.' Hackett, having affixed his dashing black pennant to signal the attack, rather than relying on the unreliable net, drew the weight of Axis fire against his own vehicle which was soon disabled, 'about three minutes after putting up the black flag'.[53]

Bir Hacheim, the pivot upon which the Axis southerly attack was to turn, proved a far tougher nut than Rommel had anticipated. His two more northerly assaults both failed to break in, stalled against minefields and determined resistance. The new Grant tanks and heavier punch of the six-pounder AT guns made their presence felt. Failure to eliminate Bir Hacheim spoilt the smooth execution of his plan, and supply lines were attenuated, vulnerable to marauding columns of light armour and armoured cars. Despite the Axis's potentially exposed position, Ritchie failed to concentrate his armour, an error which amazed his more nimble opponent: 'Ritchie had thrown his armour into the battle piecemeal and had thus given us the chance of engaging them on each separate occasion with just about enough of our own tanks; this dispersal of the British armoured brigades was incomprehensible.'[54]

Though we are concerned with the deeds of 151 Brigade, at this point 'still in our box, living our normal life, not attacked', the uses of British armour are an integral part of the defensive concept. Many of the Allied tank officers had approached this battle with far greater confidence than before, believing the improved firepower of their Grants would even the odds. Colonel G.P.B. Roberts, leading 3rd RTR, described the fighting that subsequently took place south of El Adem: 'There they are – more than a hundred. Yes, 20 in the first line, and there are six, no eight lines, and more behind that in the distance; a whole ruddy Panzer Division is quite obviously in front of us. Damn it. This was not the plan at all – where the hell is the rest of the Brigade?'[55] Despite the odds, the 75mm gun did good service in the melee; '75 gunner, enemy tank straight ahead receiving no attention – engage…Good shot; that got him – same again.'[56]

Thrown in piecemeal fashion, 2nd and 22nd Armoured Brigades, despite gallant and costly efforts, were insufficient to stem the onslaught. DAK was now within an area known as the

'Knightsbridge' box. South Notts Hussars were providing the eyes and guns for 22nd Armoured and a brace of armoured cars, one commanded by Captain Garry Birkin the CO, and the other by his brother Ivor. Sergeant Harold Harper was in the patrol (although his experience is not strictly a part of the infantry battle, it gives an impression of the nature of such ferocious combat):

> We had only done six or seven hundred yards when we heard a garbled message from the commander's radio which immediately told us something was wrong. Captain Birkin jumped out and dashed across to the armoured car and I followed him. I've never seen anything quite like it in my life. Major Birkin lay flat on the floor, obviously dead. I went to the back and opened up the doors of the armoured car. Apparently an armour-piercing shell had gone clear through the middle of the battery commander as he was standing in the turret and then chopped off the heads of the two radio operators. All you could see was the two lads, hands still holding their mouthpieces – although their heads had rolled off on to the floor; the third radio operator, who had sent the message, jumped down from the armoured car and raced off.[57]

Harper had to take charge as the younger brother was traumatised by the ghastly death of the elder. In the confusion the surviving car collided with a Grant tank belonging to the Royal Gloucester Hussars. The armoured car burst into flames and, even worse, in their mad career, they found they'd run over the surviving member of the other crew and fractured his leg:

> We then jumped on the back of a passing tank of the CLY and lay flat on it. The tank commander had no idea we were there and kept firing. We had to keep dodging as best we could when the turret and barrel kept swinging round one of the chaps fell off and we thought he'd been crushed to death, though I found out later that he lived. Most of us received wounds of some sort from the German shelling. I'd crushed my ribs as we collided with the Grant tank and later I got some shrapnel in my left knee.[58]

On 30 May the Durham's neighbouring box, that held by 150th Brigade, now left horribly exposed, was overrun: 'Help did not arrive. At first light on 1 June the enemy attacked from all sides, and platoon by platoon the brigade was overrun and captured. The last sub-unit to go down was believed to be the platoon of the 5th Green Howards commanded by Captain Bert Dennis.'[59] It was not till 1–2 June that Ritchie decided to storm the Cauldron. As the Official History tersely records: '…British operations on the night of 1st/2nd June were a fiasco.'[60] The subsequent attack put in before dawn on the 5th – Operation 'Aberdeen' – was a tragedy. The 7th Armoured and 5th Indian Division stormed their objectives only to find they'd missed the enemy and landed a blow in the air: '… evil consequences were to follow quickly'.[61]

Exposed to relentless counter-attacks, several regiments and their supporting guns were decimated. Major A.H.G. Dobson describes the fate of 150th Brigade:

> All the guns had been lost or were out of ammunition. It was just the foot soldier sitting in a hole in the ground with a Bren gun and he hadn't really much hope by that stage. I remember the sapper commander on the phone saying 'I can see the tanks coming now', and by the time they were 50 yards away he said, 'I don't think I shall be telephoning much more.' That was the end of his particular unit, and this went on all the way round.[62]

Such an apocalypse could now very easily engulf 151 Brigade.

Breakout

When the minefield barrier was finally breached and Axis support came through, Bir Hacheim was further isolated, pressure ratcheted to an irresistible level. On 9 June, the survivors, battered but unbowed, fought their way clear of the trap. Of the 3,600 who'd begun the fight, 2,700 escaped: 'The defence of Bir Hacheim had achieved several purposes. At the outset it had made longer and more difficult the enemy's temporary supply route; it had caused him many casualties; and it gave the British a chance to recover from their defeat in the Cauldron.'[63] Driver Robert Crawford described how vulnerable supply columns of both sides were to the attentions of marauding armour:

> He [a survivor] described how they were moving up towards Bir Hacheim when they ran into the tank ambush. The tanks closed

in from all sides, blazing away with their guns. The Bren guns of the supply column hardly had a chance to answer before the gunners were mown down. Then carnage was let loose as the tanks drove straight over the column, smashing lorries on to their sides in all directions; within a few minutes the column was a mass of blazing wreckage with bodies strewn everywhere...[64]

With this obstacle removed, Axis forces were freed for a further thrust, this time toward El Adem, with a demonstration to distract the British in 'Knightsbridge'. By dark on 11 June Rommel had attained El Adem having, once again, wrong-footed his opponents. Next day he moved in an attempt to surround the remnants of 2nd and 4th Armoured Brigades. There was now a very real risk the largely static infantry formations to the north could be surrounded and heavy clashes occurred in the vicinity of Rigel Ridge. Here, the Scots Guards fought tenaciously, earning high praise from Rommel. Nonetheless, relentless pressure and mounting losses forced the British from the higher ground; 22nd Armoured lost some two thirds of its tanks.

Despite the destruction of 150 Brigade, the Durham battalions had, at this point, seen little action beyond probing attacks by Italian units, commencing in the early hours of 27 May:

At first light the small garrison of infantry, anti-tank gunners and machine-gunners at Stricklands[65] under command of Lt. R. Place watched a battalion of Italian infantry debussing on B 13 Ridge. The British gunner OP at the outpost immediately called for artillery support, and as the enemy formed up to attack the British gunfire caught them in the open. For a minute or two there was chaos but the enemy force was reorganised and advanced to the attack, two companies coming in from the north-west, one from the south-west and a fourth company moving in reserve. By this time an SOS had been sent for more gun support, and as the Italians advanced across the three thousand yards of desert which separated them from the outpost, the heavy and concentrated fire of the guns in the box was brought to bear on them. The gunners sent shell after shell whistling over Stricklands to burst among the advancing companies; it was accurate and concentrated fire and tore large gaps in the enemy lines. As they wavered the Vickers guns of the 2nd Cheshires at the outpost opened fire, followed by the Bren guns and rifles of the infantry platoon under Sgt. I. McDermott.[66]

This NCO showed remarkable coolness, directing his men with great finesse, oblivious to danger. The Italians withdrew in some disorder, much depleted despite odds of ten to one in their favour.

When not otherwise engaged, the Durham battalions remained far from idle, keeping up raids on Axis transport – 'commerce raiding'. In a battle where supply was paramount, this was highly effective. Captain Freddie Cole of the Battalion and Lieutenant Philip Hampson from the 8th wreaked havoc on several columns, but they did not have it all their own way. In the course of one foray they became embroiled in a major firefight: 'Both sides fought hard, but in the end Cole's party had to withdraw, though not before he himself was severely wounded and his driver killed. In his weakened condition he was unable to move the body from the driving seat, so he held the dead man's leg on the accelerator and steered the carrier to safety.'[67]

Ian English, of 8th Battalion, was another energetic officer who engaged in commerce raiding:

I took out a patrol with three South African armoured cars, a section of carriers, a rifle platoon; this was stronger than normal and we had three-inch mortars with us. We moved out from Strickland's Post and hadn't gone far before we were bumped by an Italian MG position. We got the Brens going in reply but I rather unduly exposed myself and was shot through the neck – had to be taken back to Strickland's.

He was now out of the fight: 'I was in a bit of a bad way, had lost rather a lot of blood and, on June 5th, was ferried out to Tobruk hospital. Pretty grim there – the doctors and nurses were amazing; the place was overflowing, many of us on stretchers. Air raids were frequent but the doctors and nurses just carried on, took no notice, fantastic.'

George Chambers remembers the terrain at Gazala as 'not really sandy, a sort of sage brush country, very dusty with one or two hills; one that was prominent we called the "Pimple". It was a folding countryside, one went everywhere on map bearings – the wrecks of a Heinkel bomber became a distinctive landmark.' After the loss of 150

Brigade, an uneasy lull followed with the Durhams keeping up their buccaneering. Their carriers frequently gave chase to Italian light tanks – like hounds upon a stag, Bren guns chattering: 'Sergeant Hill ordered his driver to charge the tank. The carrier accelerated and as the gap between the two vehicles was rapidly closed, Hill swept the tanks with bursts of Bren gun fire. The Italians showed no fight, most probably because of Hill's ferocious attack.'[68] Nervous tank crews did often surrender, with one who popped out of the hatch to implore, 'No make me prisoner; me only on patrol.'

However, the constant bloodletting and attrition of British armoured forces had so eroded the Allies' capacity for manoeuvre that by the night of 13/14 June, withdrawal remained the only viable option. This was a complex affair – the South Africans and 50th Division had to be exfiltrated and the former would take up all the available space along the coast road. As the enemy had swept around behind the Northumbrians, escape would entail breaking out through their thickening lines. The plan was that 69 Brigade would head out due east but the Durhams should attack west and then hook around Bir Hacheim to head eastwards again. In the dark of desert night, shrouded in the fog of war, this was highly perilous.

Harold Sell would play a key role:

It was explained to me that the breakout must be done quickly before the enemy had time to probe our defences in greater strength. I was told I had to make a bridgehead in the Italian line and had to eliminate the German strongpoints. I was given the rough distances to the enemy troops, some photographs, bits of sketches and was given half an hour to think it over. I went back to the meeting and requested no artillery support; without gunfire, surprise would be achieved and I might be able to get into the enemy positions without being fired on by their heavy stuff. It would be in the lap of the gods after that. They agreed to my plan and I got my company ready.[69]

With Sell's men as the *schwerpunkt*, the remainder of the battalion plus the other two would pass through the gap. Major Bill Watson, acting as Second-in-Command of 6th Battalion, takes up the story:

We had to take enough food for three days and enough petrol for 300 miles. The feeling in the box then was pretty grim. Everything not wanted was buried in case the breakout failed and we had to come back. We formed up at dusk and each column was to be led by a South African armoured car and an intelligence section with a compass, plus some sappers in case we had to lift any mines.[70]

Michael Ferens found himself commanding the last of the last: 'I was put in command rearguard; didn't feel too good about it.'

Waiting, as the fierce desert sun passed its blistering zenith and began its languorous descent towards the far west, seemed interminable, the dire fate of 150 Brigade in everyone's minds. As the cool of evening descended, throwing sharp, clear light across the barren ground, Sell prepared his men to move. It was now time:

We raced forward as fast as we could. We went in vehicles and almost got to the enemy positions before they realised what had happened. My truck was hit by an anti-tank gun and blown to pieces, but I was lucky as both myself and the driver were all right. Then we went through their dugouts with grenades and Tommy guns and cleared the whole lot out. We overran the Germans with our Marmon Harrington armoured cars; shot up all their machine-guns. They were eliminated, as were the Italians…We now took up defensive positions on either side of the gap we had made. Then the 8th and 6th Battalions went through. There were only isolated attacks from the Italians as our troops got away – the whole lot took an hour. The trouble started afterwards because Joss Percy[71] came to the conclusion, after hearing all the noise of battle, that we'd been destroyed. So he turned his battalion the other way and forced his way back to Tobruk and to Mersa Matruh.

At the time I was having a council of war with my officers, wondering what the hell to do. We didn't know what they were doing and we couldn't reach them on the radio as it had been destroyed by gunfire. We stuck it out until dawn. By that time the Germans had rallied their troops and we were being heavily pounded and suffering casualties. I said to my men, 'That's it, let's get out.' So we broke out into the desert and swept round the old Free French position at Bir Hakeim, being shot up by the Germans. When I got past the minefields I had three armoured cars, myself and two other blokes. That was all, the rest of the company had been wiped out.[72]

Sell, who had just earned a well-merited MC, had perhaps the most difficult task in extracting his battered rearguard who'd fought so hard to punch the vital breach. A timely warning from a cooperative Italian POW alerted Sell to more German positions astride his route. Once again his men charged through, all guns blazing:

> As soon as they heard the approaching vehicles the Germans sent up flares, turning night into day, and in their ghostly light, for all the world like clusters of giant chandeliers, the column raced ahead with every ounce of speed the drivers could squeeze from their trucks. The enemy opened up a murderous fire and in some of the vehicles took a heavy toll of casualties. But the armoured cars and carriers managed to silence most of the strongpoint's defenders, and once past it the firing ceased as quickly as it had begun.[73]

George Chambers was of the view 'it was as chaotic as France in 1940'. Deliverance for 151 Brigade but at a price. As they filed through the gap burst by 9th Battalion, their comrades in the 6th faced an equally savage gauntlet; Bill Watson takes up the story:

> Prompt at 8 o'clock the 8th Battalion did their attack and then we started to go through their gap which was the width of the column. As we advanced, the enemy began to realise what was happening and they began shelling us. The truck of the CO went up on a mine, killing the driver. This held up my column and we were now being shot at. To add to our difficulties the armoured car in my column also went up on a mine. Somehow we managed to crawl past the armoured car without going up on a mine ourselves…When we were out I said to my chaps: 'If you stick to my tail, I'll do my best to get you through.' It was a fearfully nasty experience, driving across the German positions along the Trigh Capuzzo. We saw the German bivouacs and camp fires. We drove for 30 miles into the desert and I went on for another five to make sure we were really well clear. By now all sorts of vehicles from other columns were tacking on to me. I remember a great big German three-tonner lorry came bearing down on us in the dark and we were just going to put a shot into it when we heard a lot of Geordie voices inside – they were from the 8th Battalion and had captured it when making their escape.[74]

George Chambers recorded laconically that 'we were fortunate enough to get through without any great trouble'.

Having been deterred from following 6th Battalion through the hard-won gap, 9th Battalion had elected to withdraw via the coast road, a planned escape route in case the first proved impossible. Split into two parallel columns, each column motored towards either the pass at El Agheila or that at Gazala. Michael Ferens remembers: 'Our job was to follow 9th Battalion. Colonel Percy sent me a message to that effect. We weren't attacked. We had a troop of 25-pounders and a pair of two-pounders fired from portees, plus, as I think 'C' Company. By the time 9th Battalion had come back into the box, dawn was breaking.' Dawn brought fresh hazard when South African guns mistook them for enemy. Confusion over, they found themselves under a rain of Axis shells as they attained the coast road. There was no escaping the conclusion that, in the jumble of rough dunes rising like slow breakers from the ocean of sand, the enemy were astride their route and in force. Axis infantry, supported by tanks and guns, barred their safe passage west. Colonel Percy immediately dismounted his men, who put in a spirited attack, with carriers swooping like hussars and that single troop of 25-pounders giving much-needed fire support.[75] Only the German guns bringing down fire from the escarpment remained as an obstacle and timely assistance from the South African gunners finally opened the route ahead. On the 16th the survivors passed through Tobruk and continued their withdrawal unmolested. Michael Ferens recalls: 'We were attacked by seven, I think it was seven, and I always claim it was, German tanks. The two-pounders fired from their portees and the 25-pounders went into action. We had a rare battle and brewed up all seven tanks. Captain John Irvine, who was wounded, was the troop commander. He won a well-deserved MC.'

The retreat had been something of an epic, not without loss, and though many vehicles had been destroyed the bulk of the infantry got through, not necessarily in parade-ground order, as Bill Watson observed:

Of course trucks got mislaid but everyone knew the compass bearings and by now most of us had become experts at moving in the desert. I never stopped that night [the 14th]; we passed

Italian positions, trucks and gun emplacements in the first few miles. Under cover of darkness we travelled 40 odd miles. As daylight came I found most of my column had left me, but we travelled on for another hundred miles and halted for the night. I had picked up many other stragglers. It was a night when we could sleep in peace, and we all slept as we lay, near our trucks, with sentries prowling round the whole time...Next morning we started early to get the benefit of the cool morning. Over the first rise I found, to my joy, most of the rest of my column just making breakfast. So, joining forces, we travelled on, under a scorching sun for another hundred odd miles, and late in the evening I joined the Colonel with his party at the prearranged meeting place. Next day stragglers came in, but as the day wore on it was quite apparent that our casualties were very, very few.[76]

As the Axis so often held the field in the Gazala fighting they were able to recover many of their damaged vehicles with customary efficiency. The 8th Army could not, and those left damaged were effectively written off. Despite this, British units were improving their overall rates of recovery and repair: 'Ever since the opening of the battle the British had striven hard to get damaged tanks into action again quickly'.[77] Many damaged vehicles were recovered and innumerable roadside repairs successfully carried out. Casualties amongst experienced crews were nonetheless heavy, the tankers 'only too well aware of the shortcomings of their own tanks'.[78] The Crusader had an evil propensity for bursting into flames, immolating its crew. The lighter Stuarts, though agile, were only really suited to a reconnaissance role whilst the Grant, which had achieved successes, was hamstrung by its inability to take an effective hull-down position, limited traverse and a lack of effective AP shells. The two-pounder anti-tank gun, without AP and ballistic-capped ammunition, was useless against the up-armoured panzers.

Lieutenant Parry recounted the contents of a radio conversation he inadvertently logged on to between 30 Corps HQ – well to the rear – and an officer rather nearer the front. In this, the officer repeatedly advised that large German formations were looming, to be constantly assured no such units could possibly be in his sector:

Officer: *Through the haze I can now identify tanks, difficult to identify but possibly German Mark IVs.*

30 Corps: *We repeat, there are no, repeat no, forces in your vicinity.*

Officer: *I am counting Mark IVs – one, two, three, four, five, six, seven – there is no doubt, repeat no doubt, that this is a large German force. Mark IVs number over 30, and there are also Mark IIIs and a large number of motorised infantry. This could be, I repeat, this could be the Afrika Korps moving at a speed of approximately 30 miles per hour towards El Adem.*

30 Corps: *[with an air of resignation] There are no forces in your area ...*[79]

Very shortly afterward the transmission broke off – a most telling silence.

Tobruk and Mersa Matruh

By 14 June, when Ritchie sought permission to draw off, fall back to the frontier and save his forces from encirclement, Auchinleck was not yet ready to throw in the towel, insisting that further counter-attacks be launched to deny the approaches to Tobruk. As C-in-C he had to answer to the Prime Minister, who was already querying his intentions: '...Presume there is no question in any case of giving up Tobruk?'[80] Rommel felt a surge of confidence, which he transmitted in his daily correspondence to his wife on 15 June: 'The battle has been won and the enemy is breaking up...'[81] As early as January 1942, the joint Middle East commanders, Auchinleck, Cunningham and Tedder, had agreed that Tobruk, if isolated, should not once again be defended. By 17 June, Rommel had secured Gambut airfield and beaten off the remnant of British armour. Tobruk was again invested. Two days later there was still some ill-founded optimism that the perimeter could be held on the basis – or in the pious hope – that Axis forces would settle down for a lengthy siege. The situation now within the ring was very different from before. Hitherto strong defences had been denuded and pillaged to meet the exigencies of the now defunct Gazala Line and the garrison was badly placed to resist a sustained attack.

Rommel, scenting this weakness, unleashed the Luftwaffe, which began blasting the fortress on 20 June as the precursor to a determined attack from the south-east. By 7.45am the anti-tank ditch, equivalent to the medieval moat, had been breached and the perimeter was collapsing. There had been talk of a breakout should this occur but, in reality, no escape route was viable. Auchinleck's report to London, late on the 20th, sounded a note of impending catastrophe:

> Enemy attacked south-east face of Tobruk perimeter early morning after air bombardment and penetrated defences. By evening all our tanks reported knocked out and half our guns lost...Major-General Klopper commanding troops in Tobruk last night asked authority to fight his way out feeling apparently could not repeat not hold out. Ritchie agreed...Do not, repeat not, know how he proposes to do this and consider chances of success doubtful.[82]

Bernard Martin, a signaller serving with 67 Medium Regiment RA, was one of those immured within the doomed garrison: 'We were Stuka'd and bombed continually for two or three days prior to the fall of Tobruk. I had very mixed feelings at the time: it came as a relief because of the incessant bombing and shelling but I also think we could have held out longer, like our predecessors did a year previously. However, I don't think certain people or sections of the army did enough to defend Tobruk.'[83]

More fortunate was Captain Owen Bird, a medical officer serving with one of the South African battalions who, like many others, was determined to escape the net:

> We set off in my desert buggy and had to pass through a patrol gap on the minefield where the sappers had hastily lifted the mines. We got through safely but the ambulance just behind us was blown up. Fortunately nobody was hurt but the ambulance lay across the track and was causing congestion for the vehicles behind, which soon brought down heavy shell-fire. We tried dragging the ambulance out of the way but it was firmly in the hole made by the mine blast; all we could do was gingerly lift the mines to the side and make a new track.[84]

With the erstwhile passengers in the wrecked ambulance clinging to the sides, his own overloaded truck managed, after a hair-raising ride, to slip the Axis hounds and reach safety.

Tobruk fell; it was a disastrous defeat. The debacles in Greece and Crete combined had not witnessed such fearful loss. Churchill was in the United States, within the sanctum of the Oval Office, when the dread tidings arrived. Casey had already cabled a warning to Washington but this was a terrible blow – first Singapore and now Tobruk. It is unquestionably true that a lesser man than Churchill would have been broken. There is perhaps no more telling testimony to the Prime Minister's indomitable genius that he emerged still doggedly defiant even from this latest blow. The objective analysis provided by the US military attaché in Cairo, Colonel Bonner L. Fellers, and reported on 20 June, was scarcely complimentary:

> With numerically superior forces, with tanks, planes, artillery, means of transport and reserves of every kind, the British army has twice failed to defeat the Axis forces in Libya. Under the present command and with the measures taken in a hit or miss fashion the granting of 'lend-lease' alone cannot ensure a victory. The 8th Army has failed to maintain the morale of its troops; its tactical conceptions were always wrong, it neglected completely cooperation between the various arms; its reactions to the lightning changes of the battlefield were always slow.[85]

At the time it would have required a particular shade of optimism to disagree; the battered survivors of 151 Brigade would have been unlikely to demur.

Nemesis of 9th Battalion

Losing Tobruk had a tremendous effect on morale. The small port was the bastion of British hopes and symbol of defiance. As long as so sharp a thorn remained, Egypt and the Delta appeared safe. Worse, the dreadful mauling Allied armour had sustained in the Gazala fighting left the infantry on the frontier dreadfully exposed. By 25 June, 151 Brigade was in line south-east of Matruh. For Rommel, this was the moment – one great push and Cairo might yet be his. Il Duce might even realise his cherished dream of riding through the streets upon his white charger – the conquering fascist hero. As the panzers rushed forward, 8th Army began the final withdrawal that would take the Allies back to the Alamein line, literally a last-ditch position. The position of both the 10th Indian

Division and the Northumbrians was invidious: they were again outflanked and risked encirclement; the Durhams had escaped one trap only now to be caught in another. It was now obvious to Auchinleck that Ritchie was unsuited to command and the Auk relieved his subordinate to direct the coming battle personally. This development, though significant, had little immediate effect upon the fortunes of 151 Brigade – Harold Sell found himself in action again:

> We were all on the escarpment near Mersa Matruh. Enemy patrols were probing around, throwing grenades, with us shooting back at them. That night we were being shot at by German six-wheeled armoured cars. We had just been issued with new six-pounder guns. Nobody knew how to fire them but one of the gun crews decided to stalk an armoured car. They pulled the gun to where they could see the armoured car, opened the breech and focused on the car down the barrel. They quickly put a round in and fired. As it was only 100 yards away they blew it to smithereens.[86]

It was the turn of 9th Battalion to feel the weight of the German onslaught. By 02.00 hours on 27 June the ring was tightening, and three hours later the assault began in earnest. Early in the action there occurred an incident which soon passed into legend and is remembered by the DLI and its successors today:

> Quite early in the action a German tracked vehicle towed a light gun to within close range of one of the Battalion's two-pounder anti-tank guns, sited on a forward slope in front of the infantry positions. The Battalion gun crew opened fire and put it out of action with a round through the engine. The Germans replied with another mobile gun and either killed or wounded the men manning the two-pounder. They then moved forward towards the damaged tractor and tried to get the light gun in action against the infantry.[87]

Private Adam Wakenshaw had already lost one arm yet he crawled back to the damaged two-pounder and fired a further five rounds. The German vehicle burst into flames and the gun was damaged. Another German round struck the position, killing the single other survivor and wounding Wakenshaw again. Despite these dreadful injuries, he somehow crawled back to the weapon and managed to insert a sixth and final shell into the chamber just before a further, direct hit killed him. His body was found that evening. For such astonishing gallantry he was awarded a posthumous VC. In that day's fighting, often hand-to-hand, the 9th Battalion suffered grievous loss, with virtually all of the three forward companies being destroyed. Only the HQ elements remained to finally withdraw.

Though dreadfully depleted, 9th Battalion had exacted such a high toll that attacks on the other two did not develop. Taking full advantage of this respite, 6th and 8th Battalions participated in a major raid mounted by the 50th Division and 5th Indian Divisions that night. Inevitably such operations were prone to result in significant confusion: 'At one stage of the advance a German armoured car unwittingly glided into the middle of an 8th Battalion stationary column and parked alongside one of the anti-tank guns. The gunner could hardly believe his luck and put it out of action at point-blank range.'[88] Such 'biffing' of the enemy was impressive but, in the circumstances, a mere diversion as the Axis net was again closing around 50th Division and a further Gazala-style breakout loomed.

June 28 passed in a state of heightened tension; there was little action but RSM Arthur Page of 6th Battalion conducted a most aggressive riposte to Axis probing, mobilising a motley or rear echelon personnel into an effective instrument: 'He himself was wounded in the leg, but as well as conducting his own sniper's war against the turrets of enemy armoured cars, he got an abandoned anti-tank gun into action, knocked out the enemy commander's car and killed its occupants.'[89] To afford the best chance of escape, a series of small columns was formed. It was not going to be easy: German armour was prowling and the moon horribly bright, lighting the desert floor. Descending the escarpment involved filtering down a warren of dry wadis on to a flat plain where the Axis awaited. For 8th Battalion this was to prove a particular purgatory. Barely had they set off than the column ran smack into a well-sited ambush. Mayhem ensued as the moonlit desert turned to day beneath a rain of Axis flares, and the rattle of small arms and deadly crump of mortars added an all too familiar soundtrack. The Durhams fought back with all of their habitual skill and tenacity: 'Thanks to the RSM [Jennings] and to Private George Fearon, who kept a Bren gun in action for over an hour with remarkably accurate shooting, most of the battalion column got clear of the wadi. But of those who received the full force of the initial German fire, few survived, and most of "D" Company were either killed or captured.'[90]

It was now a race. The survivors pelted over the open desert, split into smaller ad hoc groups. Their destination was Fuka but events had overtaken them and the place was in Axis hands already. The CO of 8th Battalion had unfortunately and unwisely assured his men that, 'whatever happens, the Fuka outpost will be held…'[91] As the columns drove over the moon-drenched plain, some rode parallel to a German supply column. One of the Durhams' three-tonners motored alongside an impressive-looking German staff car and one of the occupants greeted their new neighbours with a grenade as the two parted company. Those who rolled into Fuka found their deliverance thwarted and themselves captive. Those more fortunate were channelled towards the insignificant halt of El Alamein, yet another fly-blown gaggle of scruffy buildings. If this was destiny's ground, the choice, at the outset, appeared far from congenial. The attrition of Gazala and Matruh had cost 50th Division some 8,000 casualties. It was time to rest and refit, to brace for the greater struggle ahead – as ever, the Durham men would play their part in what was to prove the vital turning point.

Notes

1   A.W. Evans, quoted in Lucas, J., *War in the Desert – the Eighth Army at El Alamein* (London, 1982), p.74.
2   Quoted in Warner, P., *Alamein – Recollections of the Heroes* (London, 1979), p.39.
3   Quoted in Gilbert, A., (ed.) *The Imperial War Museum Book of the Desert War 1940–1942* (London, 1992), p.30.
4   Ibid. p.31.
5   Ibid. p.35.
6   De Manny, E., *Silver Fern Leaf up the Blue.*
7   Gilbert, p.91.
8   Lucas, p.9.
9   Ibid. p.74.
10 DLI Sound Recording Project.
11 Quoted in Strawson, J., *The Battle for North Africa* (London, 1969), p.8.
12 Ibid. p.10.
13 Warner, p.30.
14 Gilbert, p.37.

15 Lucas, p.31.
16 Rissik, D., *The DLI at War – History of the DLI 1939–1945* (Durham, 1952), p.83.
17 Ibid. p.84.
18 Quoted in Gilbert, p.37.
19 A 'box' was an independent all-arms defensive enceinte, brigade or battalion strength.
20 Quoted in Gilbert, pp.39–40.
21 Ibid. p.77.
22 A portee was simply a gun, usually a two-pounder anti-tank weapon, mounted on a flatbed truck, then swung on and off for firing.
23 So named after Brigadier 'Jock' Campbell VC.
24 Gilbert, p.117.
25 Ibid. p.120.
26 Playfair, Major-General I.S.O., *Official History, UK Military Series, Campaigns: The Mediterranean and Middle East* (London 1962–1966), vol. 3, p.136.
27 Ibid. p.139.
28 An expression advanced by the distinguished First World War historian C.R.M.F. Cruttwell.
29 Strawson, p.96.
30 Gilbert, p.60.
31 Parkinson, R., *The War in the Desert* (London, 1976), p.91.
32 Strawson, p.96.
33 Playfair, p.145.
34 Ibid. p.151.
35 Ibid. p.152.
36 Ibid. pp.153.
37 Ibid. p.154.
38 Parkinson, p.92.
39 Ibid. p.93.
40 Playfair, p.153.
41 Ibid.
42 Ritchie had succeeded O' Connor but was completely outfought by Rommel.
43 Strawson, p.100.
44 Ibid. p.101.
45 Parkinson, p.95.
46 Ibid. p.94.
47 Ibid. p.95.
48 Ibid.
49 Ibid. p.96.
50 Playfair, p.213.
51 Gilbert, p.120.
52 Ibid. p.117.
53 Playfair, p.96.
54 Parkinson, p.103.
55 Ibid. pp.103–4.
56 Ibid.
57 Gilbert, p.97.
58 Ibid. p.98.
59 Strawson, p.104; Parkinson, p.105.
60 Playfair, p.229.
61 Ibid. p.233.

62 Gilbert, p.102

63 Playfair, p.237.

64 Crawford, R., *I was an Eighth Army Soldier* (London, 1944), p.79.

65 'Stricklands' was an outpost of 151 Brigade box.

66 Lewis, P.J., & English, I.R., *Into Battle with the Durhams: 8 DLI in World War II* (London, 1990), pp.72–3.

67 Rissik, p.87.

68 Lewis & English, p.75.

69 Gilbert, pp.106–7.

70 Ibid.

71 Percy was CO of 9 DLI.

72 Gilbert, pp.107–9.

73 Rissik, p.91.

74 Gilbert, pp.108–9.

75 Rissik, pp.90–93.

76 Ibid. pp.90–1.

77 Playfair, p.243.

78 Ibid.

79 Gilbert, p.100.

80 Parkinson, p.110.

81 Ibid.

82 Playfair, p.246.

83 Gilbert, p.110.

84 Ibid.

85 Barr, N., *Pendulum of War: the Three Battles of El Alamein* (London, 2004), p.16.

86 Gilbert, p.113.

87 Rissik, p.94.

88 Ibid. p.95.

89 Ibid. p.96.

90 Ibid. p.97. Sgt Jennings won the DCM and Pte Fearon the MM.

91 Lewis & English, p.117.

Chapter 5

'Supercharge' and the Mareth Line: Victory in the Desert, 1942–43

Were you there when the desert lay silent
And they counted the cost that was paid
To ransom a world and its freedom
Mid the sand dunes and the graves?
Well, this was the arras of battle.
The weft and warp of our strife.
With bonds that were forged forever
From the broken threads of life.

Anon, 'El Alamein Tapestry'

In his postwar memoir, Montgomery spelt out how he planned his decisive stroke:

I spent the morning [30th October] writing out my directive for SUPERCHARGE. I always wrote such orders myself, and never let the staff do it. This was the master plan and only the master could write it. The staff of course has much detailed work to do after such a directive is issued. This procedure was well understood in the Eighth Army (and later because of experience in the Mediterranean, in 21 Army Group).

1. Operation SUPERCHARGE will take place on night of 31 Oct–1 Nov. The operation is designed to:
   (a) Destroy the enemy armoured forces.
   (b) Force the enemy to fight in the open, and thus make him use petrol by constant and continuous movement.

(c) Get astride the enemy supply route, and prevent movement of supply services.

(d) Force the enemy from his forward landing grounds and aerodromes.

(e) Bring about the disintegration of the whole enemy army by a combination of (a), (b), (c), and (d).

We know from all sources of intelligence that the enemy is in a bad way, and his situation is critical. The continued offensive operations of Eighth Army and the RAF have reduced him to such a state that a hard blow now will complete his overthrow.

The first stage in the blow is the operation being staged by the 9th Australian Division tonight on the Northern Flank; success in this operation will have excellent repercussions for SUPERCHARGE.

SUPERCHARGE itself, tomorrow night 31st October/1st November, will be the second blow and a staggering one, and one from which I do not consider he will be able to recover.[1]

Thus Monty defined the crushing offensive which was to finally break the deadlock and knock the Axis 'for six'. He makes it quite plain that doubts from subordinates, his armoured commander Lumsden being clearly in the frame here, will not be tolerated. As ever, the army commander radiates optimism and purpose. All that has occurred and is about to happen is part of a plan; he's in control. He did, however, quite quickly decide to modify this basic plan:

It was clear to me that the stage management problems in connection with SUPERCHARGE were such that if I launched on this night it might fail. I therefore decided to postpone it for 24 hours to deliver the blow on the night 1st–2nd November. This delay would help the enemy. To offset this I extended the depth of penetration for a further 2,000 yards, making 6,000 yards in all – the whole under a very strong barrage. I should add that there were doubts in very high places about SUPERCHARGE, and whisperings about what would happen if it failed; these doubts I did not share and I made that quite clear to everyone.[2]

Monty was aware that his enemies weren't necessarily all on the other side of the wire and mounting frustration in Whitehall would explode if decisive results were not soon achieved.

On 1 November what was hoped to form the final crushing blow that would indeed hit the Axis for six was unleashed: 'At 1am SUPERCHARGE began and the attack went in on a front of 4,000 yards to a depth of 6,000 yards. It was a success and we were all but out into the open desert. By dusk we had taken 1,500 prisoners.'[3] George Chambers was one officer who had been impressed by the difference Monty's direct style of leadership made: 'Lots of rumours and we couldn't see Cairo for the smoke – we heard GHQ were burning all their files...Monty called all COs to a conference. He said anyone who wants to cough, do so now, not later. We were to stay and fight where we were, no more retreating. Further equipment was guaranteed and would come up – that, of course, was exactly what did happen.'

Earlier in the battle

Montgomery's offensive was to represent the largest British gambit of the war and much depended on its successful outcome; in the modern idiom, 'failure was not an option'. There was little scope for finesse. The attack would be reminiscent of the break-in battles of 1918, ultimately a slogging match which would grind the Axis down by relentless attrition. It would not be easy and the cost high. 'Lightfoot', the initial crashing blow, achieved some gains but fell far short of a breakthrough. Thereafter the battle entered what Monty referred to as the 'crumbling' phase, minor gains dearly bought as Rommel's forces were steadily ground down. As the fears of those in Whitehall grew steadily shriller, the 8th Army commander planned his knockout blow.

For the Durhams, life in the desert went on much as before, as William Ridley from 9th Battalion recalls:

> The mail parcels came up, and in a hessian sack was a circular parcel about eighteen inches by twelve – a perfect circle. Well, I know instantly it was from me mam; she sent everything, sweets and tobacco, soldered into a tin. She packed them into a half biscuit tin, soldered the lid and then wrapped it up in linen, printed me name on it. It took about six weeks to arrive and about three bloody months to open. I couldn't get the solder off! 'What you got there?' all the lads was asking. Rock of ages cleft for me,

I thought – it was a stottie cake, hard as rock mind you but it was still like a breath of fresh air; did wonders for morale through the entire battalion![4]

Food, as ever, remained an obsession. George Iceton, serving with 6th Battalion, remembers:

We had bully beef stew, Maconochie's stew, tinned fish and tins of rolled bacon, we had white army bread which always arrived full of sand – think of it every time I see cellophane-wrapped loaves on supermarket shelves today. The supply drivers did their best but everything in the desert was caked in a white film of dust, however hard they tried.[5]

For 'Supercharge' the first wave would comprise the two infantry brigades attached to NZ division and each would be backed by a regiment of Valentine tanks. Following behind, 9th Armoured Brigade with its three tank regiments would make the final bound of 2,000 yards to eliminate the enemy gun line along or by the Rahman track. 10th Corps would follow 9th Armoured with 1st Armoured Division hungry to debouch into the open and seek out Axis tanks. Though Monty had intended to begin on 31 October, General Freyberg had prevailed upon him to delay for 24 hours to allow his exhausted troops some measure of respite and permit the necessary redeployments to take place. 01.05 hours on 1 November would be the appointed hour when the massed guns would speak.

Despite the strain and tension of continuous fighting, 8th Army retained its cherished sense of humour:

One of the funniest incidents I recall was as follows: Early one morning after the start I saw one of our burly Aussie gunners walk over to his gun position's 'thunder box'. Having settled himself, he began to read, last month's *Sydney Times* no doubt, when Jerry started his morning hate. A round fell some 200 yards behind him. Without further ado he shouted a correction: 'Up 400, one round gunfire.' Almost immediately a shell whizzed overhead and landed 200 yards ahead. With complete composure, having got his bracket, he called out: 'Down 200, five rounds gunfire.' You can guess the rest. He was blown off his thunder box and sailed through the air with the greatest of ease.[6]

As ever during this battle, Desert Air Force was in the vanguard. At 21.15 hours, Allied bombers plastered Tel el Aqqaqir, Sidi abd el Rahman and Ghazal Station. Some spectacular and satisfying explosions rocked the night skies and damage to DAK signals' capacity was palpable. The RN made some demonstrations along the coast and 13 Corps, though much denuded, was still charged with ensuring the enemy believed there was some offensive activity in the south. As waiting infantry crouched under the storm of steel hurtling overhead, they experienced that particular tightening of the stomach and dry-mouthed anticipation:

> Whilst awaiting the order to move forward, we all lay down on the desert with safety catches on and bayonets fixed. Suddenly, we were all on our feet and moving forward. As far as could be seen, to both left and right of us, men were advancing with their rifles in the port position, their bayonets glinting in the pale moonlight. Full moon had been days ago so the night was quite dark...As we advanced, the feeling of pride and exhilaration was unmistakeable.[7]

Prior to the attack, the Durhams' officers had gone forward to effect liaison with their Australian counterparts:

> On the way up to the front line the battalion party saw plenty of evidence of the fierce fighting which had taken place. There were knocked-out tanks, guns and vehicles, including an Australian ambulance which had been machine-gunned from the air. It stood beside the track, its tyres punctured, the body riddled with bullets and the doors at the back swinging on their hinges...At typically German regular intervals a Spandau sent a burst of fire over the Australian HQ, and when the battalion party walked back to the waiting transport an Australian private stopped them. 'Are you the coveys who are going in tonight?' he asked. The CO replied in the affirmative. The Aussie pointed in the direction of the German machine-gun. 'Well be sure and fix those bastards,' he said, 'They think they're there for the duration.'[8]

On the left, 152 Brigade from 51st Highland Division would advance across a frontage of some 2,000 yards with, on the right, 151 Brigade covering a similar distance. The 8th and 50th RTR rumbled behind with just under 40 infantry tanks apiece. The left flank of the penetration would be entrusted to 28th Maori Battalion with 133rd Lorried Infantry Brigade securing the right shoulder. Infantry surged forward:

> There were reddish-coloured explosions ahead of us and bullets, both tracer and otherwise, coming our way. I remember seeing forms sink to the ground, but our orders were to keep going and not to stop for wounded or dying. Later we passed slit trenches with forms slouched over them facing in our direction…Above all the din, the sound of the pipes could clearly be heard, and even an Englishman can feel proud to belong to a Scottish regiment when he hears the shrill warlike sound of a pipe tune above the racket all around him.

Despite some scattered opposition, the attackers made ground rapidly:

> Our objective was about two miles ahead of us, and all too soon we were upon it. Before we reached it we met Germans and Italians coming towards us with their hands in the air, and I aired my schoolboy German, telling them which way to go. The Italians were terrified and kept yelling out, 'Madre' – it was a very cold night and we were only wearing our KD shirts and shorts, yet we were all in a sweat.[9]

Jos Percy had moved up to Brigadier and Bill Watson now led 6th Battalion. The brigade had been in reserve during 'Lightfoot' and was only moved north when it was evident that the southern sector was largely stalemated. Apart from some skirmishing and a raid by 9th Battalion,[10] the Durhams had been relatively inactive. But now, on 30 October, the three battalions moved up towards an assembly area at Tel el Eisa Station. This was an area much fought over and the detritus of battle lay everywhere. A hot meal arrived at the same time as the 8th Battalion and was dished out immediately. The troops had just settled down in bomb craters and slit trenches to enjoy the meat and vegetable stew when several German planes dived out of the sun to machine-gun the battalion, and the long column of troops a hundred yards away on the track. Bursts of fire from the planes sent up little spirals of sand but no one in the battalion was injured and the planes were driven off by anti-aircraft fire. A lance-corporal in 'B' Company had his mug of tea trodden on and upset during the excitement. He looked after the planes, shook his fist and shouted: 'Why the hell can't you wait until seconds are out of the ring?'[11]

On the night of 1 November they advanced the seven miles to the forming-up position. They ploughed forwards in the half-dark of the moon, a shroud of churned sand coating each man and every vehicle like ghostly whitewash. Just before 01.00 hours, 8th (right) and 9th (left) Battalions would attack, with 6th in readiness to mop up isolated strongpoints: 'the boundaries between the DLI and Highland Brigades were to be marked by red tracer shells fired by Bofors guns every two minutes along the line of advance; and red tracer fired from rifles and Brens was to be used as a general recognition signal.'[12]

Ian English and his company were glad of the rum ration:

Everyone had a good swig – helped with the cold – and we gave what was left to the Aussies.' [The men were by now['completely covered in dust, the mood was quiet; we knew what we were doing was important but that we would be in a fight. We were in KD shorts and shirts with pullovers; as soon as we stopped we got pretty cold. We carried extra bandoliers with pick sand shovels as well as our usual entrenching tools.[12a]

Fifteen minutes before the assault and that welcome rum ration was distributed; happily there was plenty, enough for queasy stomachs and stretched nerves, the men like laden wraiths by the lanes of white tapes marking the route – pathway to death or glory. Just after one, the uneasy calm of the pregnant night was shattered by the frenzied stabbing symphony of the guns, something Bill Watson would not forget:

In the first few seconds only a dozen or so guns opened fire and then the full weight of the barrage joined in. The infantry looked behind them to see an amazing sight. The whole night to the east was broken by hundreds of gun flashes stabbing into the darkness. The shells whistled overhead to burst with a deafening crash in the target area, and from then until the barrage closed about three hours later, the frightful shattering noise went on continually…It was as if the giants of some other world were cracking their huge whips and hurling lumps of metal through the air. In every 12 yards there was a shell hole.[13]

To their left the banshee wail of the pipes echoed the fury of the guns, now providing a creeping shield as the Durhams moved forwards. Everywhere lay evidence of the fury of the barrage: 'German and Italian dead littered the area and many of those who had survived were morally shattered and almost hysterical.'[14] Major Edward Worrall, serving with 9th Battalion, used his hunting horn to communicate and rally. Out of the murk came the lethal fireflies of MG42 tracers; Axis guns which had escaped ours joined in the dread chorus. On they swept, men falling at every pace: 'The two leading companies of the 8th Battalion had, by 2.30am – when they arrived at their first objectives – lost five officers and over a hundred men ...' In the stifling blanket of dust the battle had fragmented into a savage series of small-scale encounters between the Durhams and individual enemy outposts: 'Private James Brown of the 8th Battalion, though wounded himself, disposed of the occupants of one German post single-handed with his Tommy gun; Sergeant Albert Dunn of the 6th Battalion did the same with another, only the weapon he used was his bayonet.'[15] Ian English's company surged forward; 'their blood was up, using their weapons well and though we were thinning out weren't taking too many casualties at this point'.

George Chambers remembered the fury of the assault: 'We gradually moved forward in bursts following the barrage. We came across an 88mm gun which we could see in the distance, knocking out our tanks rapidly. Our guns and MG engaged and we found the crew dead to a man around their gun; they were very brave men.' Mopping up proved a bloody business for 6th Battalion. One determined Axis outpost demanded a high price for its destruction: the attacking platoon lost its officer, all of its NCOs and all but five of its soldiers to death or wounds. The Battalion MO, attending to RSM Page, injured in clearing a further position with the bayonet, was himself, with his patient and medical sergeant, also killed. In 9th Battalion, this loss was repeated – the MO here was a popular US volunteer.[16]

In that dismal fog of deadly night the advance continued till creeping dawn, pallid light filtering through the haze, halted the attack – all objectives had been, at heavy cost, attained and it was now time to dig in. Light would surely produce an Axis response. Ian English was very much in the thick: 'We could hear the Maoris on our right, couldn't tell if they were successful, we kept close to the barrage, German MG fire going over our heads, nothing to worry about – short halts were necessary to keep everyone together. We saw several dead Germans and Italians and we began to collect prisoners.'[17]

Kiwi sappers had cleared gaps through the mines and battalion vehicles were soon moving up unimpeded, residual pockets of resistance eliminated and prisoners taken. As ever, there was a blood price to be paid for all such gains: 'What is wrong with my arm? I look down at my middle where it feels to be. It is not there. It is lying twisted up above my head. God! It is knocked off. No. It is still joined and only as I lift it down and lay it across my chest do I feel the agony of it; the sand is stained with blood in the moonlight.'[17a] Such viscerally poetic writing was echoed by the war reporter Godfrey Talbot:

Up in front where the shells were crashing red, the noise was a diabolical mixture, with the crackling of small-arms fire and the bursting of mortar bombs. Flares went up and lit all the sandy, scrubby, hummocky ground; they burnt very bright and made you feel somehow naked. There was the crisscross of tracer fire and rocket-like bursts; through it all sometimes you heard the drone of aircraft.[18]

His recollection of armour advancing is particularly haunting:

When we saw the armour moving up it was an almost ghostly sight. Tank engines roared and tracks squealed as the columns moved forward. Black, noisy shapes in the night, each tank creating a choking fog of dust as it moved through the sand; you could hardly see them in these clouds until they were nearly on top of you. And so we saw these strange dramatic glimpses of the armed might of the Eighth Army moving into battle.[19]

Whilst we remain primarily concerned with the Durhams of 151 Brigade, it is necessary to understand how the armoured brigades fared. Prior to 'Supercharge' Montgomery had ensured 9th Armoured Brigade was restored to full strength. Moving up from base areas at 20.00 hours, familiar fog and dust soon cloaked the approaches. Enemy shell-fire, though random, scored some hits amongst the lorried infantry and AT guns. A significant number of vehicles fell by the wayside through an unhappy mix of breakdown and confusion.

Zero hour for Brigadier John Currie's tanks was 05.45 hours but this was, upon request, delayed by 30 minutes to allow some sorting out. There was thus only around a further half-hour of sheltering darkness left before the armoured regiments surged past the infantry and towards the Rahman track, supporting barrage pounding ahead. On the right, the 3rd Hussars and Royal Wiltshire Yeomanry made good ground but, as they came within range of the guns lining the track, found themselves hotly engaged. To their left, the Warwickshire Yeomanry had it rather worse and losses began to mount as the enemy gun line flamed and barked. At this point 9th Armoured was under command of the New Zealanders, though by 09.00 authority would pass to 1st Armoured Division. As more tanks from the division came up, survivors from the battered regiments grouped to fight on the right.

As you know, we should have attacked in the darkness; instead we went in at dawn. That half-hour's delay cost us dear. We were like so many targets in a shooting gallery. At one time during the attack, the dawn wind came up and blew the sand away. It seemed to me that there was a half-circle of guns firing at us, and not just a single line of guns but row after row of them. And they all seemed to be firing at once.[20]

As a gap was prised in the enemy line, two of Monty's armoured car regiments, the light horse of a desert campaign, sought to ease themselves through and break out into the open, there to wreak whatever mischief they could. At Tel el Aqqaqir, Royal Dragoons found their passage still barred but they infiltrated south of there to speed west, seeking targets of opportunity:

We left our location and passed through the minefields in single file. No shot was fired at us. The only impediment to our progress occurred when the first car ran into an 88mm gun pit filled with German dead. One or two more cars, including three petrol-replenishing lorries, got stuck in slit trenches, but most of them pulled out when dawn broke and fought their way up to us. The enemy was too astounded to do anything as we came through, or else the Italian section thought we were Germans, and the German section thought we were Italians. They waved swastika flags at us with vigour and we replied with *achtung* and anything else we could think of which, with an answering wave, would get us through their lines.[21]

It had been hoped that the attack by the Kiwi Division would bring on the seemingly inevitable counter-attacks and that 1st Armoured Division, with remnants of 9th Armoured Brigade, would be well placed to deal a significant blow against any move from either north or west. Consequently, 2nd Armoured Brigade was intended to deploy some two miles north-west of Tel el Aqqaqir where 8th Brigade was to assemble and 7th Motor Brigade took station between the two. By 07.00 hours, 2nd Armoured was moving up towards the embattled 9th, sappers leading the way. Blanketing dust and cloying, oily smoke swirled in perfect confusion. Enemy tanks and guns began to exact their toll. Just over three hours later, 8th Armoured was advancing, tasked to continue south-west, but they too were brought to a standstill by intense fire.

Taking part in the assault was 7th Rifle Brigade. Their experience of the infantry battle mirrored that of the Durhams; Sergeant D.A. Main recalled details:

In the early evening of 1 November we were told that the 7th Motor Brigade would attack at midnight to force a gap for our tanks. When darkness fell I tossed up with my particular friend, Sergeant Brine, to decide who would split the watch until midnight. I won and slept first. Meanwhile we had sent out a patrol, which could only hear enemy rations being distributed, and we were unaware whether the enemy positions were Italian or German.[22]

As they moved off, bayonets fixed, Main's platoon was behind the two leading. Initially all was calm, but some 50 yards short of the enemy all hell broke loose and men began to drop in the face of deadly accurate, sustained Axis fire:

Above the noise of the explosions I heard the company commander, Major Trappes-Lomax, shout: 'Up the Rifle Brigade!

Charge!' Trappes-Lomax disappeared through a hail of tracer bullets. I felt he couldn't go in by himself and I gave the order to charge. I went through the enfilade fire and I couldn't understand how I had not been hit. It was like daylight with the flares and mortar explosions. Sergeant Brine had run straight into a German machine-gun. He was hit all over and before he died he asked to be placed facing the enemy.[23]

Deployment was not following the plan as intended but Rommel's tanks were being drawn into the fight and worn down by grinding attrition. It was at close quarters and savage: 'Even in daylight you couldn't see the guns until they fired, and then if they missed you had to get them with your first shot or you were dead. There was no mercy shown to crews – tank crews or gun crews. We shot them up as they ran – they did the same to us when we baled out. It wasn't such a gentleman's war…'[24]

For 'war without hate' this was anything but gentlemanly. It was bloody attrition:

There was for me no excitement in the charge. I'd seen it all before, and after a certain time you look round the faces of your mates and you realise with a shock how few of the original mob are left. Then you know it's only a matter of time before you get yours. All I wanted to do was to get across that bloody ground and through the guns. As I passed one position – the gunners were prostrate, I think with fear – I saw the gun couldn't be swung round very easily. They were only good for 'action front' – well, they had a little bit of a traverse, about 15 degrees either side of a zero line, I should think; so once we were past them they couldn't really shoot us up the arse.[25]

If the fog of war assisted the Axis, daylight brought opportunities for Desert Air Force. Enemy vehicles, massing west of the Rahman track, were deluged with 163 tons of bombs. As the bombers delivered their deadly payloads, Allied fighters, mainly Hurricanes, were providing close support above the lines of British tanks. Despite the odds, Luftwaffe sorties twice attempted to intermeddle, firstly a dozen JU87s then 40 more, with fighters, which were met each time by Hurricanes and seen off; both sides lost two fighters each. For German infantrymen like Hans Schilling the dwindling of vital supplies was utterly disheartening:

> Supplies were our main problem. Before we left Alamein, during the battle after the retreat, we kept waiting for supplies to get through. The British had our lifeline throttled. We used to wonder how the British had so many submarines and planes to sink our ships. We especially needed petrol – there was constant rationing and any unauthorised use of a vehicle was heavily punished. El Alamein was a hell…[26]
>
> Oddly enough, there were patches of calm in all that frightening fury, and there were jeeps racing about, organising something or other I suppose. The infantry didn't like us [tanks]. First of all we attracted shell-fire, and many 'overs' usually pitched on to them. I felt sorry for them just sitting there in all that shelling without being able to hit back – it couldn't have been nice.[27]

As 9th Armoured's depleted tanks battled their way forward, a murderous attrition between armour and guns, General von Vaerst then put in a strong counter-attack, committing both panzer divisions, which hurled themselves at the threatened shoulders of the thin salient 9th Armoured had butted into the gun line. The desert floor was soon littered with smouldering and flaming hulks of destroyed tanks, gun barrels twisted and pointing accusingly. Majestic and aloof, Allied bombers droned overhead, seeking fresh targets.

Throughout all this sound and fury the Durhams clung to their hard-won gains, dug into the often unyielding rock of barren desert, where the chill blanket of night had been succeeded by the broiling furnace of blinding day. In the late afternoon on 2 November, British armour made a further effort to advance over ground now held by 6th Battalion, though to little avail, 'though the effect of their fire on the German positions immediately at hand was not without effect and another 90 Germans surrendered to the Battalion, including an immaculately dressed Commander of the Panzer Grenadiers'.[28] Captain Ian English[29], commanding 'C' Company of 8th Battalion, was furthest forward and had many wounded. Stocks of food and ammunition were also running very low. During that same afternoon the survivors were withdrawn and all the injured recovered, 'though a raid by Stuka dive-bombers, which occurred simultaneously, made the operation a trifle uncomfortable'. The Axis seemed unwilling to allow the brigade to be relieved without a parting gift, some very loud and heavy shelling. Bill Watson experienced the brunt: 'It fell all round Battalion Headquarters and was horrible while it lasted, but seemed rather like the enemy's final effort.'[30] Behind the enveloping shield of night, in the early hours of 3 November the Durhams marched back to their start line – they had completed their allotted task and made a major contribution to Allied victory, at some considerable cost – 'tired, hungry and triumphant'.[31] For 151 Brigade their role in the crucial battle of El Alamein – the end of the beginning as Churchill was so memorably to describe the fighting – was over. To understand the Brigade's next major blooding at Mareth we need to understand how the battle and pursuit developed.

Rommel decides to disengage

By 20.15 hours on 2 November von Thoma had given his C-in-C a bleakly realistic assessment of *Panzerarmee Afrika*'s position:

- No breakthrough had occurred; the Axis line was holding.
- Nonetheless he was outnumbered and outgunned, subject to continual air attack.
- By the 3rd he would be lucky to have more than 35 'runners' amongst his tanks and infantry strength was severely eroded.
- His AT guns had been significantly reduced in number.
- He had no reserves.
- It was therefore inevitable the 8th Army should at some point, and soon, break through.
- It was therefore time to withdraw.

Rommel concurred. British attacks were, he felt, both ponderous and predictable, therefore a planned withdrawal at this juncture was feasible and might yet be carried through without further and fatal losses. Antennae quivering with finesse and informed of enemy intentions via Ultra, the shift was already understood: 'There were indications the enemy was about to withdraw; he was almost finished.'[32] Montgomery saw the decisive moment as being at hand. What remained of 9th Armoured Brigade clung to the northern shoulder as 1st Armoured Division's two brigades deployed to attempt to hold on around Tel el Aqqaqir (8th) and ground to the north-west (2nd). The north flank of the salient was held by 151 Brigade whilst the Highlanders occupied the southern 'wall', armour facing west. The Allies had not yet taken all of their original objectives – the ridge of Tel el Aqqaqir was not completely secured nor had the full 'Skinflint' bound been achieved ('Skinflint bound' meaning the advance to and taking of the Skinflint position). Nonetheless, a decisive armoured clash was under way.

As the days of 'balaklavering' (charging) were now distant, British tanks, dug in, awaited the panzers. When these failed to make headway, Axis guns took up the gauntlet, flinging down a fearful curtain of fire. For British infantry this was a most unpleasant time:

> We were up the sharp end with a vengeance. I'd never seen any shelling like that before…the worst I'd seen, and every time it died down the tanks would roll forward again to our slit-trench line and fire their guns. Then they would pull back and Jerry would send some stuff back, all of which fell in our area. The battalion's anti-tank guns had it very bad; for a long time they were out in the open and unprotected.[33]

Monty could sense the very fulcrum of battle had been reached. He was well supplied with intelligence via Ultra decrypts and his superiority, both on the ground and in the air, was substantial. On the evening of 2 November, 152 Brigade, with 2nd Seaforths and 50th RTR, was to capture 'Skinflint' whilst, a little later, 5th Royal Sussex from 133rd Lorried Infantry Brigade was to assault 'Snipe' – the German defended area or position. Both attacks would go in under cover of a heavy barrage. In each instance the infantry secured their objectives and a respectable haul of Italian prisoners from Trieste. With these strongpoints eliminated, the prime obstacle to a westerly breakout was the Axis gun line along Rahman track. Lumsden now, in the late evening, proposed to deploy his infantry (7th Motor Brigade) in a bid to seize a two-mile stretch of ground north-east of Tel el Aqqaqir. Once they were on their objectives, 2nd and 8th Armoured Brigades would advance for three and a half miles westwards. This would enable 7th Armoured Division, early on 3 November, to leapfrog 1st Armoured and drive toward Ghazal Station.

Keith Douglas,[34] whilst a member of that charmed circle of writers based in the Delta, was very much up at the sharp end. His experiences, whilst he was not with 151 Brigade, lends colour to the action. At one point a foot patrol, led by an experienced corporal, not disposed to show over-regard for tank officers, requested assistance. They had identified Axis snipers using burnt-out hulks as cover – "them Jerry derelicts over there" – and requested the armour flush them out; "I should have thought you could run over the buggers with this," he said, patting the tank...' Douglas's troop commander gave a cautious thumbs-up to the cooperation and the target area was hosed with MG fire, at least till the weapon jammed. 'Evan cleared and re-cocked it. It jammed again. A furious argument followed; even maintaining that the trouble was due to my not passing the belt of ammunition over the six-pounder and helping it out of the box: I pointed out that the belt was free on my side.'[35] A rather unseemly slanging match followed, tempers frayed by the stress of battle. The MG now had to be stripped whilst the troop commander advised he was going back to the NAAFI for lemonade and buns. Douglas was momentarily distracted by the corpse of a Libyan soldier sprawled in the indifference of death whilst his fuming gunner was obliged to continuing fretting over his weapon. 'We got the biscuit tin off the back of the tank and mounted the gun on it loose, on the top of the turret: from this eminence, as we advanced again, Evan sprayed earth and air impartially, burning his fingers on the barrel casing, his temper more furious every minute.'[36]

Presently an infantry officer joined the tankers, replete with primed grenades: 'very good of you to help us out old boy'. The British were now closing in upon the hulks:

A few yards from the left of the tank, two German soldiers were climbing out of a pit, grinning sheepishly as though they had been caught out in a game of hide and seek. In their pit lay a Spandau machine-gun with its perforated jacket. So much, I thought with relief, for the machine-gun nest. But men now arose all round us. We were in a maze of pits. Evan flung down the Besa machine-gun, cried impatiently, 'Lend us your revolver, sir,' and snatching it from my hand, dismounted. He rushed up and down calling 'Out of it, come out of it, you bastards' etc. The infantry officer and I joined in this chorus, and rushed from trench to trench; I picked up a rifle from one of the trenches and aimed it threateningly, although I soon discovered that the safety-catch was stuck and it would not fire; the figures of soldiers continued to arise from the earth as though dragon's teeth had been sown there.[37]

More and more Germans were now virtually queuing to throw in the towel, the British gathering their captives like shepherds with the enormous dog-like tank lumbering after. This activity was now beginning to attract the unwelcome attentions of Axis guns:

As the main body of prisoners was marched away under an infantry guard, the high explosive began to land closer to us. I did not feel inclined to attack the further position single-handed so I moved the tank back and tacked it on to the column of prisoners. The mortar stopped firing at us, and some of the infantry climbed on to the tank to ride back. I reported over the air that we had taken some prisoners.[38]

Douglas's CO was hugely impressed by this burgeoning bag of prisoners and instructed the officer to ensure the POWs were sent back to the brigade commander for interrogation,

'so you'll get the credit for this'. This was unfortunately more than my conscience would stand. I felt that all the work had been done by Evan and the infantry officer and said so. This was a bad thing to say to Piccadilly Jim [the colonel] because it showed him that I did not agree with him about snatching little gobbets of glory for the regiment wherever possible. The infantry were in another brigade, as Piccadilly Jim knew. Evan said: 'You were a bloody fool to say that, sir, you've as good as thrown away an MC.'[39]

To add insult to injury, the tankers found their infantry passengers had repaid them by appropriating some choice items of loot:

We were shocked to find that the infantry had stolen all our German binoculars while enjoying our hospitality as passengers on the tank. We all bitterly reproached them and I regretted ever having wished to give them extra credit. We had left, however, a large stack of machine-guns and rifles, which we dumped. Three Luger pistols, which we kept; these are beautiful weapons, though with a mechanism too delicate for use in sandy country...[40]

For the British tanks, the task was for 2nd Armoured Brigade to bolster 2nd King's Royal Rifle Corps, allowing 8th Armoured Brigade to exploit the south-west. Axis guns and tanks dug in along the Rahman track frustrated efforts by the former brigade whilst more guns, mainly 88s, held up the latter. During the course of that afternoon the Notts Yeomanry attempted to charge the line, 'balaklavering' with no more success than previously. Though some vehicles may have reached the line of the track, the net result was more losses. The 3rd November, however, brought intimations from the Australians in the north and 13 Corps to the south that the enemy was, or appeared to be, withdrawing. As the morning wore on, 1st Armoured Division also appeared to be pushing forward against weakening resistance: 'On 3rd November one of the troop commanders and No. 1 of the battery working with the armoured brigade had the satisfaction of capturing an Italian tank; they walked up to it with revolvers, knocked on the front door, and the crew came out and surrendered.'[41]

When writing to his 'Dearest Lu' the same day, Rommel was singularly pessimistic:

The battle is going very heavily against us. We're simply being crushed by the enemy weight. I've made an attempt to salvage part of the army. I wonder if it will succeed. At night I lie open-eyed, racking my brains for a way out of this plight for my poor troops...We are facing very difficult days, perhaps the most difficult that a man can undergo. The dead are lucky, it's all over for them. I think of you constantly with heartfelt love and gratitude. Perhaps all will be well and we shall see each other again.[42]

Sensing that the dam was about to burst, Monty had already deduced that Rommel might attempt to form a fresh line on suitable ground, either at Fuka or perhaps Matruh. Rommel was indeed now seeking to disengage. At this crucial juncture, Montgomery found he had an unexpected ally in the person of the Führer himself. Adolf Hitler ordered Rommel to hold his ground and 'not to yield a step'. Mussolini, in the unlikely event Rommel would take notice, sent a similar order through Cavallero. Sick at heart, Rommel read the order out over the telephone to von Thoma, who was understandably outraged. Both he and his army commander understood that such an order spelt nothing but destruction. Though phrased in suitably flowery terms the Führer's direct order was crystal clear:

> To Field-Marshal Rommel...It is with trusting confidence in your leadership and the courage of the German-Italian troops under your command that the German people and I are following the heroic struggle in Egypt. In the situation in which you find yourself there can be no other thought but to stand fast, yield not a yard of ground and throw every gun and every man into the battle. Considerable air force reinforcements are being sent to C-in-C south [Kesselring]. The Duce and the Comando Supremo are also making the utmost efforts to send you the means to continue the fight. Your enemy, despite his superiority, must also be at the end of his strength. It would not be the first time in history that a strong will has triumphed over the bigger battalions; as to your troops, you can show them no other road than that to victory or death.[43]

This was, for Rommel, a bitter blow and yet who would dare defy Hitler? Such heroic prose, which ignored every tactical and strategic reality, promising reinforcements that did not exist, amounted to little more than insult. Monty was ready: 'At 2am I directed two hard punches at the "hinges" of the final break-out area where the enemy was trying to stop us widening the gap which we had blown; that finished the battle.'[44]

For Rommel, the scale of this defeat was enormous. Assessments differ, but the Axis had lost something in the order of 30,000 prisoners, two-thirds Italian, and perhaps as many as 20,000 dead and wounded. Most of his Italian formations had been decimated and such transport as could be found was reserved for German survivors. Out of nearly 250 tanks, DAK could barely field three dozen, and though the Italians had more runners these were inferior and no match for Shermans: 'The Italian divisions in the south, in front of 13 Corps, had nothing to do except surrender; they could not escape as the Germans had taken all their transport. I directed

Horrocks to collect them in, and devoted my attention to the pursuit of Rommel's forces which were streaming westwards.'[45] Well might the marching soldiers have lamented; many would never see Rome or Naples, Milan or Bologna again:

> *Captain, captain of the guard*
> *Summon the buglers all,*
> *Make them stand in the barrack square*
> *And sound the demob call.*
>
> *Driver, driver of the truck,*
> *Start your engine off,*
> *We're in a hurry to get home;*
> *Of war we've had enough.*
>
> *Oh driver, driver of the bus,*
> *Run through the streets of Rome;*
> *Make her go like a racing car,*
> *We're hurrying to get home.*
>
> Italian marching song

As one British officer tellingly observed, 'One remark from my diary at the time is significant. "We are throwing stones at the Italians and they are running away." There was no doubt that the enemy, at last, was in retreat.'[46]

The Allies were now seeing a collapse of Axis morale: 'Can you wonder that, the battle having lasted some twelve days and ended in complete victory, I keep saying that he [Montgomery] was in a class by himself as an army commander.'[47]

Such a victory, resounding as it was, had been dearly bought and Allied losses were heavy:

- 2,350 officers and men killed.
- 8,950 wounded.
- 2,260 missing.
- Some 500 tanks damaged, say half of which could be repaired.
- 111 guns of all types destroyed.
- 97 aircraft of all types lost (as against, say, 84 Axis, though the Allies had flown a vastly greater number of sorties – at nearly 12,000, six times the Axis's total).

For the weary soldiers still sweating it out in the 'Blue', victory, however sweet, did not alter life's daily realities beneath the relentless desert skies. Private Crimp serving in 7th Armoured found:

> the desert, omnipresent, so saturates consciousness that it makes the mind as sterile as itself...Nothing in the landscape to rest or distract the eye; nothing to hear but roaring truck engines; and nothing to smell but carbon exhaust fumes and the reek of petrol. Even food tastes insipid, because of the heat, which stultifies appetite. The sexual urge, with nothing to stir it, is completely dormant...The most trivial actions, such as cleaning the sand off weapons, making a fire or brew, or, when you're lying down by the truck, moving position into a patch of shade...seem utterly not worthwhile and require a tremendous effort to perform... Then, of course, there are the flies. Lord Almighty, that such pests should ever have been created!...At the moment of writing there are five crawling over my hands and I'm spitting as many away from my mouth.[48]

Montgomery subsequently divided the fighting at El Alamein into three distinct phases.

1. First, the break-in, which he defines as a struggle for tactical advantage. He felt that this was successful, though the record might tend to question this.
2. Secondly, the crumbling or dogfight phase, aimed at 'crippling the enemy's strength'. This did succeed; a nasty, vicious attrition that told heavily in favour of the Allies. This was as much due to the fact Rommel squandered his precious resources in set-piece counter-attacks in unfavourable conditions. Allied success was mainly due to Axis inability to learn from past mistakes and a propensity to fling men and vehicles into a maelstrom where the Allies held vital trumps in air and artillery superiority.
3. Finally, the break-out, which Monty saw as successful as it was aimed at the weakest link in the crumbling Axis chain, the juncture between Italian and German units. Rommel had taken the gamble of drawing his remaining strength into the northern sector where he was misled into thinking the final blow would be directed.[49]

If your enemy stands to fight and is decisively defeated in the ensuing battle, everything is added unto you. Rommel's doom was sounded at Alam Halfa; as Von Mellenthin said, it was the turning point of the desert war. After that, he was smashed in battle at El Alamein. He had never been beaten before, though he had often had to 'nip back to get more petrol'. Now he had been decisively defeated. The doom of the Axis forces in Africa was certain – provided we made no more mistakes.[50]

Monty was not shy in attributing the victory to his own strategic genius. In this he may have been prone to overlook that much of the strategic planning had been done previously by others such as Auchinleck, Dorman-Smith, Gott and Ramsden. These are not mentioned. Nonetheless, even his most constant critics must concede that Montgomery brought to the 8th Army cohesion, a simplicity and directness of approach that had been lacking. He restored confidence:

> Generals who become depressed when things are not going well, who lack the 'drive' to get things done, and who lack the resolution, the robust mentality and the moral courage to see their plan through to the end – are useless. They are, in fact, worse than useless – they are a menace – since any sign of wavering or hesitation has immediate repercussions down the scale when the issue hangs in the balance.[51]

As the hounds were unleashed, Robert Crisp[52] and his comrades bounded after the survivors of 90th Light Division struggling along the coastal ribbon:

> The most exciting moment of the battle was when we first cut the coast road in an effort to head off the 90th Light Division. Long columns of Italian and German transport were still swarming along the road westward. My tank was first on to the road, being in the recce squadron. It really came as a tremendous surprise to the enemy when they heard the rattle of our machine-guns… They put in one attack only with about 20 tanks, but of these only two managed to break through, the rest were destroyed. We collected a tremendous bag of prisoners, tanks, lorries and transport of all kinds.[53]

The battle was won but could the rout be transformed into *Götterdämmerung*?

Mareth

On 23 January 1943 the 8th Army entered Tripoli; in the three months since El Alamein Montgomery's forces had advanced some 1,400 miles. Rommel fell back across the Tunisian border and prepared to hold the old Mareth Line, originally constructed by the French as a buffer against their Italian neighbours. By mid-February the Allies were at Medenine, where a vigorous thrust by the Axis was seen off with loss. The 8th Army, having cleared the way, must now assault the formidable barrier Rommel had bequeathed his successor at Mareth. It was to be no picnic; the Germans were not yet defeated and the ground favoured the defender.

> Except for a few tracks running through narrow passes, these rugged, broken hills formed a natural barrier to wheeled transport and at the same time dominated the whole western end of the defence system. In the coastal sector the line had been based on the Wadi Zigzaou, a horrible obstacle, widened and deepened to form a tank trap and covered by enfilade fire along its whole length by a complicated system of concrete and steel pillboxes, gun emplacements and blockhouses. The strongpoints, formidable affairs of concrete two or three feet thick, were supported by a well-revetted trench system, linked with deep dugouts and funk holes.[54]

A formidable task awaited 50th division; their allotted sector was overlooked by the enemy without offering any equivalent vantage. Having rested and refitted at Benina, where the heavy losses sustained in the Alamein fighting had been made good, 151 Brigade was now commanded by Brigadier Beak. The respite had been put to good effect with '…the most valuable training which we had ever had and did more towards raising that high morale and confidence so necessary in battle than anything I had ever experienced either before or since.'[55] Ian English remembered the approach march: 'On 2nd March at 08.30 hours we left Benina, and covered some 60–80 miles a day in transport. Plenty evidence of the Germans thoroughness at mine-laying…we covered 140 miles to the forward areas on 13th March.'

It fell to the Brigade to assault the formidable Wadi Zigzaou. The 69th Brigade had cleared Axis outposts on 16 March, leaving the ground open for the Durhams' attack. The wadi was slow, soft and treacherous, fordable here and there but with high, slime-slicked banks; behind, a riddle of trenches were studded with redoubts. Patrols probed the dangerous ground; mines were present, predictably and in habitual abundance. Ian English again: 'The main positions were extremely strong, mines on both sides of the wadi, concrete pillboxes, gun emplacements, well-concealed communication trenches – like a small Maginot Line.' Being this far forward was obviously hazardous, even more so when the 'Brass' insisted on using your trench for observation. An exasperated section commander railed: 'I don't mind who comes up here, as long as they keep their heads down, but when Crasher [Major-General Nichols] and Beako [Brigadier Beak] came up here, they bobbed about all over the place and didn't even take the red tabs off their ruddy hats!'[56]

Once again the Durhams would advance under the deceptively benign glow of a desert moon; 69 Brigade would mount an attack on their left at 22.30 hours on 20 March. Half an hour later the DLI Battalions would engage. They were supported by 50th RTR, whose flail tanks[57] did good service as 9th Battalion was deluged with enemy fire, some wildly inaccurate but still causing casualties. Charles Goulden led 'C' Company over the wadi, soldiers scrambling up scaling ladders like their medieval forebears to greet the Italians hand-to-hand. Dennis Worrall's 'B' Company, delayed by British mines, struggled forward, hunting horn blowing. It required a human ladder to heave men up the steep, mud-rucked side of the wadi then on to the objective – the strongpoint at Ksiba Ouest. Let Major Worrall take up the story:

Here, the fire was quite bloody. I told Corporal Bell to crawl forward and cut the wire. Scotty White, Sergeant Randall, Corporal Daly and myself lay beside two palm trees and tried to cover him. We couldn't have taken those pillboxes unless somebody had cut that wire, and the bullets were missing by inches here. My horn had got bunged up with sand, so I couldn't blow the company on. A lot of them had temporarily stuck and slowed down crossing the wadi and getting up the anti-tank ditch…At last Bell said, 'I've cut the wire, Sir.' We made a dash for it and by sheer luck got into their trenches 50 yards beyond the wire. We went up these. When we got near the pillboxes, I put Randall and Daly with two Brens to fire at the slits, while White and I led a party up the trench towards them, throwing 36 grenades at each corner.[58] To my joy, suddenly about 50 Italians appeared with their hands up. I then saw that the Bren guns had set the pillboxes on fire, at least the two left-hand ones. More Italians surrendered, among them a Major and a Captain.[59]

So far so good, but the fight wasn't over and the remainder of 'B' Company was still held up in front of further bunkers on the right of their axis of advance. Worrall was undeterred:

The Italians came rushing out in our faces…I tried to make one put his hands up, but found I was unarmed; I had lost my revolver and, worse still, my hunting horn. However, no Italian fired! This time I determined there would be no need to go back and we swarmed over all three strongpoints quickly. We took about 80 prisoners and pushed them out of the fort along the trench to the road.[60]

As Worrall stormed Ksiba Ouest, 9th Battalion was tasked to storm the Ouerzi position. Again this was a hard fight and a squad of Italian diehards refused to surrender, clinging to the innermost ring of defences. Ian English, leading 'C' Company, exhibited his habitual dash when 'it was found impossible to make effective use of the sappers' mine detectors, as the noise of battle was so great that the buzz in the earphones could not be heard when a mine was detected. Besides, there were so many shell fragments lying about that the detectors could not distinguish between the mines and them so English led the way through the minefield.'[61]

Again, boldness reaped rewards and the advance was successful, with few casualties. One of these, however, was the Colonel, wounded crossing the wadi then killed, with other injured men, by a further enemy barrage. It was the CO, frustrated with slow progress, who'd spurred Ian English on: 'Get a move on and ignore these blasted Scorpions [flail tanks], there aren't any mines on this side of the wadi.' No sooner had he spoken than one of these non-existent mines detonated loudly beneath a flail! To reinforce the initial success, the reserve company now came up but suffered heavy casualties in the roaring storm of continuous Axis fire: 'the wounded had to be left where they lay on the banks of the wadi. There, for the next 10 minutes, these unfortunate men were subjected to a vicious hail of fire from machine-guns, mortars and guns...';[62] few survived.

Dawn and the Durhams, battered and bloodied, were on their objectives but 6th Battalion had been considerably impeded during its intended advance, badly delayed and harassed by shelling. The narrow bridgehead had to be consolidated and supplied, and viable crossing over the treacherous wadi constructed – all in the teeth of unrelenting enemy fire; losses amongst the engineers were considerable. During daylight no concerted counter-attacks developed but: '8th Battalion spent the day conducting a vigorous guerrilla warfare against these marauders, [Italians attempting to infiltrate the captured defences] in which three men – Sergeant William Crawford and Private William Higginson and 'Mick' Michael – played a very prominent part. Each was able to claim a satisfactory "bag" at the end of the day.'[63]

No rest, however: as the relief from 69 Brigade moved in, the Durhams moved out to press their continuing attack. It was now the turn of 6th Battalion to assault forts Ouerzi Ouest and Zarat Sudest. This was grinding, exhausting and bloody work, with the 6th attaining its objectives only after suffering significant loss, savage hand-to-hand fighting exacting a mercilessly heavy toll upon officers. Allied tanks were now across the miry gulf of the wadi but their passage wrecked the crossings. By the morning of the 22nd any favourable outcome still hung very much in the balance. Enemy snipers remained active. Axis tanks were seen to be massing but 8th Army's guns stopped them, literally in their tracks. Rain now came to the Axis's assistance, sudden sharp showers flooding the wadi, turning waterlogged gully into raging torrent. When the attack came it was from the Germans rather than Italians, well supported by armour. The British Valentines were no match for upgunned Mark IV Panzers, which disabled most of the inferior British machines.

Ian English and the remains of his company were at the front of the front:

One shell landed amongst our sappers, killed the Lance-Corporal and several of his men; our ladders were just wide enough to bridge the anti-tank ditch around 15 feet wide and eight foot deep... as we consolidated, a cone of our own fire came down, very uncomfortable; one shell landed near Harry Johnson, commanding 14 platoon and he was totally shell-shocked...At first light things seemed pretty quiet, we still had plenty [of] ammo, a packet of biscuits and a tin of bully beef. We sent out pleas for anti-tank guns to be brought forward. Our Bren guns engaged a 20mm cannon; not sure if our fire was effective...in the afternoon we saw Italian infantry, battalion-sized group forming up, the artillery commander made them a regimental target, 36 guns, the Italians were caught in the open and the attack broken up – we took about 80 prisoners.

Isolated and short of everything, the Durhams fought magnificently to hold on to their desperately won positions: 'The company of the 6th Battalion in Ouerzi Ouest received the full brunt of the attack. The company was without officers and commanded by Sergeant-Major Watts who was never heard of again; and it fought till its ammunition was used up when the survivors struggled back to the anti-tank ditch.'[64] This extreme gallantry in a rapidly deteriorating situation characterised a stubborn defence, ground down by relentless attrition.

By dusk the scattered survivors were clinging on by their fingernails, armoured support had been destroyed or driven back and the enemy were penetrating in strength at all points: 'Ammunition, too, was running out. Dick Ovenden of 6th Battalion visited Colonel Watson at Battalion Headquarters – a joint one with that of 9th Battalion – just before midnight to ask for more and was given the last box. He was killed on the way back to his company.'[65] Overall the position was desperate and the morning would surely bring further and overwhelming attacks. The Durhams had killed a great number of the enemy but he was not disposed to give up so vital a bastion. It was a bitter blow then when the divisional commander ordered a withdrawal to the east flank of the wadi; the wearied, grim-faced survivors, who were leaving so many comrades in the rubble, cut their way out and by dawn on the 23rd had fought clear.

Once again, Ian English was in the forefront:

The CO and other officers had been killed, the second-in-command wounded; 'A' and 'B' Companies had been amalgamated. Enemy tanks and infantry were forming up at

14.00 hours; he attacked in earnest, recaptured the position on our right…three German Mark IV Specials with the long gun and a Mark III…the corporal continued taking radio messages as though we were on exercise, totally undeterred. Heavy German shells, 155mm or bigger, 'flying kitbags' we called them, were causing casualties. The Germans concentrated on our tanks [Valentines] – these were completely outgunned, only one six-pounder gun per troop, 30 tanks destroyed and Colonel Cairns, their CO, a casualty. We damaged the track on the Mark III with a 68 Grenade and engaged with Brens, to which they replied with long bursts of rapid MG fire.[66]

It seemed like a defeat but it was not – 151 Brigade had pinned the enemy forces and obliged them to expend slender reserves in the vicious fighting. The Axis had fallen into the earlier French belief that the Mareth position could not be outflanked on the landward side. However, Monty had the LRDG and the Axis did not. These indefatigable raiders had cracked the key to a turning movement so the Kiwis appeared as though by mysterious alchemy on the Axis's flank. The battle was still not over but, by 27 March, the enemy had pulled back, the Germans' turn now to quit the ground across Wadi Zigzaou that had cost both sides so dear.

Regardless of the outcome, the actions of the Durhams in that terrible fight became the stuff of legend and, like most legends, came at a fearful price. The three attacking companies of 6th Battalion which had entered the fight 300-strong were reduced to 65 and the other two experienced similar losses. No finer epitaph could have been penned than that written by a Green Howards' NCO in a letter home: 'The Scots lads of the Highland Division are good lads with bags of "go"; the Aussies have plenty of dash; the New Zealanders are easily the finest soldiers in the desert; but when things are at their worst, when everything looks lost and men are going down left, right and centre, give us the Durham Light Infantry.'[67] There is nothing more that needs be said.

O, Lord, our only Master
Our victories were Yours,
Pray keep us now and after
May peace be assured.
Look up you sons of Glory,

> *The Crusader flags' unfurled;*
> *Remember our true story;*
> *'We fought to free the world'.*
> *So hoist our Banner highly,*
> *Our cause shall not be lost;*
> *For we were the proud Eighth Army,*
> *Our emblem was the cross.*

8th Army hymn

Notes

1   Montgomery, Field-Marshal, the Viscount, *Memoirs* (London, 1958), pp.121–3.
2   Ibid. p.125.
3   Ibid.
4   DLI Sound Recording Project.
5   Ibid.
6   S.J.C. Cross, quoted in Warner, *El Alamein: Recollections of the Heroes*, p.170.
7   R. Cooke, quoted in Lucas, p.236.
8   Lewis, P.J., & English, I.R., *Into Battle with the Durhams: 8 DLI in World War II* (London, 1990), p.146.
9   Lucas, *Panzer Army Africa*, p.236.
10   Rissik, D., *The DLI at War – History of the DLI 1939–1945* (Durham, 1952), p.100.
11   Lewis & English, p.147.
12   Rissik, p.101.
12a Ibid.
13   Lewis & English, p.148.
14   Rissik, p.102.
15   Ibid.
16   Ibid. p.103.
17   L.R. Symonds, quoted in Warner, op cit, p.132
17a Ibid
18   Gilbert, p.72.
19   Ibid.
20   Lucas, op cit, p.242.
21   Carver, M., *El Alamein* (London, 1962), p.168.
22   Gilbert, p.74.
23   Ibid.
24   Lucas, op cit, p.243.
25   Ibid. p.242.
26   McGuirk, D., *Rommel's Army in Africa* (London, 1987), p.60.
27   Lucas, op cit, p.243.
28   Rissik, p.104.
29   Captain English was awarded an MC for this action.
30   Rissik, p.104.
31   9th Battalion War Diary; Rissik, p.105.
32   Montgomery, p.125.

33 Lucas, op cit, p.246.
34 The poet was later killed in Normandy.
35 Lewis-Stempel, J., *The Autobiography of the British Soldier* (London, 2007), p.352.
36 Ibid. p.354.
37 Ibid. pp.354–5.
38 Ibid. p.355.
39 Ibid. p.356.
40 Ibid. p.357.
41 Colonel R.F. Wright, quoted in Warner, op cit, p.176.
42 Carver, p.173.
43 Ibid. p.177.
44 Montgomery, p.125.
45 Ibid.
46 Warner, op cit, p.211.
47 Ibid. p.171.
48 Lewis-Stempel, p.344.
49 Montgomery, p.126.
50 Ibid. p.127.
51 Ibid. p.126.
52 Crisp subsequently wrote a justly famous memoir of his time in the desert: *Brazen Chariots: An Account of Tank Warfare in the Western Desert, November–December 1941* (London, 1959).
53 Gilbert, A., (ed.) *The Imperial War Museum Book of the Desert War 1940–1942* (London, 1992), p.175.
54 Lewis & English, p.168.
55 Rissik, p.107.
56 Lewis & English, p.171.
57 'Flail' tanks were converted Cromwells or Shermans; part of Hobart's 'Funnies', the 'Scorpion' was designed for mine clearance and featured chains attached to a roller which could literally flail the ground ahead.
58 This refers to the pattern of grenade rather than any quantity.
59 Rissik, p.110.
60 Ibid.
61 Ibid. p.111.
62 Ibid.
63 Crawford received a bar to his MM; both Higginson and Michael were each awarded an MM.
64 Rissik, p.115.
65 Ibid. p.116.
66 Ibid. p.117.
67 Ibid. p.117.

Chapter 6

Sicily: Primosole Bridge, 1943

The battle was very noisy and very, very bloody. It caused us all a lot of grief. After we'd crossed the river and taken up a defensive position behind a low stone wall, I had my section dug in and we all had our heads well down. I kept telling Reg to "get your bloody head in!" but he insisted he couldn't be seen.

Sergeant R. Pinchon and Private R.G. Goodwin, 8th Battalion DLI[1]

Quite possibly the finest German troops in Sicily at the time, they fought superbly. They were troops of the highest quality, experienced veterans of Crete and Russia; cool and skilled, Nazi Zealots to a man and fanatically courageous. To fight them was an education for any soldier.

The Times, 27 August 1943

Described as an obscure speck on the harsh Sicilian landscape, Primosole Bridge was, in 1943, a 400-foot-long box-girder-type bridge not unlike a Bailey bridge, guarded by concrete blockhouses sited at both ends of the span. The Simeto River itself was perhaps 30 yards across, meandering through a fly-infested marshland of primeval aspect. North lay a pair of small farms surrounded by a tangle of ancient vines, olive gardens and orchards,[2] a landscape which the classical Greeks contesting ground with Carthaginian rivals would have easily recognised. In this setting DLI would fight one of its bitterest battles of the war. This undistinguished structure opened the way on to the vital Plain of Catania and the blood-price for its capture would be terribly high. The ground was deceptive, for the view from the south which the Allies perceived as they moved north towards the bridge concealed the fact that a sunken road ran behind at a distance of several hundred yards – a ready-made defensive line; 'indeed such cover as there was lay on the enemy side of the bridge, for the British side was completely flat and open'.[3]

Bill Watson, CO of 6th Battalion, recalled:

The width of the river was about 30 to 40 yards, came up to my waist, so for a smaller fellow it would be chest high and chaps kept slipping into deeper shell holes. It was a high girder bridge about eight feet above the water. Beyond the bridge on the left stood an oblong vineyard, no great depth, maybe 200 to 300 yards and extending for about a quarter of a mile upstream. Beyond lay a sunken road or lane – 'Stink' or 'Stench' Alley we came to call it; between this and the vineyard a dense hedge of prickly pears; on the other side, at the corner, stood the ruins of a farmhouse. Then the road, running dead straight between an avenue of poplars. From the north the ground dipped down to the bridge with some very steep 'S' bends before the bridge. There was an old quarry here with seven dead mules in it! We called the place 'Dead Horse Corner.'[4]

Sicily – the landings

Flung like a triangular boulder into the Mediterranean, separated from the heel and toe of Italy by the Straits of Messina, Sicily has been a stepping stone from Africa to Europe for a catalogue of conquerors from Carthaginians, Romans, Arabs, Normans and, in 1943, the Allies. The land is rugged and harsh, dominated by high, sharp-fanged ridges. In summer the air is furnace hot, scorching hills and terraces, oven-like on the plains. The planned Allied invasion, 'Operation Husky', began on 9 July and officially ended on 17 August. It was the first major blow directed against the Axis heartlands after victory in North Africa and formed a curtain-raiser for the subsequent invasion of the Italian mainland, hammering nails into Il Duce's political coffin and heralding the demise of his regime. The island would not be easily won.

With the Allied victory in North Africa now complete, those luxuriant cities of the Delta reverted to their peacetime calm, oases of hedonism after the harsh confines of bitter sands. For the weary warriors of 151 Brigade the relief was palpable. Their desert fighting had been long, hard, bloody and desperate. To men emerging from the cauldron, this lush indolence and abundance of plenty must have seemed almost unreal, another of the Sahara's tantalising mirages and, like such floating images, did not long endure, 'Enfidaville to Alexandria, took 20 days and more.'[5] Soon the brigade was back in training, preparing for a major amphibious operation; 'we exercised with LCAs [Landing Craft Assault], so clearly some form of opposed landing seemed inevitable.'[6] This new challenge would be directed by a fresh appointment at the top, Brigadier Beake having passed the baton to Ronnie Senior, who would see the Durhams through Sicily and on to the Normandy beaches.[7] For over a month till the end of June the whole of 50th Division practised landing on hostile shores, no target was specified and the rumour mill ground fervidly. On the last day of the month the division embarked at Port Said and, once upon the seas, their destination could be confirmed. For the first time in four grinding years of war, the Allies were carrying the fight on to Axis ground.

For these seasoned desert warriors the sea passage proved almost reminiscent of Homer's bronze-clad Achaeans on their distant cruise to the Troad. The Mediterranean summer produced halcyon sailing conditions, cloudless blue skies, untrammelled by enemy aircraft. Though the alarm rang out half a dozen times, only one actual plane was sighted, and that a mere observer.[8] 'On that first morning as we came up on deck there was nothing to be seen but ships, hundreds of them.'[9] The Allied flotilla, mighty upon seas controlled completely by the Royal Navy, steamed towards the hostile shore. Five days out and the squadron was joined by two more out of Malta and North Africa, a vast armada which crowded the sparkling waters from horizon to horizon, precursor of that great fleet which, in less than a year, would transport Allied troops in the greatest crusade of all.

Men lazed upon sunlit decks, the clamour of war's confusion and horror temporarily banished. This was not to last: on the final evening at sea a tempest arose, driving the placid waters to white-capped frenzy and wreaking havoc with carefully laid plans. At sunset on 9 July, after a day's buffeting which left many feeling wretchedly sick, a break in the blanket of fitful cloud revealed the imposing, smoke-shrouded summit of Mount Etna. As darkness descended, an aerial armada passed overhead, paratroops and airborne infantry in the vanguard. The Durhams were back in the war. In the small hours of 10 July, soldiers clambered into their landing craft. For anyone prone to seasickness this presaged a heightened degree of misery as the small craft butted against the heavy swell. There were some distractions amid the briefings: 'A page from an illustrated magazine had been pinned below the notices. It showed an attractive girl in a very abbreviated bathing costume. "Come to sunny Sicily for your holidays," had been chalked underneath, and below this someone else had written: "I bet she won't be waiting on Green Beach."'[10]

They would, in fact, form the spear-point of the amphibious assault; 6th and 9th Battalions would come ashore in the van, securing the coastal town of Avola, lying on the south-east tip. 8th Battalion would follow on to consolidate the beach-head and town, allowing the rest of 50th Division to disembark. The boats had been launched some five miles further out than anticipated and, in the storm-tossed night, confusion reigned. 'B' Company 8th Battalion found themselves leaping into six or seven feet of water, depending on their life jackets, with sailors already ashore unceremoniously dragging the weaker men in with boat hooks. If standard webbing was heavy when dry, soaking wet it was very weighty indeed.

Aside from the hazards of attacking an enemy shoreline, the heavy seas made the whole process of disembarkation difficult and unpleasant. George Chambers recalls:

The LCAs were lowered into the water by derricks, in rough conditions no sooner had we touched the sea than we were pitched upwards again by the swell, the hooks from the derricks swinging around and threatening to decapitate someone! We were in the boats for several hours, many chaps lying sick as dogs on the decks; practically had to kick people off when we hit the shore![11]

Where is this perishing battle anyway?

It was not until 04.15 hours that lead elements of 6th Battalion attained the beaches. Happily, apart from some random shooting, the Italian defenders proved incapable or unwilling to offer effective resistance. One enemy searchlight probed the darkness but was quickly extinguished by a well-aimed burst from a handy Bren. Private Ernest Kerans of 9 DLI was one of those coming ashore:

There was only two feet of pebbles between the sea and the low cliffs of Avola, where we landed, right on target. The moment I put my foot on land two enemy fighters, their machine-guns blazing away, skimmed overhead. I got awful wet diving under a low overhanging ledge in the cliff at the same time as a wave. We climbed the bank, cut the wire and ran across a vineyard to the road. Odd rounds of rifle fire did nothing to slow us down. What slowed me was falling over a couple of vines and my puttee getting wrapped around one of them. The company settled down to a steady trot up a narrow lane that bypassed the village.[12]

Kerans, like others, found the Italians to be somewhat less than fanatical:

There were a lot of Italians in the few houses we passed, a lot of them busy changing from their uniform into civvies. We could not prove it and hadn't got time to try. A big officer tagged himself on to me, I think he was a press reporter, and somebody must have told him I was in the Intelligence Section, giving him a totally wrong impression. 'What are we going to attack first?' 'There is a farm-house on a hill, about a mile ahead, to the right of the lane, we are going to capture it, 'brew-up' and have some breakfast.' 'Don't joke man, what are we on?' 'I'm not joking sir.' He left us in disgust, but that is just what did happen. We took the farm without opposition.'[13]

As they moved inland, 6th Battalion discovered an unexpected reinforcement in the guise of US Airborne, victims of a widely dispersed drop. The two units cooperated with gusto. Not all the Americans had been so fortunate, as Ernie Kerans remembered:

Then it was down the lane and on to the road for Nota. There was a thick wood to the left of the road and from each tree hung a dead Allied paratrooper (Americans I think). It was weird; we could only leave them there. A few yards further on, in a ditch following the road, was a long line of wounded Italians, screaming, weeping and pleading. I had started to leave the column to have a closer look at them when the Sergeant-Major shouted at the top of his voice 'You help that lot and I'll shoot you.'[14]

As 8th Battalion hit their beaches, they discovered the sands were not theirs at all, as another division claimed proprietorship rights. As the Battalion, still minus 'C' Company, finally marched off the beaches they ran into units from yet another division coming back. 'Landed in the wrong Div area,' these newcomers grumpily observed, 'where is this perishing battle anyway?'[15] By mid-morning, however, the two lead Durham battalions had secured the town of Avola and Union Jacks (courtesy of RN) were flying from the Town Hall.[16] Despite all of their difficulties, the Durhams were on their objectives and holding the front door open, controlling the significant heights above the landing beaches. News from the other Allied landings was encouraging and 50th Division could proceed inland. Their objective was the level plain of Catania inland from Syracuse. Their line of march lay through crowding hills till the vital crossing of the River Simeto and Primosole bridge. Beyond this narrow funnel the plain stretched for 15 miles towards Catania.

Peter Lewis with 8th Battalion found his platoon an excellent billet in an abandoned Italian encampment, their gunners having departed rather hastily leaving both guns and all equipment behind: 'Even the beds were made up as though for an inspection, far more luxury than we were used to; maps, cameras, everything you could imagine left lying about, but not for long, as you can imagine!'[17] As the Durhams settled in to these unexpectedly sybaritic surroundings:

a farm cart went by – the family all smiles, one small boy waving a Union Jack and yelling 'Viva Inglesi.' The CSM then arrived in a Fiat car. I asked if he had come by this properly and he replied he's provided the owner with a formal receipt c/o the Sporting Club Gezira, Cairo. Check if it's taxed and insured, I asked. We found the car most useful, though it got run over and flattened by one of our Priests [a self-propelled gun rather than any member of the clergy] a few days later![18]

The CO did somewhat better, picking up a rather racy Lancia, a low-slung sporty model that was both more comfortable to ride in and easier to exit in a hurry if being strafed!

Enterprising locals soon had the measure of their liberators, as Peter Lewis recalls:

Around six in the evening a small boy with a tear-stained face came in, crying that we'd stolen his bike and that his parents were very angry with him for allowing such a thing to happen. Could he have it back? We felt sorry for the little fellow and he'd brought two bottles of the local vino to trade. Eventually we found his bicycle and off he went, though I realised he couldn't reach the pedals and had to push – we then realised we'd been had and he'd likely been going around everyone with the same story – the wine was pretty dreadful too![19]

Primosole Bridge – the airborne spearhead

'Operation Fustian' was to prove a mini-Arnhem from which certain key lessons might have been learnt. Primosole was one of three river crossings that would have to be secured to facilitate the rapid Allied advance. The plan was to drop three parachute battalions but they would find their opposition drawn from German counterparts, elite Fallschirmjager.[20] A single parachute regiment under the command of Oberstleutnant Ludwig Heilmann formed the vanguard, dropped by Primosole Bridge with the express intention of denying this to the British. These highly experienced and hardened veterans wasted no time in digging in.[21] This was unfortunate; worse, the Allied drop left units widely scattered and less than 200 Paras could be assembled for the attack on the bridge defences; 'some were dropped into the sea and never heard of again'.[22] Despite this, the Red Devils pressed home their assault and subdued the few Italian defenders.

Though the British did succeed in removing Axis demolition charges, their position was soon under heavy attack from the Germans. Subsequent glider-borne landings were badly shot up and eventually the surviving paratroops, their ammunition exhausted, were obliged to withdraw. Despite the ferocious fighting both sides conducted themselves punctiliously:

It should be noted that there was a strange bond of comradeship between the German and British paratroopers fighting for Primosole Bridge. Red Devils, swinging helplessly from the orange trees, were not shot or bayoneted in their harness as one might expect in such a confused night battle: rather, the enemy paratroopers were allowed to unbuckle and fall to the ground, where they were taken prisoner. Captives were not shot, or even roughly handled, but were treated almost like guests.'[23]

The fight was hard and intense. Even *Krieg ohne Hass* between such determined and disciplined adversaries was bound to be close and bitter. Sergeant J.A. Johnstone of 2nd Para Battalion recalls:

As we lay among the vines it was soon evident that we were in the middle of a nice firefight, for from the hill above us came the solid thunk of a Bren in reply to the Spandau cobra hiss. Then we heard the swish and crump of mortars coming from the German side on to what we now know as a handful of 'A' Company on Johnny 1 [drop-zone 1]. I think I remember also identifying the bark of 88s down the valley, but whether they were ranged on Johnny 1 or the bridge which, like Arnhem later, had been gained by the brigade only to be lost because of lack of numbers and lightness of armament...[24]

Very soon the fight moved rather closer to Johnstone and his party:

For how long this went on I have no idea, nor had I at the time, but abruptly, as usually happens in war, our situation changed completely, for there was the sound of movement close in the vines and I was startled by an abrupt command in German, *'Hande Hoch'* [hands up]. I found myself on my knees, hand on Sten, and gazing at the back and left side of a stocky little figure whose Schmeisser [the German MP40 submachine carbine] was levelled at the bulky form of the CMP sergeant, who later turned out to be 'Biff' Whitehead, a professional rugby player of international standing. As I say, the German's back was half turned to me and I started to raise my Sten, to be checked by George Fisher's urgent 'Not now Johnnie!' I don't know exactly what passed through my mind at that moment. I had never killed a man at close quarters or indeed at all, that I knew for certain... Certainly I had no appreciation of the tactical situation which I suspect that the sharper-witted cockney, George, may have realised that we were about to be enveloped in the advance of German paratroopers up the hill. I saw them moving swiftly and competently each side of the little hide-out a minute or two later. Anyway I lowered my Sten and it was all over.[25]

As British paratroopers contested the bridge with their German opponents, 50th Division was toiling inland. The ground was difficult: high, steep-sided hills crowded the narrow highway, crowned with stout stone terraces, the valley floor thronged with dense and ancient groves. Though 69 Brigade were leading, the Durhams found themselves under attack from the Napoli Division, a series of largely uncoordinated assaults directed against 6th Battalion, 'first with tanks and then with infantry. Neither [of two] attacks was successful. The tanks – some five in all – careered down the road from Palazzola as the Battalion was moving forward; four were knocked out but one reached Floridia, shooting up Colonel Watson's jeep and wounding the medical officer on the way. It ended its career by running into a lamp-post .'[26]

At first light on 13 July the Durhams, having stopped Italian infantry, counter-attacked and swept through enemy positions, mopping up snipers and stragglers in the rout; 'the Battalion's casualties were light but included two company commanders, Captain Dominic Parker, wounded in the lungs, and Captain Jimmy Chapman, who was unfortunately killed – a very serious loss so early in the campaign.'[27] So vigorous was the assault and pursuit that Napoli Division virtually ceased to exist; hundreds surrendered, including the unit commander, with a matching haul of materiel.

Bill Watson was the officer who captured General Fortunare:

> He was extremely annoyed when we told him to sit on top of the carrier not on one of the seats. He was even more annoyed when we took away his pearl-handled revolver. He went back on Sergeant Raine's carrier [Raine was later killed]. All in all my patrol [six carriers and a troop of Shermans] did rather well, our haul comprised two 88mm guns, two 75mm guns, two anti-tank guns, 13 Breda MGs, six 3-inch mortars, one ammunition wagon, six motor bikes, 12 Lancia 10-ton trucks, three Fiat three-tonners and 16 light tanks![28]

Peter Lewis toiled along the hot, dusty march, his men, hardened by the desert, standing up well. That evening they were treated to 'the sound of a great deal of MG fire above the low cloud, echoing through the heavens, then six Stukas dropped out of the sky, through the clouds like leaves falling; our Spitfires had downed them all, well that really perked us up.'[29]

On this day the British paratroops attempted their seizure of Primosole Bridge. The difficulties they had encountered and the stiffness of the opposition made early arrival by 50th Division as reinforcement essential. To relieve 69 Brigade, who'd so far acted as the 'schwerpunkt', 151 Brigade leapfrogged and the Durhams began a tough forced march, covering some 25 miles in the furnace heat of a Sicilian midsummer. By late afternoon on the 14th, 9th Battalion, in the lead, was within a mile of their objective, 4th Armoured Brigade in support. Though the Red Devils had been driven off the bridge itself, their slender line held sufficiently to prevent the Axis from rewiring it with explosives.

For unexplained reasons, most of the motor transport had been sent back (bar carriers) and the men had to tramp in broiling heat on the harsh unyielding surface. Peter Lewis was marching with his men:

> We marched 25 miles from Sortino to Primosole. It was hot and dusty with the Shermans [from 4th Armoured Brigade] pushing out vast quantities of diesel fumes. We were very thirsty and weighed down by kit; this was the longest operational march since France in 1940. We'd been told the Paras would hold the bridge till we got there. We had 10 minutes' rest every hour, trudging along in a zombie-like state, platoons in single file on both sides of the road, tanks mixed up with the infantry. Well, one of the tanks stopped suddenly and Sergeant Brannigan walked right into the back of it; the blow knocked his helmet down over his face. He let rip with a stream of expletives, and the tirade continued. This produced a ripple of laughter behind that spread down the entire length of the battalion – it was incidents like this that kept you going.[30]

Brigadier Senior sensibly judged the men too exhausted from their gruelling marching to put in an immediate attack and that this could wait until morning; 6th and 8th Battalions were still strung out along the dusty highway. Intense and debilitating heat was nothing new to these desert survivors, nor forced marches, but the Durham Brigade was poised to endure one of its most severe and costly tests. The undistinguished and unremarkable bridge now lying ahead would prove a veritable Calvary. An intimation of what lay in store arrived in the shape of a brace of Paras, brimming with anger at their repulse. Ernest Kerans was a witness:

> During the night two tired and bitter paratroopers came up the road to the battalion. They had captured the bridge but could not hold it any longer. Most of their mates were dead or captured. So deep was their sorrow they tried to talk the IO and the CO into waking the lads and making the attack right away. There were tears in their eyes and anger in their voices as they talked. To the best of their knowledge they were the only ones left from the battle and it was definite that the bridge was in German hands. They swore they were coming in with us and taking no prisoners.[31]

15 July

As the men of both lead battalions (8th and 9th) bivouacked and sought to snatch a few hours' rest, their slumbers were rudely interrupted by sorties from the Italians, who, at 04.00 hours, sent in a troop of balaklavering armoured cars; 9th Battalion's anti-tank gunners swiftly brought the charge to a standstill: 'There were very few survivors and the failure of this desperate bid by the Italians to shoot up the 9th Battalion HQ was not due to lack of courage on the part of the armoured car crews.'[32] Peter Lewis remembered that, around 04.00 there was violent firing in the area of 9th Battalion: 'There had been a short, fierce action when several Italian Marine armoured cars penetrated as far as HQ Company. The AT gunners fired point blank and set all of the cars on fire. I walked down there in the morning, a frightful mess, some were still burning. It was a brave attempt, almost a suicide mission.'[33]

At 07.30 hours the Durhams advanced; two full field regiments of British guns sending ahead a wailing chorus of shells. The ground was open and horribly exposed, German machine-gun fire raked their files, bullets swarming thick as angry hornets from the tangled groves and sunken road. The crossing was a nightmare and a savage, confused melee erupted on the broken slopes. Wounded men floundered amongst bobbing corpses crowding the sullen, blood-laced water; some drowned. Like the Paras before them, the Durhams laboured and bled to maintain a precarious foothold on the north bank but the bridgehead was hammered relentlessly and could not be held.

Peter Lewis with 8th Battalion was an observer:

They had to advance some 300–400 yards and went in open formation, two companies up and one in reserve. We couldn't see the enemy, well entrenched in closed country and, at that point, we'd no knowledge of the sunken road. They were met with heavy fire long before they'd even got as far as the river bank. It was almost like watching toy soldiers. I had a grandstand view and wished I hadn't, watching as men went down. Those who got over were met hand-to-hand by German paratroopers in the vineyard. Eventually they were driven back across the river – had to leave their dead and wounded, the fight probably lasted one-and-a-half to two hours.[34]

Private Kerens found himself in the thick of it:

They [the Battalion] started to cross the river then all hell broke loose. On the other side of the river suddenly a row of heads, machine-guns and rifles popped up. Soon the river ran red, literally, with the blood of the Durhams. Some did reach the other side, clamber up the bank and engage the enemy in hand-to-hand fighting, but there was not enough to hang on to what they had gained. We in HQ Company went down to see what we could do to help; there wasn't a lot. We stopped just short of the river and fired at anything that looked *Tedescish* [German]. One or two of us went into the river to try and rescue some of the wounded. It wasn't easy, bullets buzzed about us like bees. The bloke nearest to me had himself to be rescued. I went under [the] bridge to keep bullets off me and my charges. The Padre was there too… What was left of the battalion went back up the hill to have a meal and much-needed rest. The 8th Battalion made sure we were not followed.[35]

16 July

If the bridge could not be taken by brute force then it must be possible simply to outflank and secure a wider lodgement or series of lodgements on the north flank of the river which would render the defenders' position untenable. Clearly attacking in daylight hours was unsupportable, so 8th Battalion would now go in under cover of darkness at 02.00 hours on 16 July. Lieutenant-Colonel A.S. Pearson DSO MC from the 1st Parachute Battalion was another of the airborne contingent anxious to be back in the fight.

His knowledge of the ground, gained in the earlier combat, was invaluable:

> Battalion HQ was situated in a small cave, and the CO had just started to outline the plan when a stranger appeared in the entrance. He was unshaven, his khaki shirt and trousers in stains and grime, and he looked dog-tired. He walked over and sat down beside the CO. 'My name's Pearson' he said. 'I commanded the paratroops down at the bridge and I understand you are attacking again this afternoon. I think I can help you.'[36]

He'd become aware of a suitable crossing point some 200 yards upstream. 'A' and 'D' companies would, under Lt. Col. Pearson's guidance, secure an immediate lodgement then make for the bridge whilst the remainder crossed in their wake. 'It was impossible not to feel an intense admiration for this burly Scotsman who, having fought continuously for 24 hours with his paratroops to hold the vital bridge, was now offering to lead another attack to capture it, knowing full well that he need take no further part in the battle.'[37]

'A' Company had been occupying a bivouac recently vacated in some haste by the previous tenants:

> The 'A' Company area had been a Luftwaffe rest camp for German airmen on leave from the airfields on the Catania Plain. A number of tents in the area had comprised the HQ Officers' Mess and sleeping quarters of the German pilots. Captain Beattie's Company HQ was soon established inside the mess tent, where a half-consumed meal still remained on the table. The Germans had left hurriedly, and a great deal of useful material was picked up in the area by the battalion, including cameras, air-filled mattresses, German fleece-lined flying coats, and a portable lighting plant which came in very useful later in the campaign.[38]

Any who'd seen action before knew this was no picnic. They knew their opponents were of a rather different stamp to the Italians. Peter Lewis remembered: 'there was one officer who after every CO's briefing would always spread doom and gloom, "we've had it this time" and so forth, very disheartening for the men who had nothing to do but brood till we attacked. The old sweats knew better than to look too worried, mindful of the effect this would have on those who'd not seen action before.'[39]

As ever, the guns boomed in support, sure harbingers of battle; 'it was a heavy barrage for such a narrow front and the noise was deafening'. Private Kerens takes up the story: 'At about 02.00 hours the next night [16 July] the 8th DLI went in. Allied guns had been belting away before that. By dawn the 8th had got most of their men across and gained quite a foothold. However, the Germans were Paras, well armed and they knew what to do with them. With both sides it was hand-to-hand, rifles, bayonets and plenty of Spandaus.'[40]

In the warm darkness where the heat of day still lay like a blanket, men stumbled and cursed in tangled vines. Peter Lewis recalled: 'It was a clear moonlit night, some men stepped into shell-holes in the river bed and had to be rescued; the vines were closely entwined and difficult to cross, you had to shout to ensure people kept up and all this was doubly difficult at night. I remember there was lots of tracer but that's not too difficult to dodge.'[41] These two leading companies achieved a measure of surprise and hooked around towards the bridge to establish a block across the road north of the span. Fog of war and signals' failures, despite careful preparation, delayed the remainder; 'The mortar flares had got separated from the mortars; the wireless sets had got "drowned" during the crossing and an RE carrier with wireless which came up to the bridge received a direct hit.'[42]

Providentially, an observer from the War Office chose the moment to saunter up to the bridge on a bicycle, as though he was on a country lane. He was quickly sent back as a galloper. Dawn was filtering through by now, air heavy with the promise of yet another furnace-hot morning. As the reserve companies, 'B' and 'C' pushed north of the bridge, infiltrating along the ditches lining both sides of the road. They didn't get far; all hell broke loose as the waiting Germans, carefully dug in, deluged the Durhams in fire. Men began to fall in increasing numbers as bright fireflies of tracer ripped through the still morning, the harsh, staccato rattle of MG42s contributing a truly Wagnerian dawn chorus. All through the battle the bridge itself remained a most undesirable locale, as Bill Watson recollects:

There was constant sniping and mortar fire, tanks couldn't get across for a pair of 88mm guns astride the road could fire directly down on to the bridge. All this time, although the detonators had been removed the explosive charges were still in place. The approach was an appalling scene of total havoc, tanks in flames, pillboxes smashed to smithereens and a wrecked glider on one side.[43]

Reg Goodwin and Ray Pinchin went in with 8th Battalion:

Reg was shouting that a party of Jerries were crossing our front. Sergeant Mackmin of 'D' Company ran over to him and together they had a go at them. Reg acted as a rest for the Bren by standing up with the gun on his shoulder. They fired a couple of magazines at them. It must have been a bit hard on Reg's eardrums. When the battle ended we looked over the ground and between them they had accounted for a few of the enemy...Reg was quite unflappable, never seemed to raise his voice and never, like most soldiers, used bad language. And being from the West Country his dialect was like music after Geordie twang.[44]

Reg's son Keith remembered the lasting effect on his father's hearing: 'I often wondered why dad couldn't hear the grasshoppers in the garden at home – [he] had lost much of his hearing due to the firing of the Bren gun on his shoulder.'

Now 'C' company began moving through open fields to the right, feeling a way around the flanks, 'B' company's Brens added their own fury to the rising crescendo. Lieutenant A.F. Jackman led a desperate charge – it was time for the bayonet; 'Jackman was badly wounded and most of his men killed or wounded; but the Germans withdrew. Then both sides set to with bayonets, grenades and automatics.' CSM Brannigan, he of the earlier helmet incident, swept through a squad of Germans like the grim reaper, killing roughly one Axis soldier per minute.[45]

In the scrub and tangle both sides blazed at nothing or at trees. 'It seemed as though there was a German behind every tree and vine; every bush. The situation was unreal, almost fantastic. Both sides fired at trees by mistake, thinking they were men; both sides threw grenades until it was realised that the exploding bombs were just as likely to kill friend as foe.'[46] Some from 'B' Company were mown down as they struggled forwards; others outflanked and executed their killers from behind.

This was now the classic soldier's battle; in 20 minutes the lead units were fought out and virtually wiped out. Only a couple of score of Durhams from 'B' Company were unhurt and the Fallschirmjager still held the sunken road. As the companies fell back, the paratroops emerged from cover, bayonets fixed. The fury of their charge virtually eliminated the slender rearguard, commanded by Sergeant F. Mitchinson: 'The Sergeant shammed dead to avoid capture, allowing the enemy to pass him by. One of the paratroops actually kicked Mitchinson to see if he were dead and was apparently satisfied. When the Germans moved on Mitchinson opened fire with his Tommy gun...'[47] For the battered survivors of both companies there was no hope of carrying so strong a position, so they consolidated in and around the farm left of the road; virtually every officer had become a casualty. CSM Brannigan acted as a one-man rearguard, accounting for a further tally of Germans before being shot down. As the survivors clung to their hard-won lodgement the inevitable counter-attacks developed. These tough paratroops were not overly keen to yield ground.

As dawn came, so did they; these were seasoned veterans who used the broken terrain to good effect. 'A' Company on the extreme right flank, half dug-in to the dense jungle of vines, was hit point blank. Again it was a fight reminiscent of the Western Front battles. The Durhams, heavily outnumbered, were forced back yard by contested yard, both sides leaving a slew of dead and wounded. Bayonets lunged and flicked, grenades cracked amongst the growth, small-arms fire barked and snapped. By 06.00 hours 'A' Company had either been driven back to the churned banks, where survivors had to swim for it, or were forced into the leaguer of a stout stone farm to the right of the roadway. The Fallschirmjager missed no opportunity for aggressive action, even pressing a captured Sherman into immediate service. Gallant Jackman, already wounded, was entangled in barbed wire, now caught in the tracks of a careering Sherman which had fallen prey to a well-sited 88mm gun: 'Jackman was dragged along the ground but fortunately the tank soon came to rest.' Happily, the badly injured officer was evacuated by the Germans to Catania where he was found, though in a very bad way; mercifully he survived.[48]

All through that long, hot day the Germans kept attacking, determined to expunge the shrinking bridgehead. They did not succeed: 'The battalion mortar fired over 600 bombs and accounted for dozens of snipers. To tackle a German pillbox, Corporal David Scriven at one stage led a tank by crouching outside on the top of it and from there directing the commander inside. At the end of the day the Battalion was still where it had been that morning.'[49]

Ernie Kerans would soon experience this inferno first-hand: 'While we were enjoying our well-earned rest the 8th and the Germans kept the "hand to hand" up all day. When night came the weakened 9th had to go back in and take over, there was nobody else. There had been no time for burial parties and there were dead bodies everywhere. A sunken road was paved with them...'[50] Kerens, as part of Battalion HQ, accompanied the intelligence officer and the CO.

> The rest of us went on, Nobby with us. Down the side of a big farm building where a lot of 8th Battalion wallahs were dug in, to the road. Across it in a mad dash and through to a field to a deep ditch that ran 90 degrees to it. With a CO with you there are things done more dangerous than with a 2nd Lieutenant. Now we were in the thick of the bullets and grenades. Some of our carriers had got across and were going up the road towards Catania. They weren't getting very far, like I say there was a lot of opposition. About 40 yards from us, just across the road, two enemy dashed out of a farm building and put something that exploded under one of our carriers. Charlie Sollis and self fired at them two or three times. I don't know if we hit them, they gave up the idea.[51]

Next the dreaded Tigers[52] made an appearance:

> From the other end of our short trench a 'Tiger' fired down it. I think it was. I dug myself into the side of the trench until it went away. In a battle like this nobody knows who's who. There were now less than a score of us. Nobby got the men on a carrier to ask for a 'smoke-screen'. This was put down (I think by a carrier) and we ran like the devil the way we had come. We ran back to a deep hollow about 40 yards from the bridge, bomb hole I think. The bridge was still under constant shell-fire. Nobby must have thought I was indestructible, he sent me to the bridge to make a sit-rep. There were explosions all the way to it and around it and me but I went inside. The sides were OK but the floor across was

more 'Holy than Godly'. Suddenly I got a painful 'uppercut' which floored me. A nose cap from a shell fell almost into my hand. I lay stunned for a few seconds but as sense returned I realised this was not the safest place to be and dashed back to rejoin the CO and the rest, who by now had returned to the other side of the road. It was not a big cut, I wiped the blood off a couple of times and it soon stopped.[53]

Alongside 9th Battalion, the 6th also ran into heavy opposition, their crossing paid for in blood. Fighting through the warm Mediterranean night, amongst the almost primeval scrubland, ditches and structures, they inched forward, Germans contesting every step. Lieutenant D.J. Fenner was in command of 13 Platoon of 'C' Company:

The whole battalion moved silently in single file to the attack. Rum had been issued before we left and was of some comfort in this limbo period where we had little to do but occupy our thoughts with the grim and inevitable prospect ahead. We reached a dry ditch running towards the river and began moving through a battlefield where our parachutists and the Germans had fought. All around the vegetation had been burnt by phosphorus bombs[53] and tracer bullets. Evidence of the fighting was everywhere. The ditch contained many burnt bodies. One completely blackened sat upright staring sightlessly at each member of the battalion as he struggled past in the moonlight. The only sound came from the burst of harassing fire from the Cheshire machine-gunners and the bull frogs croaking in the reeds. We paused before the leading company entered the river, bayonets were fixed, rifles and machine-guns cocked.[54]

At this point, in best British fashion the platoon runner, an old sweat, began disputing the need to fix bayonets with the NCO. This man, Private Dickinson, was loudly of the view the use of bayonets was unlikely:

I cannot remember the outcome of this disagreement but I did appreciate the easing of tension it produced amongst us. Then we were on the move to the river, sliding down the bank into chest-high water, again in single file guiding ourselves by hanging on to a wire stretched between the banks for this purpose. Below the far bank the Battalion bore left then turned to face the enemy, the three assaulting companies in line. So far all had gone well; our objective, a sunken road, was some 500 yards away through the vineyards. It needed a few more minutes to pass before zero hour when someone said, 'What are we waiting for?' Another voice said 'Let's get stuck in,' then followed a general move by all the leading companies up the bank, through the vineyard towards the sunken road.[55]

Very soon 'C' Company was hotly engaged:

My recollections of what happened after that are confused. Firing began at isolated Germans seen running away then from the direction of the road came a murderous fire from the Spandaus located there. The gunners were firing on 'fixed lines', they could not see us in the dark. Burst of tracer swept by at knee height. The line of infantry kept going on in spite of men being hit until we were struck by heavy concentrations of artillery. Some of this was probably enemy DF [defensive fire] but in the opinion of those who had been shelled by our gunners on previous occasions we were in our own. Ben Dickenson [*sic*] was clear on this point. He shouted 'When I get out of this I'll do those bloody gunners.'

As the deadly barrage finally lifted, the survivors of 'C' Company were on their feet again and pressing on: '...groups of men got up, moved on through the cactus hedge into the sunken road. There was a lot of shooting, suddenly it was over and we had taken about eight prisoners, all but two wounded.'[56]

It was time to dig in:

Mark organised what remained of the company astride the road. There were elements of two platoons and we started to provide some entrenching tools. The older soldiers acquired the much more efficient German article and were soon digging in at great speed. The place was littered with German equipment, Spandau machine-guns, belts of ammunition and corpses. Our prisoners were parachutists; one spoke good English and told us that three days ago they had been in the south of France! A fierce battle was in progress to our right where the 9th were going in. Apart from the pop of small-arms fire, where we were was comparatively quiet. In the first light of the summer's day we dug while the stretcher-bearers attended to the wounded lying thick in the vines.[57]

Bitter victory

'B' Company, led by Captain 'Reggie' Atkinson, finally took the sunken road at bayonet point and at some considerable cost. Barely a single platoon strong, they battled on, succeeding in occupying a warren of ditches and a single massive shell crater just left of the highway. This was significant; here they formed an effective cork in the bottle. Axis reinforcements could be interdicted and remnants left behind contained. All night they clung on. Predictably, at dawn the Germans threw in several strong counter-attacks to dislodge them. It was a very near-run thing but they held: 'This gallant action very materially influenced the course of the battle.'

Ernie Kerans and his comrades in 9th Battalion experienced similar tribulations:

The Battalion advanced under heavy fire, it was slow going. All day we hung on to half a mile of land, every inch of it hard won. When night came we had made some sort of position but had neither food nor water. By the moonlight, in no-man's-land, we could see a farmhouse. It was less than 40 yards ahead. With a jerry can and Charlie Sollis 'covering me' the two of us warily made our way towards it. It was a huge barn, the floor six inches deep in liquid. We tasted it and found it to be vino. There, wrecked by the enemy, were the vats with the bungs knocked out. They were all around the walls but not much left in; we only just managed to half-fill a jerry can. Suddenly there was what sounded like a loud snore. We dropped the tin and pointed our weapons at a very drunken goat that was staggering around in the corner. We enjoyed a quiet laugh, refilled our can and set off for home. As we did so others were entering from the enemy side. We did not argue with them, we did not do this killing business just for the sake of doing it.[58]

By this time 'A' Company of the 9th, led by Captain Hudson, which had set out with two platoons, had fought doggedly forward, knocking out several enemy strongpoints and taking a hefty haul of prisoners. The cost was very high indeed: when Hudson counted up he had only 15 fit men in total. They kept fighting, always under an intense Axis fire. Finally reduced to seven men standing and virtually out of rounds, Hudson ordered the survivors to withdraw; he himself was soon wounded and captured. In fact, the crisis had passed, though the desperate survivors clinging on under incessant fire might have been forgiven if they did not immediately perceive it. At first light the paratroops threw in a strong counter-attack, supported by tanks; Allied artillery drove them off. An hour later, 4th Armoured Shermans were rolling over the tortured carcass of the bridge. They stormed through the bocage of roots and vines leaving a flattened wake, their co-axial machine-guns raking every thicket. This intervention finally turned the tide and for the first time in this bitter contest, Germans began surrendering in numbers. By midday it was over: 'over 150 Germans had surrendered; and their dead on the ground numbered over 300'.[59]

For Ernie Kerans, it was to be a bitter victory:

The battalion got organised. The 'I' Section went back to the river bank. There wasn't much small-arms fire but plenty of shelling. The bridge was getting more than its share. There were still plenty of casualties. One or two Shermans got through and for the first time the Germans began to give themselves up in large numbers. Rumour had it we would be relieved tomorrow. In theory things were good but Nobby and Big Bill went round with the officers from another division of the 69th Bde when a salvo of enemy shells got both of them. I'll bet he said 'I am not showing them I dive for cover every time a shell explodes.' The sort of thing he would do. He was killed instantly; it was like losing a father. When they told us on our river bank I could not help but cry out 'If they can kill Nobby, what chance has any of us?' Visher told me to shut up or I'd have everybody bomb-happy.[60]

The field itself looked like a vision of hell, like some replay of the Somme or Hooge. Everywhere the ground was blackened and scorched, ancient vines twisted into grotesque images of souls in torment. Discarded equipment and the detritus of war lay everywhere: broken weapons, mounds of brass casings glinting innocently in clear light, torn strips of webbing and the dead.

1937

Members of the Unit photographed during a night exercise shortly after conversion from
7th Battalion The Durham Light Infantry T.A.
to 47th (The Durham Light Infantry) A.A. Battalion R.E. T.A.

Members of 7th Battalion DLI after conversion to AA role during a night exercise.
DRO D/Cl 27/278/402

Eighth Battalion personnel carrier in action in North Africa.
DRO D/Cl 27/278/402

German half track captured by 'A' Company 6th Battalion, 8th June, 1944.
DRO D/Cl 27/278/402

A group of officers standing by the original cairn erected at Primosole Bridge.
DRO D/Cl 27/278/402

Cast of the pantomime 'Robin Hood' directed by Lt. John Arnold, following the Sicily Campaign.
DRO D/Cl 27/278/402

A patrol from 9th Battalion in North Africa, 1942, pausing to eat.
DRO D/Cl 27/278/402

Gordon Worrall and Jim Kennedy from 9th Battalion, Alexandria, 1942.
DRO D/Cl 27/278/402

Gordon Worrall on board a captured Italian tank.
DRO D/Cl 27/278/402

Sixth Battalion moving forward into action. The column is heading towards a start line prior to action when the men will move into skirmishing order.
DRO D/Cl 27/278/402

Prisoners of the 9th Battalion.
DRO D/Cl 27/278/402

ALAMEIN

A rather larger haul as the pursuit unfolds.
DRO D/Cl 27/278/402

Ninth Battalion in action at St. Joost, Holland, early 1945.
DRO D/Cl 27/278/402

Ninth Battalion again in action attacking at Bakehoven and Dieteren, Holland, 1945.
DRO D/Cl 27/278/402

Corpses were everywhere, British and German, united in the anonymous comradeship of violent extinction. Singly and in heaps they sprawled, blood-garnished, hungry flies already jubilant over bloating flesh, rising miasma enveloping in a diabolical pall:

> It was a scene of terrible destruction and telling evidence of a bitter struggle in which neither side had asked or given any quarter. There can have been few better German troops in Sicily than those who held the bridge. They were Nazi zealots to a man, but they fought superbly well and as their Battalion Commander was led away into captivity Colonel Clarke of 9th Battalion quietly shook him by the hand.[61]

For Colonel Clarke the battle was not quite over, as George Chambers recollects:

> The 2I/C had gone up towards the ditch where the Germans had entrenched, 'Stench Alley', dead men, cows and animals. He was wounded in both arms. The CO had gone up to Brigade, which more or less left me in charge. A stray mortar shell hit Andrew Clarke and Bill Robinson. The colonel had a tiny wound above the heart; 'My God, they've got me,' he said and fell instantly dead. Bill was hit in the thigh and evacuated by ambulance but they couldn't stop the bleeding and he died in the vehicle, so we lost them both at the very end of the battle.[62]

As the survivors were finally relieved and retired to rest and count the cost, they found this had been very high indeed. They had won a hard-fought and famous victory for which the Brigade had paid a terrible price. Ernie Kerens: 'No Nobby, but the rest of the battalion was relieved and went on a very high plateau, not far from the river behind Plimsole [sic] Bridge. We washed and changed ourselves and were reinforced; the latter had to be: the Brigade lost 600 men. When you realise that no battalion had more than 300 men to start with, it meant that one in three had gone.'[63]

After this, a period almost of anticlimax; the Axis were preparing to fight for Catania so 50th Division remained in a largely defensive posture whilst the main action occurred further west. When Catania finally fell on 5 August it was the Durhams who took the surrender – fittingly so, for no unit in 50th Division had fought so hard to gain this particular objective. As they secured the streets and public buildings the Durham men again found themselves surrounded but this time by swarms of happy locals, pleased with their deliverance; it was an altogether different form of conquest. Instead of grenades and small-arms fire, the soldiers were deluged with flowers and ample quantities of excellent local wine. Past Catania, fighting became more contained, the advance hemmed in by high, stone-girt hills where retreating Germans could conduct a fighting withdrawal using all the advantages of ground. It was a grinding battle of attrition, not without its comic moments, for the Sicilian villagers had had quite enough of their erstwhile allies:

> ENGLISHMEN
> *We dwell at Aci S. Filippo and we have come here for telling you*
> *that the German soldiers have gone away from our country,*
> *where still are mines at the road, for this reason we caution you*
> *to be attentive and to remove the mentioned above mines. All*
> *people are happy in receiving you and they pray you to respect*
> *them.*
> *Hurra! Englishmen!*
> *England for Ever!*

The Durhams have had far worse greetings[64] and, by 16 August, Messina and thus Sicily had fallen; the campaign was effectively over.

Now, the bridge so hotly contested in 1943 has gone, replaced by a more modern structure, and evidence on the ground is sparse, though the landscape generally has not changed overmuch. On the eastern flank of the north bank a memorial to the DLI has been erected. Nearer home, in the DLI Museum and Art Gallery in Durham, is a mute artefact from the battle: a standard-issue German infantry helmet with one side savagely punctured by bullets or shrapnel. The wearer did not survive yet the helmet, mute and terrible witness to so murderous a contest, offers a most eloquent testimony.

Notes

1   BBC People's War: Sgt. R. Pinchon and Pte. R.G. Goodwin 8th Battalion DLI.
2   Rissik, D., *The DLI at War – History of the DLI 1939–1945* (Durham, 1952), p.125.
3   Ibid.

4   DLI Sound Recording Project.
5   G.P.Chambers HQ Company 8th Battalion.
6   Ibid.
7   Rissik, p.119.
8   Ibid.
9   DLI Sound Recording Project.
10 Lewis, P.J., & English, I.R., *Into Battle with the Durhams: 8 DLI in World War II* (London, 1990), p.201.
11 DLI Sound Recording Project.
12 Carver, Field Marshall Lord R.M.P., *The Imperial War Museum Book of the War in Italy* (London, 2002).
13 Ibid.
14 Ibid.
15 Lewis & English, p.205.
16 Rissik, p.122.
17 DLI Sound Recording Project.
18 Ibid.
19 Ibid.
20 German paratroopers, a Luftwaffe rather than Wehrmacht formation.
21 D'Este, C., *Bitter Victory* (London, 2008), pp.335–56.
22 DLI Sound Recording Project.
23 Mitcham, S., & von Stauffenburg, F., *The Battle for Sicily* (Mechanicsburg, 2007), pp.150–1.
24 Carver p.35
25 Ibid. pp.35–6.
26 Rissik, p.123.
27 Ibid.
28 DLI Sound Recording Project.
29 Ibid.
30 Ibid.
31 Carver p.36–7.
32 Lewis & English, p.210.
33 DLI Sound Recording Project.
34 Ibid.
35 Carver pp.36.
36 Lewis & English, pp.211–12.
37 Ibid.
38 Ibid.
39 DLI Sound recording Project.
40 Carver p.37.
41 DLI Sound Recording Project.
42 Rissik, p.127.
43 DLI Sound Recording Project.
44 BBC History – both men were subsequently awarded the MM.
45 Rissik, p.127.
46 Lewis & English, p.216.
47 Ibid. p.217.
48 Ibid. pp.220–1.
49 Rissik, p.128.
50 Carver p.37.
51 Ibid. pp.37–8.

52 The Tiger, or PzKw Mark VI, was just making an appearance; these may not have been Tigers but upgunned PzKw Mark IVs.
53 White phosphorus grenades are incendiary weapons which burn fiercely, causing extensive burns and death.
54 Carver p.39.
55 Ibid. p.40.
56 Ibid.
57 Ibid.
58 Ibid. p.38.
59 Rissik, p.130.
60 Carver pp.38–9.
61 Rissik, p.130.
62 DLI Sound Recording Project.
63 Carver p.39.
64 Rissik, pp.131–2.

Chapter 7

Italy: the Long March – the Beginning, 1943–44

It was Christmas Day, I was one of hundreds of 16th Btn, the DLI soldiers aboard a troopship. We were all excited – not at the thought of the festive celebrations but because, that day, we were setting sail and our ultimate destination was the Battle Field.

Company Sergeant-Major G. Gates, 16 DLI[1]

It was very democratic – the troops were cramped, the Warrant Officers were cramped, the NCOs were cramped, the officers were cramped.

Major Viz Vizard A. Coy, 16 DLI[2]

The decision to invade the Italian peninsula, previously and famously described by Churchill as 'the underbelly of Europe', was a backstairs child of compromise. After the North African campaign and the subsequent invasion of Sicily, strategic thinking between the Allies was sharply divided. The US, very much the lead partner, favoured an immediate opening of the Second Front against Fortress Europe: the invasion of France. Britain, as ever, preferred a more peripheral strategy. The bastard spawned became the Italian campaign. This was to last from summer 1943 to the capitulation of Germany in May 1945, and would claim the lives of 60,000 Allied soldiers.

'We began some fairly hard training. The Officers and Warrant Officers were given an idea of their future target by being taken to a geographical formation, the silhouette of which resembled what we ultimately found when we got ashore.' Major Vizard recalls that, in addition to the training, the battalion was re-equipped, lavishly so by existing standards. 'We'd never been as well equipped since we'd come abroad. We were really given everything that we could possibly have asked for in the way of clothing, boots – with a warning from the Colonel that if we got the boots wet we should not get any further boots for three weeks after arrival!'[3]

Allied Forces Headquarters ('AFHQ') under the direction of General Harold Alexander, comprising US 5th and British 8th Armies, would undertake the forthcoming campaign. The perceived benefits were that an assault on the peninsula would finally knock Mussolini's tottering regime out of the conflict. This would guarantee the Royal Navy complete hegemony in the Mediterranean, and force Germany to shift reserves from the Eastern Front. Mussolini's regime might have collapsed but German resistance was always ingenious, fierce and determined. Conditions veered from oppressive heat to freezing mud and sleet. It was here the men of 16th Battalion DLI were blooded and bloodied in a series of savage actions that frequently recalled the horrors of trench warfare.

'Nearly all the troops on board were lining the ship's rails and no doubt, like me, wanted to see as much of dear old England as they could before she faded from view, perhaps for ever.'[4] 16th Battalion was, at the outset, something of a mongrel, conscripts raised from every corner of the realm, few having any root or connection with Durham. Mainly they were drawn in drafts from other regiments without even the benefit of training together and then flung into the maelstrom. Casualties were such that frequent new drafts had to be fed into the mincer, a rate of attrition again reminiscent of 1914–18. Their identity, of which they came to be justly proud, was forged in the heat of a protracted, vicious and relentless campaign. This began rather early in North Africa for Private Kenneth Lovell of 'D' Company, though not echoing to tunes of glory:

CSM Baker had given me the job of trying to keep down the germs in our rather primitive latrines. To give some sort of privacy some big 80-gallon petrol drums had been laid longwise around their sides. He said, 'Get some cans of petrol, pour the petrol in and chuck a match on top. It won't do much but it might keep the germs down!' I did this with a couple of other chaps and we got to the last one. There wasn't much petrol left so I chucked it in, set light to it and sent one of the other chaps to get another can of petrol. When he returned I threw some earth into the pot to smother any remaining flames. Then, satisfied it was safe, I threw the contents of the can in. There was a hell of a 'WHOOSSHHH!' and a bloody great sheet of flame shot up towards me.

Lovell decided that it was less risky to try and leap through the flames as the wind was fanning them towards him. However, his panicked leap landed him on the slope into the mire and his steel-shod boots afforded no purchase: '…. Despite all my efforts, I fell back and with a splash landed into the shit! They say the more you stir the more it stinks – I can assure you that's very true!' Happily, the midden proved less damaging than the flames and Lovell's grinning mates hauled him free. 'I walked the few hundred yards to the sea and I just laid down in it for about two hours till I was thoroughly cleansed!'[5]

The landings: Salerno 9–18 September 1943

Operation 'Avalanche' – codename for the amphibious landings at Salerno – was to be carried out by the 5th Army[6] under US General Mark Clark.[7] The plan of attack was straightforward, in that once the beachhead was secured it was essential to seize the surrounding hills and establish a viable perimeter. For 16 DLI the hot North African summer had been passed with intensive bouts of training in the rugged Atlas Mountains before troops were moved to join the swelling fleet mustering in Bizerta Harbour. None of the men was as yet advised of their destination but the regular attentions of the Luftwaffe enlivened their waiting. Driver Gordon Gent of the transport section, headquarters platoon, stationed on high ground overlooking the bay, watched the nightly show till the realities came a little too close:

> Then we heard a whacking great thud – very near! We thought, 'To hell with this – we'd better get shelter!' We went and got under our trucks because they had a sheet metal base. Our lads were camped in little two-man tents and next morning they found a piece of old shell bottom, a great big lump of horrible metal, bigger than your hand with great raw gashes, had gone right through the bottom of their washing tin and was a foot into the ground when they dug it out. That had just missed a tent. So we were very cautious after that![8]

Lieutenant Russell Collins had been commissioned into the Duke of Cornwall's Light Infantry. Prior to active service he had been posted to 16 DLI attached to the support company. The role of a support company was vital, with vehicles crammed into the heavier Landing Ships Tanks (LSTs). The young officer was impressed by the artifice of experienced and worldly wise drivers:

> The drivers were very ingenious about how much they seemed to squeeze into their trucks. There was a 15-hundredweight truck which had about 30 hundredweight of stores stacked into it! It was a question of getting on everything you possibly could but only in such a way that the vehicle would still actually drive on to the landing craft and drive off again at the other end.[9]

If this was confusing to a newly commissioned officer, worse was to ensue:

> I made a bit of a fool of myself just at this crucial moment. Of course one of the biggest hazards, not only in North Africa but also in south Italy, was malaria and everyone had to take a certain quantity of mepracine tablets. They were given out at meal times and one stood in the meal queue and made sure every soldier had his mepracine tablet – and took it.[10]

Collins was diligent in ensuring his men took their required medication but, on several occasions, sitting down, exhausted, to his own delayed meal, he omitted to follow suit: 'So shortly before the invasion, unfortunately, I went down with a mild attack of malaria – I didn't get many brownie points for that!'[11] This misfortune earned him a 'pretty sound, severe ticking off' from his company commander; fortunately the symptoms never recurred but Collins nonetheless missed the first phase of the Salerno landings. These proved eventful. The vast armada of Allied ships had sailed unopposed into the Bay of Naples and the waiting troops, mainly horribly seasick, had been cheered by the news of Italy's capitulation. Nonetheless, most of the officers knew this optimism to be illusory. Naval and air supremacy were complete. As the men attended divine service, HMS *Warspite* provided more material comfort with salvoes from her 15-inch guns, huge shells whistling 'through the air making the sound of railway porter running with his devil along the platform'.

The beaches were less welcoming than the sun-drenched strand would suggest. Many of the Durhams splashed into waist-deep water, sucking at battledress and webbing. Mines had already caused casualties, wounded men struggling back, the congress of blooded and unblooded. Signallers were particularly heavily burdened. Anthony Sacco of 'D' Company decided to take decisive action:

> I had six batteries this time plus my other gear. As we were going up there was about a two-foot gap between the ship and I said, 'To hell with this, I'll never need these batteries!' And I just plonked three of them into the sea. Corporal Reynolds spotted it and he said, 'Right, you'll be reported!' I said, 'Please yourself, I'm like a flaming pack mule here, I cannot carry more than this.'[12]

Kenneth Lovell found the landings less taxing than his earlier attempts at sanitation. Being a good sailor he avoided the seasickness that afflicted so many of his comrades. 'Every officer on board was seasick, half the crew was seasick and the mess decks were absolutely awash with vomit.' Some would have subsequently drawn comfort from the bold announcement that the Italians had surrendered, 'a cheer rang through the ship'. Lovell remained unimpressed: 'I thought it was bloody stupid, we were all sort of pretty young chaps, we'd been trained up, we were tensed up, we didn't know what we were going into but we expected the worst.' The battalion officers soon knocked the edge off any false optimism: ' [they] told us to get any idea out of our mind that we were going to stroll ashore on a Roman holiday…'[13]

The chaplain was equally inspired by the hope that the Italians were surrendering and the campaign would prove the proverbial walk-over. Nothing would satisfy the Padre, Major Vizard lamented, 'but that he had a drumhead service of thanksgiving on board. I took him aside and I said, "Now look, if you do this you're going to put the wrong sort of emphasis into troops' minds. They think there's going to be the local mayor and a brass band ready to receive them…"'[14]

Though the Hampshire Regiment had stormed the beach, enemy rounds were still falling. 'They had 88mm Tiger tanks hull-down on the sand dunes and they were banging away. 128 Brigade were about 1,000 yards inland,' recalls Major Vizard; 'they'd had a lot of trouble and a good deal of the trouble was still there, because they'd over-run some of it.' Amphibious landings are even more prone than other operations to descend into chaos as men, weighed down by sodden kit, struggle ashore, '...bits were flying off the LCI [Landing Craft Infantry], we started to get off and I said to the skipper, "Well don't hang around..."'[15]

Whilst the training might have shrouded their objective in secrecy, the Major found all of the landmarks clearly identifiable. 'We had this profile of the hills and I could see it quite clearly – the training had been good, the profile was there – except all the angles were much steeper and they'd warned us about that. So I knew where we were going to...'[16]

Despite enemy fire, 16 DLI came ashore with some finesse, led by Major Vizard:

> I was the lead man off, there were two ramps. Tom Logan took one and I took the other. Then we had two subalterns, they were standing behind, and we organised ourselves into three platoons. Number One Platoon moved off to its right, rushed up the beach, Number Two rushed off moving to the centre and Number Three to the left...As one man moved in one direction the next advanced in another...so there were no solid targets on the beach at all.[17]

By dusk on the 9 September a bridgehead, somewhat narrow and precarious, had been established. This comprised a ribbon of coast 30 miles long but hemmed in by the hills lowering above, high ground upon which the German defenders were well dug in and confident.

It was not until the day following the initial landings that the battalion transport came ashore. As their vessel cruised toward the beach the soldiers found their assumed insouciance severely tested:

> We were shifted off the decks; everybody had to be piled down in the hold with the exception of the people that were concerned with the vehicles on the deck. You always get one or two smart Alecs and they'd found this large cupboard in the bulkhead. They had a light in there and they were playing cards and smoking. We were approaching this landing. The ship hove to and they dropped the anchor – now what we didn't know was that we were immediately next to the chain locker! These anchor

chains were rattling away – it sounded just like all the bombs that ever were were being dropped! It was absolutely deafening, we had to put our fingers in our ears. We crouched on the floor in sheer panic, thinking, 'We're going down, this is great, we've got here and we're going to drown before we get ashore.' It was a terrible noise! This American Chief Petty Officer was laughing his head off; he'd known all about what would happen and hadn't warned us.[18]

Over the next several days, 16 DLI edged forward, continually under sporadic fire as the build-up at the bridgehead continued. The transport arrived and the Durhams moved on toward blocking positions established on slopes above the River Grancano. As they advanced, the grim detritus of war lay around. 'Suddenly a huge cloud of flies came up and there was a horrible stink. A sweet, sickly smell, something I had never smelt before. As I went past the bush there was a German half-track that had received a direct hit from a shell. The whole lot, nine or ten men had been killed, all sprawled in grotesque attitudes, many of them black from burns. I spewed my heart up…'[19]

Committed to battle for the first time, the young soldiers suffered as much from nerves as the attentions of the enemy; 'one or two planes came over strafing and you were praying for darkness to come. It got dark – then you were praying for it to be light.' Viz Vizard shared the men's apprehensions: 'We spent a very fretful night. I don't think anybody slept at all. In fact I don't believe anybody slept for three days. It can be done when you're that age. It dulls your senses a bit but when your senses are being stretched like violin strings – it's the aftermath rather than at the time.'[20]

On 11 September they advanced toward higher ground lying just down from the local asylum – Hospital Hill. They were now front line, part of the necklace of defenders guarding the landing beaches below. Now very much the front of the front, 16 DLI became bogged down in a vicious war of skirmish and bombardment – the lightning rattle of the German machine-guns[21] and the slower response of Brens[22], Tommy guns and rifles. Fighting was confused, deadly and not infrequently hand-to-hand, a murderous mini-war of bare, fire-swept hillocks, tangled scrub and a confusion of shallow ravines. Kenneth Lovell, like many of his comrades, was aware that he and they were about to be tested: 'I wondered what it was going to be like. I wondered what my reaction would be, whether I'd be able to stand up to it.'[23]

'It' proved very rough indeed. Determined and sustained German counter-attacks were launched and Lovell was soon in the thick of it: 'We got stuck into the Germans...As we were going [into the attack] I was firing from the hip. I suddenly saw a German lying down behind a machine-gun. He looked at me and I looked at him – I pulled the trigger and nothing happened so I just swung the Tommy gun round, grabbed it by the barrel and smashed him over the head...' It was not the killing that carried the impact but the subsequent realisation. 'I went back and saw this German that I'd slammed. I don't think it was the fact that his head was stove in, but rather the idea of having killed another human being. All right, he'd have killed me if he'd got the chance, but nevertheless I was physically sick, I vomited.'[24]

Many of the Axis who surrendered after this engagement proved to be veterans. One, at least, caused Lovell a start:

> Most of them were wearing the Russian Front decoration. They were all experienced soldiers; some of them were wearing the close-combat clasp which they didn't exactly chuck away in the German Army...One of them was ranting and raving in English about the fact that the Germans were going to win the war and about the glorious Führer. At school I used to sit next to a German named Mittelhauser and I turned round, looked at this German Lieutenant who was ranting and raving and said, 'Why don't you shut your mouth, Mittelhauser, you were just the same when you were at school!'[25]

One of the principal German weapons was the fearsome rocket launcher or 'Nebelwerfer'.[26] Lieutenant Gerry Barnett: 'It was awful, really terrifying. We could hear them start off because they [the rockets] used to be fired electronically from six-barrelled mortars, we used to call them 'Wurlitzers'. They had a note as the barrels fired in rotation. Then you knew you had about 20 seconds before the bombs arrived. Terrifying it was.' Lovell meantime had a very lucky escape. 'Bill Crummock and I had a most miraculous escape – a mortar shell landed in our trench and didn't explode. It landed between our feet. It did shake us! We scrambled out of the bloody trench faster than you've ever seen anyone scramble out of a trench.'[27]

For some, the constant bombardment proved too much. Lieutenant Ronnie Sherlaw had to react when one young soldier 'started screaming'. A split-second decision: 'I just gave him a good clout in the face and he stopped. We eventually had to get him out of the line but he cooled down.' It was not always the newcomers who felt the strain. 'Some of these chaps, more the chaps who'd been in the line than the chaps who hadn't, took badly with this shelling. I suppose they'd seen more of what happened when you were shelled than we who hadn't been in action before.'[28]

Ronnie Sherlaw was now facing the same test:

> I was and am a great fatalist and I have a very strong faith too – I'm not saying that I wasn't frightened – I had the same sort of fears and apprehensions as anybody does when this sort of thing happens, but I refused to let it worry me, put it that way, so I always got through things that way. I think it's just sort of ingrained in me – my mother always used to say, 'You can't help being frightened but never show it!' And I didn't![29]

It was into this inferno that Russell Collins returned to active duty on 18 September attached to 'A' Company. He was about to undergo his personal baptism of fire, a disturbing and traumatic episode: 'It was just a question of me taking my platoon and going forward to find out how far they [the enemy] had gone and whether the ground in front of us was clear and so on.'[30]

This was to be a fighting patrol[31] with the entire platoon committed. Though Collins had carried out simulated attacks many times in training this was now in deadly earnest. The company was positioned some 200 yards from a corner of the asylum wall and the briefing intimated that supporting fire would be directed from warships, with US troops nearby. Dangerously, the tactical radio proved highly unreliable, disrupting communication with Company HQ. Dry-mouthed, Collins led his sections forward:

> I hadn't gone I don't suppose more than 100 yards, at the very most 200 yards, before we were fired on from a position beside the hospital about 150 yards down on the right. There was a light mortar detachment there and they were firing mortars in our

direction. We were on a slope leading down towards the hospital and machine-guns were also being fired at us.[32]

This was an infantryman's nightmare. An exposed position swept by enemy fire, bullets thumping into the bankside around him. He attempted to contact the company commander by radio, failed and sent a runner. Already his beginner's confidence was shaken and he could feel the situation slipping away. Circumstances seemed totally at odds with the breezy tone of his initial briefing. Should he halt or try to press on? After 10 agonising minutes, the rapid rattle of the MG42 and steady crump of mortars unceasing, the dazed runner returned – no orders. He'd not made it back to or from Company HQ. Germans had infiltrated behind. Possibly the man might have confused foe with allies, US steel helmets being mistaken for German. Equally, he might be right. One thing was certain, the enemy had definitely not withdrawn; 'they were very much on the doorstep'. In the absence of orders, Collins resolved to press his attack against this immediate opposition, attempting to circle around the right flank: 'As we approached the hospital wall all hell was let loose and our own battalion mortar platoon brought down the defensive fire slap on top of my platoon. Well, it was the first time for me; it wasn't the last time, but it was the first time. I mean one is just cringing…'[33]

He had taken some 30 men out on the patrol but only a handful was left unwounded. Things then got worse. In the fog of war Captain Pritchard, the company commander, led his remaining platoons in an attack on these supposed Germans; 'an assault with bullets and bayonets. I was screaming mad with them really.' Though already slightly wounded in the hand, Collins survived the onslaught from his own comrades, yelling, 'You bloody idiots, can't you see it's us!'[34] Signaller Anthony Sacco was a witness: 'Somebody said "Jerries". But it was Collins and them coming back. They started firing the bloody mortars at our own men...It was terrible.'[35]

Collins was loaded with a sense of total failure: 'Of course everybody was then very crestfallen', weighed with the virtual destruction of his entire platoon:

We tried to see to the wounded and pick up the pieces of those who had been blown to bits, it was that bad. In the circumstances it was difficult to see how anyone could have done better. I think if I was more experienced I might have played it differently, but I'm not sure quite how. To have gone on with, as I understood it, enemy troops around and behind me, would have been even more foolhardy. I would just have walked straight into the bag, so there was no point in doing that and I couldn't get through to the company commander.[36]

Lack of adequate radio communications had undoubtedly played a major role in the tragedy. 'I was very shaken but I felt with a few deep breaths that I would be alright again. But I was made to go back to the regimental aid post, for a check-up as they said. Then I had to go and tell the CO Johnny Preston what had happened and even then he was very sympathetic and understanding.' Truly a baptism of fire: '…the whole thing was what we also call an "MFU". If you don't know what that is, it's a Military F**k Up.'[37] Ironically, it was during that night the battalion was withdrawn from the line and the Germans began their planned evacuation of the heights, fearing entrapment by the advancing 8th Army.[38] A new defensive barrier was constructed along the line of the River Volturno[39] with strong rearguard units posted in the strategic passes which opened the way to Naples.[40]

Advance on Naples 22 September–1 October 1943 and the Volturno Line

General Albrecht Kesselring[41] favoured a stubborn tenure of the Italian peninsula. The terrain ideally suited the defender and shielding the Reich at such long distance was clearly preferable to a second front far closer to the Rhine. Besides, Hitler was convinced that the Allies would use success in Italy as a springboard to seize the Balkans, so depriving Germany of much-needed resources. As the autumn rains came to the aid of the defenders, Kesselring completed work on both the Volturno and Barbara lines.[42]

The Durhams were to be in the eye of the storm: Colonel Preston, battalion commander, developed an audacious plan to seize the vital Vietri Defile. This narrow pass was key to turning the German line and opening the road to Naples. Part of the high ground had to be taken by 'B' Company, and whilst manoeuvres in the dark were perfectly feasible in intent, the reality, as soldiers such as Lance-Corporal Virr found out, was considerably more challenging: 'We set off, all in single file. It was that dark we had to hold each others' bayonet scabbards, like elephants holding each others' tails.'[43] Despite the difficulties, this operation was an outstanding success and the road beyond soon lay open.

Naples fell and on 6 October the DLI passed through the great city to a rapturous welcome. The 'liberation' was not without attendant perils, as Signaller Ronald Elliot of HQ Company discovered:

> It was great fun; we went right through Naples in these lorries, with everybody cheering you. It wasn't the same as being on foot because they couldn't embrace you or whatever. What happened in the end was quite funny in a way – they pelted us with apples. It was the apple season, they were just collecting them and they pelted us with apples all the way along! Well apples are quite hard and people were getting hurt by them so we threw them back again! And before we got to the end of the run through Naples there was a battle going on...[44]

For the Germans, holding the Volturno Line bought valuable time whilst a further series of defences was thrown up behind to bar the road to Rome.[45] General Clark, with the dismal autumnal rains lashing the ground into a mud-soaked waste, detailed X Corps and US VI Corps to storm the line. 16 DLI as part of 46th Division on the eastern flank, slogged over a barren alluvial plain, completely waterlogged and dominated by German fire from the higher reaches of the far bank. The Durhams had been moved up to the line on 7 October and were immediately deployed, probing German defences on the south bank. Russell Collins, returning from treatment for his hand wound, found, to his relief, that the earlier debacle had not irretrievably blotted his reputation and prospects: 'When he [Colonel Preston] saw me he said, "Well, I'm glad to see you, I had asked for you back." That absolutely took the wind out of my sails – it hadn't dawned on me before, that of course, he might have decided that under no circumstances did he want this officer back!'[46]

He was determined that his next patrol should not be a repeat of the first. This time he was to lead a lightly armed reconnaissance team. 'Very lightly equipped and armed and you might wear rubber shoes and no helmets, no equipment – just a personal weapon and perhaps a compass; very little else, the idea being to see and not be seen and to take evasive action if encountering any enemy.'[47] Using aerial photographs, Collins had spent hours studying the ground. This was likely to be confusing, especially in the dark, a sprawl of dykes, raised trackways with parallel ditches and significant flooding. His patrol proceeded with maximum caution; '...mainly in single file with me leading. The next chap keeps a sharp lookout to the right, the chap behind that keeps a sharp lookout to the left, and the chap behind that keeps a sharp lookout behind.'[48]

Having completed their scouting mission without encountering any opposition, the patrol was set to return the way they'd come. Collins, hyper-vigilant, remembered the old maxim that you never came back by the same road you went in; 'so I struck another route across country. It turned out to be a very propitious one because we went right through a melon field, the place was stacked with beautiful melons and they were all ripe. We were sitting in the middle of that field, eating these melons while straight ahead of us lay Mount Vesuvius – a pillar of fire by night.'[49]

Such calm reflections were shattered by the clatter of small-arms fire. A second patrol under Lieutenant Ray Mitchell had shown less circumspection, retracing their route, and had run into an ambush; '...I felt very gratified that I'd remembered that lesson.' Collins had now begun the foundations of a formidable reputation as an infantry officer. His burgeoning skills would be much in demand during the bouts of hard fighting which lay ahead. The rugged spine of the narrow peninsula afforded Kesselring every opportunity to construct a series of strong defensive lines, with the Allies simply having to batter their way past each in turn. For the moment, 16 DLI was still probing German defences and assessing their firepower and inevitably this was formidable: 'When enemy guns fired, what one does is to take a quick bearing with a compass, the bearing from which the flash comes and the time of day. Then you count the interval between the flash and shell arriving and then report it on a little form that's handed in.'[50] By such means, Allied gunners could assess and locate their opposite numbers.

Others, like Mitchell, were less fortunate. Both Kenneth Lovell and Private Robert Ellison with 'D' Company had been ordered to support a Royal Engineers' detachment, throwing a Bailey bridge over the Regi Lagni Canal. 'We went across in our canvas and wood assault boats...we got across the canal, which was about 10 feet deep.' Ellison was convinced he saw German activity, 'running across the road carrying a machine-gun'.[51] Ellison's corporal was unimpressed. Lovell, likewise alerted, had no more success convincing Sergeant 'Soss' Martin: 'he just laughed at us and told us we were a load of bloody amateurs'. As the platoons fanned over the far bank, Signaller Elliot with the Company HQ was setting up in the rear.[52] It proved to be a classic ambush. Ellison's earlier fears were more than vindicated: 'We had to scarper back to the canal. They were lobbing these little stun grenades, and I got quite a few shrapnel wounds on my wrist and arm, only small bits in the muscle. You didn't know it had happened, just a flash at the side of you. But the other lads were getting bullets in them unfortunately.'[53]

Kenneth Lovell also found himself fighting for his life:

All hell broke loose. Machine-guns opened up on us from every bloody quarter – from behind us, from our sides, from the front. The Germans had set up a beautiful ambush. 'Soss' Martin's platoon got cut up, he got badly wounded. We had taken up fire positions, we opened up, we could see flashes! 'Brothel Baby' was next to me; he was my Bren gunner and he got a bullet through the wrist. After a little while he said to me, 'Here corporal, give us a drink will you?' I felt for my water bottle and found I'd had a burst of machine-gun bullets go through it. I cut my hand quite badly where the metal had been ripped to pieces. The Germans were just a few yards away. The buggers![54]

Collins' success in reconnaissance catapulted him to the spearhead of the assault being planned. 'A' Company would form the point:

I was detailed to lead the battalion up to the river because I'd reconnoitred the route…The outline brigade plan was that the unfortunate [Sherwood] Foresters were going to decoy for us. We were going to make the actual crossing a little bit further down the river. The Bofors light anti-aircraft gun fired tracer rounds and the scheme was that every five minutes they would fire a burst of five rounds along the axis of attack, so that everybody moving forward could keep their bearings and know that this was the direction they were to go.

This was a very great responsibility. Collins was to lead the entire battalion with the knowledge that the Germans had fighting patrols on the south or near bank, as Lieutenant Mitchell's command had discovered; 'I had it very much in mind that our patrol had been ambushed only a night or two before, and I didn't want the whole battalion to walk straight into an ambush.' Having learnt the virtue of caution, he proceeded, with due circumspection, to the mounting frustration of the adjutant, Captain Pritchard, who favoured a more bullish approach: 'we had to get a bit of a move on and so, in due course, we got to the river.[55]

Now for the crossing itself: 'Then with my platoon leading we had to make the first crossing. We hoisted our packs up as high as we could on our shoulders, put our rifles in our outstretched arms above our heads and the first few of us waded into the river…it was certainly up to my armpits, if not up to my shoulders, being a rather shorter chap.' These hardy pathfinders had some 300 feet of freezing muddied water, oozing black and evil-smelling slime, to traverse. On attaining the far bank they secured a fixed line which would guide the rest of the battalion pulling across in small assault craft. Not a shot was fired. As they emerged, frozen and soaked in foul ooze, Collins' platoon had to press on and consolidate the foothold: '… our first objective was a high dyke, 200–400 yards to the north of the river. It seemed like a mile because when we were about halfway across somebody fell into the river and cried out – that alerted the Germans and suddenly we found all along this dyke were machine-gun posts as we came under fire.'[56]

One of Collins' men, a youngster called Anderson, was chopped down by the tongues of fire. The lieutenant sought to assist the desperately injured lad who, believing himself to be dying, conveyed a series of frantic personal messages.[57] Dealing with wounded men in the field was always problematic: medical officers were frequently overstretched and getting a badly injured man back under fire was never easy. Though the German fire was intense it was largely undirected: 'Sergeant-Major Wilson was as cool as a cucumber, whenever he got an order he always said, "Very good, sir!" Major John Morant was a bit laconic and eventually he said, "Sergeant-Major!" "Sir!" "I've been hit!" "Very good, sir!"[58] By now the other companies were reaching the north bank and the fighting intensified, in pallid light ripped by the flash of detonations and the firefly hum of tracer. Snipers were active and casualties mounted. Nonetheless, a bridgehead had been established and Colonel Preston set up a temporary HQ on the northern side.

Collins found himself again in demand: 'There was a pocket of enemy some few hundred yards to the east who were holding up progress and I was to go and try and sort it out.' After a hurried conference with the company mortar officer he formed an impromptu plan of attack. The defenders were dug in behind a tall dyke, covered by ditches on both sides. Collins intended to take a storming party and approach in the cover of a dry channel parallel to the dyke. Once poised, the mortar crews would deliver a short bombardment to cover the actual assault. 'I hadn't pinpointed the machine-guns, but the Mortar Officer had seen them. So I mean it was by guess and by the grace of God really! I just said, "Right, fix bayonets!" Everybody lined up behind me and I set off. We just crept forward first of all and then down came these six bombs, one, two, three, four, five, six – and then we were up and ran full tilt.'[59]

As he and his men pelted along the ditch, he spotted the defenders scrambling for the safety of their bunkers, caught unprepared and vulnerable: 'I was right upon them and in total command of where they were. I just called on them to come out and of course they had no choice.' In all, some 16 of the Germans, forming a company headquarters unit, surrendered and were sent back under escort. Colonel Preston was voluble in his praise and proposed to recommend Collins for a decoration. 'I was as lucky in that as I was unlucky at Salerno. There's a big element of luck in these things. I mean the bombs could have fallen on us, or I could have got there and it might have been bombproof, or they might have been just 50 yards further down waiting for us as we came round the corner.'[60]

Exhaustion quickly succeeded elation. The weary, grimy soldiers of Collins' platoon bedded down in an abandoned farm building. Fires were not allowed; there was no food to be had, only the lieutenant's dwindling supply of cigarettes for comfort; '...I got down on to this bed smoking a cigarette. I woke up with the mattress burning and I was so tired that I went to sleep again without putting out the fire. I was absolutely knackered, as they say these days.'[61] Exhausted he might be but 'Winkler' Collins was becoming something of a local celebrity in 16 DLI, famed for 'winkling' out German positions.

Despite the dreadful toll in dead and wounded, 16 DLI were forged into a unit, no longer a pack of mongrels but a battle-hardened formation. Newcomers, best beware, even – or perhaps especially – cocky young officers. Tom Lister, still with transport, had seen and learnt much since his baptism of rattling anchor chains.

> We got an officer there who'd come straight from England.[62] He arrived in semi-darkness one evening and he wanted to know where his batman was and this and that and the other. He was horrified with the service! He buttonholed a bloke and said, 'bring me my tea and shaving water in the morning.' The bloke said, 'You can get your own bloody tea mate!' That attitude! He said, 'You're talking to an officer!' He said, 'Well, I'm not a batman either, I'm a Corporal – and I've got my own job to do, I'm not running about after you! We don't do that in this battalion!'[63]

The *Winterstellung* ('Winter Line')

Bad weather and stiff resistance were compounded by political and strategic differences. Attention was shifting westwards to the narrow waters of the English Channel and the vast accumulation of men and materiel being assembled for Operation 'Overlord'. The Italian campaign yielded few headlines and excited scant enthusiasm. Alexander had his sights firmly fixed on the prize of Rome but his attackers barely outnumbered Kesselring's defenders, dug in and confident. Forcing the river lines had been difficult and costly but the prepared defences behind were more formidable still. By 2 November, Allied forces stood on the banks of the Garigliano. Bridges blown, widespread flooding and a rain of death from German guns on the commanding heights removed any prospect of a viable crossing. Inland, the alluvial plain gave way to a jumble of bare, rocky outcrops and ridges collectively forming Mount Camino.

Life was unpleasant. Lance-Corporal William Virr from 'B' Company suffered in the soaking squalor: 'It came on absolutely bucketing down with rain, terrible weather. It just churned it all to mud, the lit trenches were half full of water, you were just sat in them, trying to get a cigarette going – but you couldn't.' 'B' Company was treated to a regular round of mortaring – as the Germans had previously occupied these same trenches they had little difficulty in finding the range. 'A chap in the trench next to me, he must have sat up above the level, a bomb killed him; his mate with him was badly wounded.'[64]

The strain of constant bombardment was telling and cumulative. Virr and his comrades from 'B' Company remained horribly exposed in the mud-slicked scrapes of their slit trenches:

If you're under a long bombardment I think you go mad eventually, go off your rocker. Every man has a different breaking point and some go before others. So you could never point a finger at anyone because another half-hour and it might be you. You tend to be on the brink and it takes all your striving to prevent yourself from going to pieces. I've been on the point of it a few times and I suppose everyone else had. When you feel [like] letting everything go – gabbling and screaming, gibbering away – just letting go. I just managed not to – till next time. You just curl up in a ball and hope nothing comes your way. I always lay on my left side and put my hands between my legs, my tin hat on the top and hoped for the best.[65]

On 5 November General Clark launched a divisional assault. This was no complex manoeuvre or tactical gambit, just a grim, ghastly slogging match for every foot of contested ground. In scenes that might have echoed the doomed Gallipoli campaign of 1915, the British clawed their way to the summit only to have the exhausted remnant unseated by counter-attacks. Undeterred, on 2 December in the appropriately named Operation 'Raincoat', Clark tried again. This time 56th Division, which had attacked on 5 November, was to be supported by 46th Division advancing toward the Calabritto basin and thus securing the line of advance.

The graphically nicknamed 'Bare Arse Spur' ran south from the mountain and formed the eastern flank of the basin. 'B' Company of 16 DLI was detailed to support the Sherwood Foresters and Leicesters. Russell Collins with 'A' Company was stationed amidst the battered ruin that had been La Murata village. It was grim: '... there were feet of mud on the tracks. All the roads and tracks were very badly damaged by shell-fire; any bridges or culverts, all that sort of thing, had been blown by the enemy...we found ourselves in this little village where we were concentrating and we could see this mountain range ahead – Monte Camino – which was just a bare escarpment. Hence the name "Bare Arse".'[66]

And they waited, nerves taut, with the enemy's guns playing on their exposed huddle of shell-torn buildings '... in little platoon groups just basically waiting for our turn to go into the attack. There was a wind-up gramophone, with a 78 record or two there – that's the first time I'd heard the "Intermezzo" from *Cavalleria Rusticana*. Then it was another song, "When it's Moonlight on the Colorado", and things like that. We played these for days; over and over again.'[67] It was 1 December in the dark of late evening that the attack went in, scrambling up steep terraces, before stalling some 400 yards short of the main objective. They floundered, trying to dig in during a relentless downpour as casualties mounted and German gunners flayed the slope. Driven back by this appalling fire, directed with pinpoint accuracy, the survivors withdrew. Tactically a failure, the attack fostered more strategic success by bolstering the main assault formations, which succeeded in capturing the high ground of Monastery Hill commanding the entire basin below.

The grinding attrition of war amongst the hills continued. One hard-won success merely opened up the vista for another. Now 16 DLI were to pass through Allied troops established on Bare Arse Spur and assault Cocuruzzo Spur, on the western rim of the basin and still very much in German hands. 'C' Company was to win a hillock (Point 430) by dawn and thus allow 'A' Company to leapfrog forward to seize 'Dick' Spur, enabling 'C' and 'D' Companies to finally reach a further summit (Point 420).

Sergeant-Major Les Thornton of the Support Company began the long and exhausting ascent heavily burdened. 'I had my company headquarters with me and the Captain. I had my full kit on, and on top of my pack was a coil of barbed wire – Sergeant-Majors had to do the work as well you see!' As he laboured up the slope Thornton was greeted by a senior officer coming down (considerably less encumbered): "Good morning, Sergeant-Major!" "Good morning, Sir!" I wondered what the hell he'd being doing up there – it was the Corps Commander Lieutenant-General Sir Richard McCreery – he'd been to have a look.'[68] Thornton understood that the General's going down was as necessary as his going up; so senior an officer had no place in the hazard of an assault.

Such a gentlemanly exchange preceded a very fierce reception: 'halfway up it started. Oh aye, down we got in the rocks – shellfire, mortars.' Thornton's difficulties were compounded by the collapse of his corporal: '… if you see a dog in pain with his brown eyes looking up at you, that was him, terrified, absolutely terrified. We were all frightened. When it finished I says, "Corporal, you're no use to me, man, get back, go back down and report sick!"'[69]

These neat topographical designations, dots on the map, belied the almost lunar landscape of exposed rock and scree, as Russell Collins and his platoon discovered: 'It was like climbing Snowdon, in later years. There were very steep tracks, and of course we were all carrying full battle order, 48-hour rations, full water bottles and full load of ammunition. There was no possibility of any motor transport going up there so we had pack mules which took the heavy stores up.'[70]

Reaching their start line, the troops rested, apparently undetected, in the lee of Point 620. At 03.00 'C' Company launched their attack, securing Point 430 but sending a very clear wake-up call to the German defenders, who responded with alacrity. As mortars thumped in the brightening dawn, it was 'A' Company's turn to attempt 'Dick': 'We were given an axis of advance...As we were going across there we came under a lot of small-arms fire, and a lot of artillery fire. In fact the artillery fire was extremely confusing; it was all so close to us.' This could have been either or both German defensive fire and the British supporting barrage, but small-arms fire claimed a number of casualties; 'about 18 men in 'A' Company, in the space of about half an hour, were hit individually with bullets. The medical officer did a tremendous job, because he had brought his regimental aid post forward and set up in a sort of crofter's hut down on the leeside of the mountain...'[71]

On the summit there were grim reminders of previous assaults. Dead British and Germans sprawled grotesquely together. 'A' Company was under intense and well-directed fire: 'We were under this fire and of course we were keeping pretty close to the ground, because anything that moved was fired at, we were sort of cowering behind boulders, very low drystone walls and things.' Collins worked out where the bullets were coming from, a complex of stone farm buildings to their right front. Men were being hit and the lieutenant volunteered to 'sort it out'; Mitchell, the company commander, was happy to let him try: 'sooner you than me'.[72] Collins set up a Bren section to provide covering fire, then selected a handful of bolder spirits for the attack.

Theirs was a dangerous mission and the lieutenant had no doubt as to his role. 'I led from the front wherever possible. I felt more confident that way. I felt it was my duty to tell you the truth...In war the dominant lesson I learnt was the crucial role of the junior officer, because it was quite clear to me that unless platoon commanders led their platoons, nothing happened.' The patrol worked their way around the right flank of the objective, the Bren clattering constantly behind. At this point, Collins found he couldn't remember if he'd given instructions for the gunner to desist as the attack went in, so there remained the added fear of being shot from behind by your own. 'As I ran into the target area on which our machine-gun was still firing rapid fire, the bullets were cracking over my head, but I think they saw us just in time.'[73]

In front of them now was a solid double-storey farm building '... there was no ground entrance but there was an outside staircase. I rushed straight up the staircase and there was a door open at the top. I was aware of the danger of going into an open doorway, so somehow or other I established that there was nobody in the upper room.' Collins found himself looking over a parapet and a solid outbuilding below. It was here that the Germans were lurking. His Thompson was the ideal weapon for delivering a burst of automatic fire through the timber roof covering: 'I ordered my other chaps around the side of the staircase to my left, so they were standing outside the door with their rifles at the ready.' He now had the defenders at his complete mercy. 'What came out through the door was a white flag on the end of a rifle bayonet, because there was absolutely nothing else they could do.' The 'bag' was impressive, nearly a score surrendered. 'I'm afraid that when we lined those prisoners up, if any of them had any cameras or anything like that, which we didn't want to fall into the hands of the people guarding the prisoner of war camps behind, we helped ourselves.'[74] This was done in the time-honoured tradition of the victor.

Major Mitchell was happy about the elimination of the German strongpoint but he had been incensed by the killing of two stretcher-bearers by sniper fire. 'He demanded that the sniper in the group of prisoners show himself.[75] There was only one there with a camouflage suit on; he didn't look like a German at all, dark hair.' Mitchell was getting ready to have the man shot, though the German appeared unconcerned. Such insouciance merely fuelled the Major's rage and he was all for shooting the lot. 'Then suddenly this great big fat one, right at the front, he must have been about 18 stone, he started crying. He got down and started taking all his photographs out of his wife, he was looking at them...But the other Germans were looking at him as if he was dirt.' The moment passed; the fat prisoner's gibbering appeared to calm the Major; 'he wanted somebody to show fright. I think that's all he wanted in the end.'[76]

The battle for Monte Camino was nearing its end. Next day, as 16 DLI occupied Cocuruzzo, it became evident that the Germans were again falling back. Their Winter Line proved untenable. General Clark's plan of attack, costly and unimaginative, had achieved success but at a high price and in worsening winter conditions. Ahead of the weary Allies lay the great massif of Monte Cassino[77] and the Gustav Line. The bitter slogging match seemed set to continue. However, there was the possibility of a further amphibious operation aimed at outflanking the Gustav Line and opening the road to Rome: the genesis of Operation 'Shingle' – Anzio.[78]

Notes

1   Stringer, L., *The History of the Sixteenth Battalion Durham Light Infantry* (Graz, 1946), p.17.
2   DLI Sound Recording Project.
3   Ibid.
4   Stringer, p.17.
5   DLI Sound Recording Project.
6   The 5th Army comprised British 10th Corps with 46th and 56th Divisions and US VI Corps, supported by Rangers and Commandos.
7   US General Mark Clark, second-in-command of the Allied landings in North Africa; his subsequent role in Italy proved highly controversial.
8   DLI Sound Recording Project.
9   Ibid.
10 Ibid.
11 Ibid.
12 Ibid.
13 Ibid.
14 Ibid.
15 Ibid.
16 Ibid.
17 Ibid.
18 Driver Tom Lister MT Section HQ Company, DLI Sound Recording Project.
19 Corporal Lovell, DLI Sound Recording Project.
20 DLI Sound Recording Project.
21 The German MG42 was a versatile and efficient weapon with a high rate of fire; calibre 7.92mm, air-cooled, belt-fed.
22 The British Bren gun was a .303 calibre, magazine-fed light machine-gun, portable and accurate.
23 DLI Sound Recording Project.
24 Ibid.
25 Ibid.

26 *Nebelwerfer* translates literally as 'smoke launcher' but the weapon was a multi-barrelled 150mm artillery piece that discharged six 75lb rockets over a 10-second detonation. In Sicily, where the Allies first encountered the distinctive wailing shriek of the incoming rounds, these became known as 'Moaning Minnies'.

27 DLI Sound Recording Project.

28 Ibid.

29 Ibid.

30 Ibid.

31 A fighting patrol is distinguished from a reconnaissance in that it comprises more men, with full packs and extra ammunition.

32 DLI Sound Recording Project.

33 Ibid.

34 Ibid.

35 Ibid.

36 Ibid.

37 Ibid.

38 The 8th Army had landed on the 'toe' of Italy on 3 September (Operation 'Baytown') with additional landings at Taranto ('Slapstick').

39 The route to Naples was blocked by a series of significant waterways and by succeeding east–west ridge lines. The Volturno ('Viktor') Line ran from Termoli in the east, along the course of the River Biferno, cutting through the precipitous spine of the Apennines to Volturno in the west.

40 Naples formed the immediate strategic objective; the city, aside from its obvious political value, was a major port remaining within the operational shield of Allied planes flying from Sicily.

41 Kesselring was an air force (Luftwaffe) General who, in early campaigns, commanded air fleets. He was Commander-in-Chief of all Axis forces in the Mediterranean theatre (which included North Africa). His defence of the Italian peninsula was both stubborn and highly competent.

42 The Barbara Line ran some 10 to 20 miles north of the Volturno – with the Gustav Line a further, similar distance north. It consisted mainly of a series of hilltop redoubts.

43 DLI Sound Recording Project.

44 Ibid.

45 These comprised the Winter Line from the mouth of the River Garigliano over the summits of Mounts Camino and Lungo, across to the River Sangro.

46 DLI Sound Recording Project.

47 Ibid.

48 Ibid.

49 Ibid.

50 Ibid.

51 Ibid.

52 Ibid.

53 Ibid.

54 Ibid.

55 Ibid.

56 Ibid.

57 Private Anderson died of his wounds; he was aged 20.

58 DLI Sound Recording Project.

59 Ibid.

60 Ibid.

61 Ibid.

62 70th (Young Soldiers) Battalion DLI.

63 DLI Sound Recording Project.

64 Ibid.

65 Ibid.

66 Ibid.

67 Ibid.

68 Ibid.

69 Ibid.

70 Ibid.

71 The Regimental Aid Post (RAP) was the forward medical station, immediately behind the line; often in Italy it was located in a ruined building or structure. It was essentially a first aid post where the Medical Officer (MO) would stabilise the wounded, who were sent on their way as quickly as possible to the Advanced Dressing Station (ADS) in the rear. The RAP was very important in saving lives and the MOs worked in often difficult and dangerous conditions.

72 DLI Sound Recording Project.

73 Ibid.

74 Ibid.

75 Snipers were much detested and often denied quarter.

76 DLI Sound Recording Project.

77 Monte Cassino was crowned by the imposing Benedictine monastery founded by the saint in AD524. Its subsequent levelling by US bombers was, and remains, controversial.

78 The Anzio Landings took place on 22 January 1944 and were initially unopposed. The road to Rome lay open. However, the advantage was permitted to slip away and the Germans recovered, sealing off the bridgehead. This stalemate persisted till the final Allied breakout in May.

Chapter 8

Italy: the Long March – Journey's End, 1944–45

The Colour Sergeant met me coming along and he saw we were absolutely shattered, "Come on Sergeant-Major, we've got some clean blankets!" I said. "You what, clean blankets, lovely!" So we went into this building and got down to it. Well – right outside the building opposite was a 7.2-inch artillery piece, that was the biggest gun we had. They started to fire – our building went up and down like that! I said, "Who thought of this place for a rest!" My God, every time it fired the blast was terrific, so we didn't get a great deal of sleep!

Sergeant-Major Les Thornton[1]

Sixteenth DLI was to be spared the horrors of both Anzio and Monte Cassino. After Monte Camino they were taken out of line into billets to the rear at Campo and St. Vaglie. Their role was now relegated to tactical reserve, should the Germans counter-attack to recover the hard-won ground. In reserve, their duties were confined to the unglamorous chore of assisting Royal Engineers in building and consolidating roadways. This respite, if indeed it could be so called, was short-lived. By mid-December the battalion was deployed to relieve the Hampshires in the line north-west of San Carlo.

A new draft of officers had joined, including Captain Alan Hay. He was relieved to find at least one familiar face:

Another chap I saw was a man called Duffy who was a well-built lad, a Major, MC, whom I had sent out as one of the draft officers some time ago. He had been keen to get out and had been doing the Battle Schools and that was what he was best at – he was a bit wayward in other respects; getting into trouble over larking on and not having that sort of respect. He loved the Battle Schools and so he was a natural to get abroad.[3]

Duffy welcomed Hay into 'D' Company and the Captain first saw the front line at La Vaglie, the village a shattered debris of rubble, mud and squalor, 'the most God-awful place you ever saw'.[2]

Though he had the benefit of thorough training, Hay knew he had much to learn about life in the line:

Lieutenant Critchley who came out with me was to take the patrol. I was curious and I said, 'Can I go down and see what the procedure is for them going out?' 'Oh, yes!' I went down and I saw Critchley and his men. I said 'Don't worry, good luck!' They walked into the Germans and Critchley was killed and so were one or two of our men – the new ones, first day out. I thought, all the time we've been wasting in England, why couldn't they have brought one or two of us out, just to be there to get the feel of things? Because it's a hell of a sight different going against the real enemy, particularly in small patrols where you get this nous, you get the feel and smell of the thing.[3a]

Digging in along the frost-bound slopes of Mount Maggiori was extremely difficult. Frozen rock refused to give in to pick and shovel. Here, the defences consisted of small stone-built redoubts or sangars where the men, swathed in greatcoats, huddled through cold days and colder nights. 'This really was the most horrible place I was ever in. We were on rock into which you could not dig. We had in the rear positions one or two clefts between rock which gave slightly better cover, but in the night positions on the forward slope we could only lie behind sangars – which are little piles of rocks in a circle which you try and take cover behind…it was really a hell on earth.'[4]

The men passed a miserable Christmas in these dreary conditions, no festivities till they were rotated again on 31 December:

During the morning the Padre visited Battalion HQ and all the companies taking services. Dinners, which were visited by the Colonel and Second-in-Command, can only be described as Lucullan (i.e. luxurious and profuse) and were served by officers and NCOs in an atmosphere of great joviality. Roast pork, some turkey, roast potatoes, cauliflower, Yorkshire pudding, stuffing and apple sauce, plum pudding and white sauce, formed the backbone of the menu. When the serious business was done, the diners punctuated their work among the nuts, fruit and beer, which followed with cheers for everyone from the Colonel to the cooks.[5]

By 6 January they were back on the wind- and hail-lashed terraces. Three days later the bulk of the battalion followed 'B' Company across the River Peccia and advanced on Cedra. As dense mist blanketed the valley bottoms, coiling around the grey shapes of buildings and sliding a blanket of confusion over the battlefield, long periods of boredom and uncertainty were punctuated by fierce little skirmishes. Withdrawing to previous positions south of the Peccia, there was some good news. Russell Collins had been gazetted for his Military Cross. The untried young officer who'd suffered his terrifying and confused baptism of fire just a few months beforehand was now a decorated veteran. Moreover, he was a successful and experienced infantryman:

> I don't think MCs came up very frequently for platoon commanders; they came up sometimes for company commanders who'd commanded a successful attack, but hadn't done anything perhaps too personal…The thing that sticks in mind is that I did many things which in my mind were equally meritorious[6] and some of them even more hazardous which just weren't recognised at all… it's the luck of the draw. I was quite chuffed about mine![7]

Allied landings at Anzio were to be complemented by a further push from 5th Army against the Gustav Line. The initial bright promise of the beachhead was squandered when the Allies failed to exploit the advantage of surprise. The Germans were quick to recover and a mighty ring of armour closed around 5th Army with British X Corps crossing the River Garigliano on 17 January 1944. It was at once chillingly obvious that the Germans were not contemplating retreat. Hitler moved in scarce reserves, drawn from other theatres, to shore up Kesselring's defences. At the outset, 16 DLI were spared the worst, being out of the line in billets till 25 January. In sheeting hail and biting winds they crossed the swollen Garigliano as reserve battalion for 138 Brigade. Creeping forward from the southern slopes of Mount Turlito, they advanced on Point 400 and Mount Siola. This was the infantryman's war, a dangerous slogging match for undistinguished features in a desolate landscape. Russell Collins summed up the action with a terse diary entry from 29 January:

'Moved forward to Hill 400; had a few hours rest, went forward with platoon all night. Infiltrated behind Jerry; attacked at dawn, captured seven. Two Jerries wounded. One of my men killed, Mawson.' Private Mawson was a noted loss:

> A splendid little man, totally reliable though he wouldn't say boo to a goose. I think I recommended him for a Military Medal; I know I had it very much in mind to do so. A very interesting lesson I learnt from the war was that the calm, quiet people like that, undistinguished people you might think, not extrovert in any way, were absolutely steady and reliable. Whereas other people who were showing great bravado, 'My God I can't wait to get at them!', often crumbled in an instant. I've seen this happen time and time again. The moment they're fired on they explode in a puff of smoke.[8]

Mawson had simply been unlucky; the platoon was working its way round the north side of a projecting spur and then on to Mount Siola under cover of a boulder-strewn defile:

> ...it was quite a deep patrol and we got into this gully. Well, the Germans were in it; that was the trouble, they were covering it – machine-guns certainly on one side and possibly on both sides. We were trying to make progress, but I saw that we had gone too far and were going to have difficulties in extricating ourselves. We came under fire – so we just had to get out of the gully as soon as we could.[9]

It was then that Mawson was shot, unable to move and 'some 30 or 40 yards from me to my left'. This was a classic infantry officer's dilemma:

> It was a question then if anybody could go down and recover him or not...I agonised as to whether or not I should go or send anybody to try and get him out – whether or not we should hazard more of us to try and get him out. You couldn't rely on the

Germans; it wouldn't be any good taking a Red Cross flag or anything like that. If anybody else went down there they would have been fired on as well. So he was just unlucky.[10]

'Unlucky' for the badly wounded man meant he was beyond the reach of the Medical Officer and could not be rescued by comrades. Death was virtually inevitable due to shock and blood loss.

Next day 'B' Company went up the scarred slopes of Monte Siela but the assault was savagely contested:

As the first platoon got amongst these positions all hell let loose. They threw everything at us...the three of us dived into this sangar...we were in there for the biggest part of that day...quite a few were killed. Mr Coutt's batman, Jack Vile, he was hit in the pouch, he had some flares for the Verey pistol and they all set alight and burnt. Sergeant Makepeace, he was killed and several others, some were taken prisoner. One or two lads in front of us took their packs off and slid back. It wasn't a matter of running away, you were in a position where you couldn't do a thing about it. What could you do?[11]

The Durhams clung to their hastily scraped foxholes as the fighting stalled in a grim attrition. For officers like Russell Collins this was another form of testing; correct cleaning of weapons was an essential tool of survival, personal hygiene vital to morale: 'You had to have a proper regime of weapon cleaning. Small arms are particularly susceptible to malfunctioning due to mud, ingress of mud and grit. And of course they are most likely to get the ingress of mud and grit!' Personal appearance was just as important; 'I always made my people wash and shave, and they thought it was ridiculous sometimes; you know we had no hot water. But if we were going to move the next morning, or go on an advance or an attack, I always insisted that everybody got his mess tin, put a drop of water in it from his water bottle and washed and shaved. It had a tremendous morale-boosting effect.'[12]

Throughout the hard-fought Italian campaign 16 DLI relied for fire support on 449 Battery Royal Artillery, from 70th Field Regiment; 'they were our battery. We became integrated, almost as if we were in the same unit. We knew them all extremely well personally and I think that's why it worked so well. They were brilliant!' In one instance Collins acted as his own forward observation officer, the role normally entrusted to a gunner, calling down fire on a machine-gun nest some 400 yards distant from his position:

> Well the gunners wouldn't have it that I knew where I was – but I did! The first shell they dropped was absolutely nowhere in sight. So I said, 'Well, you'd better try again!' They tried again and got one closer. Now the drill is, once you see a shell then, taking the axis of oneself to the target, in relation to that you say, 'Go right 200, go up 100', or whatever. I did that and of course it was a total fluke, rather like a hole in one at golf, but the next shell fell slap on the machine-gunner under the tree.[13]

Such triumphs were conspicuously rare. Constant attrition, the lack of any significant gains, no sign of any weakening by the enemy, the shrill and deadly chorus of mortars, and atrocious conditions steadily sapped morale.

> The men were sick, they were fed up. Normally in a war you are fed up but you could see the difference in the men. They were tired; they'd been up in those hills for three weeks, so they hadn't really had a rest. None of us had had a real rest, not what you'd call a rest – just a couple of days when you knew straight away you were going back in the line. So it wasn't a rest, your mind didn't register it as a rest at all. The men were just weary, battle fatigued and war weary…[14]

Russell Collins could also see the strain was telling: 'You know you can sense when everybody is at a low ebb; if it was necessary to detail somebody off to accompany me on a patrol then I had to think twice…'[15] On 14 February the battalion was pulled back to La Vaglie. This was a real rest, full bathing facilities, new kit, plenty of ale. Better news followed: 16 DLI, with the whole of 46th Division, was being sent to the Middle East for extended recuperation and re-training. For the moment they were missing the war.

The Gothic Line

From February–July 1944 the battalion enjoyed an altogether cushier billet in Egypt. This was not intended entirely as a rest cure. At

Quassasin, then Kefar-Yona, Tel Aviv, and Er Raima, by Lake Tiberias (perhaps better known as the Sea of Galilee), there were bouts of intensive training. Lieutenant-Colonel Preston left the battalion and was replaced as CO by Lieutenant-Colonel Worrall.[16] When rumour began to solidify, most faced the prospect of going back into line with a degree of stoicism. Russell Collins believed he accepted the prospect with equanimity.

> Yet I think I must have been subconsciously apprehensive about it for I was taken ill with a very severe gut ache shortly after we returned to Italy. It was never really fully diagnosed and was presumed to have been some bug I'd picked up in the Middle East. But I've wondered since, whether – being quite frank about it – whether it was some subconscious mechanism, telling me that I didn't want to go back there again.[17]

In Italy the war moved on, Rome was liberated and the tide of battle surged 130 miles north of the city. It was still no pushover. On the upper reaches of the Tiber the German line began to harden. On 4 August the Allies reached the River Arno – they now faced the Gothic Line.[18] Again, and as before, ground favoured the defender. Just south of Rimini the Apennines veer north-west toward the Maritime Alps. The Line derived maximum benefit from the Po Basin and mountains around, running from Spezia in Liguria all the way to Pesaro on the shores of the Adriatic. By now, however, the Allies had landed in Normandy and the campaign in Italy was relegated to a sideshow.

By 3 July the Durhams were back in theatre and advancing toward Assisi, to the unpromisingly named town of Bastardo. Here, there was more intensive training, including street fighting. This interval ended on 22 August when the battalion moved into line. By 27 August they were deployed in the region of Isolo del Piano to support the Sherwood Foresters and Leicestershires. Men were already dropping, picked off by random shrapnel and the feared 'schu' mines:[19]

> We were shelled, at first sporadically, sometimes more heavily. People got whittled away without any particular action. A couple of casualties whilst being shelled or mortared; two or three blokes standing on a schu mine moving through a field; a lad on my left

screaming out – he'd stood on a schu mine. People were always frightened of getting their balls blown off. This was this fellow's main shriek, 'How's me balls? Oh God...' He was alright as it happened; he was badly cut in the lower thigh. They were nasty things.[20]

On 28 August the battalion leapfrogged into the lead and assaulted the town of Petriano. The streets were taken but, inevitably, the Germans responded with a storm of fire.

We'd only been in Petriano half an hour before they started knocking hell out of the place. Shelling – 88s – the flat crack of a high-velocity weapon – they shelled Petriano very heavily, knocking down buildings, there were a number of casualties. A lot of us, including my company commander Frank Duffy, we were in this stone house with a very thick wall, Frank Duffy was on my left...Further to his left there was a door which led into a bedroom. We were tired and we had our packs on which we just rested up against the wall. In came this chap who remarked to Frank Duffy and myself that there was a bed there, 'Why don't you go rest on that?' Both Frank and myself said, 'Oh, can't be bothered, we're all right where we are!' Three minutes later the room, the bed and everything else disappeared in a cloud of smoke – a direct hit by a shell...[21]

Yet another of those interminable lateral waterways, this time the River Apsa, barred the line of advance, with the Germans dug in on the high ground beyond. A line of outposts was stormed but the Germans withdrew, falling back to their main defensive line. As ever, the enemy sowed a deadly harvest of mines and booby traps. A particular jury-rigged anti-personnel device was intended to damage the victim in a most ungentlemanly manner, aptly and pithily named the 'de-bollocker'.[22] Snipers, too, were active:

We found ourselves in a minefield. Goodness knows how we got there! Suddenly we were surrounded, all round us except for the way we'd come in. We hadn't suffered any casualties. Now, we had to get out, so we had to go back the way we came in – that's not to say we'd laid a white line or anything. If they were the heavier tank mines they may not have exploded but all these places were full of schu mines. So it was simply a case of retracing our steps a couple of hundred yards through this minefield. We walked back in single file and Muggins went first! That was my job, everybody expected me to apart from anything else, and that was one of the most terrifying, or numbing, experiences that I can remember.[23]

By 30 August the Durhams were over the next river barrier and preparing to assault the village of Mondaino and the high ground on the slopes of Monte Gridolfo, a daunting, heavily defended obstacle. Pressure flowing down the chain of command meant that the attacking companies received inadequate tank and artillery support. 'The CO came forward and he said, "I want you to take those buildings." Which happened to be a place called Mondanio which was in the distance, about a mile and a half; I said, "Well what is the plan, where are the tanks, what about the artillery fire?" He said, "Oh, they'll be coming."'[24]

The promised support did not arrive and Major Hay ('A' Company) never forgave Colonel Worrall for ordering the attack to go in regardless, for bowing to pressure from the brigadier. The assault was launched into the teeth of a deadly fire. 'A' Company attained their objectives, but with loss and horribly exposed to heavy fire. 'The casualties were alarming. The Gothic Line had been prepared specially for this; they had their lines of fire.'[25] The position, so dearly won, began to seem untenable. Less than a third of those who'd left the start line were uninjured. Bitter, confused and bloody fighting followed 'B' Company, who subsequently put in a brilliantly executed attack on Serra Ridge, capturing 30 POWs, a Panzer Mark IV and one of the lethal 88s. The slogging match continued until 4 September when 46th Division was relieved by 1st Armoured. In a dozen days of desperate fighting they had achieved considerable tactical successes but 16 DLI had sustained 137 casualties. Their recuperation in the Middle East was merely a memory.

Despite the awfulness of assaulting the Gothic Line, the fighting was not without its lighter moments:

Harry Mynheer was a great man for presence of mind. We were near a bridge in some little village and it was being shelled. There were semi-detached houses with a passage going through to the back of each place and we were in this passage. Harry and I were in there and several civilians had taken shelter. One of them was a big, strong Italian and as the shelling increased he started to have hysterics, 'Oh mamma mia...' Of course, Harry, with his great presence of mind, decided what to do – so he slapped this great big Italian round the face! Well it cured him – because he drew back his right hand and he gave Harry such a blow in the eye! It did quieten the Italian down because he realised the enormity of his offence of striking a British officer! How I kept a straight face![26]

Gemmano Ridge

The Gemmano Ridge rises south of the River Conca and comprises a range of hillocks and linking saddles. When 16 DLI advanced up late on 10 September the ground was already much contested – two of the most significant obstacles were two hills, designated 449 and 414, and the dip between. As the Durhams relieved the King's Own Yorkshire Light Infantry and the Lincolns, determined German counter-attacks wrested back the high ground and the Axis were in the outskirts of Borgo village. For the battalion, it was the familiar pattern of advancing into a confusion of hills, pressing ever upward whilst receiving the full and undiluted attention of the German gunners. Borgo and Gemmano were bombarded into a shattered waste. It was impossible to imagine that people had ever lived there and the men tunnelled their way into makeshift dugouts in the wreckage. These ancient hill-towns were reminiscent of the level of destruction in Flanders or Artois from the Great War. Buildings toppled and sheared, timber, stone rubble, plaster and the smashed vestiges of possessions were scattered and rearranged at random by the shelling. The bloated carcasses of dead men and animals swelled noxious and obscene.

Frequent sorties were launched to advance over the intervening saddle and wrest back the lump of Hill 449, but the defenders enjoyed a perfect firing position. Every attempt was repulsed and casualties mounted inexorably. It was the worst kind of fighting, shredding nerves, snatching men at random, sapping morale:

We were moving up when the shelling and bloody mortaring started. It was heavy, it was real nasty, the bloody place was alive then. We just kept on moving up, you know, you halt now and again, move a bit then halt a bit and then move a bit. They were stonking away all the time, mortar shells. We'd already lost one or two blokes and I passed 'Shack' on the road. I knew it was 'Shack'. I could see him lying there; I knew he would be dead. There was nothing I could do about it, I had to just keep moving...'[27]

Removing the dead also proved difficult. 'We went to pick some grub up; they had transported some up near us at the bottom of the hill and "Shack" was still lying there, my mate, still lying there on the side of that road. By then he was black.'[28]

No headway could be made and it was only gains won by other units that finally rendered the defenders' position untenable. As the Germans slipped away, 16 DLI gained the high ground: small, steep conical hills, undistinguished in all but their price in blood. It only remained to gather and bury the dead, a grisly and sobering business at best. George Bland of the carrier platoon was one of those detailed. 'I'd seen dead lying before, like, but when you come to pick them up, blokes that have been lying out in the sun and the rain two or three days, you know, the smell was terrible. They were rancid; man, their blood was dried on their faces.'[29]

However grim the prospect, bodily needs continue to arise, as Les Thornton recalled.

We were in a position where we were being heavily shelled with mortars and artillery. Naturally we all wanted to go to the toilet sometime and there was no toilet around! The shelling died down and I decided to go outside near a tree to do what I wanted to do. Well, I got my trousers down and started – and so did the Germans! There I was, lying flat on my stomach with my behind facing the sky and I daren't move. I had to remain there until the shelling ceased.[30]

Odd moments of incongruous humour stayed in the mind. Lieutenant Dick Hewlett recalled an incident involving Sergeant Jerrison: 'He was 'A' Company, I think, and I was asking him for information. It was fairly quiet, he was standing to attention as he spoke to me. There were chickens all over the place, one was on each shoulder and one on the top of his steel helmet...they were standing on top of him and it didn't seem to worry him at all, extraordinary sight.'[31]

Russell Collins had missed the attrition of Gemmano due to his stomach ailment. By the time he returned later in September the battalion was reduced to three companies, 'C' and 'D' Companies having suffered such high losses. He led his platoon out on a probing mission on 26 September. The 'Winkler' was back in business. His objective was a stone farmhouse, occupied without incident. Like any good infantry officer, Collins settled in. One room contained that most singular marvel, an intact bed; he was just about to take possession when 'Alan [Hay] turned up with his Company Headquarters. "Ah," he said, "Thank you very much, very nice Company Headquarters you've found for me!"' So Collins lost his precious bed. Captain Hay, settling himself into the lieutenant's bed, quipped that they'd all be fine unless an unlucky shell landed on their doorstep: 'We all laid down on the floor and it wasn't long before a shell fell in the doorway! Poor old Alan, because he was upon the bed, he was the only one above ground and a shell splinter went through his hand. But that was a shell splinter that really had my number on it, but he'd rubbed it out and put his own on it!'[32]

Barely two days later and Collins was again in the thick of it. Both 'A' and 'D' Companies were allotted the unenviable task of seizing well-defended buildings on the bare heights of the Casa Ricci Ridge. By now he was regarded as something of a local hero; 'he really was,' as Ronald Elliot observed, 'a very good officer indeed, very dare-devilish.'[33] This time the attack was put in with armoured support, ostensibly a bonus but Collins was not convinced of the benefit.

As a matter of fact I used not to like fighting with tanks because one relies so much on a sort of sixth sense – you can just hear and feel if there is any movement, or any shells approaching and you can take evasive action. Being in the close neighbourhood of a tank is very like being blind; you're deafened and so you just lose the capacity really to exercise that sixth sense. I always felt very vulnerable if I was anywhere near a tank.[34]

The overwhelming advantage of tanks was their ability to direct fire on to the enemy at will, but it was often very hard for the infantryman to actually convey instructions to the tank-crew:

> At command level they had radio nets but at individual foot-soldier level it's extremely difficult. The way we had to try and communicate was very complex but it worked. They installed a telephone on the outside of the tank, behind the turret, communicating to the commander inside. We were meant to run up behind the tank, pick up this phone, crank the handle and then we were supposed to be able to talk to the crew inside. But even if the tank commander had his head stuck out, it was very difficult, the noise prevented one really communicating by shouting, so it was jolly difficult.[35]

As the attack went in to the usual accompaniment of shells and mortars, the Company Commander, Captain Sherlaw, had ordered the laying down of smoke but he was injured early on by shrapnel so the baton of command passed to Collins. As the Durhams closed upon their objectives, the smoke canisters being lobbed by the supporting armour became a hazard in themselves.

> Now as we faced the two buildings, we were approaching the one to the right of the road, in fact the whole of our force was. So perhaps we were coming in by the right flank a little bit. I led the men right through the smoke area but the tanks were still firing these smoke canisters. They were things weighing about five or six pounds and dropping on you from perhaps a hundred feet in the air – it could have been very nasty. But I mean there was nothing for it but to press on.[36]

The Durhams secured the first of their objectives (a group of buildings collectively labelled as 'Johnson'). Fighting was at close quarters, and success had to be followed up immediately by consolidation against the inevitable German counter-attack: 'and you would dig in because the first thing that would happen is that you would be counter-attacked. Maybe counter-attacked immediately or counter-attacked subsequently – but you would be counter-attacked.'[37]

With this important foothold gained, Collins now had to secure the remaining buildings and it was here that he could exploit his

182 Dunkirk to Belsen

armoured support to the full. With typical elan he led a storming party against the next strongpoint; it was obvious that the defenders were housed in the bottom storey. Rushing an external stair, Collins' party gained the upper level but were still unable to bring much pressure against those below other than by lobbing grenades. To storm the place would have been near-suicidal so it was clearly a job for the tanks: 'So I gave orders for all our chaps who were in and around this building to withdraw to the other building, to clear the way.' As the infantry withdrew, the tanks hovered to blast the defenders; 'as soon as they started firing, a man came and appeared at the upstairs window...one of our chaps who had been left behind in there. One of these sort of nightmarish visions, which I've never been able to rationalise or get out of my mind since – he was waving his arms desperately – but the next shell went through the window and that was the end of him. That picture is engraved on my mind.'[38]

Tanks themselves were vulnerable to artillery fire, particularly the superb German 88, and never more so than crossing a ridge line where the exposed belly rears invitingly into the artilleryman's sights:

A tank came up, and when it got about level with us it became just exposed. The German 88 anti-tank gun only a couple of hundred yards ahead, got it with a direct hit right on the front of the turret...the shot went straight through the turret, it must have killed the commander, then the hatches went up at the back and the rest of the crew baled out quicker than you can say 'Jack Robinson' – very wisely in case it blew up...[39]

The Sherman tanks used by the Allies were frequently referred to by the Germans as 'Ronsons' – after the lighter, due to their unfortunate propensity for 'brewing-up' (catching fire when hit).

So far the company had secured its objective in taking the huddle of buildings but the survivors were far from secure. The buildings, impressively solid, were located some way below the crest. Two of three tanks had been knocked out and the last one withdrew. To exploit their gains it would have been desirable to advance beyond and establish a perimeter. Nobody doubted the Germans' intention to return. 'Obviously the Germans hadn't given it up, they'd just withdrawn to regroup.There was a sense of foreboding; that the Germans were going to counter-attack again, they hadn't given up, they hadn't withdrawn and we were very exposed there.'[40] Collins set up his machine-gun posts and established his gunnery officer. With the men in the stout buildings, supporting fire could be brought close, as indeed it was during the inevitable counter-attack. Despite the Durhams' fire and the weight of British shells falling, the Germans gained the building they'd been blasted from before. The battle became bitter, intense and very bloody, Ronald Elliot remembers: 'They fired phosphorus bombs at us, 88mm guns, mortars, the lot. There was hand-to-hand fighting.'[41]

By dogged persistence and weight of numbers the Germans managed to infiltrate the farmhouse Collins and his men occupied; 'Then they actually got into the building that I was in and the Italian family were still there in the building. There was an ordinary standard doorway about eight feet high and a kitchen dresser blocking across it.'[42] Collins could hear excited voices on the far side, Italian female and German male. The lieutenant perched on a chair and peered over the impromptu barricade. A mere eight feet away he saw an enormous German, complete with steel helmet, demanding information of the terrified housewife. Collins felt able to assist the Axis officer in his quest to know where the English were with a well-directed shot from his revolver; 'You always have to aim a little low. I tried to fire at his head but I got him in the throat actually. He fell like a sack of coal, the woman screamed and they hid under the table.'[43] To ensure he'd killed the enemy, Collins fired a burst over the door from a Thompson then, as the dead or dying man had slumped against the door, a further burst through the planks: 'A rather brave German soldier, only just visible around the doorway, dragged the officer away out of sight, and so that was that.'[44] Close quarters indeed.

This was the crisis point. Collins was painfully aware that neither Battalion nor Brigade had any reserves left to send. The artillery performed magnificently:

David Purnell [Forward Observation Officer] brought down this divisional concentration of fire all around us. Really it was very good infantry and artillery cooperation, because I knew exactly what our situation was and was able to convey it to him. Anyway, the attack was repulsed and the main thing that broke it up was the artillery fire. We were really hanging on, quite honestly, by the skin of our teeth ...[45]

Though it seemed no reinforcements were available, Collins received a radio message from the Intelligence Officer 'Giff' Footer. 'My signaller [Ronald Elliot] was trying to receive a message on the radio from the Intelligence Officer and he couldn't make head nor tail of it.' Elliot's confusion was understandable but Collins quickly divined that they were to be relieved that evening by the Divisional Reconnaissance ('Recce') Regiment; 'very good news indeed'.[46]

In fact their ordeal was not yet over. The relief was delayed until the early hours of the following morning. When the Recce Regiment did come up there was still the tricky business of withdrawing under fire. The Germans were far from giving up: 'The first elements of the Recce, a couple of troops, came up. I couldn't help feeling rather sorry for them, because it was a rather precarious position. But you know we had gained it and we had hung on there. I showed them the position and the problems. I started pulling out some of my chaps, sending them back.'[47] Winkler Collins had again justified his now formidable reputation.

One last skirmish remained to complete this action: a battle for possession of Ronnie Elliot and his radio.

The captain of the Recce troop came up, Winkler Collins showed him the position and told him where to put his people. He came in to see us and he said, 'Well this is the signal terminal if you want to put your set in here.' The Recce officer said, 'I haven't got any signal set...' I looked at Jackie Wells and he looked at me, 'Jesus Christ! We're going to get landed here...' But Winkler said this set belonged to the DLI, it was on the DLI network and therefore he would have to take it with him and he couldn't leave it – for which we were devoutly grateful.[48]

I was the last one left, which is the right and proper thing. I set out and by then I was absolutely on my uppers and exhausted. I just staggered back down the hill on my own wondering how I was going to get back to the rallying point. When along came a jeep, I recognised Harry Craggs, the Battery Commander of the battery that supported us. Dear Harry Craggs, he stopped and hauled me aboard and so we got back to the rest area, I collapsed and slept the clock round, utterly exhausted. Unfortunately when I eventually came to, the first thing I was told was that the Recce Regiment had lost the feature soon after we'd handed over.

They'd come to it, they hadn't got the feel of it, they hadn't a cat in hell's chance really, at night. So it was very bad luck on them. Whether we'd have been driven off if we'd stayed there – who knows?[49]

Collins' men, despite the murderous pressure, at least understood the feature they were holding; their successors in some ways faced a more difficult task and were driven off.

He, Elliot and the other survivors were dazed and exhausted; to have fought so long and so hard to see the position immediately lost was demoralising. By the early autumn officers like Collins could see the signs of stress rising amongst their soldiers and in them also:

I'm sure I'd reached that point myself at the very end. At the very end I was beginning to feel that, rather than saying, 'Come on chaps, follow me', I was rather saying, 'Now look, I'm going to put my headquarters here, and you go there and you go there.' Which many people had done from the beginning – but that was not my way. The thing that really weighed on my mind – it's sheer rationality really – was the number of officers and soldiers who'd been killed, wounded or missing from the start of the Italian campaign to the end. Bear in mind I was a platoon commander in the front echelon the whole time. I mean I used to regard a company headquarters as a place of comparative safety. So you reach a point 'Come in now, your time is up.' You just waver and think, 'Well this just can't go on.' Everybody else that I could think of had been killed.[50]

Once out of the line the men's thoughts turned to more immediate needs which were frequently limited to alcoholic refreshment and female company, not necessarily (though usually) in that order. In relation to the former, few were particularly choosy, as Les Thornton relates:

The men very seldom got any beer. The only time they got anything to drink really was if they got into a village and the inhabitants had a wine cellar. Very often they did. We went into this barn place and there was a little Italian lad in a barrel stomping. I said, 'What's he doing?' Of course the Italian explained that he was pressing the grapes with his feet. The mud on the floor was terrible. They just turned the tap on, put a glass underneath and drank it; it wasn't even fermented, it was just pure black grape juice – but they would drink it![51]

Women, as the Sergeant continued, were also a priority. 'They wanted a woman if they could – they were all human. They probably hadn't seen a woman for six months, and naturally if they had the chance they would. Half of the company lined up for one woman.'[52] Kenneth Lovell complained of price inflation due to the arrival of our more affluent US allies. 'The lads had the time of their lives. The ladies of the town started off at five lire and a bottle of wine was a couple of lire – the boys were having a high old time until the Yanks came in and prices went up suddenly.'[53] Whilst the army might be obliged to condone such activity, command felt the need to issue the usual strictures; Kenneth Lovell again:

> We were compelled to see a photographic exhibition showing the ravages of venereal disease. They were pretty ghastly photographs, not the sort of thing you want to see immediately before lunch. The infantryman's view is, 'Sod it, I may get killed tomorrow so why not!' But I think it put a lot of the lads off their nookie for quite some time and it made a lot more take precautions – they no longer rode 'bare-back'![54]

The Balignano Spur

Despite the numbing weight of his exhaustion and the sapping demands of combat, Winkler Collins was soon in action again. On 10 October, he was leading a fighting patrol toward the village of La Crocetta at the foot of the Balignano Spur. Collins gambled speed over caution in crossing open ground, which proved a high-risk strategy: 'I'd taken a bit of a gamble in going across a rather open space in open formation. We had all our heavy weapons and when we were in the middle of this open space the Germans opened up with artillery fire. The platoon found themselves deluged in fire. It was a very, very alarming moment – shells firing, concentrated on a given area – and there we were.' These were men who'd had their nerves frayed for months by this deadly storm: 'You just think, "My God, the next one is going to land on me."' In spite of the exposed nature of their position and the intensity of the bombardment, no-one was hurt. The men, understandably, were somewhat reluctant to continue; 'I promised them we would go around a more secluded way.'[55]

'A' Company secured their objectives but Ray Mitchell, Collins' Company Commander, was injured by a mine, the blast severing a leg. As the badly injured man, a keen footballer, was stretchered back he managed to quip, 'Bugger it, I shan't score any more goals with that foot!'[56] 'B' Company was now allotted the task of cracking the spur itself. Lieutenant-Colonel Worrall attached Collins' platoon to support Major Stringer, leading 'B' Company in the assault. The Major was glad to have the Winkler by his side. Collins himself was less than enthusiastic, particularly about the plan of attack: 'When I told the lads we were going to have to do this attack, there were groans all the way round.'[57] Men were exhausted. One veteran section commander, Corporal Vick, privately entreated Collins to be excused. The Lieutenant knew that the man wasn't shirking. He'd simply reached the end of his endurance. In the end he was talked round.

Collins had little faith in the plan of attack, the main axis being frontal with Collins' platoon working around to the right and bearing on the church. Initially, all seemed to go well. 'B' Company made good progress over the lower slopes, well supported by artillery, and many of the defenders simply surrendered. For an instant Major Stringer allowed himself to think they'd win the crest. But as they toiled up the steeper gradient, German fire intensified: 'By this time we had got up fairly close to the crest of this feature, within 50 yards of the crest, when the enemy counter-attacked from the reverse slope and from the left-hand side of the feature. They had a machine-gun firing from enfilade.[58] I was beginning to have a lot of casualties and the situation was beginning to look serious.'[59]

As Collins recalled: 'There was a tremendous lot of shooting on the central part of the attack but there was no direct opposition where we were, which was obviously the better line of approach.' Some 50 yards from the church he set up the heavier support weapons and detailed a section, Vick's as it happened, to storm the building itself: 'He got up there and just walked in the church door – he was shot – that was the end of him. The poor chap – whether it was the stress – he just forgot his drill at the moment. Instead of taking some precaution, a quick look round the door and throw a grenade in, he just walked in the doorway.'[60]

The attack in the centre had degenerated into confusion and was running out of steam. As pockets of infantry struggled toward the ridge, the well-coordinated counter-attacks drove them back. Collins had attained his objectives, but soon realised that all was not going according to plan: 'Suddenly I became aware everything was very quiet…it became apparent that the company had withdrawn, aborted the attack and gone home. I'd got no message and there I was with my solitary platoon on the edge of the village.'[61] In fact, Collins was able to withdraw in good order whilst the survivors of 'B' Company were in a more shop-worn condition. Major Stringer, in his subsequent assessment of the failure, felt obliged to agree that Collins' proposal to shift the weight of the attack on to the right flanking movement rather than 'attacking from the front' was sensible; 'He thinks we might have had a greater chance of success and he might well have been right.'[62]

Having fought and bled to win the ridge, final victory was again denied by a further enemy withdrawal and 138 Brigade passed through 16 DLI and the rest of 139 Brigade to take the lead. As the advance continued, Captain Jones, the Medical Officer, found himself in demand from an unexpected quarter:

> The fighting had moved on and I was asked by the Italians to visit a lady who was in labour. Fortunately it was her fourth and she did most of the delivery herself. The placenta took a long time to be delivered and it had me worried for I had no blood or anything should difficulties have occurred. However, all was well. The local farmer was very grateful and we were given a chicken, which was enjoyed by all.[63]

From Cesena to Cosina

Their next major objective was Cesena, no mere village but an urban centre with a population of 20,000. Ronald Elliot found his signaller's skills in demand to ensure close cooperation between tanks and infantry:

> They had decided that cooperation between tanks and infantry wasn't particularly good, which was not untrue to say the least! So they decided to have a company signaller in a tank on the company network to provide immediate communications with

the troops that were attacking. Because Jackie Wells and I were spare, we went into the tank in this attack on Cesena. The interesting part about that was that we'd always thought as infantry that the tanks had this marvellous life because every evening they pulled back to some sort of reserve position and laagered up, had food and got their heads down. We thought that was great.[64]

Elliot found that the tank crew's life was less idyllic than the infantryman imagined.

The part that really intrigued me was that I was more afraid inside the tank than I would have been outside the tank. You were more conscious of shot and shell; the shrapnel pinged on the side of the tank; it was claustrophobic; it was noisy. You felt as [if] you were the focus point, particularly of any likely attack and that you were vulnerable inside…The infantry hadn't a great deal to commend it but on balance I preferred it to a tank man's life.[65]

Major Lawrie Stringer was one of the infantry engaged in the savage and murderous fight for the streets of Cesena.

Sergeant-Major Clark, instead of following me, he crouched up against the wall and stayed and the Spandau[66] picked him up and killed him without any trouble at all. Meanwhile the tank commander of the leading tank had seen what had happened and his cupola swung around and he fired an HE shell at this house where this Spandau was firing from and the whole of the house came down into the road. It was a fantastic thing; so that finished that particular machine-gun.[67]

One or possibly two machine-guns had been silenced but:

there was a lot of machine-gun fire coming from other directions at this stage. I ran around, got into the main road, ran across the garden into the front of this house on the left-hand corner. If you go to the house today you will see machine-gun bullet holes all the way round the entrance to the house – how they didn't hit me I shall never know. I flung myself at the door and fortunately it gave way. When I got inside the house I was met by 10 screaming hysterical women! So, without being dramatic about it, imagine the situation. I was expecting a German counter-attack at any moment and I had these women to deal with. They were absolutely hysterical. Just a little way down the passage there was a cellar of some kind so I put my arms round all these women and I pushed them down this cellar.[68]

After this bitter battle for the streets, German resistance was overcome and a number of prisoners taken. Despite another defeat, the more diehard Nazis amazed Major Vizard by their continued defiance.

There were some virulent troops; the MO moved up a forward RAP and a mortally wounded Corporal from the German 91st Light Regiment[69] was brought into the RAP. It was quite clear he wasn't going to last the distance to the clearing station.[70] He'd been blown up in one of the houses in Cesena. I lit a cigarette and bent down to put it between his lips and he spat at me! This man was within minutes of death and he wouldn't even take a cigarette from me. There were some like that…[71]

Still the long march ground on. For a while the Durhams remained in support until, on 14 November, the brigade was sent forward to relieve 128 Brigade at San Varano. The baking heat and acrid dust of summer had again dampened into autumnal rain, which had swollen slow-moving rivers and choked canals. The flat alluvial landscape of the Italian flood plain, with its grid of waterways, all seemed to wash together into one dismal sea of mud. One river line replaced another: 'We got across this range of hills – and that's the end of it. Then you cross the next range, then the next range, you went from one line to another. This was the last line; they took some budging at that time the Germans. You gradually got them out of their positions and they withdrew, only for you to find that they'd got another line with another name somewhere behind it…'[72]

Lawrie Stringer was aware, as were all of the officers, that this grinding attrition was taking its toll: 'In efforts to encourage the troops that the infantry "slogging match" would soon be over and the armour would then be able to break through on to the plains of Lombardy, stories were circulated, somewhat prematurely, that "the next ridge is the last".' Troops heard this rumour so many times during this stage of the campaign that they, in turn, circulated the story that, 'The enemy had a large team of bulldozers specially trained for the purpose of creating fresh ridges as they fell back!'[73]

To these accustomed trials was added the horror of a strafing attack from the RAF, 'friendly-fire'. Lawrie Stringer again:

> ...they mistook our line for the enemy line and they came over a minute before 'H' hour and dive-bombed and machine-gunned my forward position. This was most unpleasant and it was there that Denis Worrall, who happened to be up forward, saw what was happening and he stood in the middle of the road – he hadn't got a steel helmet on – waving his stick at these aircraft to try and let them know they were machine-gunning the wrong line. There he stood in the middle of that Italian road and he was unperturbed and really didn't bat an eyelid.[74]

Having survived the aerial attack from their own planes, the troops advanced. Stringer then had to deal with an officer who had lost his nerve: 'I took him by the arm, I didn't get excited, I said, "You must move forward!" With that he left me and ran in the opposite direction, it was a very, very tricky situation.'[75] Snipers were, as ever, a constant hazard. 'We had two brothers in our company,' William Virr remembered, 'in the same section together and it was while we were amongst the rubble that the younger one lifted his head up and the sniper hit him straight through the head; his brother was there at the side of him.'[76]

After only a few days out of the line, the Battalion was again sent forward for a further assault on the Cosina Canal. Russell Collins had been reassigned to the Carrier Platoon of Support Company, though the men were 'dismounted' and fighting as infantry: 'We tried to sally forth to make an exploratory patrol across the river and they opened fire and drove us back.' It was obvious that the enemy was installed in strength, using buildings as strongpoints with an outpost line beyond:

> I went upstairs in the farmhouse to look through a window to try and locate their machine-gun posts. With my binoculars I was searching the ground and suddenly there was a great clattering and a long burst of machine-gun fire, which spouted all around

this window – broke through the plaster on the walls on either side, through the window and none of them hit me. But they might have done and you get to the point where you think, 'My Gosh! I'm leading a charmed life!'[77]

His extreme good luck held when Collins led another fighting patrol forward to the river. A German machine-gun nest barely 20 yards distant kept them pinned down whilst the Durhams lobbed showers of grenades, taking turns to stand and throw:

> …there was a soldier standing next to me, I can see him very clearly…about three or four feet away. In turn – just turn and turn about – we stood up and threw a grenade and when we had done that four or five times, there was a searing burst of fire; when it was his turn – it went right through his head…He was obviously dead before he hit the ground…the luck of the draw you see, I mean I had a fifty-fifty chance there.[78]

With his platoon retiring back to their position in the farmhouse, Collins resumed his observation. Shortly he witnessed the machine-gun team clamber from their slit trench as though surrendering and with a flag on the end of a stick. They did not come forward but retired back towards their own lines. 'I'm afraid I was very suspicious about the whole thing, and I really had very little sympathy for those chaps by then. I had a great anguished debate with myself whether we should shoot them or not.' Fearing a ruse and putting the safety of his own men first, he killed the Germans. 'There were very few people I've shot in cold blood, particularly in the back, when they're waving a white flag, but there was nothing else for it really – so that was the end of them.'[79]

A subsequent battalion attack failed to breach the defensive line on the canal, though successes along the line rendered the German position untenable. As 16 DLI again advanced, Collins was again detailed to perform his habitual magic against a further defended farm. By now his nerves were stretched to breaking point; 'I couldn't be the first man forward there. I'd done it so many times and I'd really got to the end of my tether then.' Happily, one of his section commanders, Sergeant Chilvers, was also a first-rate soldier and led this attack with such distinction he was awarded the Military Medal. Once the position had been secured it was time to dig in and establish all-round defence. As the sections fanned out to their allotted tasks Collins began his rounds. 'It was dusk and I came around one corner and a voice said, "Halt, who goes there?" "BANG". All in one moment. It was a carrier driver, who was shaking like a leaf and had his rifle at the hip. He was called Yorkie Streeton and that was the last shot that was ever fired at me in anger in Italy.'[80]

As the savage contest of the Gothic Line was slogged out in the autumn mud, the armies in the embrace of punch-drunk fighters, 139 Brigade was withdrawn to billets in the Forli area and from there they were withdrawn to Rome. They had been hoping for a prolonged and much needed rest. What they got was Greece and rumblings of civil war.[81]

Greek interlude

On a damp December morning the battalion flew into Athens. Most were simply glad to be out of Italy. Greece, whilst sliding into the throes of civil war, was infinitely less hazardous than Italy. There was unrest following the German withdrawal; furthermore, tensions between the Communist partisans of ELAS and the newly returned government-in-exile were running high. Insofar as the Durhams gave much thought to the internal politics, there was a measure of empathy with the left. Socialism was a doctrine which most espoused and even Churchill's epic wartime leadership had failed to render the Conservatives attractive.

Ronnie Elliot found himself in a city he'd long dreamt of:

In my childhood I had always been reading the classics and the thought of going to Athens was something quite remarkable to me. Something I thought I should never have been able to take advantage of. One of the companies that night was placed on the Acropolis itself. Nothing much happened and next morning I said to Signaller Tony Sacco, 'How was it, Tony?' and he said, 'Nothing else but bloody stones up there and it's freezing cold.' I thought, 'Well, that's the practical view of what the Acropolis was like!'[82]

Elliot, like many of his comrades, had some initial sympathy with ELAS:

All of the army by that time was pretty well socialist. Everyone was of the view that the Conservatives were to blame for all sorts of ills that we had in the war, the general level of the economy and the way that people felt about the future, so that, by and large, they were all pretty well Labour. Even though people admired Churchill for his ability to lead the country, his politics were completely suspect – he was a Conservative. We felt that what the government was trying to do in Greece was to restore the monarchy, which we all surmised was really not what the people wanted, but was going to be imposed upon them. Therefore in the beginning there was a fair amount of favourable feeling towards this insurgency.[83]

Such sentiments tended not to survive contact with the realities and Ronnie Elliot was soon disillusioned:

The ELAS tended to use women; they'd have women coming along the street, just as though they were housewives having a demonstration, followed by armed men behind them using the women as a shield, or even children, having children around so that you couldn't fire at them. So it got very dirty in that sense. This is about the time, as will always happen in these situations, that the soldier's attitudes changed from being politically favourable to being militarily against them…Churchill was trying to re-impose the King, the Communists were trying to impose Communist rule so that really in effect one was almost as bad as the other – and we were somewhere in between I guess![84]

As exposure to insurgent fire waned and spring returned in the halcyon days of March 1945, thoughts inevitably turned to 'what next'. The war in Italy and north-west Europe still raged; Greece had been an interlude rather than deliverance. The prospect of returning to the unending attrition of the peninsula had very limited appeal. Russell Collins certainly had no desire to go back:

All the talk and speculation was where we were going next. We were hoping against hope that we were going to be selected to go to north-west Europe, to join the much more glamorous party that was going on there. We abhorred the thought of going back to Italy again, where we'd fought two previous campaigns and had left a lot of our dead...But of course in the event we were told we were going back to Italy.[85]

'A lot of them weren't keen, which is understandable. To coin their phrase, "It was a bit late to get a wooden top coat!" They'd gone so long.'[86]

End of the march

That spring the Allies were preparing for the last 'big push' that would drive the Germans back to the Alps. Attacking on 9 April, the offensive breached the line of the Sento and Santerno rivers and pushed on toward the Po, with Verona as the objective. The Germans, battered but still resilient, were establishing their defensive line on the banks of the Adige. To 16 DLI it was all so dreadfully familiar. On 15 April they disembarked from the steamer *Ville d'Oran* at Taranto to be greeted by a stirring message from Major-General Weir, who was now divisional commander. They'd rather heard it all before and none but a fool would have relished a return to the grim, attritional warfare they'd experienced through the long months since landing at Salerno.

They were to be concentrated at La Fratta, near Bertinori, before going back into line. But this time the call to arms was never issued for, on 8 May, they sat on the lush spring grass and listened to Churchill's announcement that the war in Europe was over and that they had won.

> We all used to think, "Now one day we'll wake up and it will be over!" You used to think fantastic things. If you were in the line and you had to take wounded back to a safe place you were always happy because you used to think, "Well, while I'm here the war might be over – somebody might sign the peace!" Which eventually did happen – but it didn't happen when you thought it would. Fantastic![87]

Many felt that odd detachment, a sense of unreality. The war, however vile, had defined and shaped them, none who'd survived emerged as he had entered; it changed them all. There was a dawning relief that the horror was past, no more dry-mouths at start lines, no more clinging to a frozen hillside as mortars crashed around, no more burial details, no more grim, denuded roll-calls in cordite-wreathed dawns. Russell Collins was in no doubt: 'I was absolutely relieved, particularly as then we didn't have to go into action a third time in Italy. There was a great sense of euphoria, it was really marvellous.'[88]

For Winkler Collins and 16 DLI, the long march was finally over.[89]

Notes

1   Sergeant-Major Les Thornton, DLI Sound Recording Project.
2   Captain Alan Hay, DLI Sound Recording Project.
3   Ibid.
3a   Ibid.
4   Lieutenant Gerry Barnett, DLI Sound Recording Project.
5   16 DLI War Diary, 2 January 1944.
6   The medal was awarded for the attack he led on the Cocuruzzo Spur.
7   DLI Sound Recording Project.
8   Ibid.
9   Ibid.
10   Ibid.
11   Lance-Corporal William Virr, DLI Sound Recording Project.
12   DLI Sound Recording Project.
13   Ibid.
14   Sergeant-Major Les Thornton, Support Company, DLI Sound Recording Project.
15   DLI Sound Recording Project.
16   Originally transferred from the Dorset Regiment.
17   DLI Sound Recording Project.
18   The Gothic Line ('Linea Gotica'): Kesselring's last major defensive line along the crests of the Apennines.
19   Schu Mine 42: anti-personnel device with a 200g charge of TNT in a hinged, wooden box – being timber this was harder to detect.
20   Lieutenant Douglas Tiffin, DLI Sound Recording Project.
21   Ibid.
22   This was crude but nastily effective. A pipe, some 9 inches in length, was armed with a single round, angled upward; when trodden on, the bullet was fired; see Hart P., *The Heat of Battle* (Barnsley, England, 1999), p.118.
23   Lieutenant Douglas Tiffin, DLI Sound Recording Project.
24   Major Alan Hay, DLI Sound Recording Project.
25   Ibid.
26   Lieutenant Lionel Dodd, DLI Sound Recording Project.
27   Sergeant Tony Cameron, DLI Sound Recording Project.
28   Ibid.
29   Private George Bland, DLI Sound Recording Project.
30   DLI Sound Recording Project.
31   Ibid.
32   Ibid.
33   Signaller Ronald Elliot, DLI Sound Recording Project.
34   DLI Sound Recording Project.

35 Ibid.
36 Ibid.
37 Ibid.
38 Ibid.
39 Ibid.
40 Ibid.
41 Signaller Ronald Elliot, DLI Sound Recording Project.
42 DLI Sound Recording Project.
43 Ibid.
44 Ibid.
45 Ibid.
46 Ibid.
47 Ibid.
48 Ibid.
49 Ibid.
50 Lieutenant Russell Collins, DLI Sound Recording Project.
51 DLI Sound Recording Project.
52 Ibid.
53 Ibid.
54 Ibid.
55 Lieutenant Russell Collins, DLI Sound Recording Project.
56 DLI Sound Recording Project.
57 Ibid.
58 Enfilade fire: this is fire directed at the length of the attacking formation rather than the breadth, i.e. from the side, and far more deadly.
59 Major Lawrie Stringer, DLI Sound Recording Project.
60 DLI Sound Recording Project.
61 Ibid.
62 Ibid.
63 Ibid.
64 Ibid.
65 Ibid.
66 'Spandau': nickname for the German MG42 machine-gun.
67 DLI Sound Recording Project.
68 Ibid.
69 9th Light Infantry Division: A famous Afrika Corps formation, raised in August 1941. By 1944 it had been re-formed several times and was then 90th Grenadier Division (Motorised).
70 Casualty Clearing Station (CCS): 3rd link in the medical chain – (1) Regimental Aid Post, (2) Advanced Dressing Station, (3) CCS.
71 Major Viz Vizard, DLI Sound Recording Project.
72 Driver Tom Lister, DLI Sound Recording Project.
73 DLI Sound Recording Project.
74 Ibid.
75 Ibid.
76 Ibid.
77 Ibid.
78 Ibid.
79 Ibid.
80 Ibid.

81 The Greek Civil War 1944–49 was fought between the government of Greece supported by the UK and, latterly, the US, and the Democratic Army of Greece, the military arm of the Greek Communist party. The Communist forces comprised many who had fought in the wartime resistance organisation (ELAS), itself a tool of the Communist Party (KKE). The final victory of the government forces led to Greece's membership of NATO and is often viewed as the first Cold War conflict; the victory also affected the political map of the Balkans.

82 DLI Sound Recording Project.

83 Ibid.

84 Ibid.

85 Ibid.

86 Sergeant Tommy Chadwick, DLI Sound Recording Project.

87 Driver Jackie Milburn, DLI Sound Recording Project.

88 DLI Sound Recording Project.

89 16 DLI were sent from Italy to Austria as part of the army of occupation, from where they were gradually demobilised, the few regulars in the ranks being returned to their parent regiments. The battalion, a child of the war, did not long survive the peace and was disbanded in February 1946.

Chapter 9

D-Day: the Battle for Normandy, 1944

All of Amsterdam, all of Holland, in fact the entire western coast of Europe all the way down to Spain, are talking about the invasion day and night, debating, making bets and – hoping.

Anne Frank, diary entry, 22 May 1944

… Having seized the initiative by our initial landing, we must insure that we keep it. The best way to interfere with the enemy concentrations and counter measures will be to push forward fairly powerful armoured force thrusts on the afternoon of D-Day…I am prepared to accept almost any risk in order to carry out these tactics. I would risk even the total loss of the armoured brigade groups – which in any event is not really possible.

Montgomery, writing to Bradley and Dempsey, 14 April 1944[1]

On 19 August 1942, St. Oswin's Eve,[2] the Allies launched a major amphibious raid on the coast of occupied France aimed at seizing and then, for a limited period, holding Dieppe. This was the curtain-raiser for Operation 'Overlord'. Even at this early date the Americans, anxious to be done with war in the west so they could concentrate upon the defeat of Japan, were pressing for a full-scale invasion of Hitler's 'Fortress Europe'. Some 6,086 Allied troops, mainly Canadians, went ashore at Dieppe and, of these, 3,623 became casualties, a loss of nearly 60 per cent; the RAF lost 96 planes and the navy 34 vessels of all types. The images one retains of Operation 'Jubilee' are those of wrecked Churchill tanks hopelessly bogged down on the shingle with the bodies of dead Canadians strewn around. The raid was an unqualified disaster yet many lessons, vital to the subsequent success of D-Day, were learnt. It could be argued, though many would disagree, that the Canadians' terrible sacrifice was not wholly in vain.

Preparation

> Soldiers, Sailors and Airmen of the Allied Expeditionary Force! You are about to embark upon the Great Crusade, toward which we have striven these many months. The eyes of the world are upon you. The hopes and prayers of liberty-loving people everywhere march with you. In company with our brave Allies and brothers-in-arms on other Fronts, you will bring about the destruction of the German war machine, the elimination of Nazi tyranny over the oppressed peoples of Europe, and security for ourselves in a free world.
>
> Eisenhower's Order of the Day

Sergeant-Major William Brown, serving with 8 DLI, was one of the thousands who found the Commander-in-Chief a powerful and heartening presence:

> Eisenhower came to have a chat with everyone, he was great. The finest general there's ever been. We formed a whole square right round this great big field. And he walked into the middle of it and said, 'Right, gentlemen; when I give the signal, all come in and sit down. Never mind the officers; they'll walk in with the men. I want everyone to hear what I have to say.' That pleased everyone. There was no bullshit about him. He was immaculate; he could have been made from chocolate. He said he'd heard all about us down in Southampton, how we'd been living it up and now the time had come to get aboard ships and fight alongside each other. He did more to lift morale – certainly mine – than anything else.[3]

Not all of the Durhams enjoyed such cordial and uplifting relationships with our US allies – Sergeant George Self, also 8th Battalion, formed a rather different impression:

We moved to a camp near Romsey. We had battles with the Yanks nearly every night in Southampton. The main cause of this friction was money and their arrogant behaviour. Eisenhower came to see us and gave us a lecture about the American soldier. He agreed they were overpaid, oversexed and over here – but when we got over the other side, they would show us the road home – how to fight. That was the worst thing he could have said. That night blood flowed in Southampton.[4]

One of the Durhams preparing for the invasion was Lieutenant William Jalland, again of 8th Battalion:

I'd been on a sniping course at Llanberis, with instructors from the Lovat Scouts, Lord Lovat's private army![5] They were all ghillies and absolutely first class…Then we were moved down to Southampton prior to the invasion. I knew what we'd be doing, I'd taken part in exercises SMASH 1 & 2.[6] Well, we were open-mouthed at all the equipment; we saw part of PLUTO,[7] it was enormous, and sections of Mulberry,[8] there were crab, scorpion and flail tanks.[9] We knew we must be going, we weren't confined to base just at that point but soon we were. We finally embarked on an LCI,[10] had ramps on either side of the prow, it could accommodate the entire battalion. My company would be one of the first off and we carried loads of equipment: Ian English and his company were kitted out with bicycles, I had to carry a folding bike and extra magazines for the Bren guns. I had a plentiful supply of condoms, not for what you might think but for waterproofing grenades and other kit. Our loads were very heavy and we were given these enormous chest waders so we'd come ashore dry, in theory at least. I wore my pyjamas under battle dress, helped to prevent the wool from chafing – just as well – I didn't take mine off for 28 days as I recall![11]

Montgomery had replaced General Morgan, whose COSSAC[12] group had been planning the invasion, codenamed 'Overlord'. The amphibious landings would be supported by a vast naval armada, 'Neptune', and the enemy kept guessing by a brilliant deception plan, 'Fortitude'. American General Dwight Eisenhower would lead SHAEF.[13] Monty, in charge of land forces and abrasive as ever, wanted to expand the initial 30-mile landing zone to 50 and to commit five divisions rather than three as previously planned. British troops would land in the east on Sword beach, west of the Orne estuary, then Canadians on Juno and 50th Division at Gold. West of the British beaches, the Americans would land firstly on Omaha then Utah on the flank of the Cotentin Peninsula. Paratroops would precede both British/Canadian and American seaborne landings. In the British sector Red Devils would secure the vital Orne River and Canal crossings to be immortalised as Pegasus Bridge, the high ground by Ranville and eliminate the ostensibly formidable Merville Battery[14] overlooking Sword Beach.

Lieutenant Jalland remembers the embarkation process:

> When we went down to the harbour and embarked, it was too rough to sail that night; next day was 5 June and we had a visit from a group of dignitaries, VIPs, several cabinet ministers, Churchill himself, Attlee, Eden, Bevan and Herbert Morrison, Jan Smuts and Prince Bernard of the Netherlands, all there to see us off. Once on board we were told where we were going and we sailed past the Needles as it was getting dark. The sea was very rough and people were being sick everywhere. I started feeling queasy so I left my bunk and went up on deck; this wasn't really allowed but I found a corner and huddled down up top. We were a flotilla of three LCIs and a tiny minesweeper. An awful lot of aircraft were going over and there was clearly a great deal of bombing. Naval vessels were hooting to each other and the occasional MTB motored between us.'[15]

Sergeant William Brown was also on the LCI:

> They gave us these enormous gas trousers, they went on last over all of your kit, and we carried everything you could imagine – three days' rations, toilet paper, cigarettes, sweets and our damned folding bicycles. I went up on deck as we crossed the Channel. We seemed to be the only ones then, all of a sudden, as we rounded the Isle of Wight, there were thousands of ships, thousands of them. Downstairs, below decks, the smell was pretty horrible, vile in fact, and the chewing gum they gave you just made it worse; the spew bags were handy though and you just threw them over the side.[16]

Brown, a highly experienced NCO, was serving with Ian English:

> The 'O' – Orders Group involved all the officers and NCOs above
> the rank of corporal; Major English, Ian he was called, though he
> always got 'Pat', not sure why, asked me to sort out some tea so I
> went to find our cooks and orderlies in the bowels of the ship but
> they were too busy spewing up. I was looking for tea; the tins had
> no labels but the one I opened contained fat bacon! Well I retched
> and retched, I'd had nowt to eat really for a couple of days so I
> just retched! Now 'Pat' English was a hell of a soldier, the men
> had total confidence in him. He wasn't the smartest soldier in
> terms of turnout but he always needed to be in charge, I was sure
> he was after a VC![17]
>
> Once we were all on deck, even with these gas trousers on, it
> was easier, the air was warm but the ship was still rolling
> dreadfully. Next to us a rocket ship was blasting away, salvo
> after salvo, the recoil was juddering the ship, great bloody noise.
> The LCIs were coming in on Gold beach but we stuck quite a bit
> out, about 500 yards off, in fact – quite a swim. Major English said
> to me, 'Right, Sergeant-Major, lead the way.' 'Not bloody likely,'
> I replied, 'I'm not taking men into that depth of water.' The LCI
> captain said 'Right, we'll give it another go.' So he backed up and
> charged in again. This time we got to within 200 yards before we
> stuck, the prow of the ship digging in. 'Come on Sergeant-Major,'
> said Major English, 'Now's the time.' 'I'm still not taking men
> into that,' I replied. Just then a young US sailor offered to get a
> rope ashore, he stripped off down to his singlet and in he went,
> great lad he was. The rope was secured and we started going
> ashore, got everybody off OK, though the damned gas trousers
> immediately filled up with water. We couldn't hang around, had
> to get up that beach as quick as possible![18]

Gold beach

> Under the command of General Eisenhower, Allied naval
> forces, supported by strong air forces, began landing Allied
> armies this morning on the northern coast of France.
>
> SHAEF's Communique no. 1, broadcast by
> the BBC, 09.32, 6 June 1944

The sea at dawn is grey, sombre as metal,
With dull unburnished strength
The light expands till the horizon,
Once more defined, encircles our day.
In the tufted grass and the sea-pinks
Our rifles lie, clean, with bolts oiled,
Our pouches hard with rounds,
A metal world of rifle, sea and sky

Neil McCallum, 'Stand to' (1942)

At 07.00 hours on 6 June British I and 30 Corps came ashore on Sword and Gold beaches, General Crocker, commanding I Corps, was tasked to take Caen, and the British failure to seize this vital gateway on the first day would have serious consequences. Bucknall's 30 Corps, which included 50th Division, was to drive seven miles inland and liberate Bayeux. Within the initial and critical couple of hours some 30,000 soldiers, 300 guns and 700 armoured vehicles were landed, a magnificent achievement and, though the sands were soon choked with the mother of all logjams, exacerbated by a swelling tide, the British were firmly lodged. A bridgehead had been secured, albeit rather flimsy at this juncture. This was the moment and fulcrum of decision. None of the momentous events and titanic clashes beforehand could match this present contest in terms of overall strategic significance. These young Allied servicemen were in the prime of their youth, prepared, trained, readied, equipped and now to be tested. Seasickness, however, is no respecter of history, as Bill Jalland and most others were discovering:

They offered us breakfast but I didn't really want any, I had to lead the way down the starboard side ramp in my new battledress. The platoon was formed up and the prow of the ship gouged into the shingle. The LCIs were coming in with a series of tight circles, then peeling off as their turn to hit the beach came around, it worked like a charm. The US naval personnel lowered the ramps which crashed into the shingle. I was just to walk off and get up the beach asap. So I stepped off manfully and went straight to the bottom, the water was above my head! I was aware the prow of the boat was continually smashing into the shingle – I was afraid it would smash me. My waders were now completely full, I couldn't do a thing. I got rid of the folding bike, tore off my waders, unfastened webbing; thus I arrived on the shore of Fortress Europe, completely soaked, unarmed and on my hands and knees.[19]

This was perhaps not quite the form of heroic deliverance the Allies had in mind. Happily, some inter-Allied assistance was at hand:

Seeing me struggling a US sailor chucked me his tin hat, saying, 'Here you'll need this more than me,' which was a very nice gesture. Somebody threw a rope from the LCI – we'd not been able to get as far in as we had on exercises – but the line was secured and everybody got ashore without incident. As we went up the beach we saw frogmen dealing with the obstacles. I suppose they were from the Royal Engineers – I'd never seen frogmen before.[20]

Captain Eric Hooper, transport officer with 9th Battalion, was experiencing problems of his own:

As I was standing on top of the ramp, we hit a buried mine that exploded and blew the ramp up and made a hole in the sand. They'd issued us with oilskin trousers, which came right up to your chest, which you tied up with a string. When I got into the water, I couldn't touch the bottom and started to float. Air was trapped in the trousers and the bubble rose up to my chest and I became buoyant and I started turning over. Just then the waders burst and I sank back into the water.[21]

Another DLI officer recalled the scene on Gold beach:

Away to the east, about 800 yards from where our craft was due to beach, I could see a Sherman tank fitted with flails crashing its way through a minefield on a green slope just off the beach. What a Wellsian picture! It looked like a gigantic crab and as it crawled forward there was, every now and then, a burst of flame as it flailed a mine. Further to the right I could see orderly lines of men filing out of beached landing-craft and then converging into thicker lines as they made their pre-arranged beach exits. From that distance they resembled a nice, orderly football crowd until into their midst fell one or two mortar bombs and the resemblance ended. Yet the flow of men was in no way halted or dispersed. They looked, as indeed they were, inexorable and irresistible.[22]

Bill Jalland and his comrades passed up the beach unscathed:

As we moved inland there was, I remember, some shelling and the MO, Dr Thornton, was one of the first casualties; there was a fair bit of pandemonium but the beach, at this stage, wasn't all that crowded with supplies. We went in through La Riviere; we didn't pass much evidence of fighting, no knocked-out tanks or whatever, not much small arms either, though I know they had a rough time over at Le Hamel. There was some evidence of the heavy bombing and some houses had suffered damage. We had orders to keep moving, we had to reach Bayeux. We knew it wouldn't be long before heavy shelling started. Ian and his cyclists went off – it was harvest time, corn standing in the fields, we saw some German infantry moving in the distance but they didn't bother us and we didn't bother them![23]

Despite high drama the day was not entirely devoid of lighter touches:

Captain Phil Hampson rode along bareback on a horse he'd acquired and we took some prisoners; these were Russians and they came in yelling, 'Russki, Russki'. They had their hands high and, though some of the chaps viewed them just as traitors, none was actually shot. We treated them as POWs. They didn't seem to have any prepared positions. The landing had been very accurate and we could find our way around, we'd seen aerial photographs and could recognise landmarks, such as churches. Our job was to press on to Bayeux; we saw the odd enemy tank, they stalked us and we stalked them.[24]

Sergeant Brown was amongst the gallant throng of cyclists:

When we were at last off the beach, we met up in a 'hide' where we had a self-inflicted wound in 'D' Company. I heard a rifle shot. An old fellow of 40, a bundle of nerves, had shot himself in the hand. I said, 'You shot yourself, bastard!' He said, 'I'm sorry

Sergeant-Major. I can't go on.' 'It's alright,' I replied, 'Leave your rifle here and get yourself back. You've been hit in the hand.' I wasn't going to court martial him.'[25]

Lieutenant Jalland and his platoon had by now advanced some distance inland, though still a way short of Bayeux itself:

> As we dug in I was sent for by Battalion HQ, the Brigadier [Senior] had disappeared and we had to go and look for him. I took half a dozen men and bikes from Ian English's Company. The passwords were 'Bread' and 'Cheese'. Well, we searched copse after copse; every time we murmured 'Bread' and we got plenty 'Cheese' in reply, there was engineers, pioneers, all sorts mixed up but no sign of the Brigadier. He'd been ambushed, his signaller and driver killed, he was saved by the 'red' hat! Half a dozen Germans under a corporal held him. The men just wanted to kill him. The corporal wanted him kept alive (he spoke German) as anybody in a red hat was important and would have lots of important intelligence. Anyway, the Germans trussed him up but, at nightfall, he wriggled into a ditch; the Jerries panicked, ran and he escaped. We got no sleep and someone else took Bayeux.[26]

The bocage

> A phase without spectacle or glitter: in a week of difficult fighting which had yielded no great gains, measured in distance, the 50th Division had slowly ground the enemy into impotence. From becoming incapable of effective counter-attack he passed to the stage where he could no longer hold his line. And back he went, not in rout but carefully and steadily with the usual array of booby traps and mines in his wake. We followed pressing him.[27]

Montgomery, in his strategic plan, had envisaged the capture of Caen as a 6 June objective. This was not only too ambitious, it was seriously impractical. The strength of the German defensive posts at 'Hillman' and 'Morris' was underestimated and the attack stalled short of the city and its vital aerodrome. After the success of D-Day, the campaign of bitter attrition which followed caused mounting frustration, both with politicians and Monty's fellow commanders. His personality was not one which would be likely to endear. He would always maintain the battle unfolded entirely according to plan and that the British and Canadians drew on to themselves German reserves, thus permitting the Americans to build up and finally break out in the west. In the event, this is precisely what occurred but it was not the textbook fight Monty chose to describe. A series of British tactical initiatives to break the deadlock around and west of Caen generally foundered. For Bill Jalland and others, fighting in the close country of the 'bocage' became a dreadful, sapping ordeal:

> We were to attack a place called St. Pierre in the 'bocage' country. I was briefed by Tommy Clapton, the company commander. He said this was a 'little trip' – the place was defended only by cadets armed with pistols and maybe 'the odd tank or armoured car or two'. I was a little bit sceptical, especially as we had a full tank brigade in support. The 'cadets' of course were the Hitler Youth supported by panzers. We were attacking the join between 10th SS and Panzer Lehr, all crack troops. We rode forward over ploughed fields on the hulls of the tanks. Some of the chaps with bikes who couldn't keep up would just stick their bikes under the treads so they were crushed and then clamber up! The bikes were a waste of time really. We leaguered up at Point 103, the village was maybe one-and-a-half miles away over open fields down a gentle slope. We went in with two companies forward and two in reserve. I was with my platoon towards the rear, on the east side I think. The road was lined with poplars I recall.[28] English and Leybourne were commanding the forward companies, Chris Beatty the other with us.[29]

Sergeant Brown had also found the bikes more of a hindrance and had taken similar action:

> Cycling at marching pace was pretty hard work. So when we stopped, I attracted the attention of a passing tank commander and asked him to do me a favour. 'What do you want?' he asked. 'Run over them bloody bikes with your tracks,' I said. 'Run them over?' he said. 'Aye,' I said, so he just ran them over. And then I said to my officer 'The bikes have gone, sir!' 'The bikes have gone?' 'Aye, the bloody tanks have run them over,' and he said, 'Oh well, if you haven't got a bike, you haven't got a bike.'[30]

Bill Jalland and 8th Battalion were soon struck by a strong counter-attack:

> Next morning we were subjected to heavy shelling and mortaring, fire was coming from enemy tanks, rounds bursting in the trees and showering us with shrapnel. We pulled out of the village but the two forward companies had some sections overrun. Sergeant Wallbank took on a tank coming down the main street and halted it, blew off a track. Johnnie Wheatley, an old friend, was killed there by blast, not a mark on his body; we suffered horrible casualties. We fell back to the edge of the village but it was all open country behind us, a perfect killing zone, we had no choice but to stand.[31]

A crisis point had now arrived. The adjutant [Johnnie Walker] was in charge; we had a rather odd collection of people, cooks, stretcher-bearers and all sorts; the RSM was dropping off boxes of ammo and Johnnie told us to stay quiet till the Germans appeared. Their infantry started infiltrating through the village, jumping over walls and coming through the gardens, moving very quickly. We waited till we got the order then opened up on them with rapid fire – they were no more than 50 yards away. I saw 40 to 50 of them coming at us, well equipped, fully cammo'd up with nets etc. At some point one of their tanks was amongst us, I recall. Now, our tanks came forward from Point 103; they charged just like the US cavalry but they were butchered by 88s knocking them out like Aunt Sallies – the sky was full of dense black smoke when they 'brewed up'. We lost heavily. We never heard from our own guns, too far out on a limb I suppose.'[32]

The fight was by no means over:

> Most of the tank crews escaped and some of them got mixed up with us, they carried their revolvers strapped low around the leg. That afternoon we were attacked by German tanks, perhaps three or four only on the eastern flanks, not nearly as numerous as our Shermans. Ian English was marvellously heroic, he and a sergeant tried to manhandle a six-pounder anti-tank gun into action; he wasn't a gunner of course, not sure if he succeeded. We were ordered to pull out the next night, back to Point 103 then back to Bayeux where we rested up in a field and slept for most of the next day.[33]

And now they would find themselves in the heart of the bocage:

> After a few days out of the line we were ordered up again towards
> Villars-en-Bocage.[34] It was strange country, unlike anything we'd
> encountered before, ideal for the defensive. Pocket-handkerchief-
> sized fields, as small as 50 yards across, very high banks topped
> with dense hedges; the fighting was at very close quarters with
> the enemy no more than grenade-throwing distance. We and the
> Germans sited our Brens and their MGs to provide enfilade fire;
> they tended not to use their tanks at night but theirs were fitted
> with rubber treads which sometimes made them very difficult to
> hear. They had a tank leaguer in the Chateau de Cordillon near
> us, featured in Dumas' *Three Musketeers* I recall. Sometimes they
> would bring one up, using the cover of those high banks, get to
> about 50 yards from us unheard, then open up with their cannon
> and machine-guns, gave us a real fright![35]

This fighting in the dense Norman bocage left a vivid and searing
memory with all who experienced it. The country was narrow and
enclosed. Overwhelming Allied advantages in weight of guns and
armour were nullified by the ground, ideal for the defence, and the
Allies were up against a ruthless, experienced and highly skilled
enemy whose years of murderous fighting in the East had taught
him much. Some, indeed many, of the Allied soldiers were raw,
their baptism a harsh and bloody one. Not untypical was 6 DLI's
experience when attacking towards the Hottot–Juvigny road. The
advance, on 14 July, made some ground but was halted by intense
MG fire from well-dug enemy positions. Despite a furious barrage,
it required five hours of costly attrition to win the ground.[36] The 9th
Battalion met with similar dogged resistance in its projected advance
on Lingevres. A recce carried out by 'B' Company the day before
had resulted in the loss of every single officer.[37] The Germans held a
belt of dense woodland directly astride the line of advance. As ever,
the attack was heralded by a ripping barrage and hurricane of
rockets from 25-pounders and Typhoons:

> The wood literally danced in front of our eyes, and not 300 yards
> away. The Typhoons each did one dive and released two bombs
> and 10 rockets, straddling and plastering the wood…For what
> seemed a long time nothing happened, and then an enemy tank

in the left-hand corner of the wood fired and set on fire one of our Shermans. The fire was returned with good effect by the remaining two. Another Hun tank opened up from the right-hand of the wood, and then the wood came to life. Our leading troops were now in the middle of the stubble and were caught there by a withering fire from Spandaus (MG34/42) and snipers; but they still kept going. A dash and we were in the wood; but the Hun had his plentiful Spandaus sited well back inside the edge of it.[38]

The Germans dubbed the battle for Normandy as a *Materielschlacht* – attrition. The Allies had massive superiority in firepower and in overall numbers. The quality of certain Allied units was heavily criticised by the Axis and by ourselves. Equally, many of their units were low-grade ersatz formations made up of renegades from the Eastern Front and even some Indian Army deserters left over from the Desert War. Their veteran and Hitler Youth units fought superbly and exacted a high toll for every yard of ground won. Their tanks – Mark IV, V (Panther) and VI (Tiger) – if less plentiful, were infinitely better in qualitative terms, and their commanders, 'aces' like Michael Wittman,[39] were experienced and daring. Allied armoured units might expect to lose, say, five or six Shermans for every panzer knocked out.

Like most engaged in this fighting, Lieutenant Jalland and his platoon, immured in the close and deadly ground of the bocage, saw only what occurred in their immediate sector. That was bad enough:

My chaps spotted an armoured car or what looked like an armoured car; it was quite a way away, difficult to get messages back as the wretched radios were so unreliable, we had to send runners. We did have a six-pounder with us but the sergeant wasn't prepared to shoot as he felt the gun was too exposed. Suddenly someone yelled, 'It's coming!' It came down the lane, its turret traversing; we thought we'd have to get behind it to stop it but suddenly a loud bang and it stopped dead, Hawke's grenades had blown a track off. It was a Tiger after all! The crew thought it was going to catch fire so they baled out and pelted along the hedge fronting our line. Some of our chaps thought it was an attack and got up running ahead of them but then others came out chasing the Germans, we had quite a race! Still, we captured them and were rather pleased at having knocked out a Tiger. We had a pioneer officer, a Lieutenant Pugh, he thought we should set the tank on fire and he duly did; it created a dense column of smoke. The Germans must have thought we were about to attack, subjected us to a massive barrage that seemed to go on for ages – Lieutenant Pugh wasn't very popular![40]

Some of the more esoteric Allied innovations were not necessarily welcomed by the infantry:

We did get visits from our psychological warfare people, they used loudspeakers and microphones, we didn't think much of them and, as soon as they started, Jerry opened up with shells and mortars. We did approve of 'artificial moonlight' though. We shone searchlights from behind which reflected off the clouds above Jerry, illuminated the whole area to our front and blinded him just about completely, almost like theatre footlights! We always had good support from 74 Field Artillery; we'd known them for years, of course, but they'd lay down a barrage anywhere, really plaster the place. The same went for the Cheshires who gave us support with their Vickers HMGs. The 2nd Tactical Air Force kept Typhoons in the air, like a taxi rank, we had an air link and could call them down. They'd peel off and were so accurate they could target an individual enemy tank with rockets. We carried fluorescent panels in our battledress which we could spread out to mark our own positions.[41]

Though bogged in the close ground, this deadly attritional warfare was never completely static:

Both sides patrolled. I went out many times towards Park de la Mer and Hottot, never actually got into the place but did tread on a trip wire once; thankfully it was only tied to a flare. We did get into the grounds of the chateau through a hole in the wall, Jerry was using it as a tank repair workshop. We were in the same location for several weeks and Jerry patrols would get as near as the hedge, we could have touched them, we could smell them – German officers always seemed to wear eau de cologne, they smelt different to us. There was lots of sniping, from both sides; I remember one of our chaps came through saying he'd just shot someone on the lavatory, caused great amusement. Another shot some Germans, queuing for food, it really wasn't very pleasant.[42]

We both used mines, though the positions, slit trenches mainly, weren't wired; the Germans made a form of mine out of packets of gun cotton and a detonator, very nasty. We dug our trenches into the bankside and bored through like loopholes for firing; Jerry did the same but he always ensured he had a groundsheet over the rear of the trenches he dug so you couldn't see through the aperture and shoot. A Captain Myers, who'd been to battle school, decided MG positions could be stormed frontally with the bayonet. So we laid down smoke and covering fire from the Brens, ridiculous idea, he was badly wounded as were several men with him. We used captured German panzerfausts[43] and they were very effective as well. Most of the time they were very close and we shouted at each other, pretty ribald as you can imagine. We did maintain our sense of humour – I remember the platoon next to mine was being heavily mortared; after a long time Jerry stopped firing and we imagined they were adjusting the range to mortar us. A corporal jumped up and in broad Geordie shouted to Jerry, Same range, same target![44]

Even at local level, tactical initiatives could come unstuck through poor planning, faulty or non-existent scouting:

We were attacking Hottot and 213 Brigade were putting in the attack but the last five minutes of the bombardment was directly on our positions and we were suddenly overrun by wild Devons, Dorsets and Hampshires. Had they troubled to do a preliminary recce this would never have happened. We got on well with them, of course, but it was still a complete cock-up! We'd been in the bocage for weeks now, we didn't get much information, there was a real lack of communication, we used to hear snippets from various officers in the support or carrier platoons. Finally 6 DLI passed through us during a big attack on Villars-en-Bocage. We later motored through what was left in lorries, we were now to be fully motorised; the place was flattened, nothing above six feet was left standing; both 6 DLI and the Hampshires caught a packet.[45]

Breakout

> Call from Monty, 7pm, the Germans are surrendering,
> North and West Germany, Holland, Denmark and Norway
> – the news of the surrender was announced at 8pm on the
> BBC.
>
> Eisenhower, diary entry, 4 May 1945

That process which led to the final capitulation of Germany began as the Axis position in Normandy began to collapse. Intentional or accidental, Montgomery's battle of attrition in the eastern sector facilitated Operation 'Cobra',[46] the US breakout in the west. The Wehrmacht simply did not have sufficient available resources to counter both. In the East, a great Soviet offensive, 'Bagration',[47] was threatening to, and did, smash Army Group Centre, a blow from which Hitler's forces could never fully recover. On 20 July, a group of army officers had attempted to remove the Führer with a bomb placed in the conference room at Rastenburg, his East Prussian HQ. 'Valkyrie' was a failure with dire consequences for the plotters, including Erwin Rommel, whose legendary career ended with self-administered poison. Hitler's suspicions over the loyalty of his officer elite multiplied as Axis fortunes waned inexorably. His orders in the West to hold ground regardless and fritter away scarce reserves in pointless counter-attacks contributed substantially to the ruin of his forces there which, in August, found themselves hemmed into what became known as the Falaise 'Pocket'. What transpired there was a Norse Ragnarok of epic proportions as the might of Allied firepower winnowed the fleeing Wehrmacht, burdened with its accumulated loot.

Bill Jalland takes up the story of the fight as the Allied pressure finally began to tell:

We attacked Mt. Pincon supported by tanks, a set-piece battle, brilliantly executed though I don't remember much detail, lost in the fog of war, we did take some casualties. I remember strong opposition and the enemy were firing a big naval gun from some distance, great huge shells, you could hear them coming, sounded like a kitbag turning over and over, you had time to get into a trench or some other form of cover. After that battle we were fully motorised and we crossed the Falaise Pocket over to the northern flank. We were appalled, the German columns had been completely destroyed, a carpet of dead men and horses, the Typhoons and artillery had been dreadfully effective. We also came across dead Germans hanging in an orchard – they'd been lynching their own deserters, first time we'd seen that, the SS were responsible – the dead men were just a few inches above the ground, all swaying in the breeze. We had no time to stop so we left them, pushed on. We'd not much time for deserters, our own ran the risk of being shot. It's one thing when people get bomb happy, you can understand that, I've seen people sitting helpless in trenches and crying for days, that happens, but those who just run away, well you just had to stick it out regardless, we had a job to do.[48]

The Falaise Pocket was truly a scene from the Apocalypse; a modern parallel would be the wrack of Saddam Hussein's army annihilated as they streamed out of Kuwait during the denouement of the first Gulf War:

The Germans moved along the roads till they were choked with dead horses and men and burning wreckage. Then they took to the fields, across which they moved in columns of five or six abreast. At bottlenecks such as gateways and stream crossing-places, the traffic piled up and was then destroyed by shells and rocket-firing planes. Swiftly destruction would spread across the entire field, until it was impossible for anything on wheels or tracks to move across it. In a day or two many fields became like the roads – simply impassable owing to the carnage and destruction. It was a battlefield that decided the fate of France.[49]

This was the shattered wake of a defeated army, a cause irrevocably lost:

Both sides and often the middle of the roads were jammed with wrecked lorries, guns, horses and tanks; dead men and horses lay about in grotesque attitudes, and here and there a truck or gun limber, which had been set on fire and was still smouldering. Abandoned staff cars and many other vehicles were packed with loot: field glasses, typewriters, pistols and small arms by the hundred, cases of wine and boxes of ladies' clothing. Many of the vehicles were untouched and could have been driven away, but no one had the time.[50]

Paris was now about to be liberated as the Germans, those who'd fought so hard and bled so freely in Normandy, appeared to collapse. It almost seemed as though the war in the West might even be ending:

> We reached Vernon on the Seine and Archie Bark, the IO, and I went forward in a jeep, his I think. Paris was literally just down the road and we could even get a glimpse of the Eiffel Tower. We thought we'd be the ones to liberate Paris but it had to be done by De Gaulle and the Free French. We were held back but the Parisian resistance rose against the Germans and were dealt with very harshly, perhaps it was Archie and I who started the excitement! We were sent on towards Arras and Amiens, the V1s[51] and V2s[52] were creating havoc in the south of England. We went back along the route the battalion had retreated over in 1940, on the way to Dunkirk. Every town and village we passed through was lined with flags and the people pressed us with flowers and wine, they made us feel like heroes.[53]

Increasingly, and whilst there were many vicious and sudden skirmishes ahead, the advance was turning into a victory march:

> All this while we met very little resistance and we were taking a fair number of prisoners – not the quality of troops we'd met in Normandy, older men and young boys of 15 or 16, they were demoralised and pretty confused, generally would not stand. Though we were following the Dunkirk route, most of those in the battalion now were still at school in 1940, our officers were virtually all under 25. Then, one village we went into we found the people had stored all of the battalion's musical instruments, abandoned by the bandsmen in 1940. Everyone had saved and cherished one of these, kept them clean and polished. There was a handing-over ceremony, quite emotional except none of the chaps now could play and as not all the replacements were light infantry and could do the quick march, the guard of honour was a right shambles![54]
>
> We were driving east going hell-for-leather; you could see the

V1 and V2 trails in the sky and we even drove in two columns on each side of the highway, there was no civilian traffic and you weren't likely to meet anyone coming the other way. We were in three-tonners plus a whole selection of captured German vehicles, trucks, half-tracks and VW cars. We looked so Germanised an entire field battery of 88s followed us, thinking we were all Germans retreating; they followed us all day and at night we took them prisoner, they didn't see the funny side at all.[55]

One of the major difficulties the Allies encountered was that of resupply, particularly of fuel. Despite success in Normandy, they had yet to capture a functioning deep-water harbour; Cherbourg was still being cleared. By September these mounting difficulties and the speed of German recovery under Von Runstedt[56] would greatly slow the advance, which would bog down in the Low Countries. This did not, however, impede 151 Brigade's wild career across northern France:

We were kept supplied with fuel, coming in through PLUTO, and we got ours either in jerry-cans or disposable tins; you just created a hole in the top, poured in the fuel and threw it away. Even when we stopped at night we didn't set up a full tactical perimeter, there was some probing but nothing serious, we didn't find any of the usual mines or booby traps. Our morale was very high, bolstered by the reception we got from the civilian population. We saw how the French dealt with their own collaborators – girls were whipped or had their heads shaven in the squares; our chaps had very little sympathy for them and it was their business anyway. We did encounter groups of the Resistance, they had Sten guns dropped by the RAF and were always asking if we had spare 9mm ammunition but we needed all of ours. Occasionally we'd run into ambushes and there was some shelling and mortaring, mainly just isolated groups trying to escape eastwards.[57]

Sergeant Tom Myers from 6 DLI and his comrades were doing their bit to accommodate French civilians:

We got in about seven at night with no sign of Germans, so we went into a café and had a beer and got talking to two pretty girls. The barman said to me in broken English, 'They've been collaborating with the Germans.' I said, 'They can collaborate with whoever they want – I'm going to have that blonde tonight,' and my mate said, 'I'll have the other one.' We spent 24 hours there and then it became a mad rush. Jerry had started his real pull-out and it was on the trucks and away.[58]

The Durhams were not yet out into those broad, sunlit uplands Churchill had earlier promised. The formidable obstacle of the Albert Canal remained, as Bill Brown discovered:

…we were about to have three days' rest when we were ordered to cross the Albert Canal that night. Assault boats were there to meet us. These were collapsible wood and canvas boats and heavy to carry down the bank. We could see boats sinking and blokes getting shot by German machine-guns. Later, I was standing, talking to a section commander in a sunken road, when the enemy opened up with a machine-gun. It looked like flashing lights going past me. I fell into the sunken road. About three men were killed and my guts were oozing out. I said to a young officer, 'Give us your hand. Grip it as tight as you can.' He took my hand. I was conscious all the time; I thought, 'If I lose consciousness, I will die.' Stretcher-bearers came and they put about four field dressings on me and carried me down the road. The German machine-guns could have opened up on us but they didn't.[59]

For Bill Brown his wound was definitely a 'Blighty' one.

Though the terrible battle for Normandy had ended in a resounding Allied victory, both key and decisive, the war was far from over. Pressure upon the Allied coalition was growing, partly due to supply difficulties and partly due to Montgomery's general boorishness. If Eisenhower was not a general of the first rank, he was a constant diplomat whose intemperate subordinate taxed his capacities to the very limit and increasingly beyond. Antwerp had been liberated but was not yet usable, the Scheldt Estuary remaining uncleared. Monty came up with his masterstroke to end the war with a single massive thrust aimed at Germany's industrial heartland, the Ruhr. Operation 'Market Garden' was breathtakingly audacious and ultimately seriously flawed.

For the Durhams of 151 Brigade, they would have their hour.

They might have been denied Paris but they would have the honour of entering Brussels: 'We were moved north to take part in the liberation of Brussels, led by Guards Armoured Division, we went in on the back of their tanks. I'll never forget our reception, every building was bedecked, thousands of people waving, laughing and singing, it was a very emotional experience, we were very conscious these people regarded us as their personal liberators and personal heroes.'[60] Nobody could deny the men of Durham had more than done their bit.

Notes

1   D'Este, C., *Decision in Normandy* (Connecticut, 1983), p.71.
2   The Durham men had fought before on this vigil, against the Scots at Otterburn in 1388!
3   DLI Sound Recording Project.
4   Ibid.
5   Formed as a Highland Yeomanry regiment in the 2nd Boer War (1899–1902), the Lovat Scouts were the first designated British sniper unit after 1916.
6   D-Day rehearsals.
7   'Petrol Line under the Ocean'.
8   Mulberry was the British artificial harbour designed to overcome difficulties resulting from the Allies' inability to secure a deep-water harbour at the outset – the Germans were fixated on the idea this must be a prime strategic objective.
9   General Percy ('Hobo') Hobart's 'Funnies' saved thousands of Allied lives. The designs included the mine-clearing Sherman (flail), the flamethrower (Crocodile), bunker-buster (Petard) and swimming D-D tank.
10 These amphibious assault ships were a response to the failure of wooden Landing Craft Assault at Dieppe.
11 DLI Sound Recording Project.
12 Chief of Staff, Supreme Allied Commander.
13 Supreme Headquarters Allied Expeditionary Force.
14 Lieutenant-Colonel Terence Otway and his paras, despite a disastrous and scattered drop, stormed the battery, though the ordnance within was less formidable than feared.
15 DLI Sound Recording Project.
16 Ibid.
17 Ibid.
18 Ibid.
19 Ibid.
20 Ibid.
21 Ibid.
22 Rissik, D., *The DLI at War – History of the DLI 1939–1945* (Durham, 1952), p.241.
23 DLI Sound Recording Project.
24 Ibid.
25 Ibid.
26 Ibid.
27 Tout, K., *The Bloody Battle for Tilly* (Stroud, 2000), p.205.
28 These still remain.

29   DLI Sound Recording Project.
30   Ibid.
31   Ibid.
32   Ibid.
33   Ibid.
34   Villars-en-Bocage, scene of a traumatic British defeat; see note on Michael Wittman below.
35   DLI Sound Recording Project.
36   Rissik, p.246.
37   Ibid.
38   Ibid. pp.246–7.
39   Michael Wittman (1914–44) SS Hauptsturmführer (Captain), leading panzer ace with 168 kills; some mystery surrounds his death in action in Normandy on 8 August.
40   DLI Sound Recording Project.
41   Ibid.
42   Ibid.
43   Panzerfaust ('armour fist' or 'tank fist'): a cheap, effective, hand-held, recoilless German anti-tank weapon.
44   DLI Sound Recording Project.
45   Ibid.
46   'Cobra' on 25–26 July heralded the successful US breakout from the west.
47   'Bagration' launched on 22 June, three years to the day since the Germans invaded Russia.
48   DLI Sound Recording Project.
49   Quoted in Rissik, p.253.
50   Lewis, P.J., & English, I.R., *Into Battle with the Durhams: 8 DLI in World War II* (London, 1990), pp.272–3.
51   V1 Rocket: the flying bomb, commonly known as a 'doodlebug'; these were spreading terror in south-east England.
52   V2 Rocket: one of Hitler's 'super' weapons, its arrival caused consternation in England, though it was less effective than feared – the need to eliminate launch sites in France spurred the Allied advance. The perceived need to do likewise in the Low Countries was a spur to 'Market Garden'.
53   Jalland, DLI Sound Recording Project
54   Ibid.
55   Ibid.
56   Runstedt managed to stabilise the German position in the West – the Miracle in the West.
57   DLI Sound Recording Project
58   Ibid.
59   Ibid.
60   Jalland, ibid.

Chapter 10

Germany: the Liberation of Belsen, 1945

Here over an acre of ground lay dead and dying people.
You could not see which was which…The living lay with
their heads against the corpses and around them moved
the awful, ghastly procession of emaciated, aimless people,
with nothing to do and no hope of life, unable to move out
of your way, unable to look at the terrible sights around
them…Babies had been born here, tiny, wizened things
that could not live…A mother, driven mad, screamed at a
British sentry to give her milk for her child and thrust the
tiny mite into his arms, then ran off crying terribly. He
opened the bundle and found the baby had been dead for
days.

Richard Dimbleby (BBC), 1945

Millions of words have been written about these horror
camps, many of them by inmates of those unbelievable
places. I've tried, without success, to describe it from my
own point of view but the words won't come. To me Belsen
was the ultimate blasphemy.

Michael Bentine, 1945

113 LAA[1] Battalion RA was originally 7th Battalion DLI and had,
until 1936, formed part of 50th Northumbrian Division. In that year
it converted to an anti-aircraft searchlight formation – 47th (DLI)
AA Battalion RE (TA). On the outbreak of war the battalion was
transferred to the Royal Artillery and remained on home defence
until 1 January 1942.[2] It was at this point that it was again converted
from searchlights to an anti-aircraft role. Despite intensive training

in the south-west in anticipation of a deployment in North Africa, yet more training followed, preparatory to a role in the invasion of Europe. By the latter part of July 1944, the regiment was fully deployed in Normandy, where it found itself fighting as infantry in the hard slog towards Falaise.

It was not until the closing days of August that the weary Durhams reverted to the role they'd been trained for and took part in the hectic pursuit of the retreating Germans as they pelted towards the Belgian border. Having crossed the Seine and the Somme without contact, it was not until the early autumn that the Durhams again came into action in front of Nijmegen. Though the end might appear to be in sight, the work was still both dangerous and uncomfortable: 'At six o'clock it was getting dark, so we decided to dig in for the night. We dug down, about a foot, when we hit water. The deeper we went, the more water poured into the hole. We decided to fill the trench with branches so we could stand on them to try and keep ourselves dry. A major came along and made us dig deeper so we had to spend the night up to our behinds in water.'

For 113 LAA Regiment the greatest test promised to be the crossing of the Rhine, a major and likely very costly offensive, the British Army's last great battle in the West. They fought as field artillery, firing their Bofors[3] across the smoke-shrouded water of this last and greatest frontier, the gateway to the Reich. First to cross were the paratroops; 'When the Dakotas started to come back, some of them were on fire...' The fight proved less protracted than anticipated, a superb feat of arms complemented by brilliant engineering. Pressing on into Germany the regiment concentrated east of the river at Haldern. Resistance was sporadic but savage; 'on good days they sent in the rocket-firing Typhoons'. Here they were on 48-hour standby. When the order came to move it was to a place relatively far to the east and which nobody had ever heard of: a camp called Belsen. 113 Regiment was about to face its greatest trial and be pitched into a desperate race to save thousands of lives.

Bergen-Belsen was established initially as a prisoner-of-war camp (Stalag X1-C) in 1940 and intended to hold French and Belgian captives. By the spring of 1942 some 16,000 of these had succumbed to cold, privation and disease. In that year the place was redesignated as a concentration camp.[4] From April 1943 it was placed under SS jurisdiction. Here, Jews were herded as potential exchanges for

German nationals interned by the Allies. A year later, SS Hauptsturmführer Josef Kramer, whose previous posting had been Auschwitz-Birkenau, assumed command of Belsen, now designated as an *Erhollungslager* or 'recovery' camp. The notion was that those too ill to work could recuperate and then be returned to hard labour. As late as December 1944 the population of the camp was still below 16,000 but, as the relentless Soviet advance in the East ground on, thousands of victims from the camps there were force-marched westwards into Belsen. The population swelled prodigiously; facilities to accommodate them did not.[5]

At Haldern it was first assumed that the map reference supplied was incorrect (of course it was not) as the location given was some 250 miles to the east, into enemy-held territory. Captain Andrew Pares of 113 Regiment later collated his own and comrades' experiences of what followed: 'On 12 April 1945, following the breakthrough of Second Army after the Rhine crossing, the German military commander of Bergen-Belsen (Chief of Staff 1 Para Army) approached 8 Corps with a view to negotiating a truce and avoiding a battle in the area of Belsen concentration camp.'[6]

The truce

In terms of available intelligence the situation at Belsen was that the camp presently contained 50,000-plus 'internees' with 800 German troops, rather more than twice that number of Hungarian auxiliaries with their dependants and the remaining SS guards. There was neither power nor water and diseases, particularly typhus, typhoid, tuberculosis and gastro-enteritis, were rampant. Some quarter of a mile north of the main camp stood a tank training area with substantial barracks and ancillary buildings, a small POW camp with perhaps a further 800 Soviet survivors, and a military hospital.

The German military authorities were to erect notices and white flags at all the road entrances, marked 'Danger – Typhus' on one side and 'End of Typhus Area' on the reverse, with a disarmed German post at each notice. German and Hungarian troops would remain at their posts armed, wearing a white arm-band on the left sleeve. The Hungarians would remain indefinitely and were placed at the disposal of the British for such duties as might be required. The Wehrmacht were to be released within six days and conveyed back to the German lines with their arms, equipment and vehicles. SS Guard personnel were to be removed by 12.00 hours, 13 April and any remaining to be treated as POWs. SS Admin personnel would (if the Wehrmacht could prevent them running away) remain at their posts, carry on with their duties, and hand over records. When their services could be dispensed with, their disposal was left by the Wehrmacht to the British authorities, i.e. the Wehrmacht 'sold' the SS.[7]

These seemingly civilised, almost chivalric, rules for the handover of the camp did not prepare the British for the scenes that would confront them. Not one of the men of 112 Regiment who came upon Belsen would emerge unchanged. These were men who had experienced the full horrors of war since landing in France the previous summer. Belsen, however, manifested an unspeakable darkness and level of human cruelty undreamt of. 'It is unbelievable. There is no organisation, no food, nothing. Half-starved, emaciated, spiritless, demented, these people roaming the camp have been reduced to animal level...I have seen some sights, I thought I could take anything – but this "shook" me, made me want to vomit.'[8]

Impossible to describe was the smell, a miasma of terrible portent which clung to the air like a shroud, spreading far beyond the confines of the camp to poison the approaches. Perhaps only those who had served on the Western Front in the previous conflict would recognise the ghastly, cloying odour and all that it heralded:

> There were about 10,000 typhus-infected bodies, mostly naked and many in an advanced stage of decomposition, lying around the camp, both inside and outside the huts, which required immediate burial; and the daily death rate was 400/500...The living conditions were appalling – people were sleeping three in a bed, mainly treble-bunk beds, and huts which would normally accommodate 60 were housing 600. There were no sanitary arrangements and both inside and outside the huts was an almost continuous carpet of dead bodies, human excreta, rags and filth.[9]

One of the Jewish chaplains from British 8 Corps, struggling to come to terms with the horror, witnessed something similar in the British soldiers' reactions:

... And then, [the soldiers were humping sacks of potatoes] almost as though they had emerged from the ground itself...a number of wraithlike creatures came tottering towards us. As they drew closer they made frantic efforts to quicken their feeble pace. Their skeleton arms and legs made jerky, grotesque movements as they forced themselves forward. Their bodies, from their heads to their feet, looked like matchsticks. The two Tommies, entering the camp for the first time, must have thought they had walked into a supernatural world...they dropped their heavy sacks and fled.[10]

One question which immediately emerges is how the British were so unprepared, given that the Allies had for some years been aware of what was occurring in the camps. Anthony Eden, speaking in the Commons on 17 December 1942, had condemned the genocide of European Jewry (the intelligence came mainly from Polish sources). 'The able-bodied are slowly worked to death in labour camps. The infirm are left to die of exposure and starvation or are deliberately massacred in mass executions.' This news was greeted with widespread revulsion and members stood for a moment's silence.

Later writers have detected some element of sham, even of theatre. The revulsion felt was no doubt genuine, but did not stimulate any policy aimed at alleviating the suffering of victims. Put quite simply, the British did not perceive the killing of Jews as 'their' problem; it was viewed as a European situation and not subject to action or control from Whitehall. To be fair, there was little the British government could achieve in the short term. Montgomery's victory in the Western Desert was only a month old and if the tide of endless defeats was turning, it was a very slow and uncertain process. Britain stood with her back against the wall and the American entry had yet to have a decisive influence. Eden may well have been fearful that, had representations been made, Hitler might simply deport his Jewish captives to Britain. There is some suggestion that Eden was actively anti-Semitic. A junior minister wrote to him in March 1943, 'I am sorry to bother you about the Jews...I know what a bore this is.' The US was largely complicit in this inaction; a conference to debate the refugee problem was convened in the pleasant climate of Bermuda in April 1943 but nothing concrete resulted. Most Jewish commentators felt the conference to be mere lip service. Dr Harold S. Dodds, a relatively low-ranking member of the administration, represented the US, and the American Committee for a Zionist Army went so far as to take out an advertisement in the *New York Times* to condemn the perceived mockery.

Bergen-Belsen was on the radar of the Foreign Office's Refugees Department in summer 1944, after the D-Day landings. A picture of the camp was systematically built up utilising a number of sources. It is thought that the full state of the camp and those inside was becoming apparent to the Foreign Office by the end of March 1945, yet details of the exact location remained vague (hence the rather vague map reference). Some weeks before the truce, then, the British were aware of much of what was occurring, at least in general terms. None of this intelligence resulted in the formation of any kind of plan for dealing with the camp and its inmates. The fog of war, the impetus of the Allied advance and the lack of knowledge as to the exact location all contributed, but the conclusion remains that the problem of the refugees did not merit any degree of priority.

The camp

> I found a girl – she was a living skeleton – impossible to gauge her age, for she had practically no hair left on her head and her face was only a yellow parchment sheet with two holes left in it for eyes. She was stretching out her stick of an arm and gasping something. It was 'Englisch – Englisch – medicine – medicine,' and she was trying to cry but she had not enough strength.[11]

Though Belsen was not designated as a death camp, a ticket there was strictly one-way: 'In the other concentration camps it was openly stated by their Commandants that anyone who went to Belsen would not come back; amongst their inmates a transport to Belsen was regarded as the last journey.'[12] There was no gas chamber – 'starvation, disease, and physical degradation were the lethal weapons employed at Belsen'. Merciless violence from the male and female SS guards was commonplace.

By the time the first stirrings of spring were felt in 1945, the camp was descending into anarchy.

> Until about March the dead had been cremated but during this month the mortality rate rose sharply and the crematorium could

no longer cope. The dead were then gathered into piles and burned in the open but this was discontinued when military personnel in [the nearby] barracks objected to the smell. Large pits were then bulldozed out and the dead were dragged to them for burial...But as the death rate and the physical incapacity of the internees increased, and this was most marked in the women's laager, the dead were simply dragged as far away from the huts as possible and dumped; as exhaustion increased, the distance the corpses were dragged diminished and the piles around the huts grew.[13]

'The following are some of the facts which are corroborated by many witnesses: The daily diet in a Concentration Camp was 3 pints of swede soup and 200/250 grammes of black bread. Each day at 03.00 hours roll-call was held, regularly lasting for 4/5 hours and often longer. Those able to stand were forced to drag out the sick and the dying. In Feb, Mar & Apr 1945 numerous cases of cannibalism of dead bodies are vouched for by many witnesses. SS men and women guards beat and flogged the internees persistently at the slightest provocation. Most cases reported were for petty theft of food from cookhouses, or for failure to carry out quick enough the heavy tasks ordered. Similarly indiscriminate shooting of prisoners was a normal occurrence. Beside the entrance to the Crematorium was a pile of boots removed from the bodies before incineration; it stood 12 ft high and covered an area 36 ft x 18 ft, and must have been composed of hundreds of thousand pairs.[14]

Belsen was at once both an atrocity and a humanitarian disaster. When 113 Regiment entered the camp around half of the inmates were already ill and required immediate hospitalisation; none had received food for a week. Retribution, the administration of justice against perpetrators, was now a secondary concern, medical aid and food were priorities:

There were some 50,000 persons to supply and feed, but the cooking facilities were completely inadequate. There were five cookhouses of varying size equipped with a number of large boilers, and the only containers available to distribute the food were a few large dustbins. A large proportion of the occupants were bedridden, and many were incapable of feeding themselves…The inmates had lost all self-respect and had been downgraded morally to the level of beasts. Their clothes were in rags and teeming with lice; they had no eating utensils or plates, and at the time of the food distribution they behaved more like ravenous wolves than human beings.[15]

Typhus was the main killer. Fania Fenelon, the French musician who had played in the camp orchestra, recalled the onset of the dread disease.

The illness took me over entirely; my head was bursting, my body trembling, my intestines and stomach were agony and I had the most abominable dysentery. I was just a sick animal lying in its own excrement. From April 8 everything around me became nightmarish. I merely existed as a bursting head, an intestine, a perpetually active anus. One tier above me there was a French girl I didn't know; in my moments of lucidity, I heard her saying in a clear, calm, even pleasant voice, 'I must shit, but I must shit on your head, it's more hygienic!', she had gone mad; others equally unhinged guffawed interminably or fought. No one came to see us anymore, not even the SS. They'd turned off the water.[16]

Amazingly, Fania Fenelon survived.

From the first days of March, Kramer had been protesting that his camp could take no more – 'the reception of further consignments' was out of the question. In January the maximum had been agreed at 35,000. It was already 7,000 over this limit and thousands more were being marched in. Typhus, obligingly, was reducing the population by up to 300 per day. On 19 March, an SS team of inspectors arrived, professing themselves shocked by conditions, though the need for extra accommodation took precedence. Those prisoners who had some hostage value, the 'Exchange Jews', could be transferred but more should be crammed into the stinking barracks. One easy solution was to simply murder them all and destroy the evidence. Many of the wretched and diseased survivors thought this must indeed happen but in the event it did not.[17]

These 'Exchange Jews' constituted a special category. Even as the Final Solution was being implemented, Himmler realised that certain important Jewish people could have a 'value' sufficient to save them from immediate extermination. Normally, those who had dual nationality, bureaucratic exemption (those with certificates enabling emigration to Palestine were particularly fortunate) or were sufficiently wealthy might be viewed as candidates for exchange with German nationals interned by the Allies. When the SS first took over the former POW camp at Celle that was to become Belsen, it was intended to create an enclave for this special category, of whom some 7,000 were incarcerated there. In July 1944, 250 were formally exchanged and the remainder were kept segregated in their own 'Star' section of the camp. As the Allied armies drew near SS Obergruppenführer Pohl acceded to Kramer's request that the exchange prisoners be transferred east to preserve them as future hostages. Several trains, starting in early April, were loaded and sent eastwards, though all were stopped either by the US or Russian troops and, in one instance, bombed by the RAF. Most of the prisoners did, however, survive.

Kramer's had been a rule of terror and unbridled ferocity. His remedy for the results of gastric disorders, rife through the camp, was simple: no food; if you don't eat, you don't shit. He and his men enjoyed licence to administer savage, often fatal, beatings at will. One survivor recalled the commandant himself losing patience with a helpless female inmate. In a berserk rage he shattered her skull with a single swipe of his truncheon. Pares and his comrades were left with 49 male and 26 female SS. The electricity supply had been sabotaged, most likely by the SS, and consequently the pumps had shut down, cutting off water supplies. Aside from the camp victims, the military hospital held some 2,000 patients, mainly soldiers of the Wehrmacht. To contain disease, typhus especially, it was necessary to maintain a strict quarantine, though the Hungarians proved less than enthusiastic, being '...grossly lax and made little effort to prevent [inmates] from filtering out'.

'Ihr seid frei' (you are free) boomed from the speakers fitted to the vehicle driven by Lieutenant Derrick Sington, an Oxford-educated journalist with Jewish antecedents. Sington commanded an 'Amplifier Unit' which also boasted several NCOs fluent in a range of European languages. British soldiers, however hardened, were not prepared for what awaited them at Belsen. As he entered the camp, Sington dragooned an unwilling Kramer into accompanying him. The SS officer had disingenuously advised that the camp held 'homosexuals and professional criminals and some political prisoners'.[18] Soon, as they began broadcasting, a horde of half-starved scarecrows, 'a

strange simian throng', emerged, 'with their shaved heads and their obscene striped penitentiary suits which were so dehumanising'. He observed '...These clowns in their terrible motley, seemed barely human.' A panicky German started firing and Sington drew his own revolver when a dozen striped figures jumped into the crowd, hitting again and again with packing case strips '...like prancing zebras'. These were the trusties or *kapos*.[19] Sington and fellow officers found these creatures repellent and would not hesitate to draw their revolvers to prevent their unbridled brutality.

The scene approaching the women's camp verged on mass hysteria:

> In a few seconds the car was surrounded by hundreds of women. They cried and wailed hysterically, uncontrollably, and no word from the loudspeakers could be heard. The compounds of the camp were planted with young birch trees and the women plucked leafy springs and small branches and hurled them on to the car. One branch fell on Kramer's shoulder. He brushed it impatiently away.'[20]

One survivor recalled, 'we almost tore these poor soldiers apart... other tanks followed. Through the loudspeakers and with tearful voices they repeated over and over again in several languages, "You are free. We are the English Army. Be calm; food and medical help is on the way."'[21]

Officers who had previously been somewhat disinterested in what had been thought to be some form of routine internment camp found they had stumbled into a scene they could scarcely comprehend:

> A great number of them [inmates] were little more than living skeletons with haggard yellowish faces. Most of the men wore a striped pyjama type of clothing – others wore rags while the women wore striped flannel gowns or any garment that they had managed to acquire...there were men and women lying in heaps on either side of the track. Others were walking slowly and aimlessly about – a vacant expression on their starved faces.[22]

In March alone the death toll had topped 18,000: there were heaps of dead in every cage [fenced compound] 'and it was quite obvious that unless food and water arrived soon the whole camp would starve to death'.

Understandably, the British were revolted, reviling Kramer and his remaining guards. 'The things I saw completely defy description. There are no words in the English language which can give a true impression of the ghastly horror of this camp...' Very quickly the British began to rewrite the terms of the truce, once the magnitude of the atrocity and the scale of the problem became apparent. Kramer was placed under arrest.[23] 'The priority the first night was food, water and more troops...we really thought at first that we should only be able to keep order and prevent the spread of infection by stopping people from breaking out.' Tanks were deployed to prevent a mass breakout but none occurred, though the guards' reserves of food were plundered and Kramer's hoard of 25 fattened pigs disappeared.[24] Some disturbances occurred in the Panzer Training School, where some 15,000 inmates, mainly Russians and Poles, those 'who had any strength left began to hunt down the kapos, block captains and their lackeys[25].

By no means all of the victims were Jewish:

In the accounts I have read of the camp the impression is given that practically all the inmates were Jews...This was certainly not the case when we were there; there were 15,287 in all [in camp 1*]. The largest group [throughout the camp as a whole] was the Russians, followed by the Poles. Together they made up about 60 per cent of the inmates. There were some 500 Greeks and about the same number of French and Belgians and Czechs and 120 Dutch, plus a good number of Yugoslavs. The Germans together numbered between 1,600 and 1,800 and there were several hundred gypsies.[26]

Of the women the bulk, around 18,000 of a total of 25,000 or so, were Jewish: 'They were a large part of the survivors of families who had perished in the gas chambers of Birkenau and Treblinka.' The rest, 7,000-odd, comprised Russians (2,000), or Yugoslav, Polish, French and Belgians, most of whom had been resistance workers. (* For a description of the layout to the camp, refer to note 4 at the end of this chapter.)

Initial hopes of using the camp's five kitchens to feed the starving victims ran into difficulties and pre-packed tinned rations were given out, 'Compo rations[27]...all tinned and included such things as bacon, sausages, Irish stew (from Argentina), steak and kidney pudding, meat and vegetable, fruit, puddings, butter, cheese and jam. This heavy fare proved unsuitable for and downright dangerous to those who'd existed on below-subsistence-level rations for so long, the people ate greedily and to excess.'[28] For many, it was catastrophic, they simply could not digest such stodgy richness and 'were just falling over like flies'. This new order created new rules for survival. The younger women who'd arrived recently and were less debilitated used their charms to acquire boyfriends amongst the British. One made a conquest who 'gave her things like corned beef and bags of sugar. Up till then, right through, we'd shared everything, but for some reason she wouldn't share with us anymore, and she died of the food.'[29] In all, some 2,000 were killed by this ill-judged kindness.[30]

The plan

'The plan was to create in the Tank Training School Barracks a vast hospital area for the sick under RAMC [Royal Army Medical Corps] control, and to evacuate all the fit there, where they could be sorted out in big reception areas into national groups by sexes, and could also spend a quarantine period of about three weeks before repatriation...'

This was an enormous undertaking and involved units from transport, catering, artillery, medical, engineers and administrative units:

The whole administration of the Camp was controlled by 10 Garrison and later by 102 Control Section. In support was 113 LAA [Light Anti-Aircraft] Regt. RA [Royal Artillery] with its REME [Royal Engineers Mechanical Engineers] Workshops and 1575 Artillery Platoon RASC [Royal Army Service Corps] for general duties. The medical area was administered by 32 CCS [Casualty Clearing Station] with 11 Field Ambulance and later 9 Brigade General Hospital and 35 CCS with 107 Mobile Laundry and a host of small RAMC and specialist units. 224, 618 and 904 Military Government Detachments divided themselves between the Concentration and Reception Camp. There were also 6 detachments of the British Red Cross Society and 100 medical student volunteers from the London Hospitals.[31]

Though British soldiers coming across this catalogue of unspeakable horrors might be utterly revolted, General Dempsey, CO of 2nd Army, and his political masters instantly divined a PR coup of the first magnitude. 'From the first [the General] was very keen [the press] should see Belsen and write about it. Himmler and the SS had blundered in not eliminating the evidence, for here was the most tangible proof of Nazi inhumanity. Any moral doubts that might be expressed over the RAF strategic bombing of German cities, or any other measures, could very swiftly be countered by the awful truth of the camp.' Those further down the command pyramid and closer to the reality found very little to celebrate:

A woman too weak to stand propping herself against a pile of corpses, as she cooked the food we had given her over an open fire; men and women crouching just anywhere in the open relieving themselves of the dysentery which was scouring their bowels; a woman standing stark naked washing herself with some issue soap in water from a tank in which the remains of a child floated.[32]

Today is the 24th April of 1945 [recorded Gunner Illingworth]... I'm at present in Belsen Camp doing guard duty over the SS men. The things in this camp are beyond describing. When you actually see them for yourself you know what you're fighting for here. Pictures in the paper can't describe it at all. The things that they've committed, well, nobody would think they were human at all. We actually know now what has been going on in these camps and I know personally what I'm fighting for.[33]

A particular object of revulsion was Dr Fritz Klein, the 'mad-doctor of Belsen'. Klein, born in 1888, was Hungarian by birth and studied at Budapest before practising in Romania. A Nazi convert, he joined the Waffen-SS in 1943 and spent time at Auschwitz. He himself succinctly summed up his philosophy. 'My Hippocratic oath tells me to cut a gangrenous appendix out of the human body. The Jews are the gangrenous appendix of mankind. That's why I cut them out.'

Movietone's Paul Wyand recorded the doctor's guilt for posterity.

I posed Klein on the edge of the pit into which he had been dumping corpses, and the background showed other bodies being disposed of in like manner. Two soldiers had been detailed to assist me, and one stood on each side of the doctor. Klein was trembling with fear and was half-crazy after the work he had been doing for the past few days. The [Polish] girl [interpreter] explained what was wanted, and as he started to talk I filmed him. He had only spoken a few words when the girl cried 'Stop!' and explained that although Klein had told me his name and where he was, he had given the wrong year. On hearing this the Tommies clouted the German with their rifle butts, and the Polish girl screamed at him. Klein began again and this time he kept to the truth.[34]

As reports filtered from the camp and the British public was, for the first time, confronted by the terrible reality of Nazism against which they had been fighting for so long, newspaper editorials caught the mood: 'These Germans must not pause in the hot wind. Never before, nor ever again, will they see Englishmen so angry as are the cool, grim young men...left behind the fighting to see they do this task [the burials].'[35]

Brigadier Hugh Llewellyn Glyn Jones was chief Medical Officer in 2nd Army. It was his responsibility to find a medical solution to this nightmare situation. A lesser man might easily have given way to despair.

Some of the huts had bunks, but not many, and they were filled absolutely to overflowing with prisoners in every state of emaciation and disease. There was not room for them to lie down at full length in each hut. In the most crowded there were anything from 600 to 1,000 people in accommodation which should only have taken 100...The compounds were absolutely one mass of human excreta. In the huts themselves the floors were covered and the people in the top bunks who could not get out just poured it on the bunks below.[36]

We took a look around – there were faeces all over the floor – the majority of people having diarrhoea. I was standing aghast in the midst of all this filth trying to get used to the smell, which was a mixture of post-mortem room, a sewer, sweat, and foul pus, when I heard scrabbling on the floor. I looked down in the half light and saw a woman crouching at my feet. She had black matted hair, well populated and her ribs stood out as though there were nothing between them, her arms were so thin that they were horrible. She was defecating, but was so weak that she could not lift her buttocks from the floor and, as she had diarrhoea, the liquid yellow stools bubbled over her thighs.[37]

Another key figure was Colonel James Johnston, who commanded 32 Casualty Clearing Station and who was made senior medical officer within Belsen. Remarkably, despite all the death and despair, some of the victims, themselves doctors or nurses, had achieved what, in the circumstances, amounted to minor miracles.

> They had managed, without any assistance from the authorities and without any medical or other equipment, to maintain some sort of order out of the chaos that prevailed around them. The hut in which they lived was the only clean hut in the entire camp. I will never forget my first encounter with them. In the midst of this mass of human squalor and degradation these two women [Doctors Bimko and Gutman], physically clean, mentally whole, calm, serene, and dignified, stood out as a shining example to their fellow internees, a personification of the triumph of good over evil.[38]

One hut was in the care of a quartet of young, female Polish medical graduates from Warsaw University. These courageous women 'in spite of years of living in the most appalling filth, discomfort and brutality had lost none of their self-respect'. British officers and men were impressed by such fortitude; 'morally, they were of a tougher fibre than I had ever met before'. Respect bred friendship and a fledgling element of cultural exchange, 'to explain the status of "Public Schools" and to point out that, in spite of their name, they catered for a fraction of one per cent of the population was beyond me. [The graduates] were amused to hear that women students were not admitted to St. Thomas's Hospital.'[39]

Lieutenant, later Captain, Stanley Levitt of the DLI took detailed testimony from one of the emaciated survivors, Jeanette Kauffman:

> After being liberated by the British I contrived to creep – I couldn't walk – into the men's laager. There I heard the horrible truth that my husband had been there for five weeks and had died of starvation only three days before the English arrived...My boys

(aged now 16 and 20) were supposed to be at Ordruf camp but all reports that I have heard up to now indicate that when the area was liberated there was no camp there – only a big cemetery. I am liberated but my life is crushed.[40]

The 'human laundry'

The task was monumental and time was clearly of the essence:

> 32 CCS with the aid of 11 Fd. Amb, the British Red Cross and the other RAMC specialists created a Hospital Area from empty barrack buildings and installed in it 7,000/8,000 patients in three weeks. They also organised a 'human laundry' for the dis-infestation and bathing of all persons evacuated from the Concentration Camp. Within seven days of their arrival they carried out a complete dis-infestation with anti-louse powder (AL 63) of all the internees in all camps. 9 Br. Gen Hosp [9th Brigade's General Hospital Unit] took over the Wehrmacht Hospital, created their own hospital block from empty barrack rooms and ran a maternity home.[41]

Pares' account masks with careful objectivity the endless suffering of inmates, 'not funny having soap rubbed into a painful ulcer... very painful to those with severe conditions such as bed-sores'. Most displayed an ox-like apathy: 'Living corpses, skeletons covered with parchment-like skin, discoloured by filth and neglected sores, lay on the bath tables. Mostly they lay inert, occasionally they moaned as they were touched by the nurses. They lay with open eyes sunk deep into hollow sockets, eyes which registered little, save fear and apprehension, mainly they were expressionless.'[42]

From the horror and chaos which the British had discovered, a form of order and process began to emerge.

> Military Government in four weeks evacuated every single sick person from the Concentration Camp to the Reception Area, registered and reclothed them, and dispatched over 15,000 on the route for repatriation. They obtained all the necessary food in accordance with the medical diet ordered and arranged the requisition from the district of all stores and supplies needed for the camp...The RA [Royal Artillery] set up special organisations

to deal with burials. Between 19–26 April 9,200 bodies were buried in the communal pits and over the whole period 15,000 were buried – the highest figure was 1,700 on 21 Apr. All graves were decently enclosed, funeral services read daily, and notice boards stating the date and number of the grave were erected.[43]

There was a terrible irony in the employment of SS for this purpose: 'a tremendous emotional release for the inhabitants of Bergen-Belsen. Each morning a crowd would form near the mass grave in the sandy clearing, in the south-west corner of the camp, to howl and yell execrations at their former tormentors.' The British were not moved to show mercy.

The one thing I saw that pleased me was the SS men being bullied into work…They collect dead and infected clothing – push their carts by hand and throw the mixed loads into enormous mass graves (5,000 each). All the time our armed troops shout at them, kick them, threaten them, never letting them stop for a moment. What horrible types they were – these SS! – with their Hollywood criminal features. They are being shown no quarter – they know what end is in store for them when their work is finished.[44]

Bulldozers were brought in to speed up the dreadful labour, both to excavate the burial pits and shunt corpses; the heavy blades sliced through decaying flesh to burst the bloated cadavers in an obscene miasma.

With food stocks exhausted and utilities disconnected, the provision of adequate supplies was a key priority. The challenge was immense but DLI and their comrades, representing a gamut of capabilities and experience, rose superbly to the occasion:

Large food-stocks uncovered in the Wehrmacht barracks were immediately impounded and delivered to the Concentration Camp. In addition a dump of tentage was transported to the camp and pitched to relieve the overcrowding…Each cookhouse was made the personal responsibility of an RA Officer or Warrant Officer. At the beginning, messing strengths averaged 10,000 to each cookhouse, and in one case 16,000. A Central Messing Office was set up under an RA officer to coordinate the distribution of rations and equipment and the reallocation of cooks as evacuation occurred. An invalid cookhouse was established to prepare a special Bengal Famine Diet[45] for the very sick, which was delivered round the huts for the medical students to administer to those who could not feed themselves…Reception offices were set up by the RA under the auspices of 904 and 618 Mil Gov Detachments to assist in allocation of accommodation, registration and clothing of the evacuees, and responsible for administration of cookhouses and control of labour. In one Camp where no cookhouses were available, a wooden building was erected by RA labour and equipped to feed 4,000 in the space of five days.[46]

Even as this Herculean effort gathered momentum, the scale of the problem and administrative difficulties created delays which, as Sington recalled, could be fatal to inmates:

'Monsieur, seven more women died here today [intimated inmate Mona Georges, a French entertainer interned for resistance activity]. If we stay in this place we shall all die of the pestilence. In a few days, unless something is done, there will be no women left here…' There, amid scattered turnips, the smell of burning leather and the noises of women defecating, her logic seemed unanswerable and inexorable. One felt powerless, desperately powerless. One knew that the organisation and equipment of the reception camp and the reception hospital were being pressed forward with all possible speed. But in the meantime were these women to be left in this death-trap to contract infection and die?'[47]

Ms Georges at least did survive.

Though the British had developed a singular hatred for the SS, attitudes toward the Hungarians were more ambivalent. Some 2,000 Hungarian soldiers had been attached to the camp as auxiliaries and, with some exceptions, were not viewed as part of the regime of brutality. They did shoot prisoners and a few shared characteristics with their Nazi employers. Most were ragged and rather unmilitary, though their officers were well turned out and many had even brought their horses with them. In practice, they formed an invaluable pool of hard labour; they performed many tasks, including burial details, cleaning out water installations, delousing and clearing barracks, general fetching and carrying, accomplishing these generally with good humour and to the accompaniment of some very fine singing. They were perceived as efficient and uncomplaining. No clemency would be extended to the *'kapos'* (meaning 'foreman' in German and from the French for 'corporal'). These were vicious wretches, usually brutish recidivists convicted for crimes of violence, each of whom had a designated hut in his charge. Equipped with batons, which they used liberally, they imbibed all the savagery of their SS superiors. Lawyers, magistrates and intellectuals were particular targets. Following liberation, these creatures were hunted by those they'd tormented and put down. The British were not generally inclined to interfere.

One survivor alive in the camp at this time was Bertha Frederber from Cracow.[48] She had desperately begged medicine for her ill sister-in-law but was turned away empty-handed; there was none to be had and the sick woman succumbed. The experience left her feeling that the British Army

...excelled at one thing, collecting the dead...It has been two weeks since we were liberated and even more wagonloads are being wheeled from the camp than before. There they lie on the wagons, the liberated people, the shaven heads lolling, shaking slowly with the steps of the person pushing them...The spectacle gives me no rest...I see neither the rays of the spring sun nor the green of the trees...It is true there is a difference between the funerals of today and those of yesterday. Now it is Germans who are pushing the wagonloads of corpses. Formerly we did that. But how great is the difference, the dead are laid in mass graves whether they died as prisoners or as free men.

As she lay supine, Bertha Frederber was mistaken by an English soldier for yet another corpse and he began dragging her to the pit. '"Have patience, not yet," I answered him, as he called on a comrade to assist in the chore.'[49]

Apart from sickness, hunger and the deep scars of their savage treatment, the victims comprised this vast population of the displaced and homeless, dragged from every corner of the Nazi empire.

An Inquiry Bureau was opened by the Padres to deal with the host of enquiries from the internees, to supply them with comforts and writing material, and censor and forward their letters. The

RA took over the prison where first the SS Prison Guards were housed, and later Wehrmacht POWs who were employed on burial duties in both camps. RA personnel supervised and guarded daily large working parties of Hungarians, German POWs and civilians throughout the area, whose main duties were to clear all the barrack blocks, clean them out and refit them with beds etc., either as Hospital or Reception areas for the evacuated internees.[50]

One of the most dramatic innovations was the 'human laundry'. The desperately sick patients, barely living, stick-thin bundles of ravaged rags, were stretchered from their foully infested huts then carried by ambulance to a former stable block, located in camp 2. This had been constructed with a central drainage channel flanked on both sides by stalls. These were now equipped with table, towels, scrubbing brushes and soap. A newly delivered mobile bath unit provided the vital and plentiful supply of hot water. A German medical orderly was charged with getting the patient on to the table, where each was washed, given a shave, and treated with DDT; hair too matted to be washed was removed. German nurses also drafted in soon overcame their truculence when confronted with a medical emergency of such magnitude; by the end, all of the disparate medical professionals, regardless of nationality, had welded into a cohesive and efficient team.

Though this was a significant development, it was only the beginning of a process. Once cleaned, the patients still had to be treated; most still suffered from loose bowels. The improvised wards were at best under-equipped: 'Dirty, smelly buckets, blankets and bed pans were littered all over the building. Even parts of the floor were covered in faeces.' Electricity and water supplies were still intermittent and this with 500 new patients coming in every day; the process of creating order was a difficult one and that it was accomplished, and in such short time, speaks very highly of the medical personnel, Red Cross volunteers and students who undertook this gargantuan task.

Deployed in Belsen now were the DLI gunners, other artillery units, medical professionals, army caterers, chaplains, transport and supply, military police and investigators, administrators, translators and mechanical and services trades, without whom very little could have been achieved. 'All the electricians and fitters in the REME Workshops were organised into a team, and repaired the electricity and restored the water supply. They also repaired the plant in the Camp Bakery and the other electrical apparatus in the Supply Depot so that the bakery was able to meet all the requirements of the Camp for bread.'[51]

> ... The RASC Artillery Platoon undertook the task of coordinating all transport details, and in addition to their Regimental duties they drew all the supplies for everyone in the Camp, including rations and petrol. They supplied lorries for collecting food, clothes, beds, soap and all types of stores from the surrounding districts. With the aid of the RA butchers their supply section broke down the rations for every individual unit in the Camp, including the Russian Battalion of 850 men...Ablution benches, water points, and latrines were set up under the direction of the Field Hygiene Section, and while these were being made or during the periodical failures of the electricity, all the RA water carts toured the area continuously, bringing water to the cookhouses, huts and barrack blocks.[52]

Security was another matter of concern. Obviously the former SS guards and their Hungarian auxiliaries were scarcely a desirable expedient.

> The Russian POWs were organised by 10 Garrison into a Battalion with their own officers, equipped with rifles, issued with British Army rations, and eventually they superseded the Hungarians on the Camp Guard...Numerous guards were provided from time to time at the gates, Garrison HQ, Cinema, the DID and Supply Depot and in every cook house. Mobile jeep patrols toured the area continuously throughout the night to prevent looting etc...Two troops of RA worked exclusively under the Medical authorities, one at the Wehrmacht Hospital and the other in the Hospital Area, which they completely wired off and guarded to prevent unauthorised movement in and out.[53]

Despite precautions, it proved impossible to contain the inmates completely. 'You have to say, a Russian is a Russian. The English gave them [food] to eat, but they stole all the same.' Short of being prepared to fire on absconders or foragers, the British could not prevent inmates sneaking out and the use of lethal force was not contemplated. 'An almost continuous cloud of the inmates spread over the country. Many of these merely went out for freedom and returned after a walk. Others did not return at all or only after days and weeks. Many returned laden with loot, food, clothes, and valuables taken off the Germans who were on the whole too cowed to make incidents.'[54]

For the British labouring under difficult circumstances, battling against time and with the horrors of Belsen piled around them, the strain was considerable. After a week a tremendous amount had been achieved but 7,000 had died in that short space. Many personnel found solace in drink.

> The problems peculiar to the ladies [i.e. matters in which women were involved] would be discussed first [at the nightly review sessions], about eleven o'clock they would be dismissed, gin, brandy, and champagne would appear and we would finish our business by twelve or one in the morning – it was not a party but damned hard work those meetings produced...I am very certain it was the very considerable quantities of liquor that we got through at those meetings that kept those of us who were responsible for the administration of the place from going as mad as most of the internees in the Horror Camp.[55]

Such easy if, in the circumstances, necessary ways shocked some afflicted by higher sensibilities, including one of the attendant rabbis, Isaac Levy, who observed the staff of 32 CCS 'relaxing after a long and gruelling day...drinking heavily, sinking into a state of complete intoxication. "If we were not to drink," they said, "we would go stark, staring mad. We are doctors and are supposed to heal, but this task is hopeless. They die on us as soon as we touch them."'[56]

Coping with the daily onslaught of atrocity was a great burden. Alcohol was joined by humour and tobacco as means of alleviation. The British also had to develop mechanisms for emotional self-preservation.

> Everyone builds up a sort of mental wall against the gruesome sights...There are things here which would sound cruel and

inhuman under other circumstances. For instance, when you can't take everyone to the hospital that ought to go you have to take the ones that have a chance of living and leave the ones that are going to die anyway. And you can't be kind and sweet and gentle to every patient you handle because you wouldn't get much done. All standards of privacy and informality are, of course, gone, in the interest of saving lives.[57]

Many of the young women flung into the camp had been pregnant and, whilst death was omnipresent, new life arrived.

A Maternity Home and Children's Ward were set up under 32 CCS and later 9 Gen Hospital. A cot was made for each child by RA joiners, complete with blankets and waterproof sheets. Toys were impounded from the neighbouring towns, and swings built for the playground. It is worthy of note that a very high percentage of the babies born were suffering from congenital venereal disease.[58]

The end of Belsen

'She limped down the corridor looking old and haggard. She was 42 years old, standing a little over five feet. She was trembling as she was put on the scale. In German she said, "I have my feelings".' Thus Albert Pierrepoint wrote of the execution of Belsen Camp guard Johana Borman, killed on 13 December 1945.

The Concentration Camp was burned down hut by hut under RA supervision, and on 21 May '45 the last hut was burned to the ground. It was on 21 May that the full process of evacuation was completed. Thousands had been saved but 13,000 had perished. The huts were systematically torched as they were cleared, but it was felt appropriate to organise a ceremony around the destruction of the last survivor. A dais erected in front [of the last remaining hut] featured a large image of the Führer with a backdrop of captured Nazi banners. At 18.00 hours the camp commander and the senior medical officers mounted the platform from which the former delivered a short address. The Colonel stated that only as the last hut was destroyed would the British flag be raised, hitherto the Union Jack had not been sullied by flying over the evil that was Belsen; the DLI men, 113th LAA Regiment, then fired a salute to the dead. The Durham men were singled out for particular praise 'to whom…most honour was due in the story of Belsen'.[59]

And then we cheered. The inferno before us grew brighter and hotter every moment. Although almost all of us were openly excited, even then some of the internees present wore that sadly apathetic countenance bred in them through years of bitter inhuman suffering. The remains of what had been done to them lay smouldering with the ashes amongst where they stood.'[60]

> That night we really did celebrate [the 'Coco-nut Grove Nightclub' had been established above the 'Harrods' clothing store]…The whole of one big room had been transformed into a Night Club, complete with bar, tables and seating accommodation, shaded lights, band, and during the evening a Cabaret, the artistes being four of the fit internees all gotten up in very smart evening dresses made in the Camp sewing room…It was the best party I've ever attended, maybe because it was the first dancing one since arriving in Belsen, and certainly because it was such a surprise to find a place like that in Belsen at all.[61]

Edith Fuchs and her mother Kathe had arrived in Belsen at the end of March 1945. They had hardly any food and became very thin. Shortly after the liberation Edith developed typhus but, thanks to her mother's patient care, survived. Some weeks later she was well enough to walk in the spring countryside.

> We walked on the main road into the forest. It was the first time I felt a little better and we were sitting down with my mother on to a meadow. And then we saw all the nature. There were a lot of marguerites, flowers, round us and my mother took one and made the joke – 'I love you', 'I love you not', you know? And suddenly in this moment we both realised that we are free. Being on a meadow on our own, seeing flowers and doing how it pleases us…And suddenly, only then actually, it hit us that we have survived and now we [hugged] each other and we said 'We made it. We are here. We have survived. We are alive. And soon we go home.'[62]

The next day Kathe developed a mild case of typhus, not life-threatening, but subsequent complications set in and she died still in the camp.

Did DLI and the rest do well? The British effort was not without criticism, yet it cannot be denied that the task which confronted them was both unexpected and gigantic:

> ... the like of which nobody had any knowledge or experience... Neither had we the slightest idea of what we were to discover. All of us were in a state of utter shock – young soldiers... as well as senior officers...What SHOULD you do when faced by 60,000 dead, sick and dying people? We were in a war to fight a war and to beat the enemy. What we were suddenly thrust into was beyond anyone's comprehension, let alone a situation which could have been organised and effectively planned for.[63]

That some mistakes could be made in the initial attempts at feeding and slowness of evacuation is regrettable but understandable. The entire operation was an ad hoc business, as Glyn Hughes conceded:

> What is to be done in the future if we meet these problems? If one can have ready highly trained teams, so much the better...The cry is for bodies of men at the beginning, and we are very short in the RAMC. You must have everything – and be ready to go straight in, with water and food as priorities, and with combatant troops to supervise and guard the camp. It is necessary to impound skilled and unskilled labour if you can get it, and try to 'lay on' beforehand all the accessories in the way of supplies; if fighting is going on at the time it is not easy.[64]

Subsequent writers have observed that it is a British peculiarity that the 'very worst jobs' were not necessarily lumped on to prisoners or penal units but in fact undertaken by 'young males from the privileged elite, who alone were thought to have the sense of social responsibility, awareness of social position and strength of character to do them...the only white man [old imperial reference to far-flung district officers] for miles around.'[65]

The internees sometimes displayed a bizarre irrationality, being prepared to criticise their liberators for what might otherwise appear as minor faults:

They [the inmates] criticise the fact that the British Army here eats white bread, whilst the patients are given rye bread, which they find very unpalatable. They criticise the fact that their own doctors were not consulted before the German doctors and nurses were introduced into the camp. They criticise the fact that the British military commander drove around Camp 1 on the first day of liberation, in the same car as the German military commander, 'for all the world as though we were an exhibition'. Criticism is healthy – and the British must expect it – but praise is unfortunately scarce. Considering the immensity of the task here, my own view is that, although there are small ways in which the British might have done better, on the whole, and within a very short period, the British have brought a remarkable amount of order into this area of chaos.[66]

And what of those British, the DLI veterans and others, who returned to the UK and postwar civilian life? Conditions such as post-traumatic stress disorder were not fully recognised: 'It was assumed that most stable, well-adjusted people could come through any situation, no matter how awful, without lasting ill-effects...Equally, you were expected to put such experiences behind you, to buck up and get on with your life.' Evidence is scarce as to how deeply veterans were affected and remains largely anecdotal but the effect of Belsen was undoubtedly there and never left some of those who passed through: 'I rarely fail to recall the death of a young man found in "my" hut one morning...He was kneeling by his bed. Whenever I kneel to clean the bathtub (an agreed domestic chore), I see this young man 46 years later.'[67] Some found their belief in God challenged. 'I emerged unscathed but my beliefs did not. There is no God, either in spirit or substance, only a Devil and that Devil is mankind.'

As they prepared to leave that awful place, the British erected a sign to record what had been there:

THIS IS THE SITE OF
THE INFAMOUS BELSEN CONCENTRATION CAMP
Liberated by the British on 15 April 1945

10,000 UNBURIED DEAD WERE FOUND HERE

ANOTHER 13,000 HAVE SINCE DIED

ALL OF THEM VICTIMS OF THE

GERMAN NEW ORDER OF EUROPE

AND AN EXAMPLE OF NAZI KULTUR[68]

The reckoning

Celebrated war reporter and subsequent historian Alan Moorehead observed, 'with public horror at the stories that came from Belsen went a public demand that those responsible should be punished for their deeds'. Belsen, as mentioned, seemed to fully validate the justness of the Allied cause, such manifest evil on such a vast scale. Though Belsen, if a scale of horror can be measured, was perhaps less murderous than Dachau or Auschwitz, it exerted a far greater fascination for the British. The formalities of trial were considered superfluous by many; the obvious remedy for Kramer and the other captive SS was a swiftly convened firing squad.

Some of the accused, like Kramer himself and Dr Klein, had also spent time at Auschwitz and were accused of crimes there. As this was a designated death camp, the prosecution's job was made easier. In the case of Belsen the situation was less clear cut and the crimes were more those of neglect than deliberate intent. The defence still faced an uphill task – the classic defence was that of obeying superior orders, which was found generally invalid. It was difficult for the British to enter the mind of a man like Josef Kramer who genuinely appeared to believe that he had done nothing wrong. He saw himself as a soldier with specific and limited responsibility:

Q: Did you watch these people slowly starving and dying?
A: Yes, that is to say, I did not look at it, but I saw from the daily reports how many people were dying every day.

> Q: Did you see these people gradually dying of starvation and thirst?
>
> A: Yes, I mentioned these facts in my letter (of 1st March, 1945).[69]

When asked why he had not requested additional supplies from the nearby Wehrmacht who possessed a known surplus, Kramer replied that he lacked the necessary authority, did not have the appropriate forms of requisition. That he might have simply asked for supplies without using channels did not ever have seemed to have occurred to him.

Dr Klein was also accused of crimes at Auschwitz but alleged he had done nothing wrong at Belsen, had, in fact, done his best to alleviate the suffering. He, with Kramer and eight others, were sentenced to death. Klein did not appeal, apparently due to remorse at his role in the genocide and feeling himself unfitted for mercy. No other appeals were successful. On 12 December 1945 the 11 condemned were hanged – it had taken the jury a little over six hours to reach its verdicts.

The survivors

As the huts burned, the problem of what to do with 30,000 refugees loomed large. This was difficult enough, but the six years of war had left some 10,000,000 people stateless. British thinking was rather one dimensional. Sort out the individuals by nationality and transport them home. This seems straightforward, but the plain fact was that many survivors had no home. Their families, towns and villages had been crushed or scattered beneath the Nazi jackboot, and vast swathes of Eastern Europe had swapped those jackboots for the Russian version. For those French, Dutch and Belgian survivors the job was easier and the majority were on their way before the end of May. During the summer of 1945, the Czechs, Hungarians, Yugoslavs and Romanians mostly followed. Most simply went home, across the scorched desert that was Central and Eastern Europe; some chose to try and make homes in the West, where their descendants now live. Belsen, in this context, is a shard of the shattered mosaic of European society rent by the war.

Poles and Polish Jews had scant desire to return to an occupied homeland. The latter favoured either Britain, the US or, ideally,

Palestine. It is not necessary here to discuss the difficulties leading to the foundation of the Jewish state of Israel or the breakdown of the uneasy truce between the British, as occupier, and resident Zionists. Sweden weighed in as an unlikely paladin for surviving Jews and offered to take all the sick, retaining family groups and providing long-term recovery in Swedish sanatoria. Some commentators, including Shephard, see a degree of cynicism here as the Swedes had hitherto remained within the Nazi sphere and had shown no enthusiasm for Jews. Many availed themselves of this offer, however belated, and were united in their praise for the care they received. Around half of those who went stayed, the remainder going on to America or Israel.

Despite all they had endured, a cadre of Polish Jews were able to effectively establish a representative body which was to prove highly articulate, forceful and resilient. These, most of whom had arrived late at the camp and were therefore less debilitated, 'belonged to Zionist youth movements and were preparing for a life of pioneering in Palestine'. The Jewish committee swiftly created a newspaper and a series of cultural events to enliven the days of those still immured. Actual Jewish aid agencies were slow in arriving, in part as they faced suspicion from the military. The survivors proved dogged in their resistance to perceived British bureaucracy and indifference. American enthusiasm for assisting increased after the visit of President Truman's representative, Professor Harrison, who concluded: 'We appear to be treating the Jews as the Nazis treated them, except that we do not exterminate them.'

British commentators were less sanguine, motivated in part by the desire not to treat the Jews as different, thus perpetuating the Nazi dogma, but also alarm at further mass immigration into Palestine. The reversal of this policy was protracted and difficult but the greater part of the Jewish survivors did eventually find their way to Palestine and the new state of Israel.

Perhaps most tragic of all were the orphans of the camp; many had lost both parents, some arrived to find a relative still living only to see them succumb in the closing days. Ages were hard to establish. Jewish children had learnt to lie about their ages; to be under 10 was a death sentence, better to appear to be of working age. In other circumstances it paid to be younger. The western governments could be persuaded to accept at least some, although a measure of cynicism existed aimed at extracting the maximum PR opportunity. General responsibility was vested in UNRRA [United Nations Relief and Rehabilitation Agency]. In the event, due mainly to Zionist opposition, only 50 orphans were evacuated to England – UNRRA were outraged at the Zionist's intransigence: 'Several hundred young adolescents were given hopes…wantonly dashed by adults who seemed as cruel and lacking in understanding as their oppressors.' The Jewish perspective was different – they saw this as a function of establishing nationhood, of claiming back what had been taken, or recovering their lost young. In April 1946 the first elements of orphaned Jewish children reached Palestine, a path the rest would soon follow.

Notes

1   LAA: Light Anti-Aircraft.
2   Rissik, D., *The DLI at War – History of the DLI 1939–1945* (Durham, 1952), p.301.
3   Bofors gun: a 40mm anti-aircraft auto-cannon produced in Sweden; one of the most widely used anti-aircraft systems of WWII.
4   Concentration camp: the expression was borrowed from the term Britain applied to detention centres during the South African War of 1899–1902. Essentially, these were internment facilities for political opponents of the regime; those held for arbitrary rather than legal reasons. The camp was first built by inmates from Buchenwald and Natzweiler Camps and the original layout comprised five main areas or laagers: (1) for the prisoners building the camp (mainly Jews); (2) the camp for Polish Jews; (3) the camp for neutrals; (4) 'Star' Camp, mainly for Dutch Jews; and (5) the camp for Hungarian Jews. In March 1944 a separate section for the sick from other camps was added; that August a women's laager was also set up (Anne Frank and her sister were sent here in October 1944). Adolf Haas was replaced as commandant by Josef Kramer on 2 December 1944.
5   It is estimated in total that some 50,000 people died in Belsen, a mix of Jews, Czechs, Poles, homosexuals and gypsies, all those whom the Nazis desired to remove. Amongst these were Josef Capek, a noted Czech intellectual and artist, together with Anne Frank.
6   Pares, A., *The Story of Belsen* (County Durham CRO), p.3.
7   Ibid. p.4.
8   Cited in Shephard. B., *After Daybreak: the Liberation of Belsen 1945* (London, 2005), p.51.
9   Ibid. p.4.
10 Ibid. p.69
11 Cited in Shephard, pp.4–5.
12 Pares, p.10.
13 Cited in Shephard, p.15.
14 Pares, p.10.
15 Cited in Shephard, p.40.
16 Ibid. p.18.
17 Certain Jews were segregated for exchange; see Shephard, pp.21–22.
18 Cited in Shephard, p.40.
19 *Kapos*: inmates recruited as auxiliary guards.

20 Cited in Shephard, p.36.

21 Ibid. p.36.

22 Lieutenant-Colonel Taylor of 63 Anti Tank Regiment; see Shephard, p.37.

23 Kramer and 44 SS guards were subsequently put on trial (15 were female); of these, Kramer and 10 others (seven male, three female) were hanged on 15 December 1945.

24 Cited in Shephard, p.39.

25 Of these 150 were killed.

26 Cited in Shephard, p.40.

27 'Compo Rations' or the US equivalent 'Comp Packs'; each contained sufficient to feed one man in the field for 14 days.

28 Cited in Shephard, p.41.

29 Ibid. p.42.

30 Ibid. p.42.

31 Pares, p.4.

32 Cited in Shephard, p.42.

33 Ibid. pp.74–5.

34 Ibid. p.75.

35 *Daily Express* 21 April 1945 (D/DLI/7/404/27).

36 Cited in Shephard, p.45.

37 Ibid. p.92.

38 Ibid. p.51.

39 Ibid. pp.101–2.

40 Testimony from a survivor Jeanette Kaufmann was collated by Lieutenant, later Captain, Stanley Levitt, who'd joined 5th DLI as a territorial in 1938 and had, in 113 LAA Regiment, been promoted to Battery Sergeant-Major before being commissioned as Lieutenant-Quartermaster after showing conspicuous gallantry during the Rhine crossings, where he also earned a mention in dispatches. Jeanette Kaufmann's fate is unknown (D/DLI/7/4040/14).

41 Pares, p.7.

42 Ibid. p.8.

43 Ibid. pp.7–8.

44 Cited in Shephard, p.55.

45 A major famine struck Bengal in 1943 when several millions were affected. The British Army response was the creation of a simple dietary supplement which became known as the Bengal Famine Diet.

46 Pares, p.8.

47 Cited in Shephard, p.63.

48 Bertha Frederber and Anne Frank had arrived in the camp at the same time.

49 Shephard, pp.63–4.

50 Pares, p.8.

51 Ibid. p.8

52 Ibid. p.8

53 Ibid. p.10.

54 Cited in Shephard, p.66.

55 Lieutenant-Colonel Mervyn Gonin commanded 11th Light Field Ambulance; see Shephard, p.67.

56 Ibid. p.67.

57 Ibid. pp.101–2.

58 Pares, p.9.

59 Ibid. p.10.

60 Cited in Shephard, p.125.
61 Ibid. pp.125–6.
62 Ibid. p.121.
63 Ibid. p.194.
64 Ibid. pp.194–5.
65 Ibid. p.195.
66 Ibid. p.196.
67 Ibid. p.185.
68 Ibid. p.185.
69 Cited in Shephard, p.173.

Chapter 11

The Forgotten Army: Burma, 1942–45

The first time I smelt Jap was in a deep dry-river bed in the Dry Belt, somewhere near Meiktila. I can no more describe the smell than I could describe a colour, but it was heavy and pungent and compounded of stale cooked rice and sweat and human waste and…Jap.

George MacDonald Fraser[1]

When you go home
Tell them of us and say
For your tomorrow
We gave our today

War Memorial inscription, Garrison Hill, Kohima[2]

Few British veterans I have interviewed show much rancour towards the Germans. It was not necessarily *Krieg ohne Hass* but there was generally a measure of mutual respect. The same cannot be said of those who fought in the Far East. For them, the Japanese are still perceived as vicious and bestial beyond words. One of my own uncles by marriage who served in the Royal Army Medical Corps refused for the rest of his life to have any Japanese product and electrical goods in his house or surgeries. He married late and his intended bride, at that point, drove a Japanese car. There could be no wedding till the offending vehicle was disposed of and another acquired, any nationality bar Japanese.

Burma

It is fair to say that neither side would have chosen to fight in Burma, a country where high, tree-clad mountains plunged into dense, almost impenetrable jungle; suffocating heat, cloying humidity, disease-ridden and infested swamps alternating with baking plains of near-desert savannah. For the Imperial Japanese, conquest offered two enticing possibilities: the first was the means of severing the lifeline of the Burma Road over which vital military aid was trekked into the Chinese Nationalists fighting under Chiang Kai Shek. Secondly, Japan held the belief that if her armies were to cross into British India, the oppressed masses there would welcome them as liberators. This might seem unlikely but a turncoat Bengali politician, Chandra Bose, formed an effective fifth column and his inducements had succeeded in suborning many thousands of Indian army soldiers captured in the debacle at Singapore.[3]

Sir Archibald Wavell, hero of early operations in the Western Desert, was now in charge of India. His policy of pushing slender and ill-trained forces forward to meet the Japanese head-on proved unfortunate. Lieutenant-General William Slim found himself conducting a desperate retreat up the long spine of Burma: Burforce (the units deployed) was outnumbered, outgunned and outfought. Slim fell back along the gash of the Irrawaddy River towards the gates of India, where bitter stalemate ensued.

At this point, the Japanese appeared as some form of diabolical supermen, impervious to the dreadfulness of jungle warfare (in fact, they were not, and suffered equally). During 1943 Allied morale was raised by the costly success of Orde Wingate's (killed March 1944) Chindit raids, which began to demonstrate that we could fight in these conditions as effectively as the Japanese and use our air power and capacity for air supply to achieve an advantage. George MacDonald Fraser found: 'It seemed a terribly old-fashioned kind of war, far closer to the campaign my great-uncle fought when he went with Roberts to Kandahar (he's buried somewhere in Afghanistan; I wore his ring in Burma) than to what was happening in Europe. Compared to that or the electronic campaigns of today, it looks downright primitive.'[4]

When Mountbatten replaced Wavell, the resurgent 14th Army, led by Slim, took on a refreshed and invigorated persona. Mountbatten understood the value of air drops. No longer would Allied troops be defeated by Japanese encirclements, they would hold their positions and be sustained from the air, grinding down their attackers whose own supply lines were over-stretched. By this time in the war principal strategic direction amongst the western

Allies was coming from the Americans, who were assuming a more pivotal role in the overall conduct of operations. That Japan would finally be defeated by the campaign in the Pacific rather than by any initiative undertaken purely by the British was an undoubted reality. Burma would become the last of the great Imperial adventures, the twilight of Britain's vast overseas dominion. It was estimated that the Japanese had suffered no more than 2,000 casualties in conquering Burma. To stay there, fight and suffer eventual defeat would cost them very nearly 50,000 more.[5]

Lord Louis Mountbatten had Hollywood looks, an easy and urbane charm and close connection to the royal family. He was an ideal choice for 'front of the house' in diplomatic terms but possessed few qualities required of a senior theatre commander. His fellow officers were scornful over his strategic grasp and limited intellectual capacity. General Henry Pownall, his chief of staff, observed:

> there are so many paradoxes…his charm of manner…is one of his greatest assets; many is the time I've gone to him to have a really good showdown…he would apologise, promise to mend his ways – and then soon afterwards go and do the same thing again! [He] has great drive and initiative…He is however apt to leap before he looks…His meetings are overlong because he likes talking…And he likes a good big audience to hear what he has to say.[6]

'Bill' Slim was a different matter altogether. He had served with distinction during the Great War and exhibited that bulldog tenacity Churchill so admired in his officers, though he proved no friend to Slim or the 14th Army. The disastrous retreat through Burma was rightly considered no fault of his. Down to earth, pragmatic, unassuming, reliable, he was to lead British forces in Burma from the brink of defeat to the pinnacle of success.

Finding themselves checked, the Japanese command decided to attempt a major and crippling blow by driving deep into Assam and capturing two key bastions at Imphal and Kohima. These two settlements, the former being the principal town of the hill region of Manipur, would witness some of the most savage fighting of the war and would become the crucible in which the 14th Army would be tested. Soldiers fighting in Burma regarded themselves as the 'Forgotten Army' as attention in Europe fixed on the forthcoming invasion of France and titanic struggles being found in the East. Yet Kohima was to be decisive; neither side could afford to give ground and whoever won here must triumph in the contest for Burma. For the Japanese, this would be both their high-water mark and the rock against which their prospects for final victory were dashed – *Götterdämmerung*.

Burma was something of a sideshow all round. General Mutagachi, in command of the Japanese 15th Army, was an aggressive commander who did not permit logistical difficulties to interfere with his intentions. He had already sacked his own chief of staff for pointing this out.[7] Assam was not the place to fight if it could be avoided. The province could claim to be the wettest on earth, with some 800 inches of rain annually. Supplies had to be moved by four-legged transport, long, snaking bullock trains, tenuous, slow and vulnerable. The Japanese had a slang term for Burma, *jigoku* – 'hell'. A posting there was equivalent to being 'Stellenbosched' or 'degomme' – essentially a punishment!

Resurrection – 2nd Battalion DLI

> *Out there in the jungle, down by Mandalay,*
> *A few forgotten soldiers slowly fight their way,*
> *They dream of the girls they left back home,*
> *And soon they hope to cross the foam*
> *To see their land and loved ones…*
> Anon, 'Down by Mandalay', sung to the tune of 'Lili Marlene'[8]

After the dire finale of the Battle for France in 1940 where 2nd Battalion was virtually destroyed, no more than three officers and 180 other ranks, the MO and padre[9] could muster. Lieutenant-Colonel F.G.A. Wiele was handed the unenviable task of rebuilding the shattered unit. Some officers who had been wounded and evacuated ahead of the disaster were soon back and some 500 conscripts were added to the strength. Wiele proved to be a commanding personality who welded the new and the old to re-form a fine fighting battalion, though he himself was not destined to lead in the field.[10]

After months of training, first in East Yorkshire then at Bury St. Edmunds, the 2nd Battalion (as part of 6th Brigade) of 2nd Division sailed in the *Empress of Canada* on 12 April 1942. From Bombay, where the troopship docked on 2 June, the Brigade, formed as a discrete fighting unit with four battalions and supporting arms, moved up country to Ahmednagar. Here, over ground that bore no trace of jungle conditions, they trained for the real thing and endlessly practised amphibious operations, skills they would later use in only very limited circumstances. In December, with Lieutenant-Colonel J.A. Theobalds of the Oxford and Bucks Light Infantry commanding, they entrained for Chittagong; 2nd Battalion DLI was back in the war.

Their first taste of fighting the Japanese was to prove salutary. Wavell had devised a plan to strike a major blow and clear the foe from the Mayu Peninsula and seize Akyab Island. It was thought the Japanese had no more than a single regiment and 14th Indian Division would sweep down the mountainous spine of the peninsula, allowing 6th Brigade to mount landings on the island. On paper this looked feasible but conditions in the Arakan (the long peninsula on the west coast of Burma) were fearsome, the hills high, rugged and difficult, cut with sharp ridges and deep, scrub-filled gullies. The thin strip of coastal plain is riven by small tidal rivers or 'chaungs'. This was very bad ground for attackers, well suited to tenacious defence. The Japanese knew all about tenacity, and their capacity to construct highly efficient improvised lines of defence was very considerable. They were ferocious and fanatically brave. Later, the DLI would notice that, as morale declined, more would surrender, but the Arakan defenders were not yet at that stage. They had faith in their capabilities – they were not mistaken.

Initially the offensive produced some gains and 14th Division managed to advance almost as far as the aptly named Foul Point opposite Akyab Island, but a hiatus allowed the Japanese to regain their composure and prepare defences. Attempts to wrest the village of Donbaik, key to securing the landward side, failed and a stalemate ensued. This could not endure as it was now mid-February 1943 and the dreaded monsoon was due, a continuous downpour of biblical venom that would choke further operations. It was now the turn of 6th Brigade.

An amphibious raid by a platoon-sized unit on Myebon proceeded with clockwork efficiency:

This platoon, commanded by Lieutenant Terry Bardell, was to

embark in two naval motor launches on 20 February and carry out a raid on Myebon, a village used as a Japanese reinforcement camp some 50 miles south-east of Akyab. The camp and village lay at the head of a long, narrow waterway called Hunter's Bay. The boats sailed south from the Naf River, entered Hunter's Bay and drifted silently up to Myebon under cover of darkness. On the jetty near the camp stood a Japanese soldier. The leading motor launch approached the jetty, still drifting, and a sailor, unable to stand the suspense any longer, shouted to the Jap, 'sling out a rope.' The Jap taken by surprise and, it must be admitted, somewhat unexpectedly, complied with the request! Then he saw the troops on the deck and took to his heels.[11]

The luckless watcher was cut down by gunfire then the raiders laid waste the position and withdrew as it burnt behind – there were no British casualties.

Whilst fighting in the Arakan was to demonstrate that the Japanese were mere flesh and blood and scarcely superhuman, they remained a most formidable enemy. The Allies enjoyed superiority in the air and with artillery and armour. Japanese commanders squandered the lives of their men in reckless, suicidal, human-wave attacks yet, in defence, they proved infinitely subtle. Their bunkers were ingeniously constructed and brilliantly sited, impervious to much that Allied guns could throw at them. Even when British attacks, as the Durhams would discover at Donbaik, overran their trenches they could shelter in dugouts whilst their own mortars deluged the attackers above.

Unquestionably, the vast cultural gap between British and Japanese fuelled the latter's demonical air:

I was quite scared of the Japs, myself. I thought they were very nasty people. They would die but they wouldn't lie down. They literally did hold their positions absolutely to the last man and the last round. They were immensely determined…we used to come upon pockets of these Japs, all lying dead under a tree or something. They had either died of complete starvation, or in some cases they had committed suicide by holding a grenade to their bosom and pulling the pin out, rather than be taken prisoner. We found that their food consisted only of an old sock full of rice and some bits of raw fish – terribly smelly and nasty…[12]

F. Spencer Chapman put his experiences in Malaya into his celebrated narrative *The Jungle is Neutral*. And indeed this was so; despite contrary myth, the British suffered no more in jungle conditions than their adversaries. What was true, certainly at the outset, was that the Japanese had learnt to fight effectively in such conditions; they used infiltration tactics and cover far better. Large-scale tactical manoeuvres such as practised by British forces were ill suited to such close terrain. Part of the Japanese mystique is that they were frequently invisible, their foxholes and bunkers so carefully dug and sited, so well camouflaged, the unwary might not realise their imminent peril until it was rather too late. Sound tactical skill at junior leadership level proved critical. British forces had to learn not just to cope with the physical demands of such hostile terrain but how to meet the dual tactical challenge of ground and a skilled foe. We learnt that encirclement only meant defeat if your forces thought in strictly conventional terms; where those surrounded could be sustained from the air and an all-round, all-arms defence established then the fight was far from lost.

Captain Alexander Wilson of 2 DLI, attached to 2nd Division's jungle training school, observed:

> Most British people, like many brought up in towns, have never really been in the dark, because there are always street lamps, or some sort of light. Few of our soldiers had ever been alone at night. We have lost our sense of hearing and smell. These are basic, animal-like instincts which are vital in the jungle. The Japs smelt different to us, and you could smell them in a defensive position, or if they had recently passed down a track. The Japs smelt rather like scented powder. Indians smelt differently to us too – it depends on what you eat.[13]

That the Allies were able to dispose of more devastating firepower, both on the ground and from the air, was to confer a major tactical advantage: 'We had a tremendous demonstration of firepower one day. As 25-pounders ripped up the ground ahead of us and Hurricanes tore overhead with all guns blazing, two Gurkha soldiers standing just behind me commentated laconically, "like popcorn," said one. "More like goats farting," said the other.'[14]

Disease was the other potent enemy, often more scything than the Japanese. In one half-year period, for instance, 20th Indian

Division suffered some 5,605 sickness cases and 2,345 battle casualties, a ratio of rather more than two to one.[15] Added to the natural hazards were the improvised booby traps left for the unwary. Even an abandoned dugout could spell danger, as MacDonald Fraser discovered:

> Just inside the doorway, where an unwary foot would tread on it, was a 'punjii' which is a sharpened stake set in the ground point upwards, that point usually being smeared with something nice and rotten, guaranteed to putrify the victim's bloodstream. Some punjiis are elaborate cantilevered affairs set to swing out of a darkened bunker and impale you; I had even heard of the crossbow variety, triggered by touching a taut cord. This was a conventional one, decorated with excrement by the look of it. But how old was it? (The things one does for a living: trying to determine the age of Jap crap, for eighteen rupees a week.)[16]

Aside from malaria, the jungle had an abundance of tropical fevers to offer; misery and suffering were compounded by the fact the men were never dry. Sweating terribly in the stifling blanket of humidity, unwashed, unshaved and rank, they spent days and weeks in soaking kit; the monsoon brought most operations to a standstill as pounding, incessant rain as heavy and sharp as driving hail battered for weeks, turning every surface into a thick glutinous soup of rancid mud. In Assam most supplies had to be moved by mule. Vehicles were useless on narrow jungle trails and the overburdened beasts suffered as much from parasites as their owners. Four-legged casualties were plentiful. A first exposure to the hazards of jungle warfare was always illuminating: 'Everybody that went into the Arakan to start with would be pretty certain they'd have malaria three times in the first 12 to 15 months. Malaria was sometimes followed by jaundice.'[17]

Having left Chittagong on 13 February, perhaps an inauspicious date, the Durhams began inching towards Donbaik on the night of 2/3 March. The area was well and cleverly defended, studded with bunkers covering a snaking bend in the chaung (dry river bed) dubbed 'Shepherd's Crook'. The ground over which any attacker must pass was dominated by Japanese guns dug in on the hills beyond. Evidence of previous hard fighting was all too evident; bloated corpses crowded no-man's-land. Sean Kelly was in temporary command of 'A' Company; daily he passed a solitary cross bearing the Urdu inscription *'Rasta nahin'* – 'For some days I passed this cross with feelings of silent respect for the unfortunate Indian soldier who lay beneath it until my slowly increasing knowledge of Urdu brought the realisation that the words meant "no road this way".'[18]

During the jungle darkness the Japanese used to launch dummy probing attacks using firecrackers to keep Allied troops twitching; much ammunition was often expended on such will-of-the-wisp targets. Sean Kelly again:

There was a good deal of firing at night and it seemed to be all rifle and light machine-gun, plus 36 grenades; but try as I would I could see no sign of the Japs from the forward positions nor could I hear their fire. This 'fifth of November' attitude was clarified and my suspicions confirmed when I talked to Phil Kelly[19] in the chaung next day. His Indians fired off at least 2,000 rounds each night, he said, presumably working on the theory that any dark patch might really be moving and that lead flying about in an unpredictable way must surely discourage any snooping by the Japs. Moreover, said Phil's opposite number, they had some 5,000 rounds in reserve and they could brass it all off their last night in the line. And I do believe they did![20]

First into the attack of 6th Brigade was 1st Royal Welsh. They could make little headway and losses ran very high. 'C' and 'D' Companies went forward to secure the western sector. The Durhams fought hard and secured most of their objectives but cunningly wrought enemy bunkers defied all efforts at early capture. The defenders had to be winkled and winnowed with bayonet and grenade. In the attack 'C' Company suffered grievously. Undeterred, Lieutenant Francis Greenwell[21] stormed one bunker, blowing his distinctive hunting horn, something of a novelty in the Arakan. He, with the other platoon officer, was wounded, as was the commander Bill Hutton, hit again in the same knee damaged in Belgium in 1940.[22] The Battalion MO, nicknamed 'Joe the Joiner', was kept very busy. After this din and fury, a brief hiatus ensued.

Sergeant-Major Martin McLaine, whom we encountered in France and Belgium, was back in action:

Before the attack on Donbaik, we formed up in a dry nullah[23] bed.

There was a series of them every few yards. We were carrying an average of 60 pounds of kit. The artillery fire was going over, and everything was dusty in the early morning light. The company commander gave the order bayonets on, smoke if you want to. The men dragged on their cigarettes, and were hanging on to them for grim death, because let's not be heroic, a man is only going to do a job if he's ordered to. He's going into an attack and the chance of him being killed is tremendous. The order came; right, get ready, over the top. I had the signallers and company clerk with me. As we went over the top I saw a Jap. I levelled the Tommy gun but the bloody thing wouldn't fire. I was disgusted – here I was, a professional soldier and I couldn't hit him. He had been throwing grenades, but scarpered. I never heard our Brens firing, only desultory shots from rifles. I had been in attacks in France and knew what it should sound like. All there was, was Japanese firing – nothing of ours at all.'[24]

Confusion reigned as McLaine sought instructions from the CO by radio:

He asked what was happening. I said this is the funniest attack I've ever been in, I can't hear a Bren; I can't hear a rifle. There's nothing moving, all I can see is bodies. He said, 'Do something about it then.' 'What can I do?' 'Get the men in.' Well, I only had Company HQ with me, the other two platoons were off on their own. I found the company commander wounded. He'd been wounded in France in the knee, and his same leg had been hit again. He was bleeding badly, I dragged him back through the nullah, found 'A' Company commander and put my company commander on a stretcher.[25]

McLaine now returned to the fight:

I went to find the two rifle platoons. I passed a stretcher with Lieutenant Greenwell on it. He was full of shrapnel from a Japanese plastic grenade, lying smoking a cigarette. He said 'Well, Sergeant-Major,' stroking his old man, 'they didn't hit that.' He was newly married. I found seven of his platoon lying down. I shouted, 'Come on lads, bayonets!' A corporal said, 'Wait, wait, Sergeant-Major, these Brens and rifles won't fire.' I didn't believe him and got down behind a Bren. One round fired and then the gun jammed solid. I went through all the old drills, but nothing would work. I slung it aside in disgust. 'Give us your rifle.' I fired it, but the bolt stuck solid and I could not eject the round, except by putting the butt on the ground and booting the bolt with my foot.[26]

Dirt and wet were the causes of such malfunctions.

Colonel Theobalds recalled:

It's most deceptive during a lull, you practically never see a Jap and one can wander about quite exposed without anything happening except some occasional mortaring or shelling or the odd sniper. Their snipers were very active one day, but we certainly got four and they've been more cautious since then. Sergeant Turnbull spotted a couple only 15 yards away from his position and he bumped them both off. Sergeant Scott and Lance-Sergeant Stevenson were both killed trying to get at the Japs but the trouble is you can't find the way into their strongpoints, which really are immensely strong; after a number of direct hits by our guns, the old machine-gun pops up again, apparently quite unaffected. The chaps are all in very good heart and the principal criticism is that they so seldom get a chance of shooting at a Jap! At night the Japs wander around with crackers trying to draw our fire, but the men are very steady and refuse to be drawn.[27]

These, for the British, were costly and very modest gains, not likely to affect the strategic outcome. What would was a major Japanese counter-attack aimed at cutting off the attackers on the peninsula completely. This was a well-timed and very well-aimed thrust which succeeded in throwing a block across 6th Brigade's line of retreat by Indin. On 4 April the retreat commenced. It was to be very much a fighting withdrawal. Next day the Durhams were in action. The Japanese succeeded in capturing Brigadier Cavendish, leaving Lieutenant-Colonel Theobalds to take over Brigade whilst Major Lister-Todd led the 2nd. The fight for Indin was at very close quarters, with the enemy sheltering in bamboo thickets surrounding the settlement.

This proved their undoing. Mortars and guns hosed the bamboo, obliging the Japanese simply to be killed where they were or try to break out with the Durhams eagerly in attendance. It was a fine opportunity for killing Japanese and the battalion did not see such a gift go to waste:

> It was Hobson's choice for the Japs: either stay under cover – for they had not had time to dig in properly – and be killed by the shells; or run for it and be slaughtered by rifles and automatics positioned round them like guns at a rat hunt. Many did run for it, screaming at the tops of their voices, and were shot down as they did so. Each company took a heavy toll, though Lieutenant Pat Rome's platoon actually brought in a live prisoner – a rarity at that stage of the war as the Japs preferred to die rather than be captured.[28]

In what must have seemed an almost surreal experience, the Durhams withdrew along a sandy coastal strip; this bizarrely idyllic strand of beach must have seemed a very marked contrast to the dense, inhospitable bush. More fighting followed and the retreat, mildly chaotic, continued. For some time the battalion was isolated from Brigade. A nasty incident of friendly fire, or 'blue on blue' in the modern idiom, occurred when Indian troops opened fire mistakenly at Myinhlut. Two men were killed and Terry Bardell, hero of the earlier seaborne raid, was severely injured. Patrols were sent out into the maze of low hills, outliers of the Mayu range. One such fighting patrol drawn from 'D' Company clashed with a rather larger force of Japanese and inflicted considerable loss, though not without cost: the redoubtable Corporal Hutton was killed.

Life in the jungle demanded other arts than killing; brewing tea was something of a ritual and a serious one. MacDonald Fraser explains:

> Brewing up is not merely a matter of infusing tea, making the fire comes into it, and when you have lit and maintained fires in the monsoon, you have nothing more to learn...it was a simple business of assembling bamboo slivers, igniting them (no small thing, with Indian 'Lion' matches which invariably broke and sprayed the striker with flaming phosphorus), and bringing about a gallon of water to the boil in the section brew tin. This

was a jealously-guarded article, about a foot cubed, made by cutting a compo ration tin in two and piercing the rim for a handle of signal wire. The casting in of the tea leaves from the section box was the crucial thing, followed by the ceremonial dropping in of two broken matchsticks to attract stray leaves; remove the tin from the heat, invite the guests to scoop out the brew with their piallas[29] and tea was served...[30]

In another brush with the Japanese, Corporal McLeary suffered numerous wounds:

When he was hit he fell over a small rock-face into a jungle-covered nala (a small ravine) with four wounds in his buttocks and stomach, another four in his right wrist and with his right palm completely shot away. When he came to, and despite these grievous injuries, he made his way back some three miles to battalion Headquarters, complete with all his arms and equipment. He made his report to the colonel in a very low voice as he lay on a stretcher and was then evacuated; but he died before he reached hospital.[31]

It wasn't until 12 May, as the Allies fell back yet further, that the Durhams were reunited with the survivors of 6th Brigade. Two weeks later they were back at their starting point of Chittagong. It could be said the campaign was a rather unsound gamble and one which failed miserably. The 2nd Battalion DLI had performed extremely well under most difficult circumstances and had accounted for many of the enemy. Though battle casualties had not been heavy, jungle fevers, most notably malaria, exacted a very high toll. The Durhams had withstood their first test in Burma; now a far greater trial awaited them.

The Forgotten Army – Kohima and Imphal

We make the best plans we can gentlemen, and train our wills to hold steadfastly to them in the face of adversity, and yet to be flexible enough to change them when events show them to be unsound, or to take advantage of an opportunity that unfolds during the battle itself. But in the end every important battle develops to a point where there is no real control by senior commanders. Each soldier feels himself to be alone...The dominant feeling of the battlefield is loneliness.

'Bill' Slim[32]

Burma was a very long way from the conflict raging in Europe and, for the British public, possessed none of the immediacy. Eyes here were fixed upon Italy and the inevitable assault upon Hitler's Fortress Europe upon which the outcome of the war would surely depend. Even the Eastern Front was vague; our Soviet Allies gave little away and most of that propaganda. The Poles were in the process of building up to their doomed but magnificent rising in Warsaw. Nonetheless the 'Forgotten Army' in the Far East was coming of age. British, Indian Army and Gurkha forces had endured defeat after defeat from a seemingly omnipotent foe, yet that was changing: Wingate's raid, though of limited strategic value, had done much to restore badly dented morale and the tactical value of air supply would further transform 14th Army's prospects.

Slim was one of the Allies' very finest commanders in WWII yet even he was taken by surprise at the speed and fury of General Mutagachi's offensive. A rather bombastic officer not, one feels, highly regarded by his subordinates or contemporaries, Mutagachi had energy and ruthless determination. His conduct, as the campaign unravelled and turned into disaster, became increasingly erratic. It seemed likely he would, in best Samurai tradition, commit suicide but he abandoned the path of honour for the ignominy of subsequent dismissal.

In February the Japanese launched a new thrust in the Arakan and, next month, struck at Imphal and Kohima. Moving with great purpose and elan, the Japanese effectively humbugged Slim, who anticipated having more time to react. Kohima was but lightly held and the important rearward base at Dimapur scarcely garrisoned at all. Available troops were thus rushed into the sector on an ad hoc basis. The 2nd Division, which had trained so extensively for sophisticated manoeuvres and special operations, became a form of imperial frontier force fighting an old-style Kipling war, albeit against a skilled, ruthless and numerous foe.

The Durhams were mobilised on 21 March; Lieutenant-Colonel J.H. Brown had succeeded Colonel Theobalds, who had received further promotion.[33] By 9 April, 2nd Battalion had reached the aerodrome at Dimapur. Kohima was not fully surrounded and only one Indian Brigade had been deployed to bolster the perimeter. On 15 April the Durhams began the long climb up to the encircled garrison. Two days later they halted, in reserve lines, some two miles short of the battlefield. This fight would be spread over a lush and epic landscape: 'The scenery was superb; the Highlands without heather, the Yorkshire Fells without their stone villages, all on a colossal scale which made our trucks look very puny...On such an immense landscape, it felt like defending the Alps with a platoon.'[34]

Max Hastings quotes Brian Aldiss, then a signaller with 2nd Division:

> When our lorry was labouring to the top of a crest, we could see the thread of vehicles far away behind us, below clouds; conversely, when we were in a valley, we could look up through clouds and see that thread continuing far ahead of us, climbing the next series of heights...To be part of this aspect of war was most thrilling after dark. Dim headlights scarcely penetrated the muck we threw up. We could scarcely see the tail lights of the vehicle ahead. Speed was almost down to walking pace. The impression of an animal bent on traversing a strange planet was at its strongest. On either side, unknowable, thrilling, fearsome, stood the jungle, pale as a ghost jungle in its layers of dust.[35]

Slim's warriors were British, Indian, Gurkha and Sikh. Of the score of VCs won during the campaign, 14 went to soldiers of the Indian Army, three of these to a single Gurkha Battalion. The General himself recounted a tale of meeting Peter Rees, commanding 14th Indian Division, who was in good voice and singing a hymn in his native Welsh tongue. His Assamese soldiers were joining in but in Khasi; apparently the two harmonies blended rather well.[36]

Kohima was an unlikely battleground in that it towered in this majestic, unspoilt hill region of Assam. Politically, the settlement was the base for the district commissioner, whose neat bungalow, summer house and tennis court became key tactical features. This agreeable domestic arrangement would not have looked at all out of place in the Home Counties, yet the tennis court would witness some of the most savage combat of the entire desperate defence. Set at some 5,000 feet above sea level, the long single road from Dimapur clambers up the saddle of Kohima Ridge before cutting across the dipping crest at right angles. The ridge was banana-shaped, with the civilian buildings at one tip; beyond lay Kohima village. Running away from this first eminence were a series of summits or hillocks, the whole a few miles in length.

Garrison Hill came first, then Kuki's Picquet, next lay FSD Ridge (Field Supply Depot), along to DIS (Daily Issue Store) Ridge, now Jail Hill, and the Pimple on GPT (General Purpose Transport) Ridge:

> To begin with I look over an area overlooking the tennis court… The lie of the land made it impossible to move by day because of Japanese snipers. We were in Kohima for three weeks. We were attacked every single night…They came in waves; it was like a pigeon shoot. Most nights they overran part of the battalion position so we had to mount counter-attacks…Water was short and restricted to about one pint per man per day. So we stopped shaving. Air supply was the key, but the steep terrain and narrow ridges meant that some of the drops went to the Japs. My company went to Kohima over 100 strong and came out at about 60.[37]

The tennis court became the very cockpit of battle:

> The battle took place on the tennis court – we shot them on the tennis court and grenaded them on the tennis court. We held the tennis court against desperate attacks for five days. We held because I had instant contact by radio with the guns, and the Japs never seemed to learn how to surprise us. They used to shout in English as they formed up, 'give up.' So we knew when an attack was coming in. One would judge just the right moment to call down gun and mortar fire to catch them as they were launching the attack, and by the time they were approaching us they were decimated. They were not acting intelligently and did the same old stupid thing again and again. We had experienced fighting the Japs in the Arakan, bayoneting the wounded and prisoners. So whereas we respected the Afrika Korps, not so the Japanese; they had renounced any right to be regarded as human, and we thought of them as vermin to be exterminated.[38]

On the warm afternoon of 19 April, 'B' Company launched an initial assault on Terrace Hill, necessary to effect a break-in. Captain Allen leading his company fell in the attack:[39] 'He had been well up during the attack, and when it was over went forward to organise the defence when a burst of machine-gun fire caught him in the chest. He lived only a few seconds and his only words, as the padre reached him, were "Well done 'B' Company."'[40] Two days after that, the Durhams relieved their predecessors and occupied Garrison Hill. This was all that remained in British hands; the Japanese had possession of the rest and had their sights firmly fixed on this remaining strongpoint. By now the timber-clad ridge had become a blasted wilderness, reminiscent of the Western Front, trees ripped and scorched, just mute, tortured stumps remaining, stench, detritus and mutilated flesh of war abounding, charnel-house stink pervading. Resupply had only been possible by air so tattered parachutes hung, draped like silken shrouds, over ravaged trees.

Digging-in is not an expression that could really describe life under fire on Garrison Hill. The men existed in a warren of dugouts clawed from the surface in a desperate troglodyte existence, surfacing from bombardments to fight, Tolkien-esque brutal, bloody and filthy. These positions were euphemistically described as 'non-tactical bunkers'.[41] Across the narrow neck the Japanese occupied Kuki's Picquet, 'C' Company holding Garrison Hill with 'D' behind, 'A' and 'B' some way below. At around 01.30 hours on 23 April the enemy deluged Garrison Hill in fire, then attacked with infantry. Like shrieking banshees the Japanese came on, heedless of casualties as fire flensed the ranks. As one fell, another came forward, leaping over the piles of their own dead that clogged the neck. Fighting every bloody inch of tortured ground, the Durhams were being pushed back by sheer weight of numbers into their own Company HQ.

At this critical point Major 'Tank' Waterhouse[42] brought up 'D' Company and the fight swayed back and forwards over the narrow summit. The Major remembered:

Every now and then we managed to push forward a little, but our casualties were heavy. We were now lying shoulder to shoulder and suffering very badly from spring grenades. Martin Wilson, second in command of 'C' Company, was badly hit, but refused to be moved till the others had been evacuated. All [telephone] line had gone and most of the wireless sets. Our gunner O.P. was killed and it took nearly two hours to get any defensive fire. About 4.00am we started to counter-attack the right flank.

Bill Watson of 'D' Company was killed leading one of these. He was last seen clubbing Japs with the butt end of a Bren gun. Willie Lockhart, my second-in-command, was also killed by a burst from an automatic. But the Japs were getting a good beating too; and we could hear them shouting and screaming just below us. They seemed to have had just about enough and some officer was trying to reorganise them to attack again. There was a short lull. Roger Stock, commanding 'C' Company, and I had a cigarette together and talked of Teesdale and our next leave. Then the Japs attacked again. That was the last I saw of Roger; he went forward to his hard-pressed Company and I back to collect the clerks and cooks. When I returned I was told that Roger had been killed and Pat Rome wounded.[43]

The Durhams were a very long way from Teesdale.

Martin McLaine was, as before, in the thick of the fight:

I was woken by shouts from my company commander, Major Stock. Green phosphorus was pouring into one end of the trench. I was covered in the stuff – which causes deep, penetrating burns. I was rubbing the stuff off me with earth, then the Japs came in yelling and shouting. They were in among us and just 10 yards away there was a fearsome-looking man waving a sword. But we did for him. When the position was finally cleared, my company commander, the runners and the signallers were all dead. A shell had landed right in the shell hole they were standing in.[44]

As the British began to drive the Japanese back from the ridge they were met with a storm of mortar rounds and grenades. The fight raged till 05.00 hours, when Captain J.W. Kelly led up a fresh platoon from 'A' Company below. Now the Durhams' bayonets exacted a fresh toll from their attackers, finally coming close to restoring the position. On the hilltop the corpses of friend and foe were piled in the sack-like oblivion of violent death:

One section under Corporal Arthur Breden set about them [the Japanese] with Sten guns and grenades. Breden and [Captain] Kelly bowled grenades into one Jap dugout with telling effect. At one stage Private McLellan, a wee Scot in charge of a Bren gun, fell bottom-first into a foxhole, where he stuck, head and feet to the sky, swearing horribly. 'Gie's a hand out Maister Kelly,' he shouted; which request was complied with and, none the worse, he got his gun into action again.[45]

Captain Kelly was wounded soon after but kept going and went back to collect a further platoon. Corporal Bredon battled on, clearing more Japanese from 'C' Company's battered trenches: 'Bredon was badly wounded in the legs, but nothing daunted, continued to direct operations sitting down. He was soon hit again, this time in the shoulder and chest, but he refused to give in and, dragging himself once more into a sitting position, tried to start firing his Sten gun. Just then he was killed by a mortar burst and the battalion lost a very gallant NCO.'[46] Though Japanese fire never slackened, neither side could expect fresh gains after dawn. Through the whole long and bloody day 2nd Battalion clung to their trenches, such as these were in this lunar nightmare of devastation. Snipers added to the misery of danger. Of 15 officers from three companies, only four were unwounded; 'A' was reduced from 136 to 60 effectives.

On 27 April the Japanese attacked again. The leading waves carried only grenades, no rifles. Again, by weight of the press and regardless of casualties they reached the scarred summit: 'There, they went round and round shouting "Tojo" and blessing the Mikado; it was the old boy's birthday.'[47] The Durhams put in a strong counter-attack which, at some cost, restored their slender grip to what it had been prior to the first onslaught four days before. Lieutenant Greenwell charged, once again sounding his hunting horn, probably a first now in Kohima! The 2nd's mortars fired over 1,300 rounds, so furious was the combat. Any who had suffered the hell of Flanders would have recognised the scene along these ravaged ridges.

Fighting was murderous, no quarter asked or given and frequently hand-to-hand:

At the next bunker, a Japanese soldier rushed out. He knew if he stayed there he was going to get a grenade in, so he came out of the back door, which was behind me. I didn't see him when he fired. He got me through the side of my face. It felt like being hit by a clenched fist but it didn't hurt as much as a really good punch in a fight. I spat out a handful of teeth, spun round and he was a few paces away, facing me. He had a rifle and bayonet. I pressed the trigger but I'd got no ammunition. As he came towards me I felt it was either him or me. I was an instructor in unarmed combat, so I let him come and threw the light machine-gun in his face…Before he hit the ground I had my hand round his windpipe and I literally tried to tear it out. It wouldn't come – if I could have got his windpipe out I would have twisted it round his neck. We were tossing over on the ground. I managed to get his bayonet off his rifle and finished him with that.[48]

A gunner wrote:

There was not one tree standing that was not blasted and splintered: the more primitive houses were knocked flat and others were holed and battered beyond recognition. The place stank. The earth everywhere was ploughed up with shellfire, and human remains lay rotting as the battle raged over them. Flies swarmed everywhere, and multiplied with incredible speed. Men retched as they dug in, and a priority task was to clear up as far as possible. But even then the stink hung in the air and permeated one's clothes and hair. It made one realise once again how sub-human the Japs were. A bunker was found in which about 20 men had fought and lived for several days – a bunker littered with their dead companions and their own excreta…[49]

A brief respite followed when the Battalion survivors were temporarily withdrawn before being thrust back into the maelstrom on 4 May. Although the Japanese still enjoyed local superiority in numbers, Allied air power and armour were vastly superior. Light Stuart tanks or 'Honeys' we last encountered in the desert came into their own here; largely obsolescent in the West, their speed and agility proved invaluable in Burma. This time it was the Durhams who would assume the offensive; time to clear the Japanese from the high ground of the ridge. This proved costly; the Durhams' target was FSD Ridge lying beyond Kuki's Picquet. Lieutenant-Colonel Brown was but one of many who fell in this assault. Survivors clung grimly to a precarious grip on the summit until being at last relieved on the 6th.

Aside from the tenacity and fury of the enemy, the physical conditions were dreadfully debilitating:

The physical hammering one takes is difficult to understand. The heat, humidity, altitude and the slope of almost every foot of ground combine to knock hell out of the stoutest constitution. You gasp for air which doesn't seem to come, you drag your legs upwards till they seem reduced to the strength of matchsticks, you wipe the sweat out of your eyes…So you stop, horrified to be prodded by the man behind you or cursed by an officer in front.[50]

Heavy losses had been sustained and little of tactical value gained. Fighting in these extreme conditions was exacerbated by difficult ground:

At 22.00 got the order to move out at 22.15…This night approach, in my opinion, was most difficult – very tricky navigation and altogether rather nerve wracking, something I shall never forget…I had to navigate the column – in fact, I had to lead it. Very tricky, no defined tracks, thick undergrowth, down hundreds of feet round spurs and up hundreds of feet and across re-entrants, hacking, pushing, stumbling, and through ruined bashas[51] and so on. The gist of this local attack on to this position was an assault in line under covering fire. Pen and I started the ball rolling by whistling over some grenades…But the terrain was not easy, there being many shell-holes, horizontal tree stumps and the odd trench to negotiate. As we were going down the slope we caught the full blast of about three light machine-guns and rifle fire and, of course, grenades as we tried to negotiate the obstacles. This, I am afraid, resulted in many more men dropping…After this there followed a sniping duel, and then things happened the like of which I had never seen before. It was the nearest approach to a snowball fight that could be imagined. The air became thick with grenades, both theirs and ours, and we were all scurrying about trying to avoid them as they burst. This duel appeared to go on non-stop for an unreckonable time.[52]

Manipur was inhabited by native hillmen, the Nagas,[53] who did the Allies tremendous service acting as stretcher-bearers and porters. Their physical hardiness enabled them to perform feats of endurance our men could not, in the circumstances, have hoped to emulate. The Burmese generally were no particular enthusiasts for British rule; we had come as conquerors originally, as now did the Japanese. The sheer savagery of the occupiers, however, soon alienated the locals, who even formed ad hoc militias armed with ancient muskets and liberated Japanese Arisaka rifles.[54] The Durhams recuperated by the hill settlement of Jotsoma, a quiet sector untrammelled by enemy action. Lieutenant Greenwell found the local fleas every bit as aggressive as the Japanese[55] whilst Sergeant Hogg became a sure hit with the young women of the tribe, practising the hairdresser's art![56]

All the while fighting continued, resupply was a major logistical nightmare:

> The rain poured down upon this jungle and its narrow tracks. The mud deepened, the branches dripped in melancholy rhythm, and progress towards the...box [defended area] was slowed down most seriously...Anxious and confused men slithered on the slopes, sweated and swore as they struggled to drag their frightened obstinate mules uphill. So slippery was the muddy surface of the tracks that even when the mule loads had been taken off the saddles and laid in the slush, the mules still stumbled and kicked in their game efforts to mount the slope. Mule drivers fell to their knees and held on the saddle ropes to stop themselves from rolling down to the bottom.[57]

Even when there was no intense fighting in progress, there was always the nerve-shredding danger of patrols. Handy hints for young officers offered a view straight from Kipling: 'Jungle warfare should be regarded as a game, healthful, interesting and thrilling; the men should feel at home in the jungle and regard it as a friend. They must realise the absolute necessity for jungle training as a means to defeat the Japanese who come from one of the most highly industrialised countries in the world and have no natural advantages as jungle infantry.'[58]

Practical experience tended to assume a less cheery note:

> Any Tommy will tell you that next to making a bayonet charge, the thing he hates most are patrols...I took part in many patrols, but the one I will always remember was a listening patrol just outside of Mogaung. On a listening patrol you are away from the main body of troops, listening and noting any movement of enemy troops. On this occasion there were just four of us; lying by the Mogaung Road...It was pitch black. Time was dragging. All we wanted was to get back to the main body of troops...

Suddenly there was a movement, a sound. The usual challenge was shouted: 'Halt, who goes there?' There was just a lot of muttering. The password was shouted. More muttering; then the Bren gunner opened up, hand grenades were thrown. One could not see a thing, just flashes of bursting hand grenades. We were all lying flat on the ground. Suddenly I got the urge to urinate. To stand up was out of the question. I could not hold on any longer, so I just lay there and pissed myself. Next morning we found one dead Jap who had taken the full burst from a Bren gun magazine.[59]

A mere 10 days later and 2nd Battalion returned for a third time. Major L.A.B. Robinson, late of the Royal Berkshires, was commanding and their task now was to clear a final major obstacle, the Aradura Spur. Time was not on the British side. Already that herald of monsoon, the *chota bersaht*, was opening nature's annual offensive: a chorus of hammering, unending wet, rising to the full crescendo as the monsoon proper got under way. Slim had taken the bold decision to fight on despite the season. If IV Corps, advancing now from Imphal, could join with the troops from Kohima, the Japanese line of withdrawal to the Chindwin could be successfully interdicted, dealing a major blow, turning retreat into catastrophe. Now, 2nd Division was to advance straight down the road towards Imphal, a major undertaking in itself. The Durhams advanced by stages, one platoon leapfrogging over another. It was slow, dangerous and most uncomfortable:

The rains had now started in no mean fashion, and what with the Jap, the thick jungle, the hill and the weather, life was pretty unpleasant. However, having got practically to the top, some other units of the division got behind the Jap, who very obligingly pulled out and saved us what would have been a most bloody battle on the crest. In spite of the fact we didn't see a great deal of fighting on the way up, I liked this part of it least of all, as the jungle was very dense and you never quite knew where anybody else was; and wherever we went the Jap was always uphill, which is a beastly sensation.[60]

Mutagachi's troops were falling back but the ground as they withdrew towards Imphal, the single ribbon of road, swooped and ducked along precipitous cliff-sides, great soaring peaks crowding around. The Japanese were in retreat but still full of fight. At Khuzama, what would now be termed a suicide bomber with a magnetic mine strapped to his chest flung himself upon the hull of an Allied tank. The advance was complicated by a series of small but highly dangerous 'search and destroy' type operations, but day by day the tempo of resistance began to slacken, until it could be termed a total rout: 'It really was great fun, just like walking up partridges. We got them absolutely on the hop, the whole battalion and attached troops were plugging away for dear life at the Japs, who were making off sideways up over the hill towards the Chindwin.'[61]

Alex Wilson took part in the pursuit:

> We met the Imphal garrison coming north. We were clearing road blocks quicker than the Japs thought we could. The Japs would blow the little culvert between two ridges, and sit on the other side – there were no bunkers but foxholes and they fought hard. The technique was to fix them in their front and climb above then, and outflank them. The Japs were getting short of men. Artillery support was very important. Sometimes the guns fired direct over open sights. The Jap artillery was very sparse – they were an army in disarray…but it didn't mean they didn't fight.[62]

For the Japanese, as Brigadier 'Tubby' Lethbridge, Slim's Chief-of-Staff, noted, the rout 'must have been worse than Napoleon's retreat from Moscow. The whole jungle stinks of corruption. I counted 25 dead Japs on the side of the road, between two successive milestones. There must have been hundreds more who had crawled away into the jungle to die. In some places there are Jap lorries with skeletons sitting in the driver's seats, and a staff car with four skeletons in it.'[63] Such sights were commonplace on that road of bones:

> The air was thick with the smell of their dead. The sick and wounded were left behind in hundreds…We saw dead Japs all along the road, some in their stockinged feet, and where the hills were highest and most exhausting, they lay huddled in groups. They carried only a mess-tin, steel helmet and rifle. Some lay as though asleep, while others were twisted and broken by the bombs which had rained down on them. Five hundred dead lay in the ruins of Tamu. The pagoda was choked with wounded and

dying. They had crawled here, in front of the four tall and golden images, to die. Hand grenades littered the altar. In the centre of the temple was a dais, and carved into this was a perfectly symmetrical pattern of the foot of Buddha. It was littered with blood-soaked bandages and Japanese field-postcards.[64]

After this dreadful slogging match, the offensive now became something of a triumphal march, everywhere Mutagachi's survivors were in retreat, their losses disastrous. For a week from 15 June the Battalion swept forward – on the 22nd the Durhams shook hands with IV Corps' leading echelons at Milestone 108. The battle of Kohima was over. Now the Durhams would blazon the name of the hill station on their colours, carried as ever with pride. This honour was dear in the winning: 2nd Battalion DLI had sustained the worst losses of all units in 2nd Division; over 150 names are inscribed on the Memorial.[65]

General Grover reckoned that the fighting on Garrison Hill at Kohima was worse than the Somme, where he had fought in the First World War. The 2nd Battalion DLI had more casualties there than anyone else. In my three companies there were four officers left. Of the original 136 men in 'A' Company, only 60 were left. The pioneer and carrier platoons also lost many killed and wounded. The fighting was hand-to-hand. Men were kept going by training, regimental pride and the will to survive.[66]

On the road to Mandalay

> *Wrap up all my care and woe,*
> *Here I go swinging low,*
> *Bye-bye Shanghai!*
> *Won't somebody wait for me,*
> *Please get in a state for me*
> *Bye-bye Shanghai!*
> *Up before the colonel in the morning,*
> *He have me a rocket and a warning:*
> *'You've been out with Sun-yat-sen,*
> *You won't go out with him again',*
> *Shanghai, bye-bye!*

Sung to the tune of 'Bye-Bye Blackbird'[67]

The two battles at Imphal and Kohima, whilst immensely costly for the 14th Army, had decided the course of the campaign in Burma. The Japanese, like the flood tide, had run to their high-water mark; from now on theirs would be the ebb and the inexorable road to certain defeat. Whilst 2nd Battalion was refitting, a series of bridgeheads were flung across the Chindwin. On 3 December, the Durhams, now led by Lieutenant-Colonel C.A. Southey from the Essex Regiment, returned to the fight and, as part of 6th Brigade's advance, passed the barrier of the Chindwin on 20 December. Eight days later they encountered and beat elements of the Japanese 33rd Division. Now on the fabled road to Mandalay, on the last day of that tumultuous year, they left the soaking jungles behind and emerged on to the central plain. Now their march was on the banks of the myriad web of irrigation canals. 'Tank' Waterhouse, now Lieutenant-Colonel, was in charge. 'It must', David Rissik reflected, 'have smelt pretty opulent at this time as practically everybody was smoking the excellent Burma cheroots which were produced in the area at about three shillings a hundred.'

On the afternoon of 26 February the Durhams crossed the Irrawaddy. The Japanese, if they were badly weakened, could still fight back. Resistance, when it was encountered, was as fanatical as ever but IV Corps seized the important bastion of Meiktila and won another important victory. Mandalay fell and the Allies' triumphal advance continued. At this point the Durhams, together with the whole of 2nd Division, were pulled out of the fight to prepare for an amphibious assault on Rangoon but land forces reached the city first and the Durhams' march through the freshly liberated streets was largely ceremonial. By this time 2nd Battalion DLI had fought their final battle in Burma and the remainder of their time in theatre was occupied by less martial undertakings. On 15 August 1945 it finally ended. The final word should be left to the regimental historian – 'there has yet to be found something which, given good commanders, these men cannot do'.[68] It would be impossible to disagree.

Max Hastings, for whose analyses I have the greatest respect, takes the view that the campaign in Burma 'would be difficult, and would not bring the defeat of Japan a day closer, British and Indian soldiers must die, so that Churchill's people were seen to pay their share of the price for victory in the Far East.'[69] The Prime Minister was no stranger to realpolitik yet this view is overly cynical. The Japanese had trounced British armies in Malaya and Burma, the fall of Singapore, a humiliation and catastrophe of unparalleled dimension; not since the debacle of the First Afghan War[70] had British arms been so shamed. To prove that the Japanese were not invincible was essential to restore British pride; Kohima was the remedy for Singapore and final triumph in Burma both vindication and restoration. We simply had to do it. British commanders, Slim in particular, were not impressed by US General, 'Vinegar Joe' Stilwell's obsession with nationalist China or his rampant anglophobia!

The Kohima and Imphal battles, though never as much in the public eye as the campaigns in Western Europe, showed that the British, Indians and Gurkhas could take on the best of the Imperial Japanese armies and not just win but ultimately rout them. The names of Durham men carved into the memorial on Garrison Hill tell a very different story to the disgrace of Singapore. Their stand brought about the collapse of the Japanese position throughout the whole theatre and contributed considerably to their final defeat.

Notes

1 Fraser, G.M., *Quartered Safe Out Here* (London, 2003), p.3.
2 John Maxwell Edmonds (1875–1958); his words are said to have been inspired by the memorial to the 300 Spartans at Thermopylae by Simonedes of Cos.
3 This ragtag army collapsed when pitted against their former comrades serving the Raj and surrendered en masse.
4 Fraser, p.38.
5 Hastings, M., *Nemesis* (London, 2008), p.62.
6 Ibid. p.68.
7 Ibid. p.70.
8 Ibid. p.71.
9 The Reverend D.E. Rice; see Ward, S.G.P., *Faithful – A History of the Durham Light Infantry* (Durham, 1962), p.546.
10 He died of cancer in 1941: see Ward, p.546.
11 Rissik, D., *The DLI at War – History of the DLI 1939–1945* (Durham, 1952), p.168.
12 Arthur, M., *Forgotten Voices of the Second World War* (London, 2005), p.257.
13 Ibid. p.255
14 Cross, J.P., *Jungle Warfare* (London, 1989), p.61.
15 Hastings, p.85.
16 Fraser, p.10.
17 Arthur, p.252.
18 Rissik, p.171.
19 No relation – later killed by a sniper.
20 Rissik, p.172.
21 Numerous of the Greenwell family had served with DLI.
22 Rissik, p.175.

23   Rather like a wadi in the desert a stream or an inlet with steep banks.
24   Arthur, pp.252–3.
25   Ibid.
26   Ibid.
27   Rissik, p.176.
28   Ibid. p.179.
29   An enamelled mug.
30   Fraser, p.77.
31   Rissik, p.181.
32   Hastings, p.73
33   Ward, p.551.
34   Hastings, p.73.
35   Ibid. p.78.
36   Ibid. p.79.
37   Arthur, p.387.
38   Lewis-Stemple, J., *The Autobiography of the British Soldier* (London, 2007), pp.375–6.
39   Ward, p.552.
40   Rissik, p.186.
41   Ward, p.552.
42   Rissik, p.189.
43   Ibid. pp.188–9.
44   Arthur, p.387.
45   Rissik, pp.189–90.
46   Ibid. p.190.
47   Ibid. p.191.
48   Arthur, pp.391–92.
49   Cross, p.72.
50   Arthur, p.389.
51   Basha: a bivouac.
52   Arthur, p.389.
53   Nagas: part of a tribal grouping of peoples inhabiting Manipur and Assam.
54   Rissik, p.194.
55   Greenwell counted a full 109 bites! See Rissik, p.194.
56   Ibid.
57   Cross, p.93.
58   Ibid. p.88.
59   Ibid. pp.88–9.
60   Rissik, p.195.
61   Ibid. p.197.
62   Arthur, p.396.
63   Hastings, pp.75–6.
64   Ibid.
65   Ward, p.554.
66   Arthur, p.389.
67   Fraser, p.80.
68   Ward, p.557.
69   Hastings, p.67.
70   The First Afghan War (1839–42) ended in the destruction of British Imperial forces, the 'Army of the Indus' reduced to one survivor.

Chapter 12

The Long Road Home: Prisoners of War, 1940–45

The escapers were some of the finest characters that I have ever known or likely to meet. Their total reliance, total loyalty and total devotion to duty were unbelievable, as was their total sacrifice. So often this had passed without even recognition, gratitude or acknowledgement. This was a new brand of Christian in action.

Captain Michael Farr MBE DLI

I arrived at Feethams, Darlington bus station, and joined the back of the queue for Ferryhill. A policeman asked if I was on leave. I replied that I was a returning prisoner of war. The policemen took me to the front of the queue and told the driver not to charge me for the journey home. It was very emotional. My mother clung to me. The welcome was tremendous.

Frederick Walsh DLI

During the course of the Second World War, some 3,500 members of DLI battalions were taken prisoner throughout the theatres in which the regiment was engaged. The POWs endured much during their often very long captivity. Many had gone 'into the bag' in 1940. '…Yet whose courage and good humour rarely failed them. They and their fellow prisoners from all three services remained a thorn in the side of the enemy throughout their years of captivity, preoccupying many thousands of enemy troops during their escapes and acting as eyes and ears for British Intelligence.'[1]

'Many did not return; some did with grievous hurt or illness, but all with a part of their lives as a hidden, inner world, rarely spoken of but something that would never go away. Their superb self-discipline, which protected security by retaining to themselves only their own part and nothing of that of their neighbours, made success possible. It never broke down under duress or reprisal.'[2]

'Into the bag'

During the campaign of 1940 in France and Belgium, culminating in the evacuation of the British Expeditionary Force (BEF) from Dunkirk (see chapters 2 and 3), seven battalions of DLI were engaged. Second Battalion, all regulars, fought on the banks of the River Dyle,[3] whilst the territorials of 6th, 8th and 9th Battalions took part in the Allied counter-attack at Arras from 21 May. The 10th and 11th Battalions, forming part of 70th Brigade, also fought and, like the other formations, suffered heavy loss in dead, wounded and captured.[4] For young soldiers, surrendering proved a difficult experience. Thomas Lawton of 11th Battalion DLI recalled: 'The humiliation of a defeated army and the degradation of being rounded up like cattle and herded through France in never-ending circles were very demoralising.'[5]

Alongside the shame of capture, in many cases without even the limited satisfaction of having fought the enemy beforehand, was an element of fear as to how they might be treated. During the retreat to Dunkirk there were numerous instances of British prisoners being murdered.[6] Certain allegations of atrocities against surrendering Germans have subsequently been levelled at DLI.[7] In the main, these fears proved groundless and most of the front-line fighting men on both sides treated their prisoners with decency. Ken Lovell of 16th Battalion, captured later in the war during the Italian campaign, remembered his Fallschirmjager captors:

They were quite reasonable to me. It was amazing. You're enemies and will kill each other but between infantrymen fighting each other there is nevertheless a bond. I think it is the bond of all being in the shit together quite honestly. There are exceptions but on the whole most of the prisoners I spoke to were reasonably treated by the front-line troops. The front-line troops were quite reasonable. There is a fellow feeling; the further you move away from the front line, the worse it became.[8]

In the stress and confusion of contact within a rapidly changing battlefront units became lost or separated. Their introduction to war and capture were often brutal. Douglas Nelson of 10th Battalion, deployed near Arras on 20 May, was one of those who experienced such a harsh baptism:

> We were ordered to take up positions in a ditch at the side of a lane in Frevent, a small village near Arras. The order was, 'Watch your front.' A party of Tyneside Scottish[9] were in a ditch at the other side of the road. We saw a tank at the top of the road. After a time bullets started to fly round and we were ordered to lie flat in a cornfield. The corn was just beginning to grow. The sun was up and it was getting warm. We tried to take off our greatcoats and replace our equipment whilst lying down.[10] Some of the chaps were wounded. A young lieutenant who was a nice chap said, 'Every man for himself. Run for it and good luck chaps.' A corporal who had been a regimental policeman said, 'Follow me.' He reached a railway line and ran at speed from sleeper to sleeper. I could not keep up with him. As we were being attacked from above and all sides, I ran into a copse, followed by the others. A Frenchman and his daughter were there first. The tanks appeared and the girl ran out screaming for her mother. She was riddled with machine-gun fire. One lad said, 'Let's go out with our hands up.' We decided to and one said, 'Don't take your rifle.' I realised I was the only one still carrying a rifle. The Germans came up and collected us together. Bayonets and steel helmets were taken from us and put in a heap: that was Monday 20th May, a hot, dry spring day in France.[11]

In general the British troops found themselves in confused fighting against superior German forces, supported by armour and with few if any anti-tank guns. Rifles and grenades were not enough to take on the panzers. Confusion and lack of orders added to demoralisation. Frederick Bedlington of 11th Battalion DLI found himself abandoned:

> We got into this village. There were 16 of us who couldn't find places on the available transport. They said, 'Find somewhere to sleep and we'll pick you up in the morning.' Well, in the night the Germans took the village, though we didn't realise it. When we

woke up in the morning and eventually looked round, the Germans had occupied the village. We went into this little garden and kept as quiet as we could. We said that during the night when it is dark we'd try to get out. The next thing we knew, the Germans were searching the village. We kept dead quiet. They came up to the hut we were lying in and one of the blokes coughed. The officer with us surrendered.[12]

Alan Watcham of 10th Battalion found himself part of a small group with their small arms, a single Bren gun carrier[13] and a Boys anti-tank rifle[14] '...that we carried and none of us knew how to fire the thing'. They asked a single Frenchwoman, 'dressed in black... "*ou est les Boche*?"' The woman replied there were none near. This proved misleading as the speed of the German advance had been so rapid. ' Watcham continues... 'I remember seeing this chap leaning against this farm wall with his rifle, having a quiet smoke.' They assumed the sentry to be British but were soon disabused, they were captured just as the rest of the battalion survivors soon marched up to join them. Lined against a wall and covered by a machine-gun, Watcham and his comrades became understandably nervous but their captors intended them no harm. An older combatant was Rodney Gee, a survivor of the Great War who'd rejoined 11th Battalion in 1939. Aged 40, he had won the Military Cross in the previous war. On 20 May as the battalion was surrounded he, with a group of others, hid in a cellar beneath the lanes of Wancourt, by Arras. For two nights they hid and, on the second of these, Gee went to recce in the hope the Germans might have moved on. They had not and he was lucky to regain the underground shelter. As an old sweat he was able to snatch some sleep in even the most difficult conditions:

The next thing I knew I was awoken by a bullet hitting the wall near my right ear and a great shout of *Raus* meaning 'Out!' and I got out. Someone got out before me, one of the drivers, I was second out. We were searched for any arms on us and I saw the chap who had got out whilst I was being frisked. He was standing against a wall with a rifle aimed at him. I thought, 'They're going to shoot us are they?' Then, curiously I thought, 'I wonder if the people going to the guillotine were as carefree as I was!' I wasn't frightened or anything, only half asleep. They decided not to shoot us.[15]

Gee was interrogated and, in classic mould, would give nothing other than 'name, rank and number'. Though questioned about defences around Arras, he said nothing and was presently sent to the church at Wancourt where prisoners were being herded. Postcards were given out so the Durhams could communicate with family via the Red Cross. Quite probably these cards were a further element of subtle interrogation, the German intelligence officers hoping the prisoners might give away important details.

In the course of battle British wounded were, in the normal way, seen first at the Regimental Aid Post (RAP). Serious cases were sent back to the Casualty Clearing Station (CCS) before being evacuated to base hospitals. In the swiftly moving chaos of the 1940 battle, wounded men could expect to be caught in the momentum of the German advance. Richard Forbes, in command of Carrier Platoon 9th Battalion, was hit on 28 May in the Arras vicinity. The CCS he was in was captured, lock, stock and barrel:

> My first recollection was the Germans shouting at the top of their voices. They always liked flinging their weight about. After that we were looked at one-by-one by the various medical people who were there, including French, British and Belgian doctors. I was still lying on a stretcher and I was moved to an upstairs room with a lot of other officers. Straw was placed on the stretcher to lie on. The nuns now arrived. They were so helpful and brought us water. Everyone was desperately thirsty as a result of our wounds. Meantime the Germans had taken every item of medical supplies from us because they were short themselves. So the doctors were reduced to a treatment just using salt water, but even water was short because all the mains had been destroyed in the bombing that had taken place.[16]

After a short time the British wounded were moved to Belgian military hospitals under German control. Some of the doctors were '...very, very helpful and kind to us'. Later they were transferred to another unit in Ghent, where conditions were considerably less favourable '...unlike their British equivalents...rough and ready. This applied particularly to one of the surgeons we used to call the "Butcher" because he was so rough in treating our soldiers.'

Some were less sanguine about the treatment meted out to British casualties. Benjamin Walker of 9th Battalion was one:

It is impossible to gauge the trials and miseries of the badly wounded during the first months of capture. Hundreds of British died who need never have done so, had they been treated and given the chance of treatment immediately. There is absolutely no excuse for the Germans to say it was impossible to organise medical supplies for our men. Their own casualties were negligible; they had heaps of food, tons of supplies, but their one idea was to show the beaten enemy that they were top dogs, and he would dance to their tune, they wanted to make the British feel defeat.[17]

Both outnumbered and outgunned, the Durham battalions enjoyed no prospects for success, despite the promising commencement of the counter-attack at Arras. John Bell of 11th Battalion was another who found himself under heavy fire in a hopelessly exposed position, pinned down by tanks and infantry in ground devoid of cover: '…I'll never get out of this. I took the wife's photo out and the bairns and I kissed them and said, "That will be the last I see of them." By this time there were German tanks and all kinds coming at us. We had rifles; there were four men and myself and we had rifles against tanks and all the German Battalion.'[18]

In the circumstances he escaped relatively lightly. Injured in the head and foot by shrapnel, he then sustained a nasty arm wound. The Germans did offer basic first aid and he was later attended at the Axis equivalent of the RAP. The journey by an ambulance with solid tyres to a rear medical facility was pure agony. In hospital for half a year at Cambrai, he was treated by both captured British and French doctors. His arm wound remained troublesome, despite the expedient of introducing maggots to clean the infected area, and he never regained full use of the limb. Food was continually in very short supply.[19]

One of the hardest-fought actions in which the Durhams were to be engaged in the course of the entire war was the bitter battle for Primosole Bridge fought in Sicily during a broiling summer in July 1943 (see chapter 6). The opponents were the redoubtable Fallschirmjager (German paratroopers). Peter Lewis (later to write the excellent 8th Battalion history; see Bibliography) leading 'B' Company 8th Battalion was one of those engaged, a furious close-quarter melee in which he himself was brought down by a marksman concealed in trees:

I lost consciousness for a while. When I came round, a German paratrooper was kneeling beside me. He spoke urgently and in good English, 'How many divisions are there?" Before he had time to repeat the question, there was a burst of automatic fire and he fell forward on his face. By now it was light and I managed to drag myself a few yards to a shallow bomb crater where I propped myself up on the lip of the crater. Soon afterwards two Germans arrived and I watched them as they set up a machine-gun and fired a burst at any sign of movement. They took no notice of me and this was not surprising as the side of my face was caked in blood. I must have looked more dead than alive.[20]

As the morning progressed and the relentless sun grilled the wounded of both sides, Lewis and the other injured had to endure the additional torture of raging thirst. Sometime later two Axis orderlies approached, with some difficulty as the battle still raged, and motioned for him to accompany them to the rear. By this time he was so enfeebled that any movement was close to impossible:

Eventually, with me hanging on to one German, while the other pushed me from behind, after slow and painful progress, we made it to the sunken road where I was put on a stretcher and carried to the German headquarters. A young German officer came over and knelt beside me. 'I'm sorry, but we shall have to hand you over to the Italians,' he said. We chatted for a few minutes and I asked him where he learnt to speak English so well. He replied with a smile, 'I was at your Oxford University before the war!' Then he said, 'I must go now, old boy, your mortars are being troublesome again.'[21]

The wounded Lewis was transferred by stages to a prison hospital near Lucca. The drive from the harbour at Livorno was performed by an Italian with more interest in speed than the welfare of patients, who suffered dreadfully as the vehicle rocketed over bad roads. A young British paratrooper succumbed[22] and Lewis himself suffered agonies from his injuries, sufficiently severe to warrant surgery:

On arrival in the operating theatre I expected to find a British doctor who had spoken to me the previous day, but it was an Italian doctor, who told me to sit on the edge of the operating table whilst he smoked a cigarette. The Italians did not allow

British doctors to operate. The British MO who was there handed me a bottle saying, 'Take a swig of this; you're going to need it.' How right he was. The Italian doctor, still smoking a cigarette and without using an anaesthetic, inserted a draining tube in my shoulder and pushed until it came out under my shoulder blade.[23]

Ken Lodge was an 18-year-old serving with the 6th Battalion which formed part of 151 Brigade during the battle for Normandy following D-Day. By September 1944 following the breakout, the Brigade was fighting to establish control of the Albert Canal (see Chapter 9) in the town of Gheel:

We moved to the outskirts of Gheel and we dug-in in front of these houses, in this field. You couldn't see the back of the field for this slope. We spent the night where we were because it was pretty quiet. A woman came out next morning. There was a very heavy mist. She came from one of these houses with a jug of coffee. It was very good of her. The mist cleared. Someone said, 'Germans!' and there were these four Germans walking across the field. I couldn't believe it. We fired at them. They went down and out of sight – we must have hit them. That was it; they knew where we were then. The mortars and the machine-guns started. It never ceased. We were getting a good pounding and they attacked up the field. We were firing and they were going down. Firing was coming from all directions. We were ordered to get out of the trenches and into the houses. We were well and truly pinned down; the German attack was building up.[24]

It was time to think of escape: 'I got into this house and thought, "I'll get out the other side." All of the doors were locked. I was in this little kitchen and was banging on the doors, thinking there must be somebody in the house. Anyway, I ran out again and straight into the Germans. I was caught, that was it. I was panicking by then and my mind wasn't working very well. I was by myself. It was a terrible feeling.'[25]

Marching to captivity

Weary and demoralised, those captured in 1940 were stunned by the magnitude of defeat. Dunkirk may have been miraculous but it was still defeat and, though many were rescued, many thousands were not. Their fathers had fought over the ground for four years and, whatever their hardships and terrible losses, had never known defeat. If the German front-line troops had some empathy, this diminished the greater the distance. Of the second-line soldiers, some were themselves veterans of the trenches. Others, less amenable, were callow youths caught in the fanaticism of the Nazi creed. As Steve Barker recalled: 'They eventually put us into a column to march and if anyone was not well and dropped to the back of the column, they weren't shy of placing a bayonet where it hurt to keep you moving.'[26]

Douglas Nelson found the treatment meted out to be distinctly disagreeable.

A few thousand British and tens of thousands of French soldiers began a long, hungry and thirsty march along the line of the German breakthrough. If the Germans found we had cigarettes, they took them and gave them to the French, who were also allowed off the column to collect food from friends and relatives. On the line of march French women would put out buckets of water, but the Germans kicked them over and then took photographs of us grovelling in the gutter to get a drink – ammunition for Goebbels' propaganda. We slept in fields. I was not used to roughing it and suffered badly and had very painful feet. Eventually I could not get my socks off for dried blood, and towards the end my boots were stuck to my feet. Many times I was ready to drop out and would see my mother's face in a red mist and carried on. At the time I was a 21-year-old. I reckon that in three weeks we covered 500 miles in a roundabout way.[27]

Even when they arrived in Germany their tribulations were by no means over.

Eventually we arrived in Trier in south-west Germany on the border of Luxembourg. It was an old garrison town and we were put in a camp where some French had been kept. Here we met lice, our partners more or less for the next five years. From there we went by rail to Poland locked in wagons with just room to sit without stretching one's legs. Two days and two nights with no toilet and some men had dysentery. The train stopped and started frequently and the engine was used for shunting en route. On Monday 10 June 1940 we arrived at Stalag XXA at Thorn [Torun] on the River Vistula.[28]

Few who took part in these long, dismal marches to the echo of defeat would forget, as Joseph Weddle remembered:

There was little space. We just found niches. Within a few minutes they had machine-guns in all the alcoves of the church, pointing down towards us. The lads were beginning to get a bit edgy then. Nothing did happen. They would only allow us out to the toilet two at a time, which was nigh impossible and it was getting like an oven. No lights, just the light coming in through the windows. No shouting or anything. Nobody could settle down, we were thirsty you see. A group was around the font, which was found to be full. Each member of that group got one drink. We all got little sleep due to cramp, discomfort for the toilet and the moans of many people around us. Many were worried about what was happening at home and we all carried our memories of the terrible sights of the dead and wounded.[29]

Matters improved only slightly as the daily marching continued. Sometimes French civilians were permitted to hand over food and water; field canteens, horse-drawn and archaic, provided a thin daily ration of weak vegetable soup:

All prisoners suffered from the starvation diet given to them during the march to captivity. It is unlikely that the Germans were short of food, having their own supplies, and they had looted further food supplies during their advance through France and Belgium. It could well be argued that, allied to the depression and fear brought on by capture, this was a deliberate act to lower even further the fitness of the prisoners to attempt escape or cause any problems on the march.[30]

As they toiled, the POWs began to glimpse the realities of life ahead, scrounging and foraging, the ability to barter and, above all, forming bonds with particular comrades, as Joseph Weddle illustrated: 'Robert, me and Eddy made an agreement. If we ever got mixed up in the march, when we stopped in a field or in a barn, I found a place and stopped in it and those two looked for me or, otherwise, we moved round the camp looking for each other. From then on it worked. Whatever we scrounged that day, we made a meal of it at the end of the day.'[31] Not all bore up so well or in so comradely a fashion. Moss Waterston of 8th Battalion was not impressed:

> When the old Frenchwomen came out to give us sandwiches, the lads were so down and hungry that they sometimes almost pulled and pushed the old women. It was dog eat dog, doesn't matter what it was they would fight and scramble. I've never seen the likes of it in all my life. Blokes brought down to that level. It was hunger. We plundered as we went along and paid for it when the Germans beat us.[32]

The POWs found their guards to be frequently brutal, brutish and arrogant. They revelled in their victory as the seemingly endless march continued over minor roads and byways. Main arterial routes had to be kept clear for the advancing panzers.

Hunger and degradation were the hallmarks of the march. By the time they arrived at reception camps, most were in a pretty low way, hungry, exhausted and demoralised, arguably by design. Now they were deloused and their heads shaved, then photographed with their POW identity discs, a further stage of dehumanisation. The wounded fared little better, as Richard Forbes remembered:

> We were moved into Germany by train and went to Duisburg, which had a German military hospital. All the bedding was ersatz, made of paper, and the soap contained no fat at all because the Germans wanted the nitroglycerine for making armaments. The treatment was quite good but the food, of course, was completely inadequate for wounded individuals. The basic food every day was either potato soup, turnip soup or cabbage soup, a third of a loaf of hard, black German rye bread, which tasted very sour and soggy and gave us diarrhoea, a little bit of ersatz margarine and that was it.[33]

When the war moved into the wide, harsh arena of the Western Desert both sides, at various points in the campaign, collected large hauls of captives. Firstly the British, but latterly the Germans, took many prisoners. This was especially so after the battle at Gazala and the fall of Tobruk when some 30,000 Allied POWs came into Axis hands. Though most were captured by Germans, the Afrika Corps' agreement with their Italian partners and nominal local superiors was that all prisoners should be held by the Italians. For this, the Germans were often wont to apologise. Temporary incarceration was in crude camps or cages, with limited sanitation and meagre rations. Tobruk was particularly awful and many suffered from dysentery. Worse still was the camp at Derna, its relative proximity to the Mediterranean being no compensation. Harry Sell found the place as:

...looking like the drawings of Newgate Gaol in 1600. On arrival everything anyone possessed was systematically looted. The smell from a decrepit sewage system was overpowering and conditions were absolutely filthy. The accommodation was long stone cells with a small window at the end. Into this was crammed as many prisoners as possible. Fortunately most prisoners spent only a few days there. The guards at the Barce transit camp were native Askaris wearing red fezzes. If one did not move quickly enough, one was liable to a clubbing from these 'gentlemen'. However, the Italian commandant was reasonable, perhaps because his son was a prisoner of war in India. The captives filled in Red Cross postcards that stated they were prisoners of the Italians. One man crossed this out and substituted 'Germans'. When this was spotted, the guards went into a rage, threatening dire penalties.[34]

As the situation in North Africa was extremely fluid, with both sides conducting lengthy advances and equally hurried withdrawals, the Italians preferred to transport Allied POWs to Italy. Conditions aboard ship were frequently terrible and tensions were exacerbated by the risk of being sunk by our own submarines. Brian W. Sims was one of those who sailed on the ill-fated *Scillin*:

On Friday 13 November 1942, 1,009 prisoners were marched down to the Spanish Quay in Tripoli harbour and were to be put aboard the small 1,596-ton SS *Scillin*. It was obvious there was only room for about half the prisoners. In spite of Captain Gilbert the senior MO's complaints about overcrowding, 814 men were put on board. After a delay the ship sailed at 1pm with a pronounced list to port. Heavy planks held down the hatches to the hold. They were covered with coal dust and were so crowded that no one could lie down.[35]

Conditions were atrocious, with half the men suffering from dysentery and only allowed on deck in batches of five for sanitary purposes. The idea was to hug the coast of Tunisia then attempt a swift dash across to Trapani. Two British submarines were on patrol in the vicinity, including the P212 (*Sahib*). Sighting the ship and positioning herself for attack, *Sahib* fired a salvo of a dozen rounds from her deck gun. *Scillin* was peppered and lost way, sending out a frantic SOS.

> Some of the prisoners managed to get out of the holds, but those guards who had not already thrown away their rifles and jumped overboard put the planks back over the hatches. At 7.50pm the *Sahib* fired one torpedo, hitting the engine room of the *Scillin*, which sank in two minutes. When the submarine closed to see if there were any survivors, the crew were alarmed to find many Allied POWs in the sea; 27 were picked up...[36]

The horror of below decks as the ship went down can only be imagined. DLI lost 46 men in the wreck, of a total casualty list of 783. A further seven Durhams died when another ship, *Nino Bixio*, was sunk on 17 August 1942.[37]

By September 1943, Italy had capitulated and the Germans began transferring Allied prisoners. A number had taken advantage of the confusion to disappear before the Germans arrived. Conditions for these POWs were very like those experienced by their comrades who went into the bag during the fall of France. They travelled for endless hours in filthy cattle trucks. Quite frequently, some of the trucks held cattle which the Germans had filched from their former allies. Occasionally, the tedium, dirt and hunger were leavened by small acts of kindness. 'I do remember one incident,' recalled Jack Hawkins. 'It was midnight and the train pulled into Innsbruck. The place was deserted. I was near the small opening by the door when a hand appeared through the small gap and placed about six apples at my side. I saw no head, no one, but Alan and I were grateful.'[38]

Already weakened by their experiences with the Italians, many felt their arrival in Germany heralded an even worse experience. Jack Douglas of 8th Battalion was acutely affected:

At this time I was very despondent. I was right on the bottom. The weather was bad and I was hungry and sick. I remember, I said 'I'll step over the wire.' To step over the wire meant you would be shot immediately. Lance-Sergeant Allen said, 'You're not, Sergeant, you're not.' I said, 'I've had enough, I'm sick. I might as well finish it.' He hung on to my legs and wouldn't let go. He was lying in the mud, which was two to three inches deep, and he wouldn't let go. I hadn't the strength with being so weak. Anyway, I got over it.[39]

Life inside the camps

There was no set pattern for POW camps. The Germans were perhaps unprepared for their own success and a number of old 19th century forts were hastily commissioned. Stalag XXA at Thorn in Poland was one of these; here, a tiny population of POWs from Norway was soon swollen to over 10,000. Sergeant William Roberts of 8th Battalion was amongst many Durhams who were to pass through its gates:

> Access was by a narrow bridge, which straddled a dry moat, which went round the fort itself and this was at least 20 feet deep. The wall, which encompassed the fort, was of sheer blue-black brick without a foothold anywhere. The moat itself, I would say, was 20 to 30 feet across and then within all that was the fort itself, built up to, I think, it was three storeys. But bear in mind that the top storey of this fort was level with the land outside and the roof itself was soil, shrub and trees. The top of the fort was quite a large area and blended with the land surrounding it. There were several of these efforts. Our fort housed 1,100 prisoners, all in rooms 15 to 20 feet wide, maybe 30 feet long. There was an entrance down at one end and at the other were windows, barbed wire across them. Orders from the Germans were, 'Do not look out of the windows.' The only accessible way was across the narrow bridge, which was guarded at both ends. There was a sentry outside the door and another sentry on the other side of the bridge. The windows looked out on to the moat. There was nothing there to look at.[40]

Thorn would eventually be home to some 20,000 prisoners and was relatively well provided for, with a soccer pitch and exercise space.

Sanitation, if basic, was functional. Michael Scott went to Posen (Poznan), another aged fortress network: 'A Napoleonic fort built below ground level. We went down a tunnel and into the rooms, which were very dirty with fleas, lice and bed bugs. There were 20 men to a room and we were locked in each night. The fort was surrounded by a dry moat; the windows were barred and looked out on to the moat. We were eventually allowed out on to the grass top.'[41]

Of all the castles, one stands out with singular notoriety: Oflag IVC – Colditz. This classic medieval fortress dominated a crag above the village. Famous as being deemed escape-proof, it was here that the serial escapers, British, French and Polish, were sent. Of the 130 officers typically held there, eight were from the Durhams.[42] Michael Farr felt the chill of the place as he arrived:

> My first impression of Colditz seeing it as we drove over the hill was, 'My God, what kind of place is this?' I was weary, hungry and afraid and near the end of my tether and Colditz was the final straw. I was to find out that it was every bit as bad as I expected on looking at it. The heavy blinds at the back of the German truck were pulled back as we ground to a halt. We were unloaded and led over a drawbridge into the grey, sombre castle of Colditz. I was swallowed up by the formidable granite walls of this lunatic asylum.[43] Loud shouts of 'Qualified at last,' were blasted to us by the many British officers already there.[44]

Where the camps were purpose-built, this was habitually carried out to a universal pattern. Located away from urban areas, though often adjacent to smaller settlements, lines of timber huts were contained by a double barbed-wire fence studded with guard towers at regular intervals. A couple of yards within the perimeter a single trip marked the 'forbidden zone' beyond which prisoners were not permitted to move. Entry was very likely to be fatal. Washing and latrine facilities were present but basic. Messing areas fed by the camp kitchens were universal. Alan Wareham remembered that: 'When the weather was really bad and coal ran out, we used to get a little ration of coal for the stove which was in the middle of the hut. Every man had to sacrifice one bed board as required to keep the fire going so that by the time April came you were sleeping on four boards.'[45]

Warrant Officer Johnson of 8th Battalion, one of those POWs moved to Germany following Italy's collapse, found himself in Stalag IVB Muhlberg near Dresden. His recollection of sleeping arrangements was not untypical: 'There were three-tier bunks where the most sought-after position was the middle one. On the top one you were liable to come face to face with rats running around in the rafters and on the bottom one you were liable to have all sorts of rubbish dumped on you from the people above you.'[46] Stan McDonald recalls the hours of darkness at Muhlberg: 'We were taken to Stalag IVB at Muhlberg and it was pretty unpleasant there. We had very little freedom and very little chance to get any exercise. There were guards all over the place and searchlights as it got dark; if you wanted to sneak into another hut you had to dodge the lights as best you could.'[47]

One of those who had been both wounded and captured on Kos[48] also spent time in Muhlberg, where he was one of about a hundred officers incarcerated there:

There were 60 of them in a barrack room. Three-decked beds were grouped in banks of four, making 12 people sleeping in a space of about 18 feet by 6 feet. In the middle of the room was a large flat-topped stove upon which innumerable cooking pots were permanently steaming away. People sat around barrack tables reading and playing cards and a lot of them seemed to be on their beds for most of the day. There were two WCs and one water tap for the use of 60 officers.[49]

He was subsequently transferred to Oflag VIIIF in the Sudetenland, known with a distinct lack of affection as 'Little Siberia':[50]

I believe our camp was described in the Red Cross Directory as a camp with playing fields and a swimming pool and rooms holding 10 to 16 officers. The playing field was, in actual fact, one football ground about half-size which was usually a quagmire. The swimming pool served as a small skating rink and the rooms which contained 18 people were about the size of a drawing room in a full-sized English house. The main building was a large affair that looked like a factory. It was known as 'the Biscuit Factory' and housed about 700 to 800 officers. There were chapels, a library, an orderly room, two cookhouses, a theatre and a hospital with about 30 beds. The whole surrounded by wire and sentry towers. Spaced round about were 12 bungalows that housed the remaining 500 officers. All field officers were given the option of living in a bungalow if they wished to and so 15 or so of us took up residence in Bungalow VIII. The accommodation was good.[51]

Life may have been disagreeable for the British officers and other ranks, but their treatment was benign compared to that meted out to Russian prisoners. Wherever there was an adjacent compound containing wretched captives from the Eastern Front, the British watched in horror and disgust as these were subjected to vicious and inhuman treatment, starved and worked like cattle; 'These accursed *Untermenschen* have been observed eating grass, flowers and raw potatoes. Once they can't find anything edible in the camp they turn to cannibalism.'[52] Russians died in large numbers, succumbing to hunger, sickness, exhaustion, despair and the relentless beatings: 'Ruthless enforcement at the least sign of resistance and disobedience! Weapons are to be used mercilessly in breaking resistance…nor is softness called for against the industrious and obedient POW.'[53]

This savagery contrasted with the almost civilised mechanisms offered to the British: shoemakers, tailors and an 'in-house' credit banking facility. Roll call was sounded at 08.30 hours, lunch at 12.45, tea at 15.00 hours, final roll call three hours later and lights out at 23.00 hours. Under the terms of the 1929 Geneva Convention,[54] officers could not be put to work by their captors although other ranks could be and were. The position of NCOs was more ambiguous, but work was a less unpleasant alternative than might be imagined: foraging for food was always a possibility and the endless tedium of confinement was at least varied.

Generally the German camps were better provided for and organised than their Italian counterparts. By the end of the Desert War nearly 80,000 Allied servicemen were in Italian hands, scattered through some 72 camps and a dozen hospitals. Conditions varied usually from bad to worse. In PG52 at Chiavari near Genoa, Patrick Arnold recollected meagre rations and disagreeable conditions:

At Christmas the Pope took a special interest in us as war prisoners and we were allowed to send 10 words by cable through the Vatican to our families. I don't know whether my family received the telegram, but it was nice to know the Pope took such interest in us. Only the Catholics had religious services in the camp. Italian nuns tried to take care of us. They worked hard to make us more comfortable and do little things for us. There were no nurses around and the only company we had were the Italian sentries and orderlies who couldn't speak English and we couldn't speak Italian. We didn't get on at all. We saved enough money to buy a small secondhand piano for 400 lire, an accordion for 3,000 and drums for 2,000, so we arranged weekly concert parties. We also had talks given by South African war correspondents.[55]

Food and clothing

Hunger is an all-encompassing sensation, and food continually dominated men's thoughts. There was never enough, Douglas Nelson, incarcerated in Thorn, recollected: 'We had a bowl of watery soup made of potatoes and a small black loaf for five to seven men a day. Imagine trying to cut a loaf into five or seven pieces of equal size for starving men.'[56] Richard Forbes retained similar memories:

The basic food every day was either potato, turnip or cabbage soup. A third of a loaf of hard, black German rye bread...on Christmas Day [1940] they gave us a treat. We had the usual soup, potato or cabbage, and we got a thin slice of sausage and we thought it was absolutely marvellous. By then we were not only hungry, we were starving. We always tried – whatever we had during the day, soup and so on – to save a bit of bread to eat just before we went to sleep. If you did that you might get a few hours' sleep. You were so empty inside, not only hungry but starving, and you couldn't sleep at all and you went further down the drain.[57]

This constant poor and inadequate diet, combined with consequential lack of sleep, exacerbated by tedium and demoralisation, led to a rapid decline in POWs' physical fitness. In certain camps senior ranks enjoyed a markedly more favourable dietary regime. Jim Hawkins recollected the resentment such inequality bred:

The 10 months in PG65 (Gravina, Italy) were very depressing and unhealthy. I regret to say that the Warrant Officers[58] did not give a very good account of themselves. They had separate quarters, separate rations and no idea of the men's discomfort. Many were so weak they were unable to stand at roll call. In spite of this, an order was given that physical training (PT) must be carried out by the prisoners. I resented this order and, as a sergeant I acted alone in my refusal. I was reprimanded by the same Regimental Sergeant-Major (RSM) who was fitter and better-fed than any of the men, but he did not take part in PT. My action paid off and the order to do PT was rescinded.[59]

Most survivors recall the desperately poor rations and the enervating, debilitating effects of a prolonged poor diet in a confined situation. Officers did, from time to time, enjoy rather better fare. It was common for them to form small mess groups of say, six to eight, and pool supplies. Even in such adverse circumstances, or because of them, regimental tradition survived, as Michael Scott observed: 'To give an example, the Rifle Brigade officers stuck together. There were only two or three Guards Regiments there and they messed with those from the cavalry regiments. They were more "elite" soldiers, not to say that they were any better than anyone else but that division began to appear and make itself noticed.'[60]

With food scarce, sharing could be contentious, Moss Waterston recalled:

The bread was dished out, five men sharing a loaf. One man would get the loaf of bread and we'd all go into the hut and sit at the table. There were all sorts of ways of cutting a loaf to get the [required] slices out of it. It was ascertained that the Stalag disc we had with our numbers on would go five times equally into this loaf of bread. The bloke who was cutting it had a very sharp knife. When he was cutting it, it would be like the Merchant of Venice and the pound of flesh and you didn't have to shed a drop of blood. Well, he hadn't to shed a crumb and he had to cut it expertly. If the knife went in at an angle, dear me, there was hell on! He would have to take a piece off the next slice to put on to that one. It had to be perfect because there were five pairs of eyes watching every move he made.[61]

In such difficult circumstances, stealing from comrades (as opposed to filching from the Germans) was a heinous offence, a betrayal of trust. Enforcing discipline and meting out punishments were left to the senior British officers or NCOs present in the camp. Thomas Lawton was in just such a position:

> We once found a man who had stolen a comrade's bread ration. The Germans said this man would have to be disciplined by me. My first thought was for him to be stripped and made to run the gauntlet of lines of troops whipping him with their belts. I discouraged this and it was decided to throw him into the toilet hole, which was nearly full. This became the usual disciplinary act for this type of serious crime...We had latrines which were dug about three to four feet into the ground and these latrines were getting a bit full. The lads in his section would sling him in there. The Germans could not believe it. His section took the lad and threw him up in the air and he went 'splash' down into all that filth. Some of his mates helped him to clamber out. He wasn't fit to look at. The next thing he did was to run about amongst everybody. Even the Germans were running. His idea was that he was a socialist – share amongst everybody![62]

At all times, however, the Germans were fair game for pillaging. One POW, Stan MacDonald, put to work on the railways, remembered:

> We found out that some trains were carrying food. Some of the lads on the day shift tipped us off as to which trucks were most likely to have something we could eat. Working night shifts and when the guards were dozing, some of us would break in and swipe whatever we could and hide it in the ducts where the trains were maintained and the day shift lads would smuggle it back and into the camp.[63]

Red Cross parcels were a godsend. Channelled through the International Red Cross in Switzerland, they were distributed by lorry to individual camps and given out from a central point. The arrival of parcels immeasurably lifted the spirits, recalled Richard Forbes:

> We formed little messes of four to six officers and you shared out, say, one tin of bully beef amongst you all. The next day, it would

be some other item. Then we would divide the chocolate up and make a cup of tea. We had a balanced diet as much as one could, which lasted over a few days. Parcels may arrive, say, in May and no more for a few months, so there was no point in gorging yourself one day and having nothing for some time. Without these parcels we could not have existed. They were absolutely wonderful.[64]

Fred Arnold also remembered the joy of receiving a parcel: 'In the September of 1941, we got our first Red Cross parcels. They were marvellous. They contained the first cigarettes we had had for weeks and the first decent food we had had for a long time. The parcels did not come too regularly but when they did they were welcome.'[65]

Charles Burdon-Taylor recounted what resulted when the Germans adopted the pernicious practice of opening parcels and dumping the decanted contents into individual mess tins in an unholy mix. 'On one occasion the prisoners refused to accept Red Cross parcels when the Germans began to open every tin and empty the contents into a mess tin. In this way the tins could not be used in escapes, either as saved food or to make funnels for air in digging tunnels.'[66]

Clothing was another problem. Most men's uniforms were soon worn out and replacements hard to come by. Douglas Nelson recalled that: 'By now our clothes and footwear were in tatters and were taken from us. Our heads were shaved, we were deloused and clothing was issued. The clothing was uniform confiscated from countries overrun by the Germans. We got one shirt. I got a French tunic, Belgian trousers and a Dutch blue coat. We were given Dutch wooden clogs with no socks, painful for the feet.'[67]

Those handed to the Italians during the Desert Campaign usually went into the bag with just their light summer uniforms, which soon wore out. Some were told that Italian cobblers would repair their boots but these, once surrendered, were not seen again and the men suffered dreadfully on blistered feet in the penetrating cold and damp of captive winter. At last, Red Cross supplies began to arrive. As Michael Morgan confirmed, these were more than welcome: 'The Red Cross had sent us our winter clothing; battle dress, overcoats, socks, underpants, vest and thick shirt. Thank God! It had been so cold and we had to go to bed at 5pm and not get up till 9am. Italian clothing is like their food – no good. Now we shall be able to walk round the compound at night.'[68]

As the German camps became more organised, officers found they could avail themselves of local services, such as cobblers and laundry. Families in Britain were issued clothing coupons[69] to acquire suitable attire – guidance as to what was best was provided:

> First Parcel
> 2 vests – 8 coupons
> 2 pants – 8 coupons
> 1 shirt – 5 coupons
> 2 collars – 2 coupons
> 1 pyjamas – 8 coupons
> 1 towel – 2 coupons
> 2 pairs of socks – 6 coupons*
> 2 handkerchiefs – 1 coupon
> * These came with the helpful advice that darning the toes
> and heels with cotton would induce longevity in the socks.[70]

As this total wardrobe weighed some five pounds and the parcel could contain double that, additional items, such as shaving supplies, blanket, writing material and bootlaces, were suggested. By 5 December 1941, a Prisoner of War Fund was established in Durham: 'To give advice to next of kin of prisoners of war of the Durham Light Infantry in the preparation of parcels for dispatch to them; to give grants in necessitous cases and to raise essential monies with which to carry out all the purposes of the Fund.'[71] A whole raft of social and fund-raising events was organised to swell the coffers of the Fund. Within the first 12 months, over a thousand parcels had been sent out and some £3,500 had been raised.[72]

Treatment of prisoners could vary. On the whole, the German army maintained a 'hard but fair' regime. This did not always prevail, as Alan Wareham discovered:

> The Camp Commandant was very anti-British. He was a Captain and had been a prisoner himself in World War I. He could be very difficult. I was woken up late this night to go down as there was a very ill man, one of our own boys. We brought him into our section hut. All the sick bay attendant could give him were tablets. He was very ill and I was told to go down to tell the Hauptmann. He wouldn't listen; this man was writhing in agony.

He really was ill. I don't know how many times I went down again to see the Hauptmann in the early morning. I can see him now. He was busy shaving and he wasn't going to bring out any German doctor. He refused and went out to the works site. We had to do something about this, so I went up to the works site and told him he would have to do something about it. He eventually relented. The soldier was removed to the main camp, Stalag XXA, where he died.[73]

As many guards comprised either old soldiers, veterans of the previous conflict or younger men recovering from wounds or unfit for front-line service, some manifested the traits of the natural bully, while others were decidedly eccentric, as Michael Scott noted: 'We had a very bloody-minded commandant called Oberst Blatterban. He tried to impose military discipline. The prisoners laughed at him, chanting, "Blatters, Blatters," whenever he appeared. He was a bit of a pig. When on parade and talking to the assembled, a "quack, quack" call was put up by some of the prisoners.' The commandant of Oflag VIB was an even more dangerously odd character, as observed by Michael Farr: 'Commandant Hauptmann Radamacher was a most thorough officer but very excitable, also totally eccentric. He was immaculate in dress and was often seen strutting around with his revolver drawn. Realising his temperament, we would taunt him, shout rude names, make complaints and then would dash behind a hut. Radamacher instantly fired a volley of shots into the air!'[74]

Not all the guards were necessarily as harsh as was at first imagined, as David Parker found out:

There was a guard we later called 'George' that we first thought was a terror until one bitterly cold morning he came to us on a road job. Remember, we were all in summer clothing and had no gloves and no one could work for more than five minutes at a time. One of the prisoners challenged 'George' to work in those conditions and he ordered us to make a fire so as to get a little warmth. That was of little use and he returned us all to camp. You should have heard the German Commandant tell this soldier off. From that day 'George' became one of the best guards in the camp and when he left us we were sorry to see him go.[75]

Guards might be ridiculed:

> ...called 'goons' by the prisoners but not to their faces. Marching
> Germans were met with the Laurel and Hardy signature tune but
> they could also be handily suborned. Guards were blackmailed:
> they accepted cigarettes or chocolate, for example, as a gesture of
> friendship. Then they could be requested to obtain items required
> in the camp, say, items to build a radio. They did not dare refuse
> as it was an offence for the guards to accept presents from the
> prisoners.

Once ensnared they could cheerfully be exploited; Tom Wilson
explains: 'The prisoners often tricked them [the guards] by filling a
tin partly with soil or sand and placing coffee on the top inch. They
could not complain as it was a crime for them to do this (i.e. accept
gifts).'[76]

Tobacco, as Adam Wareham recounted, was a very marketable
commodity:

> Cigarettes were worth their weight in gold. You could get
> anything. They were the currency. Most of us took out what we
> didn't want from our Red Cross parcels. We would leave it in a
> certain place then go back and find the exchange, eggs, bacon,
> bread and that sort of thing. How did we get it back into camp?
> Well we had these stoves in the huts and they didn't supply us
> with enough coal and the supervising sergeants or corporals
> would collect wood while we were working, tie it up like a witch's
> broom and inside the pile we stowed away all sorts of things and
> marched back to camp. There we were counted. We were not
> searched very often; if we thought we would be searched, we
> dumped the stuff outside the camp.[77]

Joseph Weddle remembered how even the ritual roll calls could be
satisfactorily sabotaged:

> We were all lined up in rows of five. Some guards would be
> counting along the front row and others along the back row. We
> were standing there and someone would duck and move along
> the middle rows after being counted. So they got a miscount and
> we were counted all over again and that might go on for two or

three hours. It was just something to do. You could get awkward blokes at any time who just needled them.[78]

Such relief from monotony was a salve and not a luxury. A steady drop in morale could lead to a listlessness termed 'stalag fever'. Michael Scott commented on the symptoms:

All prisoners were a bit wacky after being locked up so long. Some were wackier than others. Some men had suffered from the stress of captivity from the earliest days. They spoke often in monosyllables and showed erratic behaviour. They did not get on well with their fellow prisoners. It was something that got into your blood; the monotony of it all, although you're forcing yourself to do this and that or the other. It is like a visit to the zoo. You see animals pacing up and down in a cage. They feel the same. They shouldn't be in there should they? That's the feeling you have. You're not exactly biting your nails but after a while you have to force yourself to do something about it.[79]

At its worst stalag fever exacerbated by bitterly cold and seemingly endless winters could drive prisoners to suicide. Men might get letters from wives or girlfriends intimating they'd formed new relationships. This was terribly galling and fuelled the depression of impotence. Others, like Joseph Weddle, simply got bad news, as did Edward Bates, both of whose sisters died whilst they were captive: 'It was a great shock to me and all day long my imagination played agony with me because I cannot help thinking of the agony that my people must have gone through, especially my poor mother.'[80]

One sure escape from monotony was through the escapism of theatre, as Charles Burdon-Taylor remembered: 'We had a theatre and set up a "Café Royal" to which the German Commandant and his officers were invited. Some of the prisoners objected to this but by promoting better relationships with the German officers, it might lead to opportunities later which may help the POWs.'[81] Theatre was not a frivolous diversion; it served both to keep up morale and hone useful skills:

First of all we had to make our own scenery from whatever we could get hold of. The YMCA used to send us timber from Sweden to make them up. A New Zealand officer and myself used to design and make the scenery. Then we got a play sent out from England. The actors were chosen and the parts were learnt. The costumes were made up. We made all the stage props and put the play on. We had a box office and you had to book your seat. We had professional actors with us, so we had to aim for a pretty high standard. The plays went down very well. Keeping yourself amused and entertained was very important. The Germans used to come and have great fun listening to us. It kept us mentally alert.[82]

Michael Goodliffe, a well-known actor in peacetime, arranged and 'starred' in an ambitious production of *Hamlet* whilst in Oflag VIIID. As the Germans believed that such activities kept prisoners' thoughts from straying to more dangerous areas, they were happy to oblige. Munich Opera House provided the costumes, props and theatrical makeup.[83] Christmas, like Shakespeare 'whom they believed was of German origin',[84] was a particular favourite of the Germans, as Joseph Weddle vividly recalled:

Christmas was coming. The lads were talking about putting on a concert. The Germans always celebrated Christmas. We put on a show. You had all sorts of men; entertainers, theatre managers, dancers and concert party men. A lad had the chance of buying a piano accordion. So the lads pooled their camp money and one of the guards took him to the village shop and he got a piano accordion. Another had a small drum and one had a trumpet. So we put on a bit of a show. Some of the lads could scrounge anything. Some wrote the songs and others a bit of a musical score. We put on *Snow White and the Seven Dwarves*. One joke was against two German guards the lads had taken a dislike to. I suppose they were a bit stricter and harsher than the other ones. They wrote one into the show with the jokes, 'The Big Ugly Brute'. When we did put the show on, all the guards were there except those on duty. The majority of the German officers from the district came. The lads had quite a bit of a band at this particular time, song and dance men, duet singers. There were one or two good singers amongst the men.[85]

Thomas Lawton, incarcerated in Stalag 383, recalled that:

There were all kinds of facilities, even an entertainments hall. There were about three bands there, including a Scottish pipe band. The entertainments hall was allocated on a monthly basis to certain people. For example, the Geordies would have it for a month and everybody looked forward to watching a Geordie show because it always went wrong. The Aussies would have it, then the New Zealanders.[86]

Nor were the camps devoid of opportunities for self-improvement. Those who felt their education or professional development had been so rudely interrupted by the war and now curtailed might find that a wide curriculum existed, with tutors drawn from prisoners. Even examinations could be held, a system John Marsh experienced: 'Eventually, when the examination time came along, it was quite a simple system. The examination papers were sent to the Germans, as they had to be, though addressed to the Senior British Officer (SBO). Knowing what they were, he called in to see the German Commandant and they opened the papers together. The Commandant examined them to see that there was nothing in the papers to aid an escape and, when he was satisfied that this was not the case, he and the SBO or his deputy got the papers from the Germans and the examination was held under strict examination conditions, where one of us had to act as invigilator. The completed papers were then collected and given to a senior German officer in the camp and the Germans had to censor them. They were then sent off to the examination body headquarters in England.'[87]

Rodney Gee was one who used his time usefully, taking the Cambridge certificate in education – he had over a score of textbooks sent out to him through the Red Cross.[88] Education was also a useful form of discipline, not just the relentless control by the Axis but internal discipline amongst the Allied troops, which was never an easy matter. Thomas Lawton explained:

There could be difficult moments when dealing with men who had lost all hope, suffering mental and physical stress. Some were not willing to accept discipline. It must be remembered that most prisoners of war were men plucked from civilian life, trained and put into action. Reasons for discipline in the positions they found themselves were difficult to accept. Occasionally, difficult situations called for desperate measures. I told my men,

'Everything you've been through, I've gone through and I'll consider myself a soldier as long as I can, even if I wear wooden clogs and raggy britches, I'll still be a soldier.' This is how you had to talk to them. You couldn't go and order them or they'd tell you to beat it, especially when they had got into a cluster. So when there was a bad one, he had lots of bad ones with him. But there was one thing certain and I proved it: physical force beats all other means of discipline. I was fortunate that way. I was a strong bloke and I'd boxed for the division. I told the men, 'If necessary I'll use force. If you'll not do a thing when you're asked to do it, you'll be given another order as in the army, then I'll use physical force and make you do it.'[89]

Solitary confinement, 'the cooler', was a punishment meted out to those who'd caused offence to the guards, anything from insubordination to attempted escape. Frederick Bedlington experienced this brand of Axis discipline: 'They locked you up in a cell and [you] were given a meal every three days. The other two days you only got your coffee and two slices of bread in a morning and the same in the afternoon. You slept on a wooden board with one blanket, and the cell had broken windows and so it was bitterly cold. The only time you got out was in a morning for a few minutes to empty your slops, which were in a metal chamber pot.'[90]

Disobedience was always certain to reap reprisal. Jim Hawkins was amongst a group of prisoners who refused to occupy a verminous hut vacated by Russian POWs:

The Germans were very annoyed and eventually sent for the SS to remove us. Before they arrived and unbeknown to the German officer, we quietly went into the vacant hut, stayed inside and watched for the arrival of the SS. They circled our hut then entered to find it empty. They were not pleased and a few days later, in November, our hut was ordered out on to the road in the early hours of the morning and marched away to spend the next six weeks in a punishment camp, Jacobsthal, a former Jewish concentration camp in 1936. The hut had no beds but long shelves. The doors opened due east. We had one filthy blanket, which was so soiled it was like cardboard. The hut had no lighting and no heating and was infested with very large rats.[91]

Reprisals for alleged wrongs inflicted on German prisoners were always possible. Rumours that such an incident had followed the Dieppe Raid in 1942[92] brought a furious riposte. Thomas Lawton was one who suffered:

> Because of the Dieppe Raid 50 per cent of the men in huts were bound by rope. Everybody rushed forward and demanded to be tied up. The Germans could not understand that. As the lads were fastened they expanded their arm muscles and when they had finished fastening [and the guards had left the huts] the ropes dropped off. The Germans did beat us in the end. They got locked handcuffs from Holland with about eight inches of chain between the cuffs. The men were handcuffed and sat on wooden forms with the chains going under the forms. They also handcuffed the men in their beds with chains going under the beds. They were really proud of themselves when they went away.[93]

For men isolated from the events of the war in agonies of uncertainty, communications took on particular importance and great ingenuity went into the construction and concealment of camp radios, as Richard Forbes and others confirmed: 'There was a radio in the camp, which enabled us to listen to the news, the main points of which were copied and sent around the different huts. The radio, of course, had to be hidden. One place was a large tin of jam. The radio was in the bottom and the jam on top, so passing German inspection. Ingenious methods were used to manufacture or obtain parts for the radio.'[94]

Thomas Lawton had similar recollections:

> There was a secret radio in the camp built from parcel materials, tins, etc. and items bribed from the Polish civilians with chocolate, cigarettes, tea and coffee. An RAF corporal drew up the plans and built it, using a battered car battery for power. At the beginning, when we began to get Red Cross parcels, we kept it in a Red Cross box on 'show'. On moving from camp to camp, it was taken apart and everybody carried a bit of it. In a tin we had powdered milk. It was very handy to put a part in it and put the powdered milk back on top. Nine o'clock was the regular time for the BBC news. So Joe Roberts, Queen Victoria Rifles, used to take the news down then he'd write it out and take it round the various huts and tell them that this is the latest BBC news from

home, but don't repeat it, because we nearly dropped a clanger when Hess came to England. We had the news before the Germans and somebody nearly dropped it. You had to be careful when the Germans were about.[95]

Indeed so; Henry Davis witnessed the guards hunting for radios: 'The Gestapo came in to try and get the radio. They cut off the electricity except for the hospital. They got patients out of bed. What did we do? We had a Guards' officer and we placed him on the operating table, on top of the radio and we had him under Pentothal anaesthetic. We were going to cut his thigh but we didn't have to. They came in and saw us operating and went out, lucky!'[96]

The escapers

Escape was the obvious dream, yet even if a prisoner could get clear of the camp he was hundreds of miles inside Germany in a Europe dominated by the German presence. Capture would merit the cooler, often with an introductory beating or worse.[97] The captives had no real contact with underground resistance networks, even after the setting up of Military Intelligence 9. Officers of both sides understood they had the right, a duty, to escape if possible. As they were spared labour, officers had infinitely more time on their hands and were less exhausted than other ranks. Escapes tied up enemy resources and the escapee might have valuable intelligence, gleaned from observation.[98]

In 1943, Thomas Lawton, an NCO in rank, attempted escape from Stalag 383:

Germans and civilians, who worked in the camp as 'trusted' men, had been bribed and brought in railway timetables. This was done by the German or civilian accepting, at first, a gift from the prisoners and then threatened later that if they did not provide information etc., they would be reported. Papers were prepared and clothing made. I was a farmer. Sergeant Jack Tingle was dressed as a woman and was my 'aunt'. We practised for some time prior to the escape, learning useful German phrases and much of it from used German newspapers and magazines. Great care had to be taken, for the Germans planted 'stooges' in the camp.[99]

It was their intention simply to abscond from a working party, their 'civvies' concealed beneath customary uniforms:

> At a pre-arranged time members of the working party caused some confusion by a miscount, which was easily done, whilst we slipped out amongst the civilian travellers in our civilian clothes. We had to keep our POW discs in case we were recaptured. It was remarkable how people tried to help us. The big test came when the ticket collector arrived to check the tickets, but we had been instructed not to show him anything unless he asked to see it. We were instructed not to speak to anyone who we thought might be Gestapo. All went well. When we arrived in Munich, we asked, 'Do we have to change here for Linz?' Three or four people told us we had to and even showed us the platform.

Amazingly, the two Durhams made it as far as Budapest and a designated 'safe' house. Less safe than it appeared: 'I do not know how long I had been asleep when I was awakened by the light coming on. I was aware that standing at the foot of my bed, and at Jack's, was a uniformed German policeman with drawn revolver and three civilians wearing trilby hats, long leather coats and wearing dark glasses. The Gestapo! Imagine our fear.'[100] Though interrogated and confined, neither escapee was harmed and they eventually found themselves back in Stalag 383.

Theirs was not the only daring escape attempted by DLI prisoners. George Anderson with a mate from another regiment was able to escape from a working party in Poland and link up with partisans, engaged in harassing the Germans: 'Our work was mainly sabotage and we went with a company of Poles, 50 or 60 in all. The Germans used to come into the Protectorate and impress labour to dig trenches in anticipation of the coming Russian offensive. Our main job was to attack the Germans and disperse the workers, thereby holding up the work.'[101]

Some officers, like Michael Farr and Michael Scott, were serial escapers. Scott, with three fellow officers, attempted to escape whilst in transit by rail:

> We were put on parade [at Oflag VB]. It was evident that they were hopping mad about the break from the train. The four of us, who had jumped the train coming from Poland, were sent for 14

days' confinement to a German army barracks nearby. We were in a cell by ourselves, solitary confinement. Food was brought to us, bread with sugar on it and a potato or two. We were virtually confined to our cells. It was a very hot period and the countryside was beautiful. We were taken down a passage to do our usual functions. We had a courtyard where we exercised. It was quite difficult. The German colonel commanding this camp and an American-speaking interpreter, who was quite a slick chap, sent for us. He was the Gestapo man, though we didn't know it then. We found out later. He questioned the four of us together with the most extraordinary comments. He was quite liable to slap you on the back and say, 'It's all OK for you now but we will win the war', making a joke but very shrewd questioning. It could be worrying.[102]

Scott knew what he was up against. He had initially been put in camp Oflag VIIC. Here, the prisoners were proscribed under dire penalty from ever looking out of the windows. Lieutenant E.L. Rees, 8 DLI, had the temerity to attempt sketching the land beyond and was promptly shot dead. Not discouraged by his unpleasant experience in Oflag VB, Scott enjoyed a more relaxed regime at Oflag VIIID. When the time came, once again, to be moved, he and his comrades hit on a novel plan:

We developed a scheme where we should be bricked into a large wall, which was the base of a chimney. We were bricked in, the three of us, P. Greenwell, K. Harmon (DLI) and myself, with water and something to eat to keep us going for a day or two. The only light was the skylight at the top of the chimney, so we could tell if it was daylight or not. We had a fat lamp to give us some light. We had one chap kneeling, one chap standing and one lying down. The space was restrictive. The idea for this was that, as we'd heard that the camp was leaving, we thought that if we disappeared before this happened, they would clear the camp out and, as we were bricked into this place, we knew how to get out and we would set a course to the nearest friendly frontier. We all got packed into the chimney and put in our water and everything. It was funny because we had cans of water and we drank and peed exactly the same amount. Extraordinary, everything came up to the same level. We sat and waited. We couldn't hear very much but we had a little slot and a message could be pushed through. The last message we got from outside was that they heard the new inmates would be Russian women prisoners, replacing our chaps. Anyway, we laid low and Tacksi, the security chap, knocked the place to pieces. We heard him say as he did so, 'I know damned well you haven't escaped anywhere, you'd be here somewhere.' He had been all over the place and, in the very end, he saw from the top of the chimney right down to the bottom, 60 or 70 feet I should think, our fat lamp. So he came and tore the brickwork out and got us out. As a matter of fact we were glad to be out for it was a damned uncomfortable place.[103]

Another 14 days in the cooler followed at their new camp, Oflag VIB.

Scott was far from done. His skills as a former mining engineer were employed to facilitate a mass escape from Oflag VB – some 43 men got 'over the wire' though all but three were recaptured. Despite the high failure rate, these escapes were never futile for the searching tied up hundreds of German troops. In the autumn of 1942 he again made a bid as part of another ambitious breakout. Oflag VIIB at Eichstatt was viewed as absolutely secure. Scott and his fellow escapers were determined to prove the Germans overconfident:

All the experienced escapers were to go out. Some were in civvies, some in casual uniform dyed with coffee, ink etc. They had maps, compass, porridge, biscuits, cheese and KLIM tins. The ventilation pipes were made from empty KLIM tins. All was ready by the end of May 1943. The escape was delayed by fears that an unstable POW officer might warn the Germans and the first breakout was cancelled. On the night of 3/4 June, they broke the surface well beyond the perimeter. The whole operation was very extensive and was conducted in a manner that got men into the 'Top Henry' hut to wait their turn to be called out.

It had been agreed that 34 would go out and later, as it turned out so well, the whole 65 got out. You lay quietly in the roof up there. There was a lot of sweating, a lot of tension. Once you left there and your number was called, you went to the 'Little Henry' and picked up your pack and the rope. You went down the stairs where a fellow prisoner was waiting to encourage you. There was a great esprit de corps. You now went down the hole and another prisoner was waiting there with a carbide lamp, who said, 'Off you go'. You went up the tunnel to the 'coffin', which was a massive stone in the tunnel, and you squeezed round this. When you got up to the 'Piccadilly' area there was another good friend cheering you on, nothing to do with the escape himself, and he would say, 'You're alright now'. The sod of earth will have been removed and the movement have started proper. The night air came pouring in. It was sweet smelling. It was a June night. The exit was intended to be covered up to use again but I think that was being a bit hopeful.'

Freedom for Scott and Harmon, with whom he'd attempted escape before, was fraught with tension:

We reached and sheltered in a railway hut near a tunnel and ate a meal. Two people arrived, a gamekeeper and his young daughter. The former ran off leaving the girl, to whom we gave some chocolate. We were dressed as workmen. We hid in a cornfield and a cutter arrived but, though we could hear the voices of the farm workmen, we remained undiscovered. On the third night we were heading for Stuttgart when two farmers with shotguns spotted us and we were recaptured. Hitler Youth arrived, mostly aged eight to 10 years, and threatened to shoot us. The farmers pushed them away. We were taken to a police station and then sent to Willibaldsburg Schloss, an old baronial hall, very unpleasant and primitive. There were 20 men to a room and an armed guard in each room. Even so, three men escaped, which made the Germans extremely angry. It was a frightening time.[104]

At last this serial escaper was consigned to Colditz on 26 July 1943. The search for him, Harmon and the other escapees from Oflag VIIB had tied down thousands of Germans.

Coming home at last

During the course of the war the badly wounded, in accordance with the terms of the Geneva Convention,[105] were to be exchanged on a one-for-one basis. Richard Forbes was one of these: 'The badly wounded, together with doctors and padres, were collected in one camp and told we were going to Rouen, which we did in November 1942. It was a one-for-one exchange, one badly wounded Brit for one badly wounded German.'[106] At this point, though, the negotiations faltered, then collapsed, and Forbes, with all the others, were returned to their original POW camps. It was not until October 1943 that he was repatriated through Sweden, arriving at Trelleborg: 'HM Minister, the Staff of the British Legation, and all members of the British Colony in Sweden, send their warm greetings to you on the completion of a stage in your journey. We are all proud to be the first link with home for which you have suffered so much and where your return is eagerly awaited.'[107] With these pious sentiments no doubt warming, they were finally transferred by Red Cross ship to Leith and a rousing reception and the welcoming fare provided by WVS.'

For the rest, the unending tedium and discomfort of camp life continued, enduring till the final German collapse. The speed of the Russian advance after the successful summer offensive of 1944[108] led to hurried evacuation of the more easterly camps westwards. This would be a forced march, any distance from 300 to 800 miles through the teeth of a continental winter. Some were to be moved by train but this, of itself, posed dangers as the RAF now controlled the skies; '… the senior British officer said we would not move under any circumstances unless the top of the cattle trucks were painted in white "POW", in order to avoid being shot up …' Rodney Gee was less fortunate: he had to march. He was considerably older than his fellow captives, being in his mid-forties:

> To carry my goods, I made a rucksack from a pair of trousers. Columns of marching men attracted the Allied aircraft overhead that could not recognise the columns as marching POWs. We refused to march by day due to the danger from the air and we marched by night. After two nights we refused to go on as we were too weak. The Germans feared an uprising of Poles, internees and forced labour people.

Deliverance was nearer than these weary survivors realised, when, as a result of the US forces' rapid eastwards advance, they bumped into an American column: 'As we got a little further on, towards the village, our German major came and knelt down in the middle of the road and handed his sword to the American officer. The

American took it but didn't know what to do with it. We moved round a corner and there were all the German guards, 20 to 30 of them, all had handed their weapons over to us.'[109] That was it. Rich American food gorged on shrunken digestive systems proved an unexpected hazard to men who had lived at subsistence level for so long. They were flown to the Channel and then back across to England, a country they had not seen for five long, terrible years of war and captivity.

Frederick Bedlington was another who endured the long, freezing march west as the Germans scurried to avoid the Soviets' inexorable advance:

> The roads were lined with the dead of concentration camp prisoners, many of whom had been shot as they got too weak to walk. We made sledges in the camp prior to the march on which to carry our goods. The march took us into the Czech mountain region. The people were very friendly. When the food ran out we had to live off the land and what we could steal from the farms and houses. I was beaten up for attempting to steal a pigeon at one farm. I entered one Czech household and was fed by the family. We marched into Bavaria. We broke into a potato cellar in one farm then made a fire and roasted the potatoes. The Americans met us in a village square just west of Bayreuth. It was April 1945. We were told to occupy any house in the village. I moved in with a German couple for two or three days. He was ex-World War I and very friendly. We were taken by trucks to Munich airfield, showered and deloused, and then flown to Brussels and a few days later on to England.[110]

Joseph Weddle was another who endured the harsh journey west in the unrelenting cold of January 1945:

> Some of the lads coming into the camp, especially the Indian soldiers, were in a bad way. The lads had a whip-round to give them some of what we had. The German officers got us lined up. We had a flat float, the kind of cart with tyre wheels pulled by a small pony. This carried the Germans' equipment. We didn't know where we were going, just moving away from Danzig because the Russians were pushing through. We were told to keep together

and see what happens. When you got tired, you just rested. Even the refugees, Germans and Poles were on the roads with their horses, carts, barrows, marching, marching, marching!

Weddle and his pals stuck together, a close knit team: '…it was bitterly cold, and the wind!' Jokers, grousers and habitual aggressors stumbled on together…Most of us had British overcoats, which were a godsend.' Even the most brutal of the guards began to relax the iron bonds of discipline. It was becoming obvious to all the war was coming to an end:

> Sometimes we went into large barns, no lights. You had to be there to believe it. When you're cold you always want to go to the toilet and you're in the middle of a crowded barn. You couldn't see. Somebody would try and light a match! The barn was full of straw. You couldn't find your pals on the way back. Some shouted, 'Stop down there and go to sleep.' Then you got somebody's boot in your face. Some didn't bother, just pissed in the straw where they were. That was the worst part in the larger barns.[111]

Fred Walsh found himself on the road toward Vienna in a vast mixed column of POWs, fleeing German military and civilians:

> On the second day we got a German Sergeant-Major in charge of us. 'Tomorrow' was always the day you were going to get rations and 'tomorrow' never came. This man said to us, 'I'm sorry but you're getting the same rations as me.' We were given a handful of beans, that's all we were given. One lad was called by a strange name, Haven John Collins, from New Zealand. He said to the Sergeant-Major, 'Don't bother about us on the march. Turn a blind eye and we'll feed you!' So the first thing we did, we were going through a little Austrian village, about 20 houses, and it was obvious that a large column of people going through attracted the occupants of the houses, who came out to see us. During the time they were out in the front, one of us ran round the back and into the pantry getting bread and that was how we fed. We started to steal like that.
> We were greatly burdened carrying our packs and we went through one village and, in a little farmyard, there was a hand cart, which finished up in our possession. There were 12 of us in

our party. We had ropes and you had to pull for an hour. When there was a long pass through the mountains or a hill that was heavy going, you all got on the ropes. When not on the ropes there was a period of rest for an hour and you might use this time to scavenge for food. Another trick, if you had a pair of socks you 'sold' them to a farmer at the side of the road for a chicken or eggs, anything he had to sell. You would fold one sock into a ball and threw it to him, but he only got one sock. We kept the other one and that was sold as a 'pair' in the next village. One night we had nothing to eat until this John Collins came in carrying a dead pig. This was how we lived for about five weeks. The German Sergeant-Major used to come for his meal every night.

One of the big towns we went through had an SS camp and by now the SS were desperate. They were really wild people. The German Sergeant-Major said, 'Do not do anything today because we are in SS country.' That night, believe it or not, we had a dixy of soup out of the SS cookhouse, because they were on the roadside watching us go by and one of the lads called Wilkinson went in and got this dixy of soup and we had this. Mind you, you were up at 5am the next morning and on the march out of the way of the SS.[112]

Another on these long marches was Alan Watcham, gasping towards Magdeburg, his column strafed by US fighters. The dire cold of winter gave way to a wet thaw, the driving rain plastering chilled clothes against their wasted limbs:

The actual end came quite unexpectedly. I remember I had gone to this German farm and I'd got a bag of meal and some molasses, of all things, treacly stuff. I went down the garden and found a tin sheet and I lit a fire and was eating, Indian fashion. I could see these German guards walking down past the fence. All of a sudden a cry went up, 'The Americans are here.' I remember kicking this fire out and running down the village and into the little square. There, bang in the middle, was this jeep and you couldn't get near it for the German civilians, shouting and laughing. Some were crying. You almost thought they were being liberated.

Gorging, being sick, washing and delousing followed. Watcham and his comrades were moved by truck into former Luftwaffe barracks then flown to Le Havre and from there into England:

The Americans were very good and allowed us to go into the co-pilot's seat. We flew over Chesil Beach. God! What a sight. You picked out the little church spires, cows grazing in the fields: 'This green and pleasant land'. If ever I felt proud to be British, it was then. After five and a half years a prisoner, it was absolutely perfect. 'This green and pleasant land'; it is true. I went back to my seat with a lump in my throat.[113]

They were met at Westcott field in Buckinghamshire by the redoubtable WVS. Watcham was able to send a quick telegram to his family – he was debriefed, issued with new uniform and documents, together with voting instructions for the forthcoming general election and then, next morning, was on a train for Newcastle and home.

And so the POWs came back.

> I always used to tell my mother, 'When I come home I'll open the door and throw in my cap, and you have that corned beef pie ready.' I got back into Durham and met a lad from Murton. He asked me to go to 'The Neville' for a drink. I said, 'No, the last drink I had was with my dad at home. The next one is going to be with my dad.' I got on to the bus and the conductor came for my money and someone shouted, 'I'll pay his bus fare.' It was a lad I used to work with down the pit. I then bumped into a lad who was in my section at Warlus[114] called Morgan Metcalfe. We got off at Houghton-le-Spring and just as I got off the bus, the church clock began to strike 10 o'clock. Oh, what a lovely sound. I sat on the curb and listened to it. Morgan said, 'Howay, let's have a pint.' I said, 'No I'm going home to my mum and dad.' We were just going past the pub and he walked in and my dad was sitting there. He said, 'Your Moss has just walked past.' My dad got up and upset the beer and came out shouting along Newbottle Street. When we came to the house, the bunting was out, 'Welcome Home'. I opened the door, took off my cap and slung it in. My mother was standing there and said, 'I'm not going to throw it out.' We pulled the chairs up to the table and my mother went to the oven and said, 'Here it is' – a great big corned beef pie.
>
> Moss Waterston DLI

Notes

1   Major Ian R. English MC, TD, cited in English, I.R. & Moses, H., *For You Tommy the War is Over* (DLI Durham, 2006), preface.

2   Colonel Harry Sell OBE, MC, TD, DL, cited in English & Moses, foreword.

3   It was during the course of this action that Lieutenant Richard Annand won the VC; see chapter 3.

4   The last of seven battalions was the 12th but which was designated 1st Tyneside Scottish in February 1940, later transferred to the Black Watch.

5   DLI Sound Recording Project.

6   On 27 May elements of SS Totenkopf perpetrated the infamous Le Paradis Massacre when 97 British POWs from 2nd Battalion Royal Norfolk Regiment were murdered in cold blood.

7   See chapter 2.

8   DLI Sound Recording Project

9   Formerly 12 DLI.

10 One of the prime drawbacks of the type '37 webbing was the inability to access the ammunition pouches effectively from a prone position.

11 DLI Sound Recording Project.

12 Ibid.

13 The Bren gun carrier or Universal carrier was a small British-manufactured tracked vehicle produced in large numbers (113,000) during the war. It was the successor to the earlier Carden-Loyd Mk. IV tankette and was primarily utilised to transport men, equipment, supporting weapons etc. around the battlefield.

14 Correctly, the Rifle, Anti-Tank .55 Boys, named for its creator. A heavy, rather cumbersome weapon with a five-round magazine capacity operated by bolt action, it came with a bipod and was accurate over a range of some 300 yards (280m).

15 DLI Sound Recording Project.

16 Ibid.

17 Ibid.

18 Ibid.

19 English & Moses, pp.13–14.

20 DLI Sound Recording Project.

21 Ibid.

22 English & Moses, p.21.

23 DLI Sound Recording Project.

24 Ibid.

25 Ibid.

26 Ibid.

27 Ibid.

28 Ibid. Anywhere between 50–70 men, sometimes more, were crammed into each truck.

29 Ibid.

30 Ibid.

31 Ibid.

32 Ibid.

33 Ibid.

34 Ibid.

35 Ibid.

36 Ibid.

37 English & Moses, p.37.

38 DLI Sound Recording Project.

39 Ibid.

40 Ibid.

41 Ibid.

42 These were: M. Scott, M. Farr, J. Hyde-Thomson MC, J. Beaumont, K. Harman, J. Lace, B.S. Walker, Lt.-Col. Stallard DSO MBE; see English & Moses, p.42.

43 Colditz had previously been a mental health institution.

44 DLI Sound Recording Project.

45 Ibid.

46 Ibid.

47 Ibid.

48 1st Battalion DLI had the misfortune to form the backbone of the Allied garrison on Kos that was attacked on 3–4 October 1943. The Allies had sought to take control of the Dodecanese following the Italian collapse (Kos had been in Italian hands since 1912). Antimachia airfield on Kos was central to the defence of the islands and was taken by the Germans after bombardment and landings; the surviving garrison, some 1,388 British, surrendered. A number of Italians, including the commandant, were executed.

49 DLI Sound Recording Project.

50 English & Moses, p.50.

51 DLI Sound Recording Project.

52 Colonel Falkenburg commanding Stalag VIIIF.

53 Instructions for Guarding Soviet Prisoners of War, September 1941.

54 Article 27.

55 DLI Sound Recording Project.

56 Ibid.

57 Ibid.

58 A warrant officer is effectively a form of senior NCO who inhabits a separate class of ranks between the NCO and the commissioned officer.

59 DLI Sound Recording Project

60 Ibid.

61 Ibid.

62 Ibid.

63 Ibid.

64 Ibid. Red Cross parcels typically weighed around 11 pounds and might contain tined sardines, fruit, chocolate, sugar, Christmas pudding, baked beans and pork, stew, condensed milk, cheese, cake and tea; see English & Moses, p.65.

65 Ibid.

66 DLI Sound Recording Project.

67 Ibid.

68 Ibid.

69 For the first parcel the sender was allowed 40 coupons and 20 for each one thereafter.

70 English & Moses, p.69.

71 Cited in English & Moses, p.70.

72 Ibid.

73 Ibid.

74 Ibid.

75 Ibid.

76 Ibid.

77 Ibid.

78 Ibid.

79 Ibid.

80 Ibid.

81 Ibid.

82 Richard Forbes; ibid.

83 English & Moses, p.86.

84 Rodney Gee, cited in English & Moses, p.88.

85 DLI Sound Recording Project.

86 Ibid.

87 The list of qualifications which could be earned was impressive: City & Guilds, Institute of Bankers, Institute of Cost and Works Accountancy, Institute of Brewing, School of Oriental and African Studies, Royal Horticultural Society, Institute of Electrical Engineers, Chartered Institute of Secretaries, Institute of Chartered Shipbrokers and Institute of Structural Engineers.

88 English & Moses, p.90.

89 DLI Sound Recording Project.

90 Ibid.

91 Ibid.

92 'Operation Jubilee', launched on 19 August 1942, was a raid on Dieppe by primarily Canadian forces; of the 6,000-odd men put ashore, over half became casualties. The disaster did provide many lessons for subsequent Allied landings in North Africa ('Torch') and Normandy ('Overlord'). It was rumoured that German prisoners being transported to Britain were handcuffed.

93 DLI Sound Recording Project.

94 Ibid.

95 Ibid.

96 Ibid.

97 The 'Great Escape' – 76 prisoners, led by Roger Bushell, got out of Stalag Luft III; of these, 73 were recaptured and 50 of them were murdered by the Gestapo. The book, by Paul Brickhill, was the basis for the 1963 film.

98 For instance, prisoners noted the vast flow of men, vehicles and materiel eastwards in the spring of 1941 which presaged 'Barbarossa' – the invasion of Soviet Russia.

99 DLI Sound Recording Project.

100 Ibid.

101 Anderson had many adventures, at one time joining with the Russians and hunting Germans with the Polish police. When the Russians, confident of victory, turned on the hapless Poles he, with a small group of other escapees, made their further escape to Czechoslovakia and finally reached England in June 1945: see English & Moses, p.116.

102 DLI Sound Recording Project.

103 Ibid.

104 Ibid.

105 Article 68.

106 DLI Sound Recording Project.

107 WVS: Women's Voluntary Service, established in 1938 by Stella Isaacs, Dowager Marchioness of Reading; this became a voluntary relief organisation, though its original defined function was as support for local ARP (Air Raid Precautions) services.

108 Operation 'Bagration'.

109 DLI Sound Recording Project.

110 Ibid.

111 Ibid.

112 Ibid.

113 Ibid.

114 Near Arras.

Chapter 13

'Dad's Army':
the Home Guard, 1940–44

Great Britain stood in danger
From the Bully from Berlin
Oh! How the Home Guard was founded
Why it even staggered him.

With prongs and sticks and shotguns
There was John and Joe and Tom
Right through the bally country
The Home Guard was formed and strong.
'Winkle' Ayling, Ode to the Home Guard[1]

The primary object of the Home Guard is to have available
an organised body of men trained to offer stout resistance
in every district, and to meet any military emergency until
trained troops can be brought up.
Home Guard Manual, 1941[2]

'Dad's Army' was immortalised by the BBC television series of that
name which ran from 1968 to 1977 and is much repeated even today,
so a generation of students whose understanding of the Second
World War is limited, at best, has some idea of the Home Guard.
Captain Mainwaring and his platoon are not the only screen
representation. George Formby appeared as a Home Guard Lance-
Corporal in the 1943 film *Get Cracking*. In the same year Colonel
Blimp made his screen appearance in Powell and Pressburger's
The Life and Death of Colonel Blimp. More recent small-screen
offerings such as *Foyle's War* have played to the demand for wartime
nostalgia.

This is largely legend. *Dad's Army* does contain a great deal of truth: the muddling amateurishness, chronic shortages of weapons and equipment, Heath Robinson hardware and wide divergence of personal backgrounds all strike a factual chord. But the Home Guard remains affectionately risible because it was never tested. Those who fought alongside workers' militias in Spain had witnessed a very different reality. In the event of an actual German invasion, the Volunteers of 1940 would have been expected to fight and almost certainly they would. A memorable scene from the TV series features Mainwaring's ill-assorted heroes manning a makeshift barricade, doling out their few shotgun cartridges and awaiting German tanks. Obviously, these never came; had they done so the results would have been swift, brutal and anything but comic.[3]

If one tours the north-east coast and inland, evidence of past martial activity abounds: Northumbrian beaches are studded with tank traps, concrete and steel gun emplacements, pillboxes[4] and some superbly restored batteries, particularly Blyth[5] and Hartlepool[6]. The latter did indeed see active service in the previous war: in the battle of December 1914 when the part-time gunners fought a good fight against marauding German battle-cruisers, a dozen British soldiers died, as did 80-odd civilians in the town, which was shattered by the bombardment; needless to say, this is not the stuff of comedy! In quiet Northumbrian lanes and in most unexpected places one comes across further emplacements, seemingly in the most random pattern. These are, in fact, traces of the various 'stop' lines set up as a defence in depth against invasion. It was anticipated the Home Guard would be charged with resisting the initial onslaught on the beaches then holding a series of fallback positions to blunt the overall attack till a successful counter-attack could be launched. Most would have died or been captured.

Formation

> It helped to save the country
> Although some were old and bald
> It put the wind up Hitler
> For he was heard to say 'Good Lord'.

Ode to the Home Guard

'We shall defend our island whatever the cost may be; we shall fight on the beaches, we shall fight on the landing grounds, we shall fight in the fields and in the streets, we shall fight in the hills; we shall never surrender.'[7]

Sergeant John Williams, serving for most of the war with 9 DLI, did a stint with the Home Guard: 'We were sent to guard Vaux Brewery, which we did and, in the process, consumed a good deal of Vaux Ale! The Major, can't mind his name, was an old-type DLI bloke. Did some training with the 3-inch mortar – well, that was love at first sight!'[8]

The LDV – Local Defence Volunteers – legally came into being on 17 May 1940. At the outset, this process did resemble 1914 and Kitchener's volunteers in that there was a near-absolute dearth of weapons, uniforms, materiel and officers. Many who had seen service in the last, and indeed previous, conflicts found themselves back in command of troops, except their current companies were little more than an enthusiastic but untrained mob. Under the provisions of its initial statutorily defined role, the LDV was not paramilitary but an 'armed police constabulary'. Their primary function was to observe German troop movements in the event of an invasion rather than resist, whilst maintaining a security presence at key strategic locations. This was rather too passive for the martial ardour of volunteers and commanders, who preferred a more proactive stance. Churchill, now Prime Minister, endorsed this and, by late July 1940, had instructed Eden to rebrand the volunteers as the Home Guard. The latter's resistance was based entirely upon the pragmatic argument that a million LDV armbands had been purchased and were now to be wasted.

Thomas Myers served as an NCO with 6 DLI but spent time as a Home Guard instructor; he was not entirely overawed:

The Home Guard I saw never had a regular instructor with them, they were very inexperienced; most were overage and very unfit. I did my best but half them were generally laughing at me and usually just said, 'Come on, we're going to the pub.' Well that was usually the end of training for that day! Some of them had been in the last war but this one was very different, you see we'd learnt a lot from the Desert and from Sicily; it was no longer a matter of just digging trenches. They didn't have many weapons other than rifles and whilst they were fine for guarding bridges and the like, you can't expect men like that to go running round the countryside rounding up paratroopers can you?[9]

Not wishing to be excluded, women, initially denied a role in the Home Guard, took to forming their own units such as the Amazon Defence Corps.[10] Those ladies of a less overtly martial inclination might have preferred membership of the Women's Home Defence,[11] which, though not official, had branches all over the country. Women were latterly admitted to the ranks of the Home Guard, though strictly in non-military, supporting roles. Once the first terror of invasion had passed and as the Allies began to gain ground, the Home Guard units continued in a domestic security role, permitting regulars to take up active service overseas.

Organisation

Once the initial rush, in clouds of confusion and frustration, had subsided and the Home Guard was officially in existence as a full citizen's domestic reaction force, provision could be introduced for its proper establishment. Organisation came into the hands of Lord-Lieutenants of individual counties together with the senior military area commanders. These then appointed area, zone and group delegates. Those who had seen service were permitted to retain their unit badges in addition to the LDV armband. After August 1940 the HG units were affiliated to their local county regiments and used their cap badge; thus all Durham formations wore the DLI bugle. Each community would field a platoon, grouped into companies and battalions in the usual way. County Durham was a region with many men, miners and farmers in particular, in reserved occupations. These now came forward in large numbers to volunteer. Of those who offered to serve, perhaps half had military experience from the Great War. There was no medical test or examination as such – a core level of basic fitness was simply assumed.

Durham, in fact, raised some 26 Home Guard Battalions, one of which was the 1st Durham (Blaydon) Battalion Home Guard. Its catchment area was spread through a rash of small settlements: Byermoor, Marley Hill, Sunniside, Whickham and Swalwell. Some larger factories and businesses even had their own 'in-house' platoons – the Derwenthaugh Coke Works and Vickers Armstrong, just over the Tyne, were prime examples. Larger settlements were often able to raise more than one battalion; Gateshead and Sunderland each raised two and Newcastle could boast three. In 1943 the original zonal structure was altered so that battalions were brigaded in sectors, divided into sub-districts and districts. The Blaydon Battalion thus joined with Chester-le-Street, Lanchester, Consett, Hamsterley and Stanley to form the Consett Sector with its HQ in Hamsterley Hall. Consett Sector, together with Houghton-le-Spring and Weardale plus Sunderland garrison, comprised a sub-district, one of three in the Northumbrian District of Northern Command.

From an assortment of 'civvies' and old items of uniform, some of which had last seen service on the Veldt or North West Frontier, the HG were issued with denim battledress, standard ammunition, boots and forage caps. These gradually gave way to standard wool kit with usual impedimenta and caps carrying the coveted DLI badge. Webbing rather predated '37 canvas pattern; it even predated the venerable '08 pattern which had sustained Tommy Atkins in the trenches. This leather gear had been volunteer pattern pre-Haldane's reforms and came in a rather jaunty lighter shade. Efforts at darkening the colour proved tricky and varied – the clear favourite being an overnight soaking in a chamber-pot (full)! At the outset the volunteers still wore the HG armband on battledress until distinctive shoulder flashes were provided. Some units, like the Rowlands Gill platoon, echoing the fads of Victorian forbears, also sported the DLI green lanyard. All wore the letters 'DHM' with the battalion number stitched below.

Albert Shippen served with the 4th ITC (Infantry Training Centre) at Brancepeth from 1941–44. He remembered small arms and bayonet training:

> Well, we used the long 17-inch bayonet and we lunged at sacks stuffed with straw. We did bayonet drill where you had your bayonet and the other fellow had a kind of six-foot pole with a boxing glove on one end and a loose ring on the other. He was there to parry and you had to get your point through the ring; if you weren't smart enough the glove would come round and belt you! I also remember grenade throwing. We had a nasty accident when one fellow simply panicked after he'd pulled the pin and the lever flew off, he dropped the grenade back into the pit and another private and NCO couldn't get out quick enough; both were very badly injured, had to be rushed to hospital.[12]

From knobkerries and pikes to shotguns and rook rifles, the
volunteers arrived armed with an antique arsenal of weapons, none
suitable for fighting the Wehrmacht. One early suggestion was a
form of pike constructed from a length of pipe fitted with a long,
sword bayonet, effective if the enemy was obliging or chivalrous
enough to permit the volunteer to get within stabbing range.
Gradually a supply of rifles was sourced, some old US P17s from
1917, a reliable weapon though the round was incompatible with
that used by the Lee Enfield.[13] Some of the US .45 cal. Thompson or
'Tommy' guns[14] were provided, the sort of gun most Englishmen
had only witnessed in the hands of James Cagney or George Raft.
The lack of a reliable 9mm submachine-gun to combat the German
MP38/40 was remedied by the introduction of the British Sten,
backstairs bastard of wartime expediency. Improvised rifle ranges
appeared like a rash as usually the units did not train with live
rounds. The Rowlands Gill men practised on the riverside by
Lockhaugh Viaduct, and local lads would dig the spent bullets from
targets as souvenirs. After 1941, grenades became more readily
available in reasonable quantities.

Ernest Harvey served as a private in the DLI depot though, at the
outset, he was too young to join up:

I was 16 when war broke out, working as a trainee grocer. I'd
wanted to join the navy but ended up for a while in the Home
Guard. We used to meet in a local hall – no rifles in those early
days; we drilled with broom-shanks. Can't remember where I
joined, wasn't the police station; you just had to be 16, no
medicals. We met twice a week and I had to do some nights fire-
watching at the Coop. We didn't see many raids over Hetton but
Sunderland caught it quite regularly. Most of those who joined up
seemed to be businessmen. Major Sharp, who was in charge, had a
shoe shop in Hetton I recall, and there was Norman Land, he was
the foreman at the pit. We had no rifles to start with, none at all,
and they only arrived in dribs and drabs; it was quite something
when you got your rifle mind! We did an exercise in woods once, I
remember, and a pair of us got captured, not surprising as we'd
spent the whole time catching rabbits. We had no live firing really,
only got up to a range at Hetton Colliery every two weeks. The
training was quite tough but, as we were volunteers and not paid,
if you didn't fancy turning up you just sent in your apologies. But

most of us looked forward to it, it was very social, you met your friends and by the end we were ready for anything I'd say.[15]

Machine-guns, Brens and mortars were in very short supply and some typically Heath Robinson devices for the Home Guard comprised the Northover Projector which could lob Molotovs[16] or phosphorus bombs. The 'Blackie Bomber' was defined as a 29mm spigot mortar, and there was also the 'sticky bomb', a form of self-adhesive explosive device which could be affixed to the flank of an enemy vehicle or tank. The HG manual contained much helpful advice on the manufacture and use of improvised grenades:

> To prepare a jam tin grenade, take a small tin (jam tin, malt tin, or any other tin of about 1lb or 2lb capacity) and place in it a stick of gelignite in which a hole has been made as above. Now pack nuts, nails, bolts, stones or any other similar material into the tin around the central stick of explosive. When full replace the lid, in which a hole has been made through which the detonator may be inserted. Strap the lid on with a length of adhesive tape…To throw, place detonator and fuse into the gelignite through the hole in the lid, secure them with a piece of adhesive tape to the tin. The grenade may then be lit and thrown.[17]

One of the more ambitious and potentially cataclysmic surprises in the volunteer arsenal, was the exotically named 'Flame Fougasse'[18] which, though it sounds like a TV recipe, was a rather nasty compound of tar, lime and petrol mix served up in 40-gallon drums. These, in modern military parlance, would be classified as Improvised Explosive Devices (IEDs). The drum was buried by the roadside then detonated by pressure on a string triggering a small charge and sending a jet of the highly flammable mix spurting across the surface, igniting a raging wall of flame. Safe storage for quantities of explosives and flammables became something of a headache; few villages boasted purpose-built armouries and, as ever, it was a case of making do. The High Spen platoon employed a sealed container sunk in a local pond. Not perhaps the ideal choice as this was the local community's ad hoc swimming pool!

At the other end of the lethal spectrum was the humbler but potentially deadly booby trap, an art the Germans themselves excelled in:

BOOBY TRAPS – There are several devices for releasing a striker and so firing an explosive charge, when a door is opened, a box picked, etc. Ingenious engineers will be able to make up designs of their own. An effective release for booby traps either 'trip' or 'souvenir' can easily be made from an ordinary 'breakback' rat trap…Bore a hole through the wood just large enough to take the metal end of a 12-bore cartridge. Braze a bar, carrying a striker pin, across the backbreaker so that on release the striker hits the cap of the cartridge. A short piece of instantaneous fuse, a detonator and a charge of explosive complete the trap.[19]

Units might meet once or twice a week. For Rowlands Gill platoon, weekends sometimes meant exercises at Gibside or Lockhaugh, the 'enemy' came in the guise of the Special Constables or sometimes exercises were carried out with regular battalions.

Into action

Tanks are big and strong and bullying in their use, and like most bullies, have some very vulnerable points. Trained tank-hunters, chosen for their courage, coolness and readiness to carry the fight to the enemy, can become such a pest and potential danger to tanks and their crews that the value of both as fighting units can be reduced by more than half.[20]

With this rousing if rather vague advice, the warriors of the Home Guard were exhorted to take on panzers. Precisely how they were to strike terror into their armoured foes depended on the use of available weapons. These are listed in the Home Guard Manual as: 'Hand grenades, issue or home made, petrol bombs, smoke candles, anti-tank mines, axes and saws, explosives and demolitions, crowbars (for breaking tank tracks) and shotguns (for firing into driver's and gunners slits).'[21] Any Tommy who'd fought the same panzers in France might have had some trenchant observations. How you got close enough to ram your 12-bore through the driver's slit was not rehearsed.

On 7 December 1941, on the same day the Japanese struck at Pearl Harbor, Rowlands Gill platoon was in action against an unspecified 'enemy' seeking to infiltrate Derwent Valley. The volunteers were cautioned on the uses of camouflage – 'white face and hands give position away, the need to maximise cover – see without being seen, avoid if possible, positions that are obvious.'[22]

Exercises were numerous and varied:

The Rowlands Gill Platoon had to take the Battalion HQ at Blaydon. The Blaydon lads dutifully manned their lookout posts protecting every approach to Blaydon but the attackers chose a rather unorthodox route – they hung on to a rather slow-moving coal train at Derwenthaugh, jumped off at Blaydon and entered the Blaydon HQ without ever meeting a defender. The opposition CO then foolishly accused them of cheating and he was promptly inverted and his head ended up in the wastepaper basket, an action which nearly led to the demotion of George Willis.[23]

This was not the Rowlands Gill lads' only sparkling use of initiative:

The object was to attack a building near Burnhopfield – it was probably at Byermoor. Many of the Rowlands Gill lads were miners and their knowledge came in useful because this time their chosen route was underground. They entered a drainage tunnel on the side of the valley and came out behind the 'enemy' defences. Both exploits were apparently led by a corporal who is variously described as either 'resourceful' or 'quite mad.[24]

Highfield platoon scored a spectacular own-goal during one such exercise:

They were apparently part of the force defending their HQ at High Spen. The 'enemy' were from Chopwell and Blackhall Mill Platoons and to add a touch of realism they were dressed in German uniforms. During the course of the exercise the defenders captured one of the opposition and took him to their HQ for questioning. Unfortunately they had forgotten to search him and, when he produced a 'hand grenade', the umpire – the man who judged the exercise – declared the HQ blown up. The excitement was not over. As the attackers made their way home they caused quite a stir among the residents of Towneley Terrace at High Spen – a crowd of German soldiers casually walking across the golf course, laughing and joking as they went, was not an everyday sight in those parts.[25]

Though serious injuries were mercifully rare, minor accidents inevitably abounded:

> Scalded neck and shoulder from water jacket of machine-gun after firing at Whitburn: Gunshot wounds in right arm and chest. Accidentally shot by Volunteer L whilst on patrol: West Hartlepool; four Volunteers injured when police car collided with marching patrol: Leadgate; cleaning bread cutting machine on duty, sliced off little finger, right hand: West Hartlepool; collided with an air raid shelter whilst returning from parade, split open nose, West Hartlepool again; bayonet wound in chest, walked into sentry: Easington, jumped off a lorry and landed on barrel of machine-gun and injured buttock.[26]

It was sometimes suggested, perhaps unkindly, that certain of these injuries were the result of excess imbibing after an evening's drill.

From the outset, the HG had provided support to gunners manning coastal batteries but, from spring 1942, they also manned their own anti-aircraft (AA) batteries. These included a number of heavier guns (3.7-inch) and AA rocket batteries. These rather hush-hush formations, initially called 'Z' Batteries, delivered a majestic barrage comprising a gross of six-foot missiles. Manpower requirements were considerable: eight night-shifts, each with a total complement of 178, had to be found. These heavier batteries were under the overall aegis of the Royal Artillery whilst the lighter AA batteries were formed as part of HG battalions. Typically, their role was to defend vital industrial installations and the guns were served by workers trained to the task. Light AA batteries were armed with the famous Bofors[27]:

> Runciman, always the professional, was giving sharp orders to the seven men of the gun crew, so sharp there was scarcely an echo, and Bevan went to stand at the door to witness the soldiers go through the pantomime around the Bofors. The two gun layers, Purcell and Brown, wound the handles for elevation and for line from bucket seats on each side. Bairnsfather, the loader, said they reminded him of his mother and the woman next door, both swinging their mangles on opposite sides of the back fence. It was Bairnsfather who loaded the ammunition, clips of four shells, into a hopper and operated the firing pedal. Cartwright

and Ugson were the ammunition carriers, Ugson being relieved of his duty of observer once they were in action. Then Sergeant Runciman watched the sky and controlled the gun from his position to the right of it. Hignet's task, to his intense embarrassment, was to sweep up imaginary empty shell cases.[28]

Signaller Ronald Elliot was one young man who had experience of the rocket batteries (this is the same R. Elliot who later served in 16th Battalion). He was a working-class lad who had made the jump to grammar school in South Shields:

My father was a miner, so I had quite a hard childhood in those days; times before the war were tough. My father was very politically active, became a councillor and was pleased when I got into the grammar school, very few of the boys I knew did. You asked to what degree were we aware of the rise of fascism before 1939? I think we were more generally aware of German and Italian territorial expansion. Father was both a committed socialist and a pacifist, he saw the Spanish Civil War as a battle between communists and fascists. I remember the day war was declared. I was too young to join up at that point and, of course, like everyone I wanted to be in the RAF. That was far more glamorous than the Home Guard![29]

Ronald won an apprenticeship as an electrician in the naval yard:

I really wasn't cut out for this I'm afraid. I was at Vickers Armstrong in Elswick and we were building a warship, can't remember which. The yards were pretty robust, a great deal of foul language and roughness, not bullying as such but, as an apprentice, you were bottom of the heap and everyone made sure you knew it! I left to seek a temporary clerk's appointment and secured a position in the borough treasurer's office in South Shields Town Hall. My father was a councillor of course, so that probably helped. We worked from high sloping desks, like a scene from Dickens, with great big, yard-wide ledgers, pen and ink in those days, of course, and you added everything up in pounds, shillings and pence. I wasn't called up till late '42 so I joined the Home Guard beforehand; I was impelled by the need to be doing something.[30]

And so it was that Ronald Elliot came to understand the intricacies of a rocket battery:

My rocket squadron was based on the top of the cliffs overlooking South Shields; we were set out in a square formation and our target area was based on a grid system, the idea was you fired all of the rockets into this grid area in the hope you'd bring down an enemy plane. The firing platform had two rocket launchers, each missile around five or six foot long. We set the fuses once the rockets were loaded, swung the tubes around and set the elevation – we were advised by the AA batteries. Then we fired a salvo, whoosh and you kept out of the way of the missiles. I think we brought down one aircraft. We worked in two-man teams, alternating as loader and firer, we were on maybe two or three nights a week and you shared the battery with other units. I did spend some time in the control centre; we were part of the civil defence response, with fire, police and utilities. We used to plot activities on to maps if there was a raid, otherwise we could sleep. I remember our basic uniform and drill and coming home one day boasting I was going the next day for a FFI inspection, I thought this was a kind of exam. Actually, it just meant dropping your trousers while the MO looked for parasites in your nether regions![31]

Invasion from the skies

A particular and, for a while, near-hysterical fear was of enemy parachutists. These were likely to descend in the form either of agents or mass air landings. The art of paratroop warfare – 'aerial envelopment' (conquest entirely from the air) as one of its Axis champions, General Kurt Student, defined as his ultimate ambition – was new. Both the Nazis and Soviets had considered the use of both parachutists and airborne troops. That is, glider-borne infantry to spearhead attacks by seizing vital installations by *coup de main*. In practice, the Germans achieved some brilliant successes; the capture of the Belgian redoubts in Eban-Emael in 1940 was a stroke of genius, as was the later British descent on Pegasus Bridge, curtain-raiser to the Normandy landings. Larger-scale operations – most notably Student's intended masterpiece, the conquest of Crete by airborne units alone in

May 1941 – proved disastrous and, though ultimately successful, a Pyrrhic victory which persuaded Hitler to abandon further attempts.

It was, as much as anything, the fear of paratroops which commended the idea of the volunteers to Anthony Eden and the War Cabinet:

> I want to speak to you tonight about the form of warfare which the Germans have been employing so extensively against Holland and Belgium – namely the dropping of parachute troops behind the main defensive lines...In order to leave nothing to chance, and to supplement from our forces yet untapped the means of defiance already arranged, we are going to ask you to help us in a manner which I know will be welcome to thousands of you. Since the war began the government have received countless inquiries from all over the kingdom from men of all ages who are for one reason or another not engaged in military service, and who wish to do something for the defence of their country. Well, now is your opportunity.[32]

In 1940, in the wake of Dunkirk, this threat appeared very real. Home Guard units thus set up observation posts to watch the threatening skies. Shotguns were the handiest of weapons, devastating at close quarters. German paratroops, *Fallschirmjager*,[33] did not jump carrying small arms other than pistols; their weapons were dropped in separate containers, thus individuals were vulnerable as they initially hit the ground. 'Cromwell' was the code word indicating airborne assault was in the offing; 'Oliver' meant the parachutists were in fact landing. As their silk chutes billowed in mild summer skies, church bells, traditional alarum, would be sounded by the volunteers. In typical British fashion this led, in best *Dad's Army* style, to some strenuous disputes as to who should have custody of belfry keys.

When the immediate threat of invasion receded, the Home Guard drew breath and continued. As weapons, uniform and kit began filtering through, a number of motor-coach and transport companies were formed. Their function, in addition to maintaining vehicles, was to sweep up requisitioned transport when need arose; both Northumberland and Durham had Home Guard Transport

Columns by 1944. The former county, following yeomanry tradition, also formed a mounted patrol. Neither of these Kipling-esque formations was ever tested in earnest.

William Weightman was from good yeoman stock: his father, who had Middle Herrington Farm just west of Sunderland, was a noted Friesian cattle breeder. Young William would serve with 2 DLI in Burma and finally attained the rank of Lieutenant-Colonel:

> Morale remained high in the north during 1940; we didn't get such a fearful pounding as the south, you see. I went to Durham School, which was very much inclined to pacifism; so you couldn't join the OTC [Officer Training Corps] till you were 15. The 2nd platoon was a signals unit – part of 11th Battalion based in the old Gilesgate drill hall. We thought, at that point, that Jerry paratroopers were going to come, tumbling out of the skies. Many blokes in reserved occupations who couldn't join the regulars were able to join the Home Guard. All we had then was flesh and blood and pikes. Pie in the sky, we'd have all ended up under Nazi occupation. We joined through the school, Captain Ramsden was our CO, no need for a medical; at that age we were as fit as lops.[34]

Bill Weightman and his schoolmates were now ready for anything:

> We were given khaki forage caps with the DLI badge and we wore 'em dead straight.[35] We had battledress, ammunition, boots, gaiters and armed with Ross rifles.[36] We had Boer War pattern webbing and, after 1941, we were given some pretty antique Italian bolt-action rifles, very long barrel, probably captured by the Abyssinians at Adowa [1896]. We did tactical training, section and platoon attacks, some map reading and, on Sunday, exercise; it was my job to go up to the pigeon loft, duckets we called them, and collect messages in tiny cylinders, bring them back for the intelligence officer to read. We did train with the 2-inch mortar but we also had the Northover projector and the spigot mortar, this had a pair of racing-bike-type handles and the bomb was a large fat cylinder with the propellant in the tail section. You fired this at a tank ideally, had a range of about 400 yards, your first would probably be your last.[37]

Training was followed by more training:

> we marched at the light infantry pace of course; we did route
> marches on field days, instructors were drawn from No.4 ITC at
> Brancepeth camp, DLI and the Wellies [Duke of Wellington's
> West Riding Regiment]. We used to have mock skirmishes over
> the old golf course in the south-west corner of Houghall Woods.
> We were given '37 pattern water bottles – didn't matter how
> often you washed 'em out, water tasted foul. We scrambled
> through mud, brambles and cowpats. This is it for the infantry I
> thought, I'm for the RAF, though after my first flight I wasn't so
> sure. I later served with the Paras so you could say I combined
> both. At Brancepeth, we got a regular instructor and we did a lot
> of drill and some weapons training with the 3-inch mortar, 36
> pattern grenades. I remember the instructor drilling a platoon
> maybe 45 to 50 strong and when they weren't moving fast enough
> he'd tell them off. 'You haven't worked down the bloody pit all
> day', came a voice from the back. 'I've worked down plenty
> bloody pits an' all day,' replied the sergeant. 'Aye but not down
> a seam where you're doubled up all flamin' day you haven't,'
> from the same voice. 'Lad I've worked all day down seams where
> a mouse would come out bowlegged,' came the definitive reply.
> Nothing more was heard.[38]

The Auxiliary Units

> In order to stay behind we needed somewhere to stay; and by
> sucking up to the Sappers we had already brought into being
> what might very loosely be called a network of subterranean
> hideouts in which not only the striking force – Strix and about 15
> other idiots – but our far-flung, hand-picked collaborators in the
> Home Guard, would bide their time before emerging to wreak, in
> a variety of ill-defined ways, havoc among the invaders.[39]

For those members of the Home Guard who showed a special
aptitude there was a secret guerrilla army; highly trained to cause
maximum disruption to the invading Germans. Little is known
about the Auxiliary Units, even today, but there were three
battalions covering Scotland, Northern England and Southern
England and full of the cream of the Home Guard. These men, all

hand-picked volunteers, laid down months of supplies of both arms and food, ready to go into hiding the day the invasion started. Their job was to slow the invasion down by blowing up arms and fuel dumps, bridges, railway lines and generally causing confusion to the invaders. Most knew if the invasion came they would be on suicide missions.[40]

Anyone who has read Owen Shears' atmospheric novel *Resistance* will have experienced the conditions of active service for these behind-the-lines, last-ditch commandos. The book is both fiction and counter-factual but nonetheless paints a very intriguing picture of what might have been. The plot assumes a successful German invasion and a group of Welsh hill farmers, as Auxiliaries, take to the heather, leaving their wives to fend for themselves. We must be thankful the reality never occurred. Resistance movements sprang up everywhere the Nazi jackboot prevailed, most famously in France but more concertedly in Poland. Here resistors, the Home Army (AK), did rise in August 1944 and bled dreadfully in the grim attritional fight for the tumbled streets of Warsaw. Otto Skorzeny, Hitler's personal gladiator, was ordered, as the end drew near for Germany, to activate a 'Werewolf' network to harass the encroaching allies, plans that happily came to nothing.

> At our most forlorn moment when our army was pouring back from Dunkirk through gates we could never have shut against the invading enemy, Colonel Grand conceived the plan of organising through Britain a closely co-ordinated sabotage and intelligence network among the civilian population who would be left behind in any territories which the German armies might temporarily be able to occupy.[41]

Members of 202nd Home Guard Battalion were trained to act as behind-the-lines saboteurs and assassins in the event of a German invasion. A total of 39 specially constructed underground operational bases – bunkers – were excavated in the region, 27 in Northumberland, the remainder in Durham. This was a highly secret war in waiting; those who took part were thoroughly trained in the arts of killing and mayhem. Recruits were neither the old nor bald, these were younger, very fit men, generally drawn from farmers and gamekeepers; an intimate local knowledge and skill at concealment was essential, as was the willingness to kill. Their role would have been to spread terror amongst both the invader and those who might be tempted into collaboration, from active Mosleyites to women favouring 'horizontal collaboration'. No mercy would be extended. Such was the level of secrecy employed that, as the northern bunkers were being dug, dummy air raids were laid on to cover the sound of blasting.[42]

A seemingly innocuous publication, *The Countryman's Diary 1939*, covered a whole range of topics not normally associated with field sports – the Auxiliaries, mostly trained at the Guerrilla Warfare School at Coleshill in Oxfordshire, were after rather larger game:

> There was an Auxiliary Unit just four miles from Rowlands Gill; it was in the woods to the north of Beamish. The man in charge was the colliery engineer, Joe Harker. He recalled that when he was first recruited he had to go down to Sunningdale, between Bracknell and London, for an initial briefing. Naturally he was told not to talk about the reason for his journey, and when he arrived he was rather surprised to see that among the other recruits were the three men who had shared his railway compartment all the way from Newcastle.[43]

Command of 202 Battalion and its fellows, 201 (south of the Thames) and 203 (Scotland) Battalions, was exercised by Colin Gubbins, more famous as the founder and paladin of SOE.[44] The clandestine activities of Auxiliaries in the northern region have never been fully examined by historians. In charge was 'the Intelligence officer for Northumberland', Anthony Quayle, latterly famous as an actor:

> He assigned a unit to attack his car which he parked on a remote road; after waiting beside his car for 2½ hours he decided that the men were not going to make it, but when he got back into the car he found two of them in the back seat and then he noticed that two more were under the car and the remainder had him covered from a ditch on the other side of the road…the men of the Northumberland units were so highly regarded that they were given the job of protecting the Royal Family when they were staying at Balmoral.[45]

The Auxiliaries were advised at the outset that their life expectancy, once they were behind enemy lines, would be unlikely to exceed 14 days. Reprisals for their actions against the civilian population were inevitable and would, given the German penchant for brutality, be draconian. The network could only function with the active cooperation of civilians, who would share equal risks in the event of capture: 'For instance, a schoolmistress had ripped the treble hammers out of her upright piano to create a hidden space. A chicken farmer dug chalk out of his land to make an underground room in which to use his [radio] set: and a vicar told me no one would find his radio. It was hidden in his pulpit; "who else but me goes up there".'[46]

Secrecy was everything: 'There was one ex "Y" Service [Signals] chap who told his wife that he was going out to a meeting and his wife said that was fine because she had an appointment too. And they met up at Bletchley Park for a reunion. It was only then that they realised that they had both served in the war in a secret role without ever telling each other.'[47] Removal of all traces and destruction of most of the hideouts was an act of policy following the end of the war. The Auxiliaries had been officially stood down in November 1944, by which time their numbers had swelled to around 3,000, and a cloak of secrecy thrown over their operations: 'What is the most frequent question asked by visitors to the Museum of the British Resistance Organisation? Answer: why is it still so secret?'[48]

The assassination of potential collaborators had been finessed to a level where, it is said, each unit had a death-list, people targeted for killing in the event of invasion. This is a long way from Captain Mainwaring's war. People would live after the war in their communities knowing that they had possessed instructions to eliminate without trial or process – simple murder – numbers of those who might easily be neighbours and who went through the conflict with no inkling of this particular sword of Damocles hanging over their heads. All in all this was a very sensitive business!

I remember as a lad, I think it was 1951, we were scouting in the park, camping and we came across what was clearly a bunker, very well camouflaged amongst the trees. We were really excited as there was a ladder down into the interior but the gamekeeper, a youngish fellow, chased us off, told us to keep away. Next day, would you believe a big concrete mixer turned up and filled the bunker in completely, sealed off the hatch and they dumped soil and vegetation over the site; I couldn't find it now.[49]

On 6 September 1944, as the savagery of the Normandy battle had receded and with Paris now liberated, the HG were clearly no longer needed and partially demobilised, finally disappearing on 1 November. Theirs had not been a glamorous role though always a vital one. The crowning mercy was that they had not been put to the final test. Had this been so then their history would have been very different. As the threat of invasion faded and finally evaporated, the way was clear for the affectionate legend of Dad's Army to grow. Those secret bunkers of the Auxiliaries quietly mouldered in deliberate obscurity, the death-lists discreetly disposed of, but not necessarily forgotten.

Notes

1   14 May 1943 by 'Winkle Ayling'. http://www.bbc.co.ukk/ww2peopleswar/stories/22/a4392722.shtml
2   *Home Guard Manual 1941* (Reprint 2007, Stroud), p.7.
3   We merely have to consider the fate of the Polish AK or Home Army in their desperate struggle in Warsaw during the later summer of 1944.
4   Pillbox: a small, squat concrete bunker constructed, usually at key tactical points, after 1940.
5   See http://blythbattery.org.uk
6   See http://www.heughbattery.com
7   Winston Churchill speaking in the Commons, 4 June 1940.
8   DLI Sound Recording Project.
9   Ibid.
10 Amazon Defence Corps: a martial organisation where experienced female shots taught others marksmanship.
11 A rare example of the badge can be viewed at: http://www.iwm.org.uk/server/show/Con MediaFile.5690
12 DLI Sound Recording Project.
13 The P17 was .300 cal. whilst the Lee-Enfield was .303.
14 The Thompson used a .45 cal. pistol round and served Allied forces through WWII and after.
15 DLI Sound Recording Project.
16 Molotov: named after the Russian defence minister, a crude but effective petrol bomb.
17 *Home Guard Manual 1941*, pp.73–4.
18 Referred to by Vauban in the late 17th century.
19 *Home Guard Manual 1941*, p.75
20 Ibid. p.215
21 Ibid.
22 DLI Museum No. 2081.
23 There is an excellent website on this subject built by Brian Pears: http://www.bpears.org.uk/Misc/War_NE/w_section_04.html
24 Ibid.
25 Ibid.
26 Deary, T., *Dirty Little Imps – Stories from the DLI* (Durham, 2004), pp.42–3.

27 Bofors: a 40mm anti-aircraft auto-cannon of Swedish origin.
28 Thomas, L., *Other Times* (London, 1999), p.8.
29 DLI Sound Recording Project.
30 Ibid.
31 Ibid.
32 BBC Radio Broadcast 14 May 1940.
33 The German airborne arm, unlike the British, came under the aegis of the Luftwaffe.
34 DLI Sound Recording Project.
35 Forage caps were normally worn at a rakish angle.
36 Ross rifle: a robust Canadian design of .303 cal. manufactured from 1903 which saw service in WWI.
37 DLI Sound Recording Project.
38 Ibid.
39 Peter Fleming writing in the *Spectator*, 8 July 1966.
40 *Home Guard Manual 1941* – introduction by M. McCutcheon
41 Warwicker, J., *Churchill's Underground Army* (Barnsley, 2008), p.25.
42 Brian Pears' website (see above).
43 Ibid.
44 SOE: Special Operations Executive – their mission from the Prime Minister was to set Europe ablaze.
45 Brian Pears' website (see above).
46 Warwicker, p.208.
47 Ibid. p.202
48 Ibid. p.223
49 Interview in Prudhoe Library, March 2010.

Last Word

Few writers have summed up the personal experience of World War Two better than the late George MacDonald Fraser, who served in Burma and recorded his time there in a brilliant memoir *Quartered Safe Out Here* – from him then, the final word:

> ...if any young soldiers of today should chance to read this book, they may understand that while the face of war may alter, some things have not changed since Joshua stood before Jericho and Xenophon marched to the sea. May they come safe home to bedtime, and all well.

Glossary of abbreviations and acronyms

AA – Anti-aircraft

AFV – Armoured fighting vehicle

AP – Armour piercing

AT – Anti-tank

ATS – Auxiliary Territorial Services

BEF – British Expeditionary Force

Bivvy – Bivouac

CIGS – Chief of the Imperial General Staff

C-in-C – Commander in Chief

CO – Commanding officer

CP – Command post

CSM – Company Sergeant-Major

CWGC – Commonwealth War Graves Commission

DAF – Desert Air Force (RAF)

DAK – Deutsches Afrika Corps

DCM – Distinguished Conduct Medal

'Delousing' – minefield clearance

Div – Division

DLI – Durham Light Infantry

DSO – Distinguished Service Order

ELAS – The Greek People's Liberation Army

ENSA – Entertainments, National Service Association

EP1 – Egyptian pattern mark one mine

FANY – First Aid Nursing Yeomanry

FAP – Forward Aid Post

FOO – Forward Observation Officer

GOC – General Officer Commanding

HE – High explosive

IO – Intelligence Officer

I-Tank – Infantry Tank

KD – Khaki drill

LAA – Light Anti-Aircraft

LOB – Left out of battle

LRDG – Long Range Desert Group

MC – Military Cross

MG – Machine-gun

MO – Medical Officer

MM – Military Medal

MP – Military police

NAAFI/EFI – Navy, Army and Air Force Institutes/Expeditionary Forces Institute

NCO – Non-commissioned officer

O Group – Orders Group

OH – Official History

OKH – Oberkommand des Heeres

OKW – Oberkommand der Wehrmacht

OP – Observation Post

QM – Quartermaster

RA – Royal Artillery

RAF – Royal Air Force

RAP – Regimental Aid Post

RAC – Royal Armoured Corps

RAOC – Royal Army Ordnance Corps

RASC – Royal Army Service Corps

RE – Royal Engineers

Regt – Regiment

REME – Royal Engineers Mechanical Engineers

RN – Royal Navy

RSM – Regimental Sergeant-Major

RTR – Royal Tank Regiment

SAS – Special Air Service

Scarper – Disorganised and precipitate retreat; verging on rout

SIW – Self-inflicted wound

SOE – Special Operations Executive

SP – Self-propelled; refers to artillery

TA – Territorial Army
TCL – Tactical Command Liaison
VC – Victoria Cross

WD – War Department
WO – Warrant Officer
W/T – Wireless telegraphy

Bibliography

Published sources

Adair, R., *British Eighth Army, North Africa 1940–1943* (London, 1974)

Agar-Hamilton, J.A.I. & Turner, L.C.F., *Crisis in the Desert May–July 1942* (Oxford, 1952)

Alexander, Field Marshal the Earl, *The Alexander Memoirs 1940–1945* (London, 1962)

Arthur, M., *Forgotten Voices of the Second World War* (London, 2005)

Bailey, J.B.A., *Field Artillery and Firepower* (London, 1989)

Baldwin, H., *Battles Lost and Won, Great Campaigns of World War Two* (London, 1967)

Barnett, C., *The Desert Generals* (London, 1960)

—*Engage the Enemy More Closely: The Royal Navy in the Second World War* (London, 1991)

Barr, N., *Pendulum of War: the Three Battles of El Alamein* (London, 2004)

Beale, P., *Death by Design, British Tank Development in the Second World War* (Stroud, 1998)

Bennet, R., *Ultra and Mediterranean Strategy 1941–1945* (London, 1989)

Bidwell, S., & Graham, D., *Firepower, British Army Weapons and Theories of War 1904–1945* (London, 1982)

Bierman, J. & Smith, C., *Alamein, War Without Hate* (London, 2002)

Bingham, J., Wordsworth, K. & Haupt, W., *North African Campaign 1940–1943* (London, 1969)

Bishop, C. & Drury, I., *Combat Guns* (London, 1987)

Bond, B., *France and Belgium, 1939–1940* (London, 1975)

Braddock, D.W., *The Campaigns in Egypt and Libya* (Aldershot, 1964)

Bradford, E., *Malta 1940–1943* (London, 1985)

British Troops Egypt, *Official Handbook for British Troops in Egypt, Cyprus, Palestine and the Sudan* (BTE, 1936)

Bruce, C. J., *War on the Ground 1939–1945* (London, 1995)

Bryant, Sir Arthur, *The Turn of the Tide* (vols I and II; London, 1957–59)

Bullock, A., *Hitler, a Study in Tyranny* (London, 1952)

Calder, A., *The People's War, Britain 1939–1945* (London, 1969)

Carver, M., *El Alamein* (London, 1962)

—*Tobruk* (London, 1964)

—*Dilemmas of the Desert War* (London, 1986)

—*The Apostles of Mobility: The Theory and Practice of Armoured Warfare* (London, 1979)

Chalfont, A. J., *Montgomery of Alamein* (London, 1976)

Churchill, W., *The Second World War* (6 vols; London, 1948–54)

Clark, A., *The Fall of Crete* (London, 1962)

Connell, J., *Auchinleck: A Biography of Field-Marshall Sir Claude Auchinleck* (London, 1959)

Cooper, M., *The German Army 1933–1945* (London, 1978)

Crawford, R.J., *I was an Eighth Army Soldier* (London, 1944)

Crimp, R.L., *The Diary of a Desert Rat* (London, 1971)

Crisp, R., *Brazen Chariots: An Account of Tank Warfare in the Western Desert, November–December 1941* (London, 1959)

Cross, J.P., *Jungle Warfare* (London, 1989)

Cruickshank, C., *Deception in World War Two* (Oxford, 1979)

Deary, T., *Dirty Little Imps – Stories from the DLI* (Durham, 2004)

Defence Operational Analysis Centre, *The Combat Degradation and Effectiveness of Anti-Tank Weapons – Interim Analysis* (vols I & II Study 670)

—*The Effectiveness of Small Arms Fire* (Defence Study no. M 83108)

—*Historical Analysis of Anti-Tank Battles – the Battle of Snipe* (Study N 670/201)

De Guingand, Major-General Sir F., *Operation Victory* (London, 1963)

Delaney, J., *Fighting the Desert Fox* (London, 1998)

D'Este, C., *Decision in Normandy* (Connecticut, 1983)

—*Bitter Victory* (London, 2008)

Die Oase – *Journal of the Afrika Corps Veterans Association*

Divine, A. D., *Dunkirk* (London, 1945)

Dodds-Parker, D., *Setting Europe Ablaze, Some Account of Ungentlemanly Warfare* (London, 1984)

Douglas, K., *Alamein to Zem Zem* (Oxford, 1979)

Ehrman, J., *Grand Strategy, Volume V, August 1943–September 1944* (London, 1956)

—*Grand Strategy, Volume VI, October 1944–August 1945* (London, 1956)

Ellis, J., *Brute Force: Allied Strategy and Tactics in the Second World War* (London, 1980)

—*The Sharp End of War: The Fighting Man in World War Two* (London, 1980)

Ellis, L.F., *The War in France and Flanders 1939–1940* (London, 1953)

English, Major I.R. & Moses, H., *For You Tommy the War is Over* (Durham, 2006)

Fergusson, Sir Bernard, *Wavell, Portrait of a Soldier* (London, 1961)

Fletcher, D., *The Great Tank Scandal: British Armour in the Second World War Part 1* (HMSO, 1989)

Foot, M.R.D., *SOE in France; An Account of the British Special Operations Executive in France 1940–1944* (London, 1966)

Ford, K., *El Alamein* (Oxford, 2001)

Forty, G., *The Royal Tank Regiment – A Pictorial History* (Tunbridge Wells, 1989)

—*World War Two Tanks* (London, 1995)

—*The Armies of Rommel* (London, 1997)

—*British Army Handbook 1939–1945* (Stroud, 1998)

Fraser, D., *Alanbrooke* (London, 1982)

—*And We Shall Shock Them: The British Army in the Second World War* (London, 1983)

—*Knights Cross: A Life of Field Marshal Erwin Rommel* (London, 1993)

Fraser, G. M., *Quartered Safe Out Here* (London, 2003)

Garret, D., *The Campaign in Greece and Crete* (HMSO, 1942)

Gilbert, M., *The Holocaust; the Jewish Tragedy* (London, 1986)

Greacen, L., *Chink: A Biography* (London, 1989)

Greenwood, A., *Field Marshal Auckinleck* (London, 1990)

Griffiths, P., 'British Armoured Warfare in the Western Desert 1940–1945' in Hamilton, N., *Monty: The Making of a General 1887–1942* (London, 1982)

—The Full Monty: *Montgomery of Alamein 1887–1942* (London, 2001)

—*Master of the Battlefield 1942–1944* (London, 1983)

Harris & Toase, F.H. (editors), *Armoured Warfare* (London, 1990)

Harrison, F., *Tobruk: The Great Siege Reassessed* (London, 1996)

Harrison-Place, T., *Military Training in the British Army, 1940–1944: From Dunkirk to D-Day* (London, 2000)

Harmon, N., *Dunkirk, the Patriotic Myth* (London, 1980)

Hart, P., *The Heat of Battle: The Italian Campaign* (Barnsley, 1999)

Hastings, M., *Nemesis* (London, 2008)

Hinsley, F.H., *British Intelligence in the Second World War* (abridged ed. London, 1993)

Hogg, I.V. & Weeks. J., *The Illustrated Encylopedia of Military Vehicles* (London, 1980)

Horrocks, Lieutenant-General, Sir B., *A Full Life* (London, 1960)

Howard, M., *Grand Strategy, Volume IV, August 1942–September 1943* (London, 1972)

Humble, R., *Crusader: Eighth Army's Forgotten Victory November 1941 to January 1942* (London, 1987)

Irving, D., *The Trail of the Fox* (London, 1977)

—*Hitler's War* (London, 1977)

Johnson, M. & Stanley, P., *Alamein: The Australian Story* (Oxford, 2002)

Joslen, Lieutenant-Colonel H.F., *Orders of Battle: Second World War* (HMSO, 1960)

Keegan, Sir J., *Six Armies in Normandy* (London, 1978)

Kippenburger, Major-General Sir H., *Infantry Brigadier* (Oxford, 1949)

Latimer, J., *Alamein* (London, 2002)

—*Deception in War* (London, 2001)

Lewin, R., *Rommel as Military Commander* (London, 1968)

—*Montgomery as Military Commander* (London, 1971)

—*The Life and Death of the Afrika Korps* (London, 1977)

Lewis, P.J., & English, I.R., *Into Battle with the Durhams: 8 DLI in World War II* (London, 1990)

Lewis-Stemple, J., *The Autobiography of the British Soldier* (London, 2007)

Liddell Hart, Sir B.H., *The Tanks: The History of the Royal Tank Regiment and its Predecessors, Heavy Branch Machine Gun Corps, Tank Corps and Royal Tank Corps, 1914–1945* (2 vols; London, 1959)

Lucas, J., *War in the Desert – the Eighth Army at El Alamein* (London, 1982)

—*Panzer Army Africa* (London, 1977)

—*Hitler's Enforcers; Leaders of the German War Machine 1939–1945* (London, 1996)

McKee, A., *Caen: Anvil of Victory* (London, 1984)

MacDonald, C., *The Lost Battle: Crete 1941* (London, 1993)

MacDonald, J., *Great Battles of World War Two* (London, 1986)

Macksey, K., *Rommel: Battles and Campaigns* (London, 1979)

Majdalany, F., *The Battle of El Alamein* (London, 1965)

Mayer, S.L. (editor), *The Japanese War Machine* (London, 1976)

Mitcham, S. & von Stauffenburg, F., *The Battle for Sicily* (Mechanicsburg, 2007)

Montgomery, Field Marshall the Viscount B.L., *Memoirs* (London, 1958)

Moorehead, A., *Mediterranean Front* (London, 1942)

—*Years of Battle* (London, 1943)

—*The End in Africa* (London, 1943)

Moses, H., *Faithful Sixth: A History of the 6th Battalion DLI* (Durham, 1998)

—*Gateshead Gurkhas: A History of the 9th Battalion Durham Light Infantry 1859–1967* (Durham, 2002)

Myatt, F., *The British Infantry 1660–1945: the Evolution of a Fighting Force* (Poole, 1983)

Neillands, R., *The Desert Rats: 7th Armoured Division, 1940–1945* (Lonson, 1991)

Nicolson, N., *Alex: The Life of Field Marshal Earl Alexander of Tunis* (London, 1971)

North, J., *NW Europe 1944–1945: The Achievement of 21st Army Group* (London, 1953)

Osprey Elite Series 105: *World War II Infantry Tactics: Squad and Platoon*

—Elite Series 122: *World War Two Infantry Tactics: Company and Battalion*

—Elite Series 124: *World War Two Infantry Anti-Tank Tactics*

—Elite Series 162: *World War II Desert Tactics*

—Battle Orders 20: *Rommel's Afrika Corps – Tobruk to El Alamein*

—Battle Orders 28: *Desert Rats: British 8th Army in North Africa 1941–1943*

—New Vanguard 28: *Panzerkampfwagen IV Medium Tank 1936–1945*

—New Vanguard 33: *M3 and M5 Stuart Light Tank 1940–1945*

—New Vanguard 46: *88 mm Flak 18/36/37/41 and Pak 43 1936–1945*

—New Vanguard 98: *British Anti-Tank Artillery 1939–1945*

—New Vanguard 113: *M3 Lee/Grant Medium Tank 1941–1945*

—Campaign 158: *El Alamein 1942*

Parkinson, R., *Blood, Toil, Sweat and Tears* (London, 1973)

—*A Day's March Nearer Home* (London, 1974)

—*The War in the Desert* (London, 1976)

Philips, C.E.L., *Alamein* (London, 1962)

Pitt, B., *The Crucible of War 1: Wavell's Command* (London, 1986)

—*The Crucible of War 2: Auchinleck's Command* (London, 1986)

—*The Crucible of War 3: Montgomery and Alamein* (London, 1986)

Playfair, Major-General I.S.O., *Official History, UK Military Series, Campaigns: Mediterranean and Middle East* (Vols 1–4; London, 1962–66)

Quarrie, B., *Afrika Korps* (Cambridge, 1975)

—*Panzers in the Desert* (Cambridge, 1978)

Rissik, D., *The DLI at War – History of the DLI 1939–1945* (Durham, 1952)

Rolf, D., *Prisoners of the Reich, Germany's Captives 1939–1945* (London, 1988)

Rommel, E., *Infantry Attack* (London, 1990)

Russell of Liverpool, Lord, *The Scourge of the Swastika, A Short History of Nazi War Crimes* (London, 1954)

Salmond, J.B., *The History of the 51st Highland Division* (Bishop Auckland, 1994)

Samwell, H.P., *An Infantry Officer with the Eighth Army: The Personal Experiences of an Infantry Officer During the Eighth Army's Campaign Through Africa and Sicily* (London, 1945)

Schmidt, H. W., *With Rommel in the Desert* (London, 1951)

Shephard, B., *After Daybreak: the Liberation of Belsen 1945* (London, 2005)

Shirer, William L., *The Rise and fall of the Third Reich, a History of Nazi Germany* (London, 1960)

Slim, Field Marshal Sir W., *Defeat into Victory* (London, 1956)

Smith, M., *Station X – The Codebreakers of Bletchley Park* (London, 1998)

Stewart, A., *The Eighth Army's Greatest Victories: Alam Halfa to Tunis 1942–1943* (London, 1999)

—*The Early Battles of Eighth Army: 'Crusader' to the Alamein Line 1941–1942* (London, 2002)

Strawson, J., *The Battle for North Africa* (London, 1969)

Swinson, A., *Kohima* (London, 1966)

Terraine, J., *The Right of the Line* (London, 1983)

Toase, F.H., & Harris, J.P., *Armoured Warfare* (London, 1990)

Tout, K., *The Bloody Battle for Tilly* (Stroud, 2000)

US Command & General Staff College, *Selected Readings in Tactics* (vols I & II, April Virginia, 1974)

Van Creveld, M., *Supplying in War: Logistics from Wallenstein to Patton* (Cambridge, 1977)

Verney, G.L., *The Desert Rats: History of 7th Armoured Division 1938–1945* (London, 1954)

War Office, *Military Report on the North-Western Desert of Egypt* (London, 1937)

Warner, P., *Alamein – Recollections of the Heroes* (London, 1979)

—*The Secret Forces of World War Two* (London, 1985)

Wilmot, C., *The Struggle for Europe* (London, 1952)

Wilson, P., *The War Behind the Wire; Experiences in Captivity During the Second World War* (Barnsley, 2000)

Young, D., *Rommel* (London, 1950)

Unpublished: Defence Academy Shrivenham

TRDC 02954; Notes from Theatres of War, vol 1; Cyrenaica November, 1941

—05407; The Retreat to El Alamein, 22nd June 1942–30th August 1942

—05408; The German Assault on the Alamein Position 31st August 1942–7th September 1942

—05408; The Battle of El Alamein part II – Opr. Lightfoot

—05408; Campaign in the Middle East Part 3, September–November 1942

—05889; Defence in the Land Battle

—06347; Tactical Deception

—07315; Charles Turner Saga

—08225; Pace of Operations
—09153; The Battle of Snipe
—09657; Engr. Aspects of N. Africa 1940–1943
—09787; Battle of El Alamein
—09995; Passage Operations, El Alamein 1942
—10728; Culminating Points
—11964; The Manoeuvrist Approach
—12114; Tactical handling of Artillery
—12274; AFM vol. 4, part 3, Historical Desert Supplement
—12546; El Alamein BFT
—12686; Armour in Battle 1939–1945
—13054; The Battle of El Alamein Part III
—13535; Info. Brief on Tactical Deception
—13711; Conquest of North Africa
—13846; North Africa Extracts
—14118; Air Power at El Alamein
—14221; Desert Warfare: The German Experience of WWII
—14258; Effectiveness of Anti-Tank Weapons in Combat vols. 1,2, & 3, parts A & B
—14543; Breakthrough and manoeuvre Ops vols. 1 & 3, parts A & B
—14903; Exercise Sphinx Ride – JFHQPXR
—75123; Air Power at El Alamein

Unpublished: private sources

Akam, E.A., *A Memoir*
DLI Association: Papers, correspondence and statements relating to the alleged atrocity by 6th & 8th Battalions DLI at Arras, May 1940
Durham County Council: The Durham Light Infantry's World War Two Oral History Collection
Kelly, Major R.C., *Diary 1940 – Sir David Kelly*
Pares, A., *The Relief of Belsen DCRO*
Pinkney, M., *Maurice and Mary*

Index